A History of the First Christians

A History of the First Christians

Alexander J. M. Wedderburn

T & T CLARK INTERNATIONAL
A Continuum imprint
LONDON • NEW YORK

T&T CLARK LTD
A Continuum imprint

The Tower Building
11 York Road, London SE1 7NX
United Kingdom

15 East 26th Street
New York, NY 10010
USA

www.continuumbooks.com

British Library Cataloguing-in-Publication Data
A catalogue record for this book is available from the British Library

ISBN 0 567 08413 2 (Paperback)
ISBN 0 567 08423 X (Hardback)

Typeset by BookEns Ltd
Printed and bound in Great Britain by
MPG Books Ltd. Bodmin, Cornwall

FOR FOUR EDITORS!

Contents

Preface

One might think that enough had been written on the history of the earliest Christians and indeed much has been. However, I must admit that, when I provide students with introductory reading on the subject, the works that I most recommend are by now somewhat dated, however well they may have worn the passage of time. Rather than general surveys there has been a steady stream of individual studies either of individual personalities, not only Paul, but also of figures like Jesus' brother James and Philip, or of groups like the 'Hellenists', or else of the history of the early churches in particular centres such as Antioch, Rome, Ephesus or Philippi. It is not that more recent works covering a wider field do not exist, but that I find they are in one way or another unsatisfactory as an introduction to the subject and could present the beginner, who has little idea of other possibilities, with a misleading or confusing impression of what we know and do not know about it. In that gap, as I perceive it, lies part of the justification for yet another work on the subject.

A further part of that justification is perhaps also to be found in a certain amount of reflection, both upon what one is doing in writing a history of the earliest Christians and how one should do it, and upon the implications of that history for Christian faith. The latter is the more necessary if one believes, as I do, that that faith, if it is to be recognizable as Christian faith, is integrally linked to that history and must find in that history its justification and its orientation, as well as being called to account and cut down to size, so to speak, by that history. I must confess here to a considerable unease at attempts which seem to wish to bypass this by appealing to a new understanding of history. Too often these seem to lose sight of the ambiguity of our word 'history' (or equally of the German 'Geschichte') which can refer both to the course of events and to our attempts to reconstruct, understand and narrate those events. 'History' in the latter sense is, it is true, a subjective, human construct and access to 'history' in the former sense is also mediated by witnesses whose testimony is itself, for the most part, an interpretation of past events. It remains, however, the goal of a critical 'history' in the latter sense, or 'historiography' if that term is less ambiguous, so to investigate those witnesses that one gains insight into, and a better understanding of, the likely course of events, the actual course of 'history' in the former sense. That being so, as long as Christianity lays claim to be rooted in history, then it is legitimate and necessary to pose the question what those roots, historical in all probability, really were and not to be content with the traditional version or versions of the story of those origins. For implicit in the description of Christianity as a 'historical' religion is surely the claim that it is rooted, not in a possibly at least partly fictional story preserved in its canon, but in events which actually happened. Otherwise one is left with a Christianity which is a pure 'book religion', either in the sense that the Christian Scriptures have been directly inspired by God or that, as a collection of literary works, they exercise an influence comparable to that of other great works of literature. And that would involve a fundamental shift in the understanding of what the Christian faith is about.

It is, then, with history that I am primarily concerned and not with that 'history of theology' or 'theological history' (*Theologiegeschichte*) which has been the theme of a number of German works over the last few years. In thus restricting the subject-matter of this book I remain aware, however, that theology and theological ideas are both born of history and in turn themselves important causal factors in history. Historical events and circumstances may often be the catalyst for theological insights and ideas, but such ideas can then become an important driving force and influence upon the course of history. To that extent it will be impossible to leave theological ideas out of the reckoning in the following account, nor would I want to do so. However much proponents of a socio-historical approach to the New Testament texts may deplore the way in which the New Testament has been studied for its ideas alone, in isolation from the social and cultural realities in which those ideas are rooted, it would be equally one-sided to ignore the impact and the formative influence of those ideas upon the life of the early Christian community.

I have tried to ensure that this study is both readable and of manageable proportions and that necessitates a certain self-restraint in entering into dialogue with divergent views and also in drawing upon material from other ancient sources. One is therefore constantly confronted acutely with the question of what to include and what to omit, particularly when a work such as this touches on a vast number of issues, in order that it may be reliably informative without overwhelming the reader with a mass of details. What is not mentioned in the text or the notes has not necessarily been overlooked, although eye problems in the latter stages of the preparation of the work necessarily curtailed what was possible. Decisions were often agonizingly difficult and in trying to tread a middle way between superficiality and a comprehensive treatment of the many subjects I am aware that I may displease or exasperate many who would have liked either something simpler or something more thorough. In particular I have avoided certain areas on the grounds that the data do not warrant sufficient confidence about the historical reconstructions that some have wrested from them, and thus there will be plenty of scope for argument about what I have or have not included. At the same time, because I often put forward a contentious line – and when so much is a matter of reconstruction and reading between the lines of one's sources, controversy is hardly to be avoided – it is necessary to warn the unwary, through references in the main text or through endnotes, that it is contentious, but without always recording *all* the divergent possibilities, let alone all their protagonists. Often I have been only too aware of them, but had to restrict my arguments in order to keep in focus the essential elements of the historical reconstruction I am attempting. On the other hand, the contentiousness of some of the views has also led me sometimes to quote other scholars in my support, lest it be thought that the views expressed are altogether too idiosyncratic to be credible! (Many of the German works cited, but by no means all, have been translated and, where practicable, I have referred to the English versions, but that was unfortunately not always possible in this corner of the world.)

My warmest thanks are due to many who have helped in various ways with the writing of this book, but especially to Alexis Bunine, Ingrid Imelauer, Claudia Kemper, Nadine Kessler, Jens-Uwe Krause, Henning Lang (particularly for his invaluable help with the indexes), Enno Popkes and Christian Witschel, and in connection with its publication I owe an especial debt of gratitude to Geoffrey Green and also to Ben Hayes, Karen Parker, Katherine Savage and a whole series of others at T&T Clark for all their help and encouragement.

PREFACE

I am aware that the dedication of this volume is somewhat unusual and cryptic. The 'editors' in question are the four colleagues who very kindly and generously organized a most impressive volume of essays to celebrate my sixtieth birthday: Alf Christophersen, Carsten Claußen, Jörg Frey and Bruce Longenecker. This dedication is a small 'Thank you' to them.

Munich, May 2003 A. J. M. Wedderburn

1

Introduction

1.1. When to Stop?

It may seem a curious way of proceeding, to start by asking where to stop, but any attempt to write a history of the first Christians, of the earliest Christian community, poses the question: where is it appropriate to end the history? For any historian who writes the history of an epoch or of any period of history faces the question when the period began and when it ended; often the answer seems relatively straightforward, as with a history of Tudor or Stuart England: the period to be studied is demarcated on the basis of the family and lineage of the rulers of England. Other histories may find that their beginning and end is not so sharply definable (e.g. a history of the Reformation or of the Industrial Revolution). It is, however, a problem recognized already before the beginnings of the Christian movement by Dionysius of Halicarnassus when he describes it as the second task of the historian 'to decide where to begin and how far to go' (*Letter to Gn. Pompeius 3*).[1]

A history of the earliest Christian movement may have little difficulty in deciding upon its beginning in the rise of the belief that God had raised Jesus of Nazareth from the dead, so that his movement had not died with him at his crucifixion, but had a future – although even that can be contested, as we shall see. Determining where such a history should end is far more difficult and far more controversial. Is there a point of time such that one can say of it that it marks the end of an epoch, of the initial phase of that movement? One possibility is the destruction of Jerusalem in 70 CE at the hands of the Roman legions under Titus, an event which robbed early Christianity of that focal point which the church in that city had hitherto provided. That point is the one for which Wilhelm Schneemelcher decides in his influential little standard work.[2] Or one could opt for a far less clearly definable point of time, when the last representatives of the first generation of the earliest

Christians died out. Or one could opt for a still later point of time, as François Vouga does when he includes the whole period up to the time of writing of the latest New Testament writings, around 150 CE.[3] The first of these options is based upon a clearly recognizable cut-off point, and the second has a measure of plausibility, particularly when one chooses 'A History of the First Christians' as a title. The third really extends the scope of such a work as this too far, even if one recognizes that the endings offered by the first two are of necessity open and incomplete, in that they prepare the way for, and lead into, the next phases in the rise of early Christianity. I will, accordingly, concentrate primarily on the period up to 70 CE, but will also, as far as the sources allow it, attempt to say something about the decades immediately after that.

This period can be roughly divided into *three phases*. The earliest phase is a somewhat obscure one, since most of what we know about it is to be gleaned, with considerable care, from the first chapters of the Book of Acts as well as perhaps from certain hints in Paul's letters. For as far as Paul himself is concerned, this period also covers his largely hidden early years as a Christian, to which he alludes briefly in Gal 1. With the beginning of Paul's missionary journeys, particularly those after the conference described in Gal 2.1–10, the information available to us becomes somewhat more plentiful, even if rather one-sided, in that it is above all Paul who provides it; this period, with all its achievements and its setbacks, can be counted as a second phase, a phase dominated by the story of Paul's work and struggles. As Paul is finally imprisoned and then presumably eventually executed, a new phase begins. It begins, however, not just for the Pauline churches and for those who had worked with the apostle, but also for many of his opponents, for, about the same time, in 62 CE, James, the brother of Jesus, was also executed, and the leading counterbalance to the influence of Paul in the earliest church was thereby removed. Shortly afterwards the Jewish revolt against Rome in 66 and its tragic consequences in the downfall of Jerusalem four years later underline the removal of this counterbalance and confirm that a further phase has now begun. It is a phase which is no longer dominated by any particular figure, as the second was by Paul and James, with their two differing interpretations of the Christian message. It is, correspondingly, a phase in which varying traditions and interpretations of Christianity assert themselves – even the legacy of Paul is interpreted in strikingly different ways. It is, too, a phase in which the majority of the New Testament writings apart from the genuine letters of Paul were composed, as well as other texts like 1 Clement; correspondingly, these writings also bear witness to this variety in early Christianity, since they stem from this period of increasing diversity. And yet, despite these many witnesses, Hans Conzelmann can describe the four decades between 60 and 100 as a gap in our knowledge.[4] This paradoxical judgement stems largely from the nature of these writings, which lack an assured historical setting such as the letters of Paul offer us in so far as they can be located within the framework of his missionary work. Even those writings which claim to interpret Paul's legacy are beset by such difficulties: conclusions about when and where they were written and by whom, and which historical situation they reflect, remain at best tentative.

The diversity to be found within these various writings will continue to manifest itself long after the period on which we are concentrating here, but more and more it will be offset by increasingly strenuous efforts to enforce unity, efforts like the very gradual formation of a canon of Christian writings recognized as authoritative and binding, or the rise of a tradition of office-bearers who are to preserve and guarantee the legacy of the first leaders of the church and to determine what belongs to the content of that faith and what does not. For it is, too, a stage in which some of the writings reflect their authors' consciousness that they no longer have a direct contact with the founding events of the Christian movement (cf., e.g. Luke 1.1–4; Heb 2.3). Already in some of the later writings of the New Testament we can see signs that this process of consolidation and demarcation is getting under way, signs which at this stage serve more to throw into relief the extent to which the various traditions of the earliest Christians were still far from fixed and static and unified.

However, the choice of the *title* 'A History of the First Christians' also needs some justification. In particular, there are certain possible titles that have been avoided. The phrase 'the early church' is usually interpreted as referring to a far longer period, perhaps up to the fall of the Roman Empire and the onset of the Dark Ages. Often a German textbook will refer here to 'Urchristentum', which then can be translated into English, not wholly happily, as 'primitive Christianity'.[5] With some justification Vouga points to dangers lurking in the German term: it is not merely a description of a period of time, but carries with it the evaluative connotation that the time of the beginning determines the very nature of Christianity.[6] Also to be avoided, for similar reasons, are references to an 'apostolic age' or 'apostolic times', despite the titles of studies like those of Leonhard Goppelt or George Caird and despite Eusebius' use of the latter phrase.[7] For such a description also has evaluative connotations: an 'apostolic age' is not just the time when people called 'apostles' lived, but 'apostolic' can all too easily mean that it was not just a formative period for later Christianity, but also normative for it.

On the other hand, I have not steered clear of using the terms 'Christian' and 'Christianity', despite the protests of some that at the earliest stages these words are anachronistic, for the followers of Jesus regarded themselves as part of Judaism, as yet another group within a Judaism which was at this point of time anything but a monolithic institution.[8] And it is true that the designation 'Christian' first arose, according to Acts 11.26, in Antioch and that it is otherwise a term which is rarely used in the New Testament and then in relatively late works (Acts 26.28; 1 Pet 4.16). Yet it is undeniable that these followers of Jesus from the first had at least this in common, that they believed that Jesus of Nazareth was God's promised Messiah, the anointed one or the Christ (Greek *Christos*), however much they may have differed among themselves on other matters. This distinguished them from those Jews who did not share that belief and these terms are therefore a succinct way of designating that shared belief and those who shared it. And it is not unreasonable that these believers came to feel the need for, and the appropriateness of, such a shared designation, for it corresponded to a reality which united them and distinguished them from their fellows, initially from their fellow Jews but then also from the non-Jews around them.

1.2. A Fragmentary Story

Allusion has already been made to the limitations of the sources at our disposal, and it must be recognized from the outset how patchy our knowledge of earliest Christianity is. Our knowledge of the life and work of Paul and of Pauline Christianity is relatively extensive. This apostle is easily the best-documented figure in the Christianity of the first century; yet there are very considerable gaps in our knowledge of him, as we shall see, and many more in the information which we have for other traditions within the earliest church. The variety of reconstructions of the history of the Johannine community, which otherwise might seem to offer the best hope of gaining knowledge of another group of communities than the Pauline one, and the similarly divergent accounts of the relation to one another of the traditions which this community preserved, underline the deficiencies of the information at our disposal.

Or, if one seeks to write a history of the spread of Christianity community by community, one can glean some information about various centres; above all, again, those centres where we know that Paul was active, and we can draw upon the none too plentiful information offered by his letters, supplemented, perhaps, by the account of the Acts of the Apostles. These sources offer some information, too, about the church in Jerusalem, which is hardly surprising in the light of the importance of that Christian community in the history of the earliest church up to the fall of Jerusalem in 70 CE, but it is striking that we know next to nothing about the survival of any Christian communities in Galilee, the birthplace of the Jesus movement, let alone have reliable information about the earliest origins of Christian communities further to the east, for example in the area of Edessa. It is true that Acts at least presupposes the existence of Christians in Galilee in 9.31: after the conversion of Paul, who seems to have become the sole persecutor of the church, the churches in Galilee as well as those in Judaea and Samaria enjoy peace. Yet otherwise we are told nothing more.[9] It is true that many scholars are prepared to treat the evidence of the Gospels as a source for post-Easter Galilean Christianity, but caution is here advisable.[10] Even if the traditions contained in these documents reflected the views of the communities which preserved them, that in no way entails that these communities were located in the same place as the events and scenes depicted in the Gospels. And even the principle that the traditions reflect the beliefs of the communities that transmit them is questionable:[11] there are, for instance, traditions which seem to have occasioned the early church almost as much difficulty in comprehending them as they cause us. (A particularly clear example is the Parable of the Unjust Steward, Luke 16.1–13, where vv. 9–13 are in all probability originally independent sayings now attached to that parable in the hope of offering a suitable interpretation of Jesus' purpose in telling such a story, which on the face of it seems to present a message of dubious morality.) And the evidence of Matthew's Gospel shows that it could reflect a situation in which the mission of the Jesus movement was directed solely to Jews, whereas the triumphal climax of the Gospel clearly presupposes a mission to gentiles (cf. Matt 10.5–6; 28.19). This author, at least, seems perfectly capable of depicting a situation during the earthly ministry of Jesus which he knew was different to that which applied in his own day. Similarly, Luke 22.35–6 implies that the disciples' way of life after Jesus' death would be different from before. In that case we cannot simply assume that the sayings and stories of the Gospels must reflect the situation of a later period rather than that of Jesus' earthly ministry; with that observation hopes of recovering information about post-Easter Christianity in Galilee or elsewhere receive a considerable setback. Only if it can be shown that a particular passage *must* reflect a later, post-Easter situation can one use it as evidence for the history of the earliest church, but then usually without any too clear knowledge *where* that tradition is to be located. The theories with regard to the regions in which the communities of the various evangelists are to be located are too varied to allow us to assign their traditions with confidence to a particular area.[12]

Similar uncertainties surround other writings of the New Testament as well and mean that they can only be fitted into the picture with considerable hesitation, if at all. The Letter to the Hebrews, for instance, which some treat with confidence as evidence for the history of the Roman church, might seem to offer some handholds for locating it, but only if its epistolary conclusion is of a piece with the rest of the document. The lack of an epistolary beginning, combined with a shift in style in the last chapter and with other differences, render that questionable, and in the main body of the letter the reference to the addressees not having borne witness to the point of shedding their blood (12.4) is odd if they are the survivors of the Neronian persecution of the Roman Christians (see below, Ch. 11), as some suggest. The point could simply be that those still alive to hear the message of the letter have self-evidently not lost their lives under Nero, but that argument would be undermined by 10.32–4, which refers not only to their own sufferings but to their sharing in those of their fellows; and amongst these there is again no mention of death. The situation or situations presupposed by this letter do not allow us to use it with any confidence to fill out the picture of earliest Christianity.

The fragmentary and incomplete nature of the story we can tell is also clear from three further pieces of evidence: Paul's catalogue of his sufferings in 2 Cor 11.23–8, the lists of the addressees of 1 Peter (1 Pet 1.1) and of the letters to the seven churches in Rev 2–3. For it is clear from Paul's own listing of what he has suffered that there is much which we do not know, and the same is true of the list in 1 Clem 5.6 which mentions seven imprisonments endured by the apostle. For Paul himself tells us that five times he received the Jewish punishment of 39 lashes, three times the Roman scourging with rods, was once stoned (Acts 14.19?) and was thrice shipwrecked, and that before the time of the one and only shipwreck of which Acts tells us in chapter 27.[13] 1 Peter is addressed to those resident in the Roman provinces of Pontus, Galatia, Cappadocia, Asia and Bithynia. Of the spread of Christianity in Galatia we could perhaps know something if we could be more certain about the relationship of Paul's letter to the Galatians to the various pieces of information in the Book of Acts. About Christians in the province of Asia we know all too little apart from some references to Paul's activity in its capital, Ephesus. Our first information about Pontus and Bithynia comes from the letter of the Roman governor Pliny the Younger to the emperor Trajan in the early second century and by that time the Christians there are numerous – far too numerous in his eyes. About the evangelization of Cappadocia we are fully in the dark. The seven churches addressed at the beginning of the Book of Revelation (Ephesus, Smyrna, Pergamum, Thyatira, Sardis, Philadelphia and Laodicea) are less widely distributed than the addressees of 1 Peter – they are all to be found within a single province, that of Asia – but again our knowledge about how they came into being is scanty or non-existent.[14]

1.3. Sources

It will already have become clear that the nature of the sources at our disposal is a critical factor in writing a history of the earliest Christian movement. In a sense any history can only be as good as its sources allow it to be. If the sources are tendentious or fragmentary then the historian must discipline herself or himself to remain within the limits of what those sources allow her or him to say. It is true that one may have to read between the lines and that one may, and indeed should, seek to establish the connections between attested events and episodes even when the sources themselves do not make those connections. That belongs to the discipline of the historian, but it must at the same time be made plain where the evidence ends and the historian's reconstruction begins, for the latter will usually have no higher status than that of a more or less likely hypothesis. Its probability as an hypothesis will in large measure depend upon its explanatory capacity; the more attested data it helps to explain, the more likely it is.

For the history of the earliest Christian movement two sources are above all relevant, the letters of Paul and the Acts of the Apostles. In view of the fact that so much of the latter also concentrates upon the the story of the apostle Paul it will be apparent that much of what one can say with any degree of certainty about the history of this earliest period will then inevitably revolve around the figure of Paul. In view of the importance of Paul for the subsequent history of the Christian church it is important that we should at least be able to say something about his life and work, however frustrating and disappointing it may be that our knowledge of his contemporaries in the faith is so much patchier or indeed in many cases non-existent.

If the story which we can tell is often incomplete, there are also areas where we cannot really even begin to tell the story. A striking example is the founding of Christian churches in North Africa. We hear of the preaching of Christians from Cyrene in Acts 11.20, but Cyrene is not one of the places where they preached. Is it presupposed that they had already learnt of the gospel in their home city? (The Synoptic Gospels mention a Cyrenian, Simon, playing a role in Jesus' passion, i.e. in Jerusalem.) And even later we hear of the Alexandrian Jewish Christian Apollos (18.24), but we are not told whether he first encountered the gospel in his native city or not. Otherwise, it is 180 CE before we encounter our first literary evidence of Christianity in North Africa.[15]

1.3.1. The Pauline letters

Of prime importance are obviously those letters which are generally acknowledged to stem from the apostle himself – Romans, the two letters to the Corinthians, Galatians, Philippians, 1 Thessalonians and Philemon. Other works in the Pauline corpus must accordingly be used with care, if at all, even if one sees reason to criticize this critical consensus.

In English-speaking scholarship there is, for instance, a far greater readiness than in the German-speaking world to acknowledge the authenticity of 2 Thessalonians, and the reasons for doubting it are indeed very different from the arguments against the authenticity of the other letters in the Pauline corpus, so different that one must ask how persuasive they are. Colossians, again, is treated by many, once more particularly in the English-speaking world, as Pauline, despite the marked differences in style and thought in comparison with the generally acknowledged letters; the close relationship of this letter to the tiny letter to Philemon, whose genuineness is mostly accepted (for who would want to compose such a pseudonymous letter?), poses, however, a problem which some have sought to solve by granting that it was indeed written while Paul was still alive, e.g. by his co-sender Timothy.[16] If Paul was in prison at the time of writing, then it is easy to imagine that the circumstances of his imprisonment might in this instance, if not in other cases, have meant that he had to delegate more of the composition of a letter to a trusted friend.

It is, however, doubtful how far admitting the authenticity of any of these disputed letters would greatly increase our knowledge of the history of the earliest Christians, so insoluble are the problems which beset any attempt to determine the setting of any of these letters. In the case of the three Pastoral Epistles one might hope to use them as evidence for a further period in Paul's life beyond that covered in other letters and in Acts, but in their case the arguments against Pauline authorship are so strong that any attempt to treat them as written by him must be seen as precarious in the extreme.

Although the authenticity of the seven letters mentioned above may be generally recognized, there is one factor which further complicates their use as sources: it is often supposed that a number of them are composite letters, made up of parts of a number of smaller letters. If that were the case, then each of these smaller original letters would presuppose a different situation and setting from those which other parts of the composite letters reflect. And yet these partition theories perhaps raise more questions than they solve:[17] the motivation for the often quite complex scissors and paste operation which produced the letters in the form in which we have these letters today has not been satisfactorily explained; the absence of any trace of the original shorter letters in the manuscript tradition of the New Testament is also puzzling.[18] It seems better, therefore, to start from the assumption that the letters were originally written and sent largely in the form which we have and that their various parts were therefore written over a relatively short period of time, even if one must reckon with the possibility of fresh developments taking place within that timespan.

For many the generally recognized letters of Paul are our prime source of knowledge of Paul's life and of that period of the history of the earliest church in which he played such an important role. That is certainly true: they are a firsthand witness written by an active participant in the events which he describes, and that places them in a different class to all those other sources which are at best witnesses at one remove from the events which they depict. That is the great strength of the Pauline letters, but it is at the same time their greatest weakness: as the work of a participant in the events depicted and as works which themselves are designed to play a role in the unfolding history of Paul's relations with his churches, they are very far from being neutral or dispassionate witnesses to those events. On the contrary, they are often uncompromisingly partisan accounts. Nowhere is that clearer than in the account which Paul gives of his quarrel with Peter and the other Jewish Christians in the church of Syrian Antioch in Gal 2.11–14: that is immediately clear in the charge of hypocrisy levelled against Peter and the others there, as well as the motivation due to fear of 'those of the circumcision' attributed to them. It is hardly to be imagined that this is a description of their behaviour and actions with which they themselves would have concurred. Without an alternative version from the hand of Peter or one of the others, however, it is left to us to try to reconstruct as best we may how they would have interpreted and defended their actions.

1.3.2. The Book of Acts

It is often asserted that the evidence of the Book of Acts is of secondary value and to some extent this assessment is correct. Yet, even if it is of lesser value, that does not mean that it is worthless, and the use of its evidence is not, in my opinion, to be treated with the extreme scepticism which one sometimes encounters, as if its account could never be correct.

Traditionally the work was attributed to a travelling companion of Paul's and the striking phenomenon of the 'we'-passages was, and often still is, seen as confirmation of this.[19] That traditional view in turn led to a high estimate of its historical worth, for it was regarded as written by one who was close to the apostle and indeed a participant in at least some of the events that he describes. The literary phenomenon presented by these passages, which alternate with a narrative in the third person, is a striking one and one that is not easily explained or paralleled. On the other hand, the discrepancies between the portrayal of Paul, his thought and his life, in this work and the self-portrayal which the apostle himself offers in his letters are serious enough to make us hesitate to accept the traditional authorship and the traditional explanation of the 'we'.[20] I have, accordingly, argued elsewhere that we are dealing here with a rather unusual phenomenon, the witness to a witness to Paul's work, and that this witness at second hand signals the presence of the original witness, who may well be the Luke who is mentioned elsewhere in the New Testament, by breaking into the first person plural at the relevant points in the narrative.[21] In this way one can at least do justice to this stylistic feature while at the same time explaining the distance which seems to separate this author from the Paul of the letters. For both the theology which this writer attributes to Paul and the account which he gives of the course of his ministry seem to be, at a number of important points, at variance with the letters.

Such a theory – and it can never be more than a theory – not only helps us with the dilemma posed by the distance between the Paul of Acts and the Paul of the letters on the one hand and the sheer oddity of the 'we'-passages on the other; it also seeks to do justice to the fact that more than a quarter of our New Testament has traditionally been ascribed to this rather obscure figure mentioned but three times in the New Testament. Such a theory has the merit of explaining how the tradition incorporated in the Acts (and also in the third Gospel) came to be associated with this name, yet without requiring that this otherwise obscure travelling companion of Paul himself actually wrote either work. It is true that one could explain that attribution as a piece of detective work by some early Christian: in 2 Tim 4.11 Luke is the only one with Paul,[22] and the 'we' in Acts seems to indicate that the author travelled with Paul to Rome. Yet the careful reader should also have noticed that the 'we' ceases in 28.16 and does not recur during the second half of that chapter; would that not suggest that whoever was indicated by the 'we' may not have been with Paul during this period in Rome?

Accordingly, even if, in the following, the author of Acts is referred to as 'Luke', it must be remembered that this is no travelling companion of Paul's, but more probably someone seeking to write in his name, in much the same way as, say, later writers wrote in the name of prophets such as Isaiah.[23]

It is, however, a further question how far this writer intended to give us an accurate impression of Paul and his work. Some have stressed the literary and edificatory purposes of the Book of Acts, and have compared its writer's techniques with those of ancient historical novelists, even if not going so far as to assert that Acts actually is just a novel.[24] Yet it is widely agreed that this work is by the same person who wrote the third Gospel, and it is therefore arguable that the preface to the latter work (Luke 1.1–4), which is picked up and echoed in the briefer preface to the Book of Acts (Acts 1.1), also applies to the Book of Acts as well. In that case the writer of this double work seems to evince a seriousness of purpose alien to historical novels in the ancient world:[25]

> I too decided, after investigating everything carefully from the very first, to write an orderly account for you . . ., so that you may know the truth concerning the things about which you have been instructed. (Luke 1.3–4, NRSV)

That does not, of course, mean that the author was successful in achieving this serious purpose, but it does suggest that what he was setting out to do corresponded more to the aims of historians in the ancient world than to those of novelists. At the same time it must be recognized that what was expected then of historians was rather different to the standards by which we measure historians' work today; their art may have been at certain points nearer to that of the novelist than we ourselves would like.[26] It should also be recognized, however, that we are dealing here with a would-be historian whose literary skills and intellectual tradition differed from those of the literati of the Graeco-Roman world. Although those skills may be greater than those of most other New Testament writers, they are not to be compared with those of the probably considerably more highly educated writers of his world by whose achievements we tend to measure ancient historiography, from Herodotus and Thucydides on. And, furthermore, he was also heir to a tradition of historiography foreign to them, that of the Old Testament and early Judaism, which had developed its own conventions for describing the course of human history under the direction of the hand of God. Those stylistic features which earlier led some to suppose that parts of Acts were a translation from a

Semitic original, but have more plausibly been explained as reflecting the language of the Greek Old Testament, point not only to this author's knowledge of the Old Testament in that language, but probably also to the fact that he felt himself to be writing a similar work, with a comparable subject-matter.

In using the testimony of Acts we must make allowance for the fact that its author in all probability had access to, and made use of, various sources of different sorts.[27] Indeed, one of the main criteria for gauging the presence of sources in Acts' account is the presence of tensions between the author's apparent purpose and goal and the material to be found in his account. Consistently he portrays and emphasizes the unanimity and singleness of purpose which reigned in the earliest community in Jerusalem (e.g. 1.14; 2.44–6; 5.12), yet also mentions a dispute which arose between two groups in the Jerusalem church in 6.1 as well as the violent altercation which arose between Paul and Barnabas in 15.39. Other criteria include breaks and unevennesses in the narrative[28] and the presence of often seemingly gratuitous or at least not properly explained, but nevertheless often quite detailed, information, like the lists of names mentioned in 6.5; 13.1 or 20.4, or the strange group of prohibitions incorporated in the so-called 'Apostolic Decree' (15.20, 29; cf. 21.25). In using Acts as a witness to the history of the earliest church it will therefore be particularly important to ask, case by case, whether the author is speaking on his own account or quoting a source of some kind, and then, of course, to ask what sort of source it is and to distinguish its content carefully from the use to which the author of Acts puts it.

For the sources which he uses may be no more reliable than he himself is, or perhaps even less so; they may, at least, be equally tendentious or more so.[29] Nor should we assume that the author of Acts always understood what he found in his sources or evaluated them and used them correctly. We should not assume that with any historian, ancient or modern, nor should we assume that in the case of this author just because his work has found its way into the New Testament canon. For very often our assessments in such a matter are weighted one way or the other by the theological assumptions which we make about the canon and canonicity, and it is important not to let such a theological judgement dictate our historical verdict on Acts' reliability. Unfortunately, the opportunities for a direct comparison with other sources for the history of the period, which would offer us a better chance of gauging the reliability and the trustworthiness of Acts' account according to the standards of its own time, are few and far between. Yet, when that does prove possible, the results are telling and the differing reactions of New Testament scholars to these results are equally revealing. A particularly clear example is the speech put on the lips of the prominent rabbi Gamaliel in Acts 5.35–9. To persuade his fellow members of the Jewish council to take no further action themselves against the Christian movement, but to stand back and let events determine whether it was of God or not, he points to two recent, comparable movements which came to grief: first there had been the rising under a certain Theudas, and then, after him, that led by Judas the Galilean at the time of the census. Now both disturbances are seemingly also mentioned by the Jewish historian Josephus, that under Judas in 6–7 CE as Archelaus' territory was annexed, after his deposition by the Romans, as the Roman province of Judaea, and that under Theudas in the time of the Roman governor Cuspius Fadus (44–?46 CE).[30] The twofold problem is immediately apparent: not only is the order of the two disturbances reversed, but that under Theudas took place after the probable date of the events in Jerusalem to which Gamaliel's speech is a response. A theologically conservative scholar might resolve this problem by suggesting either that a different Theudas is meant or that Acts is more reliable than Josephus, a more critical one might admit that Acts was wrong.[31] However, if one grants that Acts may be mistaken, then the mistake would be a serious one: the writer would betray a disconcerting confusion with regard to the course of events in Palestine in the first half of the first century. Whoever the author of Acts was, he would show himself ill-informed about this area at this period. Such an ignorance would, on the other hand, be less intelligible, and therefore less likely, on the part of the Judaean-born Josephus, even if he had still been only a boy when Fadus was governor. The suspicion remains, then, that it is the author of Acts who is mistaken, and this mistake would raise serious questions about his knowledge of the true state of affairs, at least in that part of the Roman Empire at that period and above all in matters of chronology. If he does get anything right, then that may just as well be due to the fact that, in a given instance, he can draw on reliable sources of information. At times, he may even do that without properly understanding or appreciating those sources and their meaning. In turn, however, that means that each individual case must be assessed on its own merits, and sweeping judgements about Acts' reliability in general are out of place.

At the same time, we cannot dispense with Acts entirely if we are to have any success in writing a history of the earliest Christians nor, in practice, should we, for we will find, if I may here anticipate the findings of the rest of the book, that in many cases the writer of Acts, sometimes perhaps despite himself, has given us credible or worthwhile information. In other words, a healthy dose of caution and critical scepticism is called for in approaching this document, but we may nevertheless approach it in the hope that much in it will survive this sceptical scrutiny and prove of value.

In other words, the task of this work will be a limited one, focusing on those areas of early Christianity where we have something on which to base our reconstruction, rather than trying to fashion historical building blocks out of nothing or next to nothing. The evidence at our disposal will mean a heavy concentration on Paul because of the centrality of his letters amongst that evidence and because the Book of Acts devotes so much attention to him. Those letters may be our primary source, but Acts is not to be neglected; instead its information must be weighed carefully, item by item, in order to determine whether credible tradition is present or not, making all due allowance both for the distance which probably separates its author from the events described and for the perspective of a later period which his work reveals.

2

The First Beginnings

Just as it was appropriate to raise the question where a history of the first Christians should stop, so too it is legitimate to ask where it should begin. For some histories of the earliest church will include an account of the life and work of Jesus,[1] and that makes some sense, the more so as one sees lines of continuity between the history of the Jesus-movement before and after Easter. And indeed, however great the transformation which the Easter events necessitated in the life and thought of Jesus' followers, it would be surprising indeed if what had gone before were of no relevance to their life and thought after Easter. For in connection with the investigation of the life of Jesus some lay weight upon what they call a criterion of historical plausibility: what is affirmed about Jesus should be plausible in a Jewish context *and* make the rise of the early Christian movement intelligible.[2] A corollary of this is then that Jesus' life, work and teaching is indeed, at least in some respects, relevant to, and causally connected with, the life of the earliest Christians, and that aspects of Jesus' life and teaching help to explain how the earliest Christian movement developed subsequently. In other words, a historian should initially seek to present a coherent picture of the whole course of events, before and after Easter, in such a way that the postulated course of Jesus' life throws light upon the variegated life of the earliest Christians. Only when that attempt fails would one be justified in supposing that Easter ushered in something so totally new that it is impossible to trace any continuity whatsoever between events before and after that date.[3] One should begin, however, with the assumption that it should be possible to establish some measure of continuity, and work with that assumption until it proves unworkable.

Nevertheless, if this study is to remain within manageable proportions, it is advisable to limit its scope somewhat and for that reason I have chosen to begin the story with the Easter events or, more precisely, with their impact upon Jesus' followers.[4] However great the continuity with what went before, there is, nevertheless, a recognizable new start here, and all would grant that the movement gets going again under new presuppositions, unless they wish to deny that it was in any way the same movement. If one accepts that what got going was in some sense a continuation of the former movement, then it is to be expected that there are aspects of the life and thought of the renewed or reborn movement which are most easily to be explained by recourse to their antecedents in the movement under the earthly Jesus before his death, and these factors must be noted in the course of the following account.

2.1. Appearances of the Risen Jesus

Whatever one believes about the resurrection of Jesus,[5] it is undeniable that his followers came to believe that he had been raised by God from the dead, that the one who had apparently died an ignominious death, forsaken and even accursed by his God, had subsequently been vindicated by that same God. That remains true whether one believes that early Jewish expectations, for instance about the vindication of the righteous, had predisposed the disciples to expect some such vindication in the case of Jesus, or prefers instead to follow the Gospels in seeing the disciples of Jesus as thoroughly demoralized and disorientated after his death and as being, consequently, completely taken aback by the subsequent course of events. Whether they expected it or not, they came to believe that God had in fact raised Jesus and this was for them a truly revolutionary conviction.

It was certainly revolutionary in the sense that otherwise the world continued to be much as it had been before, whereas the concept of resurrection was in Jewish expectations either a temporary restoration to life in this world or, as something permanent, very much bound up with the end of history and the breaking in of a new age. Jesus' followers did not regard his new life as a temporary phase, but as something of enduring validity, and yet the end had not come and the world went on its way. Something that should have been part of a cosmic transformation or renewal had taken place without any of those cosmic concomitants which one would normally have expected. That is in itself a factor that should cause us to question whether current expectations could be a sufficient cause of the rise in the belief in Jesus' resurrection.[6]

The New Testament does not allow for any current expectations which might have contributed to the rise of this faith in the resurrection and does not even portray the disciples as predisposed to expect it on the basis of Jesus' alleged predictions that God would raise him, even when he had apparently sometimes specified that this would happen 'after three days' or 'on the third day'.[7] Instead it attributes the disciples' belief to the discovery of the empty tomb, together with an announcement by a heavenly messenger or messengers that Jesus has been raised and is therefore no longer in the tomb,[8] and to a series of appearances of the risen Jesus to his disciples. In other words, it is something outside themselves which called forth this faith on the part of the disciples.

In the case of Paul this is perhaps less clear, although he himself clearly believes that the source of the vision which led to his conversion lay outside himself: God showed him the risen Son of God.[9] It is modern critics who have suggested that inward, psychological factors may have induced an equally inward vision,[10] but this way of interpreting the appearances is obviously harder if they were in fact such tangible events as the Gospels describe. On the other hand the Gospel accounts of these more tangible resurrection appearances are beset with difficulties: in particular the motif of non-recognition[11] raises serious questions about the identity of this apparently this-worldly body which the disciples allegedly see and its relation to the crucified body of Jesus.[12]

Whatever this 'something' was, it was believed that God had acted, enabling that which Jesus had set in motion before his death to resume its progress with renewed impetus.

The twofold basis of the early Christian resurrection belief, empty tomb and resurrection appearances, does, however, have certain implications for reconstructing the earliest history of the Christian movement. On the one hand there is the tradition that Jesus was raised on the third day. It might be argued that this was simply a deduction from Hos 6.1–2,[13] although the earliest church does not seem to have found this passage a useful proof-text to interpret the resurrection of Jesus. If, however, this dating arose because something in fact happened on that third day, then it is likely that it happened in or near Jerusalem, for the intervening sabbath would not have allowed Jesus' followers to get very far from Jerusalem since Jesus' death by crucifixion, however dangerous it may have been for them in that city. They would only have attracted attention to themselves by setting out on the sabbath, particularly if they did so with great haste, whereas it would presumably have been reasonably easy to merge with the massive crowds which flocked to Jerusalem at Passover time. Yet some of the Gospels also contain accounts of resurrection appearances in Galilee,[14] and in view of the paucity of evidence for the continued existence of Christian groups in Galilee this is a tradition that calls for some explanation.

John 21 is here strikingly at variance with the previous chapter and thereby highlights this problem of the disciples' departure from Jerusalem. For according to John 20 not only has the empty tomb been discovered, but Jesus has already appeared to his disciples on two successive Sundays, and yet in chapter 21 we find some of them resuming their work as fishermen as if nothing had happened, let alone the commissioning of John 20.21–3, and they seem to be taken completely by surprise when Jesus does eventually appear to them on the shore; had nothing prepared them for this possibility? As a narrative sequence John 20–21 therefore raises more questions than it answers.

The author of Luke–Acts' concentration on Jerusalem, indeed his deliberate removal of any trace of Galilean appearances from the tradition, is, on the other hand, far more easily intelligible in the light of the prominence of that city as a later centre of earliest Christianity, indeed *the* centre until its removal by the sack of Jerusalem by the Romans. It must be asked whether, if the tomb had been discovered to be empty and if it had immediately occurred to anyone that this pointed to Jesus' resurrection, it is likely that the disciples would then have made their way back to Galilee. It is even less likely that they would ever have done so, had Jesus actually appeared to them in Jerusalem. That line of argument leaves unexplained, however, what had happened in Jerusalem: the Gospels are agreed in mentioning the discovery of the empty tomb, even if they are divided over the question whether this discovery was immediately followed by encounters with the risen Jesus in Jerusalem or its neighbourhood. Paul makes no mention of this discovery in 1 Cor 15.4–5, and that is for many sufficient cause to doubt the reliability of that tradition. Yet the discovery of an empty tomb is in itself ambiguous and can be interpreted in various ways. Perhaps more significant is that the Gospels consistently attribute this discovery to women and this is a feature which is perhaps unlikely to be a later invention. More to the point may be the question whether they found the tomb empty or merely failed to find the body of Jesus.[15] The traditions of Galilean appearances, at any rate, give us good reason to suppose that nothing which would particularly encourage belief in Jesus' resurrection had occurred before the disciples could leave Jerusalem without attracting too much attention, and that they did indeed then leave that tragic and perilous city in order to travel home. That suggests that it is whatever they experienced there, in Galilee, that is responsible for the persistent traditions of appearances of the risen Jesus there.

On the other hand it is clear that Jerusalem was later to become the centre of the earliest church and Paul implies that it was a place where one would expect to find the apostles gathered, even if he did not meet many on his first visit after his conversion.[16] Galilee was not to become the centre of the Christian movement and indeed fades from sight as the history of the earliest church proceeds. Does that then presuppose a sequence of events in which the disciples first returned home and then experienced something there which convinced them that what Jesus had started had not been finished off? If so, they must then have concluded that, despite the personal danger to themselves, they must return to Jerusalem, that focus of their people's religious hopes, as the place where they must be, as the fulfilment of God's promises and Israel's hopes unfolded.

The two-volume Lucan work, we have seen, avoids this problem of the disciples' return to Jerusalem by having them remain in that city and by emphasizing that they are expressly ordered to do so (Luke 24.49b). It also adds something further to the accounts of the other Gospels by adding a further event, the ascension of Jesus, as the termination and climax of the resurrection appearances – at least that is how the fuller account in Acts (1.9–11) depicts it; the account at the end of Luke's Gospel is less easy to interpret and can only with difficulty be harmonized with Acts, for Luke 24 on its own would lead one to suppose that the ascension took place on the same day as Jesus first appeared to his disciples (v. 51), whereas Acts inserts the period of forty days which has become enshrined in our ecclesiastical calendar.

The theological problems and problems of understanding which this author's account presents are also considerable: what does the event of the ascension add to Jesus' status and nature? Did the event of the resurrection usher in what was solely an interim state, somewhere between the world of the dead and his final glorification? And how is the state into which he now enters to be distinguished from that state in which he was between the individual appearances to his disciples? It is hard to avoid the suspicion that this extra event which 'Luke' has inserted is a somewhat artificial construct, marking the end of the period of the resurrection appearances, at least for him if not for Paul (cf. 1 Cor 15.8), but one beset by conceptual difficulties. It has, however, probably a particular significance in this writer's presentation of his message for a church still waiting for its Lord's return, assuring it that he would indeed return, despite the absence of appearances of the risen Jesus in the interim, and at the same time refocusing its eyes, not on this expected future heavenly event, but on the missionary task which it is to carry out in the power of the Spirit.

2.2. Regrouping in Jerusalem?

Whether they had stayed in Jerusalem all the time or had initially left Jerusalem after Jesus' death, which seems far likelier, it is clear that, sooner or later, a nucleus of Jesus' followers gathered in Jerusalem. In all probability many of them had accompanied him on his travels in Galilee or had responded in other ways to his preaching there. In that case it is evident that there is from the start an element of continuity between the Jesus-movement before and after Jesus' death, a continuity based on the persons of his followers.

The Book of Acts narrates here, with particular emphasis, the story of the refilling of the circle of the Twelve, which had been depleted by the defection and subsequent death of Judas Iscariot (1.15–26). It is again a story which probably has a particular importance for the author of Acts, in that it cements the continuity between the Jesus-movement before and after Jesus' death. It is striking that the criterion which decides who is eligible to be put up for election is one's having accompanied Jesus from the time of his baptism till the time of his ascension (1.21–2); yet had all of the Twelve or indeed any of them been with Jesus right from the start, from the moment of his baptism? The Gospels describe the various calls of Jesus to those who are to become his disciples as happening at some point after his baptism and, in the case of the Synoptic Gospels, after he had returned to Galilee from that part of the Jordan where John had been baptizing. It is, at any rate, a criterion which would debar the recipients of any future revelations of the risen Jesus, like Paul.[17] It is also a criterion which, strictly speaking, is not necessary for the task which is here mentioned, namely witnessing to Jesus' resurrection. For that role, so long a contact with the earthly Jesus was not really essential. Perhaps it would help one to verify that the risen Jesus whom one had witnessed really was Jesus, if one had had at least some contact with Jesus before his death, although that depends on whether the risen body of Jesus was sufficiently like the one which his disciples had known before.[18]

Are we, however, correct to speak here of a '*re*grouping', at least specifically with regard to the group of the Twelve? For there are those who doubt whether the circle of the Twelve, which is apparently here reconstituted, was in fact a pre-Easter phenomenon. Instead the formation of this group is regarded as something which first came about after Easter, and often it is thought that it was Peter's experience of seeing the risen Jesus which acted as a catalyst for this.[19] The major problem for this view is the persistent tradition that this group originally included Judas Iscariot: why should his name have been included after Easter? That can perhaps be explained by reinterpreting his deed: rather than delivering Jesus up to those who wished to arrest him, his fault was rather to desert the band of Jesus' followers at a later point of time, after they had formed themselves around a nucleus of twelve after the resurrection, and this apostasy was then projected back into the lifetime of Jesus.[20] Yet is such a theory not an act of desperation?[21] Is it not in every way simpler to accept that the Twelve existed during Jesus' lifetime and that Judas was one of them? That is, however, no easy answer, for the first Christians had then to explain how it came to be that Jesus could have chosen someone who was going to fail him so drastically. Could he, should he, not have foreseen that?[22]

At any rate Acts and the first three Gospels list twelve persons who made up this group of twelve, even if the lists do not agree with one another at all points.[23] That in itself points to one significant aspect of these lists and of the tradition about the Twelve: by no means all were natural candidates who were to play a prominent role either during the time of Jesus' ministry or in the life of the later church. Of some we know nothing more, at least from early traditions, than that they are mentioned in these lists. That applies, too, to the new member of the group who is appointed to succeed Judas – Matthias – as well as to the other candidate who is mentioned – Joseph Barsabbas Justus (Acts 1.23). That all points to the probable use of traditions here, even if the author of Acts has adapted them to heighten the continuity between Jesus and the earliest church. The presence of some names in the list is, in view of their relative obscurity, most easily explained by their having indeed been members of this group. And the obscurity of most members of the Twelve is in itself an argument for the origin of this group before Easter; for, if the role of the 'apostles of Jesus Christ' stems from their commissioning by the risen Christ, as we shall see, then it is unlikely that the group of the Twelve arose at the same time. Being an 'apostle' remained significant for quite a considerable time, far more so than being one of the Twelve, and played a more important role in the formation of the early church, as far as we can judge from the records. That the role of the Twelve paled into almost complete oblivion is easier to explain if it was an earlier institution which was superseded by a new and wider circle constituted by the risen Christ, which nevertheless probably also included the surviving members of the circle of the Twelve as well as others.[24]

The presence of these persons in the circle of the Twelve, coupled with the silence of the tradition about their activities, raises the further question of their role and purpose. For the writer of Acts, these lie in their function as guarantors of continuity, but it is likely that their original function was another one, particularly if the formation of this group is to be traced back to the ministry of Jesus. Whether or not one can do that, however, it is likely that the number twelve was deliberately chosen: by its very number this group represents and symbolizes the nucleus of a reconstituted and renewed Israel. The reconstitution and renewal of Israel is itself to be regarded as a sign of the presence of the end-time and of the eschatological intervention of God. The link with the twelve tribes of Israel is explicit in at least one saying from the Synoptic tradition, Matt 19.28 par.: '... you ... will also sit on twelve thrones, judging the twelve tribes of Israel' (NRSV).[25]

The eschatological significance of the group of the Twelve may help to explain one feature of Acts' account: whereas the vacancy left by Judas' death is carefully filled, later vacancies are seemingly left unfilled, for example, when James, the son of Zebedee, is executed on the orders of Herod Agrippa in Acts 12.2.[26] For James, as a martyr, could still fulfil his role as eschatological judge; indeed, he might be thought to be all the better qualified to fill that role, and his premature death meant simply that he was able to take his seat on his throne rather earlier than the rest of the Twelve. Judas, on the other hand, had disqualified himself from ever exercising this function.

Acts implies that the Twelve are not only 'apostles', but '*the* apostles': Matthias is elected, by God's guidance through the drawing of lots, to join 'the eleven apostles' (1.26).[27] This view also seems to be reflected in Rev 21.14.[28] It has often enough been noted that Acts, for all its veneration of Paul, mostly withholds the designation 'apostle' from him. The designation which he shares with the Twelve is rather that of a 'witness'.[29] The sole exception, in 14.4, 14, stands out, in that Barnabas and Paul are referred to as 'apostles'. It may be easiest to explain this as evidence of the use of a tradition, perhaps even a tradition which uses 'apostles' simply in the sense of 'delegates, emissaries', using it here of Barnabas and Paul as emissaries of the church in Syrian Antioch.[30] The silence elsewhere in Acts with regard to Paul's apostolate is the more striking in view of the emphasis which Paul himself places upon his apostleship. This emphasis, however, probably points in turn to the fact that his claim to be an apostle was a disputed one.

Gal 2.8, particularly if this passage, as some suggest, alludes to, even if it does not quote, the terms of the agreement reached in Jerusalem, may be significant, in that Paul speaks of the recognition of Peter's apostleship for the circumcision, but only of God's working in himself for the good of the gentiles. Paul's 'apostleship' may not have been recognized in Jerusalem and the most likely reason for that may be a more restrictive understanding of the term. The implication of Acts' silence would then be that this work, in large measure, shares that narrower interpretation of the title.

At any rate, it is important to recognize that 'apostle' could mean different things in different circles in the earliest church. Already the traditions quoted by Paul in 1 Cor 15.5 and 7 seem to imply a different definition to that presupposed in Acts 1, since the recording of appearances to 'Cephas and the Twelve' and then 'James [i.e. the brother of Jesus] and the apostles' suggests that 'the apostles' are a different group to 'the Twelve' and not synonymous with them.

And, whereas Acts defines the prerequisite for belonging to the Twelve as having accompanied Jesus during the entire time of his ministry, Paul's criteria are very different: having seen (the risen) Jesus and performing the works of an apostle, especially in the founding of new Christian communities, whose existence are evidence of the reality of his apostleship (1 Cor 9.1–2). The first of these criteria would actually fit the task of the Twelve in Acts 1.22, namely witnessing to the resurrection of Jesus, better than the criterion which Acts in fact names. That criterion reflects instead an attempt to restrict the title solely to those who had been with Jesus in his earthly ministry, and it is unlikely that the author of Acts was the first to try to impose such a criterion. It is more probable that he has taken up a traditional understanding of the title, but one which Paul himself would strenuously oppose, and the irony is that such a usage has prevailed in a work which otherwise so extols Paul's role and work.

2.3. Pentecost

At some point or other Jesus' followers reassembled in Jerusalem, having probably returned thither from Galilee. One can legitimately infer a certain sense of expectancy on their part which brought them back to this city on which so many of the Old Testament promises centred, despite the danger to themselves. The Book of Acts attaches a particular significance to the Feast of Pentecost, in the Jewish calendar the pilgrim feast fifty days after Passover and the following Feast of Unleavened Bread, and there is a certain plausibility in the suggestion that this festival did indeed bring them back to Jerusalem, perhaps even expecting the end to come at that time. Given the significance of resurrection as an event of the end-time, it is likely that the belief that Jesus had already been raised from the dead would encourage the expectation that the remaining events of that time were near at hand. Acts, at any rate, clearly regards what occurred at that festival as eschatological, as a sign of the presence of the end-time, 'the last days', a phrase which this author adds to the quotation from Joel 2.28–32 at the beginning of Peter's explanatory speech in Acts 2.17–21.

Others, however, try to explain the motivation for the choice of this date as theological: the Jewish festival celebrating the giving of the law at Sinai is the occasion for a new gift of God, the gift of the Spirit.[31] And, even if the evidence that Pentecost was regarded as celebrating the giving of the law is somewhat later, there is evidence that it had, for some time, been particularly associated with God's giving of the covenant, and it might reasonably be thought that it is a short step from that to commemorating the giving of the law.[32] A contrast such as we find in 2 Cor 3.6–18 between the old covenant of the letter and a new one of the Spirit could, therefore, lie behind the depiction of this festival as the occasion for a spectacular outpouring of the Spirit. Yet there is little sign that 'Luke' himself was aware of this symbolism of the feast. It is true that some of the imagery used in Acts 2.2–4 is reminiscent of the Old Testament accounts of Sinai and of subsequent, imaginative elaborations on that event, although it has, at the same time, to be admitted that phenomena of fire and wind were frequently associated with theophanies.[33] Nevertheless, it is hard to resist the conclusion that the points of contact between this passage and the language-miracle implicit in it on the one hand, and the exegesis of the Sinai-event by the first-century Jewish philosopher and exegete Philo of Alexandria on the other, are more than a coincidence.[34] If, then, this symbolism of the two covenants has determined the choice of this date, then it had probably already done so before 'Luke' received it and he was very likely unaware of it.

Whether or not an outpouring of the Spirit took place on this occasion, it is clear that the centre of the reborn Jesus-movement moved to Jerusalem at a fairly early point in its history. It is also possible that at some point of time, though not necessarily on this day, some mass ecstatic experience took place.[35] Despite the protestations of those who insist that appearances of the risen Jesus are something different from experiences of the Spirit, it is still possible that Acts' Pentecost is a doublet of that event which Paul mentions in his listing of resurrection appearances, in which Jesus appeared to 'more than five hundred brethren' (1 Cor 15.6).[36] For, after all, Jesus' appearance was in Paul's case clearly a visionary one and Paul does speak of the risen Jesus in such a way as to give the impression of a partial identification of the two: the last Adam became 'a living spirit' (1 Cor 15.45). In turn such an identification of the two events would imply that early Christianity was from the start characterized by ecstatic spiritual gifts and experiences and that seems highly probable, although there have been those who maintain that such experiences were a peculiarity of the Corinthian church.[37] That is unlikely in that Paul claims to speak in tongues more than the Corinthians (1 Cor 14.18) and his remark does not suggest that this was something which he first began to do when he came to Corinth or which he only did when visiting the Corinthian church. It is equally likely, perhaps likelier, that this was a feature of the earliest church, which Paul had known from the beginning of his Christian experience, just as he seems to assume that the Galatian Christians had had distinctive experiences of the Spirit from the first (Gal 3.2–5).

Exactly when and how this movement first gathered again in Jerusalem after Jesus' death is, therefore, hard to say with any certainty, but there is a certain plausibility in the suggestion that this pilgrim-festival of Pentecost brought them back, perhaps expecting the final consummation would take place.[38] At any rate, as Weiser and Jervell point out,[39] it needs to be explained why early Christians adopted Pentecost as one of their festivals, assuming that the Acts account was not reason enough. Did that festival also have a Christian meaning over and above its meaning for Jews? It is not impossible that the early Christians' gatherings were marked from the start by ecstatic experiences, and the occasion of their celebrating this Jewish festival might conceivably have been accompanied by some such experience. If there is anything in such suggestions, however, then it has probably led early Christians, before the writer of Acts, to depict the event in the light of Jewish speculations about the law-giving at Sinai.

On the other hand the picture painted in Acts 2 is not to be accepted uncritically, for the account of the ecstatic phenomena which we now have in that chapter contains a number of features which are puzzling and do not seem to fit together. In particular, the identity of the audience and the nature of the phenomenon of languages cause difficulties. On the one hand, Acts 2.5 tells us that there were devout Jews living in Jerusalem, but when they come to speak they identify themselves as living in Mesopotamia and other places (2.9–10); in other words they seem to live in two places, for the Greek word used is the same in both cases, even when translations often get round this problem by so rendering them that v. 5 refers to a temporary visit and vv. 9 and 10 to the countries where they are permanently settled.[40] It is doubtful, however, whether 'Luke' means that, since the converts from this event are to provide the nucleus of the new church in Jerusalem and are not meant to scatter in all directions after the festival is over.[41]

The other puzzling feature in this account is the nature of the wonder which so impresses this audience. It would seem, in the first place, that 'Luke' understands it as a miraculous endowment which enables the audience to hear the message of the disciples in the many native tongues of the various regions from which they come. That would be impressive, but superfluous in the sense that the hearers would probably have understood it just as well, if not better, in either Greek or Aramaic, and the disciples would be conversant with one or other or, at least in some cases, both of these languages. Were the audience Jews, then they more likely came from urban centres of those regions where one or other of these two languages was widely spoken. Nor is it clear why they should be so amazed that Galileans in particular could speak so (v. 7); some have remarked that Galileans were noted for their poor pronunciation of Aramaic, but surely more is meant here than an instantaneous elocution lesson? It is, however, also puzzling that some should suggest in response that they were drunk (v. 13). Now conceivably the babble of competing languages could confuse some so that they heard nothing aright, but it is worth noting that in 1 Cor 14.23 Paul fears that utterances in unintelligible tongues may lead to the comparable verdict that the Corinthians are mad. 'Tongues' are for this apostle only useful in public when someone can translate the utterances, but of that there is no word here, and the following speech of Peter interprets not the content, but the eschatological and salvation-historical significance of the phenomenon. Whereas Paul fears that tongues may hinder evangelism, the phenomenon in Acts 2 serves greatly to advance the spread of the gospel. Such comparisons, along with the tensions in the account in Acts, have led some, plausibly, to suggest that a description of a phenomenon in the earliest church similar to that which was to be found later in the Corinthian church, of utterances in unintelligible, perhaps allegedly angelic or heavenly, tongues has been reinterpreted, by 'Luke' or another predecessor of his, as a supernatural gift of an unlearned ability to speak human languages which are recognizable at least to some. The existence of such a tradition would, in turn, be a further argument in favour of regarding ecstatic utterances as a characteristic of the life of the earliest church from an earlier period.

2.4. A Jewish Group?

Our only source for the history of the very earliest Christian community in Jerusalem is, for all practical purposes, the Book of Acts. And yet, if the evidence of Acts is suspect for a somewhat later period, when it can be compared with Paul's own account in his letters, it is doubly so with regard to this earlier stage. For at this point the report of an eyewitness, either direct or more likely as a tradition upon which the author draws, probably does not come into question. Moreover, it is precisely this time which would be most formative and normative for the life of the later church, and we should therefore expect that the author might have given expression here to his vision of what the church should be, to an even greater extent than is elsewhere the case. We shall in fact see traces of an idealizing tendency, even if not perhaps so extensive as one might have feared.

A further problem is the episodic nature of Acts' account and this feature of the writer's methods is particularly pronounced at this point. Over against this there are a series of summaries, which seem to offer a more general account of the life of the early church (2.42–7; 4.32–5; 5.12–16). But are these more than editorial generalizations from isolated incidents? For it has been suggested that, for instance, 'Luke' knew of the episode of Barnabas' generous gift of the proceeds from the sale of his land (4.36–7) and made out of this a general principle of the sharing of goods, to which 'all' contributed (2.44), whereas the story was told precisely because it was a prominent and memorable exception.[42] Moreover, it is to be doubted how many had such properties at their disposal. In addition, all clearly did not sell what they had, for 12.12 presupposes that John Mark's mother Mary still possessed a house in Jerusalem. Such a property was doubtless more useful to the church, as a place to meet, if it remained unsold.[43] Besides such generalizations scholars have detected this author's idealizing tendencies at work in these summaries, above all in the sharing of goods; this reflects not only the Graeco-Roman philosophical ideal that friends have things in common,[44] but also, in the averting of poverty (4.34), the fulfilment of an Old Testament ideal (Deut 15.4). A further feature of these summaries is the degree to which material is repeated, both from summary to summary (e.g. the community of goods in 2.44–5 and 4.34–5) and to some extent also within a single summary.[45] Yet it is likely that these summaries are not simply the author's composition but, as elsewhere in Acts, show how the author has taken up traditional formulations and fitted them into his text, while at the same time freely composing other parts. That is suggested most clearly by 5.12–16, for v. 15 does not seem to follow on naturally from v. 14: that they carried sick out into the streets in the hope that they might be healed by Peter's shadow falling upon them is not a logical consequence of the increase in the numbers of believers, despite the introductory 'so that', but would make better sense after v. 12a which tells of the many signs and wonders performed through the apostles. Such a note about popular expectations of Peter's wonder-working powers may therefore be traditional, but at the same time this example shows the limitations of such accounts for gaining a comprehensive picture of the life of the early church.

The presence of such idealizing features does not mean, however, that these accounts are worthless or offer no information about the earliest Christian community in Jerusalem.[46] Many features of them are too intrinsically probable to be lightly dismissed as the invention of the author. It is, for instance, highly probable that the earliest community was taught by the apostles (2.42) – at least by them among others. For if it was necessary to teach them about Jesus' life and teaching as well as about the events following his death, then the circle of those who could impart such information was not limited to the Twelve. That is admitted by the account in Acts itself, not only by the fact that there was a second candidate to succeed Judas Iscariot in the circle of the Twelve besides Matthias, Joseph Barsabbas (1.23), but also by the fact that 1.15 speaks of a group of around 120. For those who had newly joined the community such instruction and information was not only necessary, but it would also have been astonishing if the new members had not asked for it.

Again, if *communal meals* had played an important part in Jesus' ministry and had indeed served then as a demonstration of the inclusive nature of God's kingly rule, then it is only to be expected that such meals would continue to form a prominent part of the life of his followers (Acts 2.42, 46), even if they and their symbolic and theological importance were a theme particularly dear to 'Luke's' heart.[47] It is equally probable that such meals took place, indeed had to take place, in private houses or in a private house (2.46) and that this community was therefore dependent, as the Pauline churches would be at a later stage, upon the generosity of at least one member or sympathizer who had a house in Jerusalem which could be placed at the disposal of the group.

At the same time it might seem unnecessary to deny another feature of the account in Acts, namely that the first followers of Jesus also attended the worship of the *Temple* (2.46; 3.1; 5.21, 25, 42), even if they also used the opportunity of their visits to the shrine to spread their message among their fellow-worshippers. For without question they would have felt themselves to be still part of Israel.[48] The earliest community was entirely a Jewish one; even if Acts 2.5 reflects an earlier tradition which spoke of an ethnically mixed audience at Pentecost,[49] it is clear that for the author of Acts only Jewish hearers come in question at this stage and on this point he was in all probability correct. We will see that in the listing of the Seven in 6.5 it is expressly mentioned that one of them, Nicolaus, was a proselyte; that means that the other six were Jews, and it is probable that the fact that one of the group was a Jew by conversion, not by birth, was still something exceptional. At so early a stage it is not to be expected that Jesus' followers felt themselves to be no longer part of Israel, and it is in fact more likely that they considered themselves to be the truest part of Israel, in that they had recognized and followed Israel's Messiah. That Messiah had sought to call Israel back to its God and it was only to be expected that his followers would be equally Israel-oriented in their aims.[50] Whether they could have seen any necessity to be critical of the institution of the Temple and its cult is more than doubtful, particularly if it is most uncertain whether Jesus had in any way challenged the validity of the cult.

It is true that Jesus' action in the Temple (Mark 11.15–17 parr.) is often interpreted as prophesying or even symbolically enacting the destruction of the Temple,[51] but, if Jerusalem with its Temple were not still a focus of the disciples' hopes, it must be asked why they based themselves in this city, despite the danger to themselves. If, on the other hand, Jesus' action was a criticism of the way in which the cult was abused by the Temple authorities,[52] and in fact expressed a deep concern for the holiness of the Temple and a veneration for its worship, then it is readily intelligible that his followers continued to take part in its rites. Equally, whatever he may have said about destruction coming upon the Temple (Mark 13.2; 14.58 parr.) may reflect, not a critique of the Temple itself, but indignation at its misuse by the Jewish aristocracy.

There is, however, in this account in Acts a tension, not only with certain interpretations of Jesus' action in the Temple, but also with the view that the new community of Jesus' followers regarded itself as the new, the true temple of God. There are parallels to this idea among the Essenes, as Grappe points out,[53] but many of them distanced themselves from Jerusalem and its Temple, rather than making Jerusalem their headquarters as the earliest Christians seem to have done. And how soon this idea or the view that Jesus' death replaced all cultic sacrifices arose among the early Christians is far from clear.[54]

Is there any truth, however, in Acts' repeated references to a *sharing of goods* or is this simply an idealizing feature invented by the author? For a start it is not clear whether he envisages property being sold and the proceeds distributed to the needy (so in 2.45; 4.34–5, 37) or whether the property is retained but the use of it is shared with other members of the community (cf. 2.44, 'all things in common'). Yet even this uncertainty is most readily intelligible if at least one of these variants is traditional; if anything is to be attributed to the author's idealizing tendency it is the motif of 'all things in common', but, as we saw, the mention in 12.12 of the house of Mary, John

Mark's mother, points to a concrete example of something not sold, but held in common. If Barnabas possessed a field (4.37), on the other hand, then this is not likely to have been so immediately useful to the Jerusalem community, particularly if it was in his native Cyprus; yet it has been suggested that it was near Jerusalem (and may first have been sold when Barnabas was despatched to, or left for, Antioch – Acts 11.22).[55] Some would certainly regard the whole picture of this sharing, in whatever form, as the product of the author's imagination, but it is to be noted, not only that what he imagines is not wholly clear, but also that there are contemporary parallels which suggest that such a sharing is by no means unthinkable. As far as the Qumran community is concerned, it seems that the possessions of members were in stages absorbed into the common property of the community (esp. 1QS 6.19–23; cf. 1.13), but this model differs from that found in Acts in that the sharing of the early Christians is portrayed as voluntary: the sin of Ananias and Sapphira was not that they withheld something, but that they pretended to have given all (5.3–4).[56] A closer comparison is rather to be found in those Essene groups which lived, not in a separate community in the desert, but in towns and villages in Palestine. So Philo describes '*Essaioi*' living in villages and working as farm-labourers or craftsmen; they pooled their wages and received in return food and clothing.[57] He also mentions Essenes who lived in cities as well,[58] even though the account in *Every Good Man Is Free* suggests that they avoided cities because of the wickedness of the inhabitants of the latter (§76). Whatever the early Christians thought about cities – and perhaps Jerusalem might be regarded as in many respects different from other Graeco-Roman cities – they evidently thought it important to be there, and the form of their communal life there can legitimately be compared with that of these Essenes whom Philo mentions in the *Hypothetica*. Of these, too, he says that they have no private property but pool everything and use it in common, living in clubs (*thiasoi*) and eating together (11.4–5, 11), and paying their wages to a treasurer who then buys what is necessary for the community (11.10); even their clothing comes out of a common pool (11.12). However, they go so far as to eschew marriage and the begetting of children (11.14–17), but there is no evidence that the very earliest Christian community went so far, even if this asceticism and the reasons by which Philo justifies it have several points of contact with the asceticism which is reflected in 1 Cor 7.

Another point at which the earliest Jerusalem church would probably have differed from most Essene groups is to be found in the fact that the nucleus of the Christian group came from Galilee. Whereas the Essene groups seem to have been able to support themselves through the work of some of them on the land or in trades and crafts, this would have been more difficult for those like former fishermen, who could not ply their trade in Jerusalem, and who anyway were preoccupied with proclaiming their new faith. Inhabitants of Jerusalem who joined them could doubtless often contribute something to support the community, by continuing to practise their previous trade. It is, however, likely that some degree of pooling of resources and of hospitality would be necessary, if only to provide those who had come from Galilee with food and a roof over their heads. This would, in itself, mean that the early Christian community might well find that the resources at its disposal were more stretched than in an otherwise comparable Essene community formed from inhabitants of the city in question.

Martin Hengel also observes, following Ernst Bloch, that there was probably an added dimension to this sharing, one to which Acts does not do full justice in its account, namely an eschatological dimension. Those who were convinced that the end of this world was very near at hand would not have felt the need to steward their resources so as to make them last. Influenced, too, by the teaching of Jesus, they would have felt free to tear down the barriers which the unequal distribution of wealth erects between people. This lack of long-term planning and stewardship of their resources may well also have contributed to the financial vulnerability of the Jerusalem community, making it more heavily dependent on the gifts and subventions of others.[59]

Philo's accounts of the Essenes therefore indicate a number of similarities between them and the early Christian community, not only the sharing of resources, but also common meals (but not with regard to the Temple cult), and it is important to recognize that many aspects of the early Christians' life together would not have struck their contemporaries as anything out of the ordinary. Others, however, were less usual, and are important both for the impression which they would make on outsiders and also for their effect on the self-understanding and self-awareness of the Christian community. Even elements which were not peculiar to them, like their sharing of possessions or shared meals, would naturally enhance their own sense of cohesion amongst themselves, just as they undoubtedly served to bind together other groups with similar practices. But distinctive elements would undoubtedly contribute to a sense that they were different, even if they still felt themselves very much part of Israel. At the same time, it must be stressed that, since the Judaism of the period was so varied, such distinctive elements would not immediately suggest to them, or to their Jewish contemporaries either, that they had placed themselves beyond the pale of Judaism.

First and foremost there is naturally their *faith in, and allegiance to, Jesus*, their belief that, despite his shameful death, he was the promised Messiah, God's anointed one, whom God would send to usher in the new age. They could not but be aware that this distinguished them from the majority of their fellow Jews who remained hostile or at best sceptical with regard to their claims. That they claimed someone as Messiah who had already come, let alone someone who had died so abjectly, was of course highly unusual, but nevertheless, a century later, R. Akiba was to see in the revolutionary leader Bar Kokhba a fulfilment of the messianic prophecy of Num 24.17; many of his contemporaries may have thought the rabbi's belief to be misplaced, but they did not condemn him as untrue to his Jewish faith because of it.[60] Likewise the early Christians' belief did not make them any the less Jews, for they believed Jesus to be the fulfilment of the promises made to Israel. Nor was this belief as such something that would call their status as Jews into question in the eyes of their fellows, any more than the loyalty of the Qumran community to the Teacher of Righteousness and its belief in his role in God's purposes cast doubt on the Jewishness of its members.

The use of *baptism* as an initiation rite, marking the entry of new members into the community, would doubtless have distinguished the Christian group from almost all other contemporary Jewish groups. Their rite was similar to that of John the Baptist in very many respects, above all in the fact that it was a once-for-all washing which was administered by another, as opposed to the repeated self-administered washings of Jewish ritual, and in that it signified the repentance of the baptized and the forgiveness of her or his sins, in anticipation of God's imminent judgement. John's rite had been so distinctive in contemporary Judaism that it had earned him the name of the Baptist, and this distinctiveness would also apply to early Christian use of the rite. Most are agreed that the rite was adopted by Jesus' followers early on, but there is less agreement how early it was adopted and why. It is difficult to gauge how far its use by John would have encouraged Christians to use it or not. For, on the one hand, the fact that Jesus submitted to it could encourage them to do likewise; on the other hand, a couple of passages in Acts reflect the view that John's rite was inadequate (18.25; 19.3–5) and certainly the significance of that baptism for John, as a preparation for God's coming judgement, would have needed to be reinterpreted in the light of the conviction of Jesus' followers that God had already intervened in kingly power in Jesus' work, and that Jesus was now enthroned as Lord. It is, correspondingly, for them a baptism 'in/into the name of Jesus' and placed the baptized in a special relation to their Lord, whose name and power they invoked at their baptism, placing themselves under his protection, consecrating themselves in his service and binding themselves to him. Despite this shift of meaning they were, however, evidently prepared to adopt John's rite, and Jesus' own baptism by John may well have been a crucial factor in this decision.[61]

At this point, however, the tradition of the Fourth Gospel is worth noting, even though many dismiss its witness as worthless at this point: Jesus and his disciples also baptized during his ministry (John 3.22, 26; 4.1).[62] More puzzling is the qualification in 4.2, that only the disciples baptized and not Jesus himself, for it is unclear why he should have refrained if they were administering this rite.[63] The motives which could have led to these conflicting statements are unclear and are further complicated by this Gospel's reticence about the fact that John baptized Jesus himself; John's witness to the descent of the Spirit upon Jesus (1.32) appears to presuppose the Synoptic tradition of that baptism or one like it, but does not describe it as they do. Were it true that Jesus' disciples had administered this rite during Jesus' earthly ministry, then it is readily intelligible that they would have continued this practice, more or less without a break, after Easter, as is depicted in Acts 2.38, 41. If that were not the case, then we must assume there was a certain delay in introducing the practice. In either case the necessary reinterpretation of the rite, to take account of the new role played by Jesus after his resurrection, would not have taken place overnight, so that one must reckon with a gradual crystallization of the beliefs and expectations now associated with it. And if John's baptism was distinctive, then it follows that the rite administered by Jesus' followers was even more so, not only in that it was seemingly practised in Jerusalem as opposed to the Jordan valley, with all the symbolism of that place, and its plentiful supply of water, but also in that it added to the already distinctive features of John's rite its own, distinctively Christian features, with the reference to the name of Jesus and the linking of the rite to the eschatological gift of the Spirit.[64]

For a further distinguishing feature of the Christian practice was the association of this rite with the bestowal of the *Spirit*. Even if the sayings attributed to John which distinguish his water-baptism from the Spirit-baptism to be administered by the 'coming One' (Mark 1.8 parr.) are not authentic but reflect early Christian belief,[65] they are at least evidence for the linking of this rite with this eschatological gift. Again, however, it is hard to determine how early this belief arose, but, as we have already seen, there is little reason either to doubt that from very early on the Christian community was, at least in part, characterized by ecstatic and charismatic manifestations or to suppose that such phenomena first arose later in a more pronouncedly Graeco-Roman context or were even limited to the Corinthian church. Yet, if such phenomena were characteristic of the earliest Christian community, then this would set its life and worship, and not only its initiation rite, apart from that of the majority of its Jewish contemporaries. Not that inspired figures were unknown in the Judaism of that day, but they were, if anything, the exception, isolated prophetic figures and holy men – and women, if 'Luke's' depiction of Anna in Luke 2.36 is to be believed. The difference between such figures and what seems to be reflected in early Christian circles is therefore quantitative rather than qualitative, but the more widespread charismatic activity in the earliest Christian community would have been distinctive, and all the more so if it was claimed and expected that all Christians would be filled with the Spirit. That was bound to have an impact on those Christians' self-perception and their conception of their place in God's saving plan, for such an outpouring of the Spirit on the whole community was, if anything, to be expected in the renewed people of God of the end-time, as indeed Peter's speech at Pentecost claimed, although the wording of the Joel text which he there quotes could lead one to expect a universal outpouring of the Spirit and not one limited to just one group (Acts 2.17–21).[66]

In other words, although the earliest Christian community had said and done nothing to indicate that it was no longer part of Judaism or that it no longer felt itself to belong to it, there were in all probability sufficient features of its life and practice, above all its belief in Jesus, its practice of baptism, and its manifestation of spiritual gifts, to give it a distinguishable and recognizable profile among the various Jewish groups of the time.

Yet a recognizable and distinct profile amongst a series of movements and groups competing with one another in first-century Judaism does not explain how it came about that the Christian movement gradually parted company with Judaism. Were the Christians driven out by non-Christian Jews and, if so, were they rightly driven out, because they no longer belonged there? Or did Christians, or at least some of them, also decide that they were no longer part of Judaism and that they no longer wanted to be lumped together with Jews as part and parcel of the Judaism of the day?[67] These are questions that must probably be differently answered in relation to various strands within early Christianity in the following chapters, but some preliminary points may perhaps be made here.

One first, general observation is most important: the parting or partings, to imitate the very apt title of Dunn's study,[68] even though he is thinking more of several stages, one after the other, must have taken different forms for different strands of early Christianity: the different partings could take place concurrently in different parts of the early church. Whether one was a devout Jewish Christian, rooted in the life of a Jewish community, or a gentile who had hitherto known Judaism from the sidelines, so to speak, or had had little experience of it at all, made an enormous difference in the way in which the recognition of a separate identity from that of Judaism would be experienced and affect one's life. For the former the effects would be traumatic in the extreme, and that seems to have been the experience of the Johannine community; for the latter the difference was slight, so that some gentile Christians found it difficult to recognize anything which bound them to the Jewish roots of Christianity at all – for that seems to be the point of Paul's rebuke in Rom 11.13–32. If there had been any break for such Christians, now at least they hardly seem to be aware that they had ever been attached.

That is to speak of differing Christian perceptions of the break.

But how did it appear from the Jewish side? Since we do not have any Jewish sources telling us why the separation occurred, as seen from the Jewish side and from inside, as it were, it is legitimate and helpful to seek here the aid of sociological models which may explain the unarticulated forces and pressures that were possibly at work. J. T. Sanders provides here a useful survey of some possible models:[69] a discussion in terms of 'sects', which he considers inappropriate and unfruitful in view of the variety of forms of early Christianity, none of which 'seems to fit into the appropriate model of what a sect is' (124–5);[70] 'conflict theory'; and finally the model of 'deviance'. If it holds good that '[p]unishment of deviants occurs when a society experiences difficulties leading to an identity crisis' (134), then one can see here an explanation of the increasing pressure on the early Christians, at first principally from the side of the priestly authorities and then, after 70 CE, in the face of the identity crisis of Judaism after the fall of Jerusalem and the destruction of the Temple, and in the midst of the attempts of Jewish rabbis to establish Jewish faith and life on a new basis.

Plausible, too, is the point that it was the early Christians' attitude towards the gentiles which made their 'deviance' a particularly serious matter, at least as long as the identity crisis was intimately connected to the danger posed by a Graeco-Roman world which threatened to undermine or swamp Jewish culture and identity. That is especially true of the latter part of the period up to 70 CE. Yet one must differentiate here, as Sanders himself implies when he rejects talk of a single 'break' between Christianity and Judaism (85). It is true, as Sanders argues, that at times it was the priestly authorities who were responsible for action taken against the early Christian community and its leaders. In all probability, then, it was not just the latter's attitude to the gentiles which provoked this action, but also their attitude towards those authorities. Acts' picture of a priestly aristocracy which felt itself being 'got at' by early Christian proclamation of a Jesus to whose death they had contributed (cf. Acts 3.13; 4.10; 5.30) is intrinsically plausible. Sanders, however, mentions another possible source of friction between the Christian community in Jerusalem and the Jewish priestly aristocracy: the former were charging the latter with 'impurity and impropriety' (138). Here it is above all the death of Jesus' brother James which comes to mind, a death which, as we shall see, seemingly offended pious non-Christian Jews as well as other Christian ones.[71] And the issue of relations with the gentiles is unlikely to have been as decisive here, for James and the community which he headed were apparently particularly circumspect in their dealings with the gentiles, including gentile Christians.

The situation with the death of James, the son of Zebedee, and the arrest of Peter in Acts 12.1–3 is somewhat different, in that it is a Jewish authority of another sort who acts here – the Jewish king, Herod Agrippa I, who had not been directly implicated in the death of Jesus. As Acts suggests and as other sources confirm,[72] his motivation seems to have been to court the favour of Jews zealous for the Torah.[73] However, this could, in large measure, be put down to a sort of personal identity crisis or at least an image problem, for here was a Jewish ruler who could be viewed as hopelessly compromised, religiously speaking, by his long years spent at the Roman court and by those tendencies towards the usual trappings and ideology of a Hellenistic king which seem to be manifest in the circumstances of his death.[74] But a dimension of national self-identity comes into play as well, for, as Sanders notes (141), Agrippa owed his royal power initially to the favour of Caligula, that emperor who at the end of his life endangered the sanctity of the Jerusalem Temple by proposing to set up there an enormous statue, thus threatening to defile the Jewish faith at its very heart.[75]

Then, after the fall of Jerusalem and the destruction of the Temple, the situation changed, for the priestly aristocracy was no longer in charge, and the pace was set by lay exegetes of the Jewish law. Here again, in a situation where it was necessary to define Jewish identity afresh over against a rampantly triumphant pagan world, it is understandable that a movement which included many Jews and which seemed in danger of merging with that gentile world and of abandoning the distinctive emblems of Jewish identity would be viewed with considerable suspicion and hostility.[76]

Up to now, however, we have spoken as if the impetus for a break in relations came solely from the Jewish side, and not that of the Christians, Jewish or non-Jewish, and to consider early Christians as 'deviants' implies the perspective of the Jewish side which regarded them in this way. The 'deviant' group does not usually describe or regard itself as such. To a certain extent the concentration on the Jewish initiative in this break may be correct, but we will see that there is a tendency on the side of some early Christians, too, to break with Jews, if not with Judaism – a tendency to break with

Jews who hold that their institutions and culture are the sole guarantee of belonging to the one, true people of God, while at the same time claiming that it is Christians, both Jews and non-Jews, who are the rightful interpreters and heirs of Israel's traditions and legacy, and in their turn saying that Jews can only belong to God's people by accepting the Christian definition of the identity of that people and of that faith. In other words, the break is not one-sided, even if, from the Christian side, it is primarily a reaction to the hostility and the uncompromising attitude of at least some on the non-Christian Jewish side, and not a move which Christians initiated.[77] To that extent, then, talk of a 'sect' may still be appropriate if that term expresses, *inter alia*, an element of protest and rejection of a hitherto dominant culture.

In investigating the very earliest stages of the rise of the Christian church in Jerusalem, we have seen that the Book of Acts paints a picture which, though in many respects idealizing and generalizing, nevertheless contains a number of features which are intrinsically plausible. Not the least of these plausibilities is the picture of a thoroughly Jewish group whose belief in the Messiahship of Jesus by no means set it outside the bounds of a Judaism which was at that stage a far more variegated and diverse phenomenon than was later the case. In keeping with that, Acts portrays a Christian community which was not at odds with its fellow Jews (although Acts puts it far more positively than that); the only friction is between it and the Jewish authorities, and one can well understand that; after all, the early Christians were proclaiming as Messiah one in whose death those same authorities had in all probability played a significant role, even if the last word was spoken by the Roman prefect. Yet the picture was soon to change, and one central question, though by no means the only one, must be to ask what led to that change.

3

Stephen and His Group

The picture painted of the internal life of the earliest church in the early chapters of Acts seems an idyllic one, marred only by the transgression of Ananias and Sapphira, which is turned into a blessing in disguise, at least for the Jerusalem church, if not for Ananias and Sapphira: the punishment that falls upon them only serves to enhance yet further the reputation of the church in the eyes of all who hear of this event (5.11). It is a period characterized by a remarkable harmony and singleness of purpose (e.g. 1.14; 2.46; 4.24). It comes as all the more of a surprise, then, when we are suddenly confronted by an internal quarrel at the beginning of chapter 6, between two groups, the 'Hebrews' and the 'Hellenists' (6.1). Yet the nature of this quarrel is somewhat mysterious, for the circumstances of the quarrel are never properly explained, and some features of it may either not have been properly understood by the author or may have been unwelcome to him. That he does record a case of such internal dissension is, however, a strong reason for supposing that this passage contains traditional material, and many of the details recorded here, like the list of names in 6.5, increase the likelihood that this is the case. But not only must 'Luke' admit to strife in the church; it is also seemingly the end of that honeymoon period in which the church enjoyed the favour of the people, even while they were in disfavour with, and persecuted by, the Jewish authorities. For in 6.12 we read that the accusers of Stephen stirred up the indignation of the people, and, even if 'Luke' wishes to portray the proceedings against Stephen as if it were a matter of a formal trial before the Jewish Sanhedrin, his execution has more the character of a popular lynching.[1] That it was the Jewish authorities who earlier had a particular interest in curbing the new movement is in itself plausible: it was they who stood condemned by this new movement's continued faith in the Messiahship of that Jesus to whose condemnation and death they had contributed. Whether or not one should contrast this hostility of the authorities with the good-will of the rest of the people is another matter; this may rather betray yet again the author's idealizing tendencies. Whether the change was so pronounced, however, it is clear that by the end of Acts there is considerable general hostility on the part of the Jewish populace, at least towards Paul, as chapter 21 makes clear, if not towards those Christians who have remained in Jerusalem under James, the brother of Jesus.

In short, in order to understand this account and its true significance it may well be that with regard to some matters we have to read between the lines and to supply information which this author either did not possess or wished to suppress.

3.1. 'Hebrews' and 'Hellenists'

It is striking that we are never told who the 'Hebrews' and the 'Hellenists' are, who are involved in this dispute, and the meaning of the two terms is far from self-evident. Nowhere else does Acts mention the 'Hebrews', but on two occasions Paul does use the term, in 2 Cor 11.22 and Phil 3.5. From the first of these passages we can infer that others, too, have applied this term to themselves and that with pride, and Paul affirms that he, too, can apply this term to himself; he is even, as he puts it in Philippians, again with pride, a 'Hebrew born of Hebrews', but unfortunately he never explains what he means by a 'Hebrew' and what were the criteria for being one.

Can one then attempt to define this term from the contrasted 'Hellenists' of Acts? Acts uses the latter term two or possibly three times, as far as we know for the first time in the Greek language, but its use of the term is not uniform. The third instance of the term, in Acts 11.20, should probably be left aside, since the text is uncertain, even though it has in the past been made the starting-point for a discussion of the meaning of the term.[2] In the first of the other two instances, in 6.1, it seems that the term refers to a group within the Jerusalem church, for the dispute mentioned there is settled within the church. In 9.29, however, the second instance of the term, this sense is unlikely: the converted Paul returns to Jerusalem and disputes with the 'Hellenists'. They then plan to kill him, and Paul is hustled away for his own safety. This account makes very little sense unless non-Christians are meant and in Jerusalem it is likely that they are non-Christian Jews.[3] So both Christians and non-Christians can, it seems, be 'Hellenists', and 'Hellenists' who are converted to faith in Christ remain 'Hellenists'.

Why were they so named? A number of suggestions have been made, ranging from Jews who have adopted a Hellenistic way of life and thus compromised their Jewishness, to a number of suggestions involving only the language used by this group. In view of the potentially violent opposition to Paul shown by some 'Hellenists' in 9.29 it seems unlikely that adopting a Hellenistic, non-Jewish way of life was characteristic of all who bore this name. A distinction based on the language which they used therefore seems likelier. Yet it will not do simply to say that they spoke Greek, while the 'Hebrews' spoke a Semitic tongue, although many go no further than this distinction.[4] For Paul calls himself a 'Hebrew' and yet undoubtedly could speak Greek and must regularly have spoken it (and at times have written it) in the course of his missionary activity. That even makes it difficult to say that the two terms refer to the language which one usually spoke, for Paul, at the time when he describes himself as a 'Hebrew' in his letters, was undoubtedly mostly conversing in Greek. Another possible, more precise definition therefore seems preferable: whereas 'Hellenists' were Jews who knew little or no Hebrew or Aramaic, 'Hebrews' could use a Semitic language; in some cases they might know little or no Greek, but in other cases, like that of Paul, they also knew Greek and could often even use it with considerable fluency. In competing with other Jewish Christians it might well be an advantage to emphasize that one could speak one's Semitic mother-tongue, as Paul does on those two occasions when he calls himself a 'Hebrew'; it showed not only one's Jewishness, but also one's more immediate contact with, and access to, the traditions of one's people. The designation of some Jews as 'Hellenists' may well have sprung up in a Semitic-speaking environment, for, if this definition is correct, they presented a particular problem in this environment: provision had to be made for them to worship God in a language which they could understand. In the Diaspora, on the other hand, it could be expected that all could understand Greek, more or less.[5]

It is, accordingly, no coincidence that we encounter Stephen arguing and disputing in the context of a synagogue for freed Jewish slaves and for Jews from Cyrene, Alexandria, as well as with those from Cilicia and the Roman province of Asia (6.9).[6] The language used in such a synagogue would be Greek.[7] The evidence of Acts 9.29 should remind us, however, that those with whom Stephen was arguing would also be 'Hellenists', like the opponents of Paul slightly later, and that such 'Hellenists' could well be fiercely conservative; that they had compromised their Jewishness or adopted Hellenistic ways simply because Greek was their language is in no way a necessary inference. Many will have returned from the Diaspora to Jerusalem, often perhaps at some cost and with some hardship and inconvenience, precisely because of their devotion to Judaism. It may well be that some 'Hellenist' Jews in the Diaspora did compromise their Judaism in various ways, but we are talking here of 'Hellenist' Jews in Jerusalem, where the motives for such compromises and accommodation were far more limited. And even if some of those Jerusalem 'Hellenists' who came to believe in Jesus were more progressive and liberal, it need not follow that all were. For, if there is any truth in the picture of a Jerusalem church in which Jewish Christians zealous for the law were dominant (21.20), is it not possible, and indeed likely, that some of them came from the Greek-speaking Jewish community in Jerusalem?[8] In other words, generalizations about '*the* Hellenists' are to be avoided at all costs,[9] since it is in principle unlikely that they shared much beyond the language which they used and, in the case of Christian 'Hellenists', some sort of belief in Christ.

3.2. The Problem and Its Solution

A quarrel arose because the widows of the 'Hellenists' were neglected in the daily distribution of aid. This is depicted as an internal squabble which had to be settled within the Christian community and that implies that the earliest Christian community already had its own poor-relief system. Some have doubted that and therefore regard this account as anachronistic.[10] Yet it is to be noted that it hangs together with the account of the pooling of resources mentioned earlier in Acts: the church had the means to offer aid and, indeed, if it did not use what was offered to it in some such way, it is difficult to see how it would otherwise have used such funds. Yet it would probably be anachronistic to treat this as an exclusively Christian relief-system, for the demarcation lines between Christian Jews and other Jews were not yet so sharply drawn. In other words, it need not only have been Christian Jews who could have been helped by these distributions. If that is the case, however, that would make it even more puzzling that the 'Hellenist' widows were left out. The question also presents itself, why, if the 'Hellenist' widows were neglected by the Christian 'Hebrews', they were not eligible for non-Christian poor-relief.[11] Yet unfortunately we know only too little about how such relief-systems operated at this time or about who was eligible.[12]

Even if it is not clear how and why this problem arose, it seems at first sight a relatively trivial matter, even if not for the widows affected, although that has not prevented the episode being labelled 'the first confessional schism in church history'.[13] That presupposes that the 'Hellenist' widows were left out on religious, rather than just practical, grounds, but that 'Luke' has played down or suppressed this dimension to the problem, trivializing the issues at stake here. And yet, if the 'Hellenists', even perhaps the Christian ones, were far from uniform as a group and indeed represented a considerable spectrum of beliefs, is it to be expected that all of their widows would be discriminated against for such a reason? In short, it seems to me that a simpler, and theologically less sinister, explanation lies nearer to hand: the 'Hellenist' widows were left out simply because the distribution took place within the gatherings of the Aramaic-speaking Christians, and the 'Hellenist' widows did not take part in these because they could not follow what was said. Instead they attended their own Greek-speaking gatherings elsewhere, just as Greek-speaking Jews would gather in their own synagogue and conduct their worship and their affairs in Greek. Perhaps, indeed, the aid took the form of meals which were held within the two, linguistically separated communities.[14] On the other hand, the account in Acts suggests that it was the Twelve who initially received the money offered, even when it came from members of the 'Hellenist' community, according to 4.32–7.[15] That is intelligible if they were at this stage regarded as the leaders of the whole community, regardless of what language its members spoke or where they met together. However, even if some of the Twelve could speak some Greek, it is likely that it was the gatherings of the Aramaic-speaking Christian community in which they took part, and over which they presided, and also that they were, as the recipients of these offerings, responsible for distributing them within their gatherings. If the widows of the Greek-speaking community were then not present when these resources were distributed to the needy, then the 'Hellenists' definitely had good cause to feel hard done by.[16]

One might have thought that those then appointed to administer poor-relief would include representatives from both sides, but on the face of it this is not the case here. Seven men are appointed with Greek names, and one of them is even a non-Jew, although a convert to Judaism, the proselyte Nicolaus from Antioch. (One should infer from this information that the others were not proselytes, but Jews by birth.) In a group drawn from both constituencies one would also expect a mixture of Greek names and Hellenized Semitic names such as one finds among the Twelve. Instead they all have purely Greek names, well attested in Greek literature and inscriptions, with the sole exception of Prochorus; this name perhaps means 'leader of the dance' – hardly a likely candidate for a representative of the 'Hebrews'![17] It remains probable, then, that all were drawn from the ranks of the 'Hellenists'.[18] That in turn raises the question whether this group of seven men were in fact created as the solution to this problem. Or were they, instead, already the leaders of the 'Hellenist' group?[19] Their role and their activity, at any rate, were not limited to 'serving tables',[20] at least in the case of Stephen, for we find him proclaiming the Christian message every bit as much as the Twelve. One cannot argue that so cogently from the case of Philip, for, at least according to Acts' account, his missionary activity takes place after he has been driven from Jerusalem and would thus be unable to supervise the work of poor-relief in that city.

Particularly suggestive here is the proposal that this may be the same Philip who is also named as one of the Twelve. Julius Wellhausen, appealing to this apostle's role in bringing 'Greeks' to Jesus in John 12.20–1, declares forcefully that the Philip of Acts 6.5 is no deacon, but an apostle.[21] Christopher Matthews points out that, were it not for Luke–Acts, we would have assumed that anyway; the name is not that common in Palestine and the four instances in Josephus are all connected with 'aristocratic, hellenized, and diplomatic families'.[22] From the second century on the tradition is unanimous,[23] and Matthews surmises that 'Luke' was simply mistaken in assuming that the Philip mentioned in the list of the Twelve differed from the one named in the list of the Seven. Yet unquestionably an identification of the two would cause acute difficulties for the division of tasks which 'Luke' envisages in 6.2–4, so that he may well have had motives for this mistake.

If Acts 11.30 is to be believed, it was then the 'elders' who took over the role of supervising poor-relief, and no longer the apostles as in 4.37. Yet the Seven might well have also provided a solution to the problem of the 'Hellenist' widows as long as they remained in Jerusalem, if money supplied by members of the 'Hellenist' community were now put in their hands, instead of those of the Twelve, and if they had now been responsible for distributing it to needy members of their own group. But it seems that they were not allowed to do so for long, since one of their number, Stephen, was soon to arouse violent opposition.

3.3. Stephen

Particularly prominent among the Seven is the figure of Stephen, seemingly the first martyr of the new community, and yet at the same time an enigmatic figure. What was it that he said or did which so provoked his fellow Jews and led to his death? Was he alone in saying and doing it, or was he merely more outspoken than his fellows, or perhaps just unlucky in that it was his activity which triggered off a reaction which others might equally well have precipitated? Acts portrays him as an outstanding personality, without saying how typical his attitude was or how much others shared it. It does not even follow that the other members of the Seven shared it, let alone all the other members of the 'Hellenist' Christian community. Yet it is also true that, according to Acts 8.1b, 3, his death was the signal for punitive action against other Christians. Even if some were unjustly caught up in this persecution, although they did not share Stephen's views, this still suggests that it was thought that others were tarred with the same brush; if Stephen were a loner, it unfortunately does not seem to have been recognized and others seem to have suffered too. And Acts also indicates what the charges were which were levelled against him, although its account immediately complicates things by attributing the charges to 'false witnesses'.[24] Does that mean the charges were actually false or merely that the author does not want us to believe in their truth? Or, to put it in a more nuanced way, if these charges were levelled against Stephen was there any element of truth in them, which would make them seem plausible? Does the fact that 'Luke' mentions them, but immediately neutralizes them by attributing them to false witnesses, mean that he found these charges in the traditions available to him, but did not like what he found there?[25]

It would be unwise to use the following speech of Stephen in chapter 7 to answer questions about the historical Stephen, even if it would be equally unwise to attribute all the views expressed in that speech to the hand of 'Luke'; for instance, the reserve expressed there with regard to the institution of the Jerusalem Temple (cf. esp. 7.48–50) contrasts with the seeming endorsement of it as a place of worship at the start of both the Gospel and Acts, even if not only the Isaiah text quoted in 7.49–50, but also other passages in the Old Testament caution against the notion that God could ever be confined to an earthly dwelling-place (cf. 1 Kings 8.27, 30).

Yet, if Stephen were the first martyr of the new movement, that is in itself an important factor and raises the question what it was in this movement, at least as Stephen represented it, which provoked this violent response. How was it perceived by contemporary Jews, even if this perception were incorrect? It is here that Acts offers us, three times, a summary of the charges levelled against Stephen. Despite the repetition, however, it is by no means easy to gauge what was meant. He is first accused of speaking blasphemous words against Moses and God (6.11), then, before the Sanhedrin, of speaking against 'this holy place' – presumably primarily the Temple rather than the city – and the law (6.13), and finally of saying that Jesus would destroy this place and change the customs which Moses had handed down (6.14). Unless it is supposed to be the provocative speech which Stephen subsequently delivers in his defence which leads to his death, then it is these charges which are regarded as worthy of death.

Again it needs to be asked whether it was just the way in which Stephen put his case which led to his death or whether these charges, if proven, were really enough to justify it. He was neither the first nor the last to speak against the Temple and indeed could have appealed to prophetic precedents, even if those prophets had made themselves unpopular at the time. Nor did their criticisms lead to their deaths nor did the woes pronounced against Jerusalem and the Temple by a certain Jesus ben Ananias in the explosive years immediately before the outbreak of the Jewish revolt in 66, even if they earned him such harsh treatment that it is a wonder that he lived to prophesy again; yet he did and continued his prophecies for another seven years and five months, until his death during the siege of Jerusalem.[26] It is to be noticed that it is not stated that Stephen, any more than Jesus ben Ananias, ever said that he himself would do anything to the Temple, only that he had said that Jesus would do so, as well as altering the customs inherited from Moses; it was, on the other hand, alleged at Jesus' trial that he had said that he himself would destroy the Temple, although we are assured that this, too, was a false accusation, which Jesus' accusers could not substantiate.[27] To say that one would do such a thing oneself may invite the violent response of killing the person who would do such a thing in order to ensure that he cannot do it; the same logic does not demand the execution of one who announces that another will do it; the death of the prophet does not remove the threat of the prophecy's fulfilment.

It is also questionable whether to announce that one who is regarded as Messiah will change the Mosaic *law* is a crime punishable by death. It is true that this particular candidate for Messiahship, Jesus of Nazareth, would have been rejected by the majority of Jews at that time, but that is to shift the gravamen of the charges against Stephen. And was it, anyway, likely that Stephen would ever have suggested such a thing, or was this charge indeed false, as 'Luke' says it was? Often it is asserted that Stephen (and other 'Hellenists') were critical of the Jewish law and that this was the reason for their persecution, but, if this is the historical truth behind these charges, one needs to ask how Stephen (and others) could have come to take up such a stance. That they should do so is all the more surprising if one doubts whether one can really speak of Jesus as criticizing that law, let alone rejecting it. Certainly, if Jesus' attitude to the law had been unequivocal, then it is hard to see how his followers should later be divided over the question whether it was still binding upon them and should be followed. What then could have led Stephen to adopt such a clear position in opposition to the law?[28] It would be apparent why he did so if Jesus had indeed spoken out clearly against the law, but it would then become correspondingly harder to explain why other Christians should later seek to insist upon observance of the law. Had they forgotten what Jesus said or did they wilfully ignore it?

At this point, confronted by such a dilemma, a hypothesis may help us forward, a hypothesis which can find its justification in its potential to solve problems like the present one (and we shall see that it may solve others, too, when we come to look at Paul's conversion). The hypothesis is this: Stephen's offence lay in anticipating already, at least to some extent, Paul's attitude towards the observance of the law, particularly as it concerned relations with non-Jews. Stephen, and probably others too, showed already some of that openness towards the gentiles which was later to characterize the Pauline mission, an openness which involved a relaxation of those commandments of the law which regulated contact with non-Jews and safeguarded the purity and integrity of God's chosen people.[29] That is not really a criticism of the law,[30] but a readiness to grant that the will of God and the service of God might justify one in waiving some of the demands of the law in the service of a higher good. And immediately there springs to mind the attitude of Jesus towards the law and towards Jewish traditions which is displayed in a saying like that of Matt 8.21–2 par., in which Jesus seems to place the urgency of the call to follow him in the service of God's kingdom above even so basic a requirement of the law as that honour for one's parents shown in burying them. In other words, there may be a higher priority and a yet higher good than keeping the law.[31] This is not so much a critique of the law as a relativizing of it in the service of a higher good. And the suggestion of a parallel in the teaching of Jesus leads us on to a further point where Jesus' ministry may shed light on the question as to how early Christians might have been led to relax their attitude to their relations with non-Jews. Jesus himself had apparently been noted for his openness towards 'sinners', and his fellowship, including especially table-fellowship, with them. In his world of the Galilean countryside that meant, above all, those Jews noted for their immorality and laxity with regard to observance of the law, but, as Paul's unexpected use of the term 'sinner' for non-Jews in general in Gal 2.15 shows, in a more urban or cosmopolitan setting the word would apply more widely to the non-Jews by whom the early Christians found themselves surrounded.[32]

This analogy and impetus to be found in the ministry of Jesus is all the more suggestive if Jesus had already shown an unusual openness towards such non-Jews as he encountered in the course of his work. The story of Jesus and the Syrophoenician woman in Mark 7.24–30 par. is the most obvious example of such an encounter, and, in view of the initially dismissive way in which Jesus responds to the woman's request (v. 27), there is a strong case for the authenticity and thus the antiquity of this story. Even if Mark's interpretation of Jesus' action in the Temple as preparing the way for the gentiles to pray there (11.17) is secondary, like the saying in 13.10, the tradition remains of a Jesus who was, at least eventually, open towards the needs and the potential for faith of gentiles, even if there are very few examples of such encounters.[33] Although Hahn may go beyond the evidence in seeing Jesus' message, mostly rejected by Israel, as becoming 'a direct promise for the Gentiles', he is probably correct to regard Peter's actions (as reflected, for instance, in Gal 2.11–12) as similar to those of Jesus.[34] While Hahn does not go so far as to say that Peter was actually aware of this similarity, or motivated by Jesus' example, that is probable, at least on the level of a feeling for what was fitting for a servant and follower of Jesus, and the same feeling may have led Peter to lodge with a tanner in Joppa (Acts 9.43; 10.6), even if the ritual purity of such a lodging may have been questionable in the eyes of those zealous for the keeping of the Jewish law.[35] But must Peter have been the first to see this and to act in this way? Could not others, who were aware of the character of Jesus' life and work, have felt similarly about their calling?[36]

Now, if it is going too far to suggest that Stephen and others were criticizing the law, it is also going too far to suggest that they were already engaging in a mission to the gentiles as Paul was later to do, in the sense of actively striving to win non-Jews, although Philip's mission in Samaria in Acts 8.5–13 is an important step in this direction. A situation is, however, readily intelligible in which non-Jews would approach Greek-speaking members of the early Christian community, even in Jerusalem, and ask them on what terms they might join their fellowship. And because these Christians were Greek-speaking and used that language in their gatherings, it is more likely that they would be approached before their Aramaic-speaking fellow-Christians. The question would therefore be more likely to present itself for them before the latter were confronted with it. And in answering it the example of Jesus' behaviour and attitude might well commend itself as showing the way to follow. If, however, Jesus' conduct in relation to 'sinners' from within the people of Israel was offensive to more scrupulous Jews, how much more so would be a similar laxity with regard to contact with non-Jews. For Jesus' example might threaten to compromise Israel's holiness from within, but laxity towards unclean non-Jews broke down those external barriers which separated Jew from non-Jew and undermined Jewish identity over against the other nations of the world. Yet, if it was a matter of responding to an approach by non-Jews, then, rather than speaking of 'mission' or even of 'outreach' on the part of these followers of Jesus, we would be better to speak of an 'inreach', so to speak, of non-Jews wishing to participate in the life of these followers of Jesus or, as Hengel and Schwemer put it with regard to non-Christian Jews of the time in relation to the gentiles,[37] of the 'attraction' of those non-Jews to this group of Jesus' followers. One should not assume that Jesus' followers too quickly adopted a more active role than their fellow Jews in their relations with non-Jews.[38] For the former, taking their cue from Jesus' treatment of the 'sinners' of his world, made the 'sinners' of theirs welcome.[39] In acceding to their wishes and waiving those demands which Jews would otherwise make of non-Jews wishing to join their fellowship fully, these Jewish Christians were implicitly taking a step which could be regarded as betraying their national identity.

It is sometimes argued that nothing more was involved here than was normal practice in Jewish communities which allowed the presence of sympathetic and interested non-Jews ('God-fearers') at their meetings. Indeed, it may well be that the existence of these sympathizers on the fringe of the synagogue is one reason, perhaps the main reason, why the practice of the Antioch church did not become an issue earlier. In its openness to non-Jews it would not be so immediately evident that it was going further than the Jewish synagogue in breaking down the barriers between Jews and non-Jews. Although our information on the position of this group within Jewish communities, both in Palestine and in the Diaspora, is not great, it seems likely that the matter of table-fellowship was an important factor in making into an issue the conduct of Jewish Christians offering entry into their fellowship to gentiles; questions of food-regulations and purity would then arise, which were not raised by non-Jews being present to pray and listen.[40] In other words, it is because the focus of the community life of the earliest Christians was no longer just a matter of teaching, preaching and prayer, but also involved above all fellowship at the Lord's Supper, that the issue of participation by non-Jews presented itself for early Christians in a different and more acute way than was the case for other Jewish communities. It is, moreover, an issue that could in theory present itself in any Greek-speaking synagogue community where there were both gentile attenders and, as a sub-group within the Jewish community, Jewish Christians who, in addition to their participation in the normal life and worship of the synagogue, also met as Christians in order to eat together. The question might arise more quickly in a Diaspora synagogue where Jews found themselves surrounded by a non-Jewish majority, but such were the communications of the nearer Diaspora communities with Jerusalem that it is not to be expected that an issue that had arisen in Antioch would not soon also be discussed and argued over in Jerusalem too.

It is, at any rate, the matter of table-fellowship which is raised later in Antioch (Gal 2.11–14). It may be asked why it only crops up so much later if it had already contributed to this outbreak of persecution, but at least in Jerusalem the question would have been removed from the agenda by the persecution and flight which followed Stephen's death. Arguably such an issue was also a less sensitive one in other centres, where Jews often had to arrive at some sort of *modus vivendi* with non-Jewish neighbours and where the conduct of the Christian group would not immediately strike their Jewish neighbours as out of the ordinary, and when the issue does arise again, in Antioch, it is, significantly, envoys from Jerusalem who raise it, not local Jews in Antioch. On the other hand, that gentiles were originally admitted to the church only after submitting to circumcision (if they were male), even in Antioch, as some suggest,[41] makes it very hard to explain why Stephen and his fellows should ever have been thought to be speaking against the law, and also leaves open the question why the practice of the Antioch church ever became more open, as it evidently had by the time of the events which Paul describes in Galatians 2. When did this (revolutionary) change come about and what occasioned it?

On the other hand, it would be rash to postpone this step of openness to gentiles until the persecuted reached Antioch and other cities outside Jerusalem.[42] Thus J. T. Sanders argues, above all on the basis of 1 Thess 2.14–16, that the evidence of Paul's letters suggests that 'Jews in Judaea persecuted Jewish churches in Judaea for admitting gentiles without requiring circumcision, or at least for promoting such a policy'.[43]

It is also possible, although perhaps less likely in Jerusalem than in other centres in the Diaspora, that some Greek-speaking Jews who had come to believe in Jesus had brought with them a 'spiritualized' concept of loyalty to the law which made it easier for them to waive the literal demands of the law upon themselves and upon any non-Jews who wished to join their fellowship. For Philo of Alexandria complains of some among his fellow Jews, perhaps also in Alexandria, who regard the laws as merely symbols of intellectual truths and neglect the provisions of the law in favour of these truths.[44] Some of the 'Hellenist' group may have come in touch with such an intellectual tradition, may indeed have come to Jerusalem from Diaspora communities where such views circulated, and may have applied it to their new-found faith, but on the whole such influences are unlikelier in Jerusalem than in Alexandria, and it is more likely that it was above all the openness of Jesus to religious 'outsiders' which guided their actions.[45]

It was, moreover, in all probability a step which threatened to impoverish other Jewish communities, for the likeliest source of these interested non-Jews were probably those who had already some contact with Jewish communities and Jewish traditions and who came into contact with Jews who believed in Jesus within those communities, who still belonged to those communities even when they also had their separate gatherings as Christians, as a distinct group within the larger group. Accepting them unreservedly into the circle of the Christians offered them something, a degree of belonging and integration which the non-Christian Jewish community could not and did not wish to offer. Such a move threatened to detach their loyalties and perhaps even their financial contributions from the Jewish community and to channel them into the Jewish-Christian one, and that was likely to provoke resentment and criticism of the seeming laxity which offered these non-Jews something which should not be offered. That was not only disloyal, it was unfair competition.

The other charge against Stephen, of speaking against the *Temple*, is a further problem. It might be regarded as reflecting the belief in the atoning power of Jesus' death, which thereby rendered the Temple cult redundant. That would presuppose that this interpretation of the death of Jesus, along with its implications for the Temple cult, had arisen very early indeed.[46] Or one could see Stephen and his group as carrying on the critique of the Temple implicit in the words of Jesus against the Temple (Mark 13.2 parr.) and in his action in the Temple (Mark 11.15–17 parr.).[47] Yet the words of Jesus are enigmatic and, as far as we can tell, may have prophesied the destruction of the Temple, but not necessarily that Jesus would do the destroying, although his accusers alleged that (Mark 14.57–8 par.). Equally, Jesus' action in the Temple is sometimes interpreted as a prophetic action, which again prophesies that destruction, even though none of the Evangelists then seems to have seen its purpose.[48] If, on the other hand, Jesus' action was instead directed against the Temple authorities and their abuse of their position, then his action, so far from criticizing the Temple, is an effort to uphold and preserve its sanctity, and it becomes far harder to explain Stephen's alleged speaking against the Temple in this way.

It is a problem that, while Stephen is charged with speaking against the Temple, it is hard to find echoes of such a critique amongst his potential successors, at least until we come to Hebrews' criticism of the sacrificial cult (couched, however, in terms of a criticism of the ritual of the tabernacle in the wilderness – a divinely ordained institution according to Stephen's speech: Acts 7.44). If Paul adopted the beliefs of Stephen and his fellows, then it is striking that he is silent regarding the Temple cult and its relevance or irrelevance. It is, on the other hand, amongst various Jewish-Christian groups that one does later find a polemic against the Temple and its cult or a rejection of sacrifices,[49] but these are hardly the obvious successors and heirs of Stephen; rather, if anything, they have otherwise more in common with those Jewish Christians who remained in Jerusalem when Stephen's group was driven out.

The explanation of the charge of speaking against the law offered above suggests, however, another way of understanding what lies behind this charge: Stephen and any others who thought like him were suggesting, not only that non-Jews were welcome to join their fellowship, but also that they were entitled to join that of the Jews in their worship in the Temple, that is, in the inner courts of the Temple beyond the point to which non-Jews were admitted.[50] Indirectly one can see support for this view in the suspicion voiced in Acts 21.28 that Paul has admitted Greeks into the Temple beyond this point.[51] Why should they suspect that Paul might do such a thing? One possible explanation is that those whom Paul had once persecuted, but whom he had later joined, had advocated such a thing, and that it was assumed that Paul, as their spiritual heir, had also adopted such a programme. Yet it is, of course, one thing to hold such a thing to be in principle legitimate, another to put it into practice. And even if the quotation of Isa 56.7 in Mark 11.17 is not a historical word of Jesus, it is nevertheless significant that it is quoted there in the fuller form (in contrast to Matthew and Luke's version), 'My house shall be called a house of prayer *for all nations*.'[52] It is unlikely, however, that Stephen or any of his fellows had yet advanced beyond arguing for such a thing; had they attempted to put it into practice, then one would have read of further martyrdoms besides Stephen's, just as the suspicion that Paul had done this all but cost him his life. Yet Stephen and others too may have advocated such a step, and so, in their openness towards non-Jews, may have caused two of the pillars of Jewish identity to totter – not just the law, particularly with its prescriptions which set the Jews apart from their neighbours, but also the Temple, that focus of Jewish piety and devotion. For a people who felt themselves beleaguered by pagan influences, under the thumb of a pagan power, and who treasured their Temple as a badge of their identity (as well as a vitally important financial factor in the life of their capital), such proposals must have seemed to be nothing short of treachery.

3.4. The Outbreak of Persecution

Stephen dies and his death is the signal for the outbreak of persecution directed at other members of the Christian community, although Acts does not suggest at this point that any others were put to death (but cf. 22.4; 26.10). This persecution of others besides Stephen does not prove that they actually shared the views which Stephen held and which led to his death, but only that they were presumably thought to share them. Gal 1.23 seems to confirm that more than just Stephen suffered on this occasion and that the persecution was a more general one. Acts sees it as nevertheless advancing the Christian cause, for those who fled from this persecution preached the gospel in those places where they now found themselves (8.4; cf. 11.19–20). And, moreover, at the moment of his persecution Paul is about to carry the persecution to another city, Damascus; there is, however, no specific mention of persecution occurring, or about to occur, in another place besides these two cities, Jerusalem and Damascus.

There is, however, one particularly odd feature of Acts' account: the Christians in Jerusalem were scattered 'apart from the apostles' (8.1b). Why should they, of all people, be exempted from the persecution? Indeed, one would expect them to be the first victims of it, as is the case later when Herod Agrippa I arrests James, the son of Zebedee, and Peter, and has the former executed (12.1–5).[53] Such a strategy to stamp out the troublesome new movement is a thoroughly logical one. Yet why should 'Luke' choose to invent such a strange detail in 8.1b? Was it because the 'apostles' must remain in Jerusalem at all costs, just as they were told to remain there to await the outpouring of the Spirit in Luke 24.48b and Acts 1.4? But they have now received the Spirit and they do not remain in Jerusalem according to Acts:[54] Peter and John are sent to Samaria to ascertain what is going on in Philip's mission there (8.14) and in 9.32 Peter is to be found in Lydda and then in 9.39 travels to Joppa and in 10.24 to Caesarea. It is therefore likelier that 'Luke' found this detail in his traditions, and it is indeed so odd that it is unlikely that anyone invented it. On the other hand, it seems that one might still expect to find some representative of the 'apostles' in Jerusalem when Paul visited that city again three years after his conversion (Gal 1.18). Perhaps, then, they did not have to flee on this occasion. (For Peter, at least, it was another matter after his arrest by Agrippa I: cf. 12.17.)[55]

As a result most are persuaded that the persecution only affected the 'Hellenists',[56] but, because the 'Hellenists' are almost certainly not to be regarded as a homogeneous group, we should limit this and say that those who were primarily affected were the group around Stephen, even if others were wrongly suspected of belonging to it and sharing its views and suffered accordingly.[57] Certainly the following references to particular persons who were driven out and scattered support the claim that they belonged to Stephen's circle. It is true that only Philip is mentioned by name (8.5), but it is probable that those who flee to Phoenicia and Cyprus and Antioch and who are, some of them at least, from Cyprus and Cyrene were also 'Hellenists' and, if they preached the gospel to Greeks, that they shared that openness towards non-Jews for which I have argued in the case of Stephen (11.19–20).[58]

The 'apostles', on the other hand, were not 'Hellenists' and belonged rather to the circle of the 'Hebrews'. That in turn makes it altogether more likely that the 'Hebrew' group as a whole was spared on this occasion, and not just their leaders.[59] Yet that could only be the case if it was in principle possible to distinguish the views and quite probably also the actions of Stephen and his group from those of other Christians: the one group was held to be worthy of persecution, the other not.[60] That distinction, that differing perception of the two groups, is of the utmost importance for gauging what is going on here.[61] It was not the linguistic difference alone which could account for this different treatment. What Stephen had said was not thought to be endorsed by other Christians, including the leaders of the 'Hebrews', and the latter were accordingly spared at this point.[62] That means that, whatever else it was that led to the persecution, it was not just belief in Jesus as Messiah, for the 'Hebrews' and the 'apostles' believed in that too. Nor was it even the message of a crucified Messiah, for that was the common basis of the Christian message of both groups.[63] Again, Paula Fredriksen's suggestion that the persecution arose because of Diaspora Jews' fear of the implications of the messianic enthusiasm of the early Christians in a Diaspora setting and when preached to a gentile audience is coupled with denying that Paul persecuted Christians in Jerusalem.[64] Yet it is Judaean Christians who speak of him as their persecutor in Gal 1.23. Moreover, it might be thought that messianic enthusiasm was equally dangerous in a Jewish context.[65] Now it may be that Stephen's group was singled out in this way because they had been approached by non-Jews because they were Greek-speaking, and that the 'Hebrews' had not been so approached, so that this question of accepting non-Jews into their fellowship had simply not arisen for them. It was a question, however, which would arise for them if they, for instance, visited Christian communities in the Diaspora as Peter does in Gal 2.12. And on that occasion his answer seems initially to have been the same as that which I have suggested for Stephen and others: they could admit non-Jews into their fellowship and eat with them. But at this point of time the 'Hebrews' and their leaders escaped persecution because they had not yet been called upon to declare their position, whereas Stephen and his fellows had had to face this challenge, and that in the context of their belonging to a Greek-speaking synagogue which also included many Jews zealous for their ancestral traditions.

The step which Stephen and his fellows took, according to this hypothesis, was a momentous one, all the more momentous if it was a step which incurred the wrath of Paul in particular, for, as will be argued below, it means that theirs was the form of Christianity with which he was most familiar and at the same time that form of Christianity of whose rightness he was subsequently persuaded by his experience on the way to Damascus. And if the example of Jesus had indeed guided them in making this step then Stephen and like-minded Christians can with some justification be described as a 'bridge' between Jesus and Paul. At the same time, it is important not to read too much into this incident, as if a grave internal division within early Christianity had already arisen, in addition to the hostility towards part of it shown by their non-Christian neighbours. There was a division, but a linguistic one, and not a theological one, and yet that may have contributed as much as anything to determining which Christians had to decide first on their attitude towards interested non-Jews and thus to risk the wrath of their fellow Jews. Some at least in the community of the 'Hebrews' may have been equally sympathetic to the line taken by Stephen and his fellows, but have had little occasion to show it; such an attitude would, at any rate, better explain the later conduct of Peter, as we shall see.

4

The Spread of Christianity

The Book of Acts shows us, at first sight, a very orderly and schematic spread of Christianity outwards from its centre in Jerusalem, according to the programme outlined in 1.8: Jesus' disciples will be his witnesses in Jerusalem, in all Judaea and Samaria, and to the ends of the earth.[1] And at first their activity is confined to Jerusalem, before, in chapter 8, the message is carried to the rest of Judaea and to Samaria following the outbreak of persecution against the church in Jerusalem (8.1); it is carried to Samaria, however, by one who was, in 'Luke's' eyes, not one of the Twelve, but, as we have seen, may in fact have belonged to that circle.[2] And, according to Acts, the spreading of the gospel is also very Jerusalem-centred in the sense that Jerusalem determines the authenticity of the churches that are established in the process (8.14–25). Again, it is the initiative of the Jerusalem church that sends Barnabas to Syrian Antioch to consolidate the work there (11.22).

And yet Acts' own account suggests what we might otherwise have expected anyway: this scheme is far too neat and tidy and is certainly no complete account of developments, as can be seen in the unexpected reference to churches in Galilee in 9.31.[3] For, in the first place, a scattering of believers that takes place through a persecution such as that mentioned in 8.1, 4 and 11.19–20 is impossible to control and direct, and yet has the very greatest significance for the spread of the faith, as Acts itself acknowledges in these verses. Furthermore, when the newly converted Paul comes to Damascus, he finds Christians already there. Some of these might merely be refugees from the persecution in which he had participated in Jerusalem, but the way in which Acts speaks of Ananias in the church there suggests otherwise: he has heard of what Paul has done to the believers in Jerusalem (9.13); nothing suggests that he was there himself or experienced this persecution firsthand.[4] And, looking ahead, we discover that, when Paul arrives in Italy, there are already Christians in Puteoli and Rome (28.13–15). How they got there we are never told. There were, however, 'visitors (*epidēmountes*) from Rome' among the disciples' audience at Pentecost (2.10); did they, at least, return home after the festival?[5] Or was it that some of those scattered when persecution later broke out (8.1; 11.19–20) made their way to Rome?[6] And, once one doubts whether all the list of peoples and lands mentioned in 2.9–11 really refers to inhabitants of Jerusalem who remained in that city after their conversion, then it is possible to recognize the potential for a dispersion of Christians in every direction if Jews and others came to Jerusalem as pilgrims, were converted there and then returned to their homes. But none of that would fit the scheme which the author of Acts wishes to portray.

Again, the author of Acts evidently wishes to portray a systematic development from a preaching to Jews to a preaching to gentiles. Therefore the evangelizing of non-Jews by the anonymous Greek-speaking Christians of 11.20 must be preceded by the account of the pioneer work of the apostle Peter in the conversion of the gentile Cornelius and his guests in 10.1–11.18. But, quite apart from the doubts as to whether Acts 2.5 originally referred only to Jews, other steps in this progression are less certain as well. The spread of the gospel to the Samaritans may be regarded as a stage in between the mission to Jews and that to gentiles, as an evangelizing of those who were ethnically and religiously nearest to the Jews, despite the often bitter hostility between them. But how are we to fit the conversion of the Ethiopian eunuch (Acts 8.26–40) into this scheme of things? His position was religiously ambiguous, and for some commentators 'Luke' deliberately leaves it so.[7] That he travelled to Jerusalem and was reading Isaiah on his way back suggests that he is likely to have been a God-fearer or sympathetic to Judaism, like Cornelius in the following chapter. But as a eunuch he would have been debarred from a full membership of the Jewish people (cf. Deut 23.1), unless 'Luke' saw this prohibition as abolished by Isa 56.3–5.[8] Yet it remains unclear how 'Luke' regards his status; the story of his conversion is presumably set where it is because it also involves Philip, like the preceding mission in Samaria. But whether he can be regarded as any closer to Judaism than the God-fearing Cornelius, whose conversion is not described until chapter 10, is far from clear.[9] So, had the momentous step, which was supposedly first taken by Peter, in fact already been taken by Philip? Does Acts, against the plan of its author, implicitly grant this?[10]

In other words there is a whole series of possibilities for the informal, uncontrolled dispersion of the Christian faith, by pilgrims as in this instance, but also by trade and other means, including the movement of slaves from one part of the Empire to another, possibilities which are, however, ignored by Acts with its programme of a systematic advance steered and regulated from the centre. Fortunately, Acts' account allows us to observe a sufficient number of discrepancies and anomalies to assure us that what common sense would anyway suggest to be the case in fact corresponds better to the evidence which Acts itself presents. In other words the spread of the Christian faith was probably far more haphazard and unplanned than the author of this work would have us believe, far more dependent on other factors like trade-routes, the slave-trade or the directions taken by those fleeing from persecution. At least the first two of these factors were highly influential in the spread of other eastern religious cults in the Roman Empire and early Christianity would have been no exception to this.

At the same time it is to be noted that the slave-trade may not have been quite so influential as it would have been with some other cults and at a slightly earlier period: Christianity was no ethnic religion which could be deported *en masse* with the deportation of whole groups of the population of a given people, and the time of the mass-enslavement of whole peoples or parts thereof as a result of fresh military campaigns and conquests had abated in the period of consolidation that was typical of the early Julio-Claudian period; that was to remain true in the areas where the new Christian communities arose, at least until the time of the Jewish risings of 66 and 132 CE. Many Jews were enslaved then and presumably a number of Jewish Christians among them.

If Acts' picture is over-schematic, the same is also true of another pattern which used to dominate many descriptions of developments in earliest Christianity, both historical and theological; for it used to be the case that one identified three phases in this development, an Aramaic-speaking Jewish Christianity, a Greek-speaking Jewish Christianity, and, finally, a gentile Christianity. That schematization has rightly been criticized as misleading, for, in the first place, Acts 6 suggests that the first two phases existed side by side in Jerusalem at a very early period; it may be true that the group of the Aramaic-speaking Christians came into being there very slightly before the Greek-speaking, but the important point is that they were both in a position to influence one another and that this influence need not just have flowed in the one direction; developments in the Greek-speaking community could also affect the Aramaic-speaking one. More important still, however, is the point that the third phase is a relatively late one, if by 'gentile Christianity' one means Christian communities which contained no Jewish Christians at all. Certainly we have no certain knowledge of any Christian communities in the period before 70 CE which contained no Jewish Christians. It is even less likely that any of them remained free from the influence and the leadership of Jewish Christians like Paul and his fellow-workers, many of whom were, like him, Jews. And if a considerable number of the non-Jewish members of these communities were former adherents of the synagogue, as seems likely, then it is probable that Jewish influence remained strong there, even among the non-Jews. To describe such communities as examples of 'gentile Christianity' is therefore highly misleading.

A more modest version of the phrase 'gentile Christianity' might be plausible, even though the designation is still misleading. It could refer to those Christian communities which had relaxed or abandoned those customs which distinguished Jews from non-Jews, and which therefore lived 'like gentiles' or 'in a gentile way' (cf. Gal 2.14). Such a term is, however, misleading because it may hide the fact that at least some Jewish Christians belonged to such communities. That was true of the Antioch community before James's emissaries came (Gal 2.11–14) and afterwards, and it also remained true afterwards of a number of those communities which Paul had founded, as well as those where his Jewish-Christian fellow-workers were active.

4.1. Samaria

According to Acts the first area to be affected by the dispersal of the persecuted following the death of Stephen was Samaria, which was then, with Judaea itself, part of the Roman province of Judaea. For immediately Acts goes on to tell us of the activities of Stephen's colleague, Philip, in that area.

Further interest in the area of Samaria in early Christian tradition can be detected in the Fourth Gospel, in addition to scattered references to Samaritans in the Synoptics, for in John 4.4–42 there is a lengthy account of Jesus' contacts, first with a Samaritan woman and then, through her testimony, with many inhabitants of Sychar where she lived. If this tradition has any historical basis (despite Matt 10.5), then it is to be expected that the ground had already been prepared in this area for further evangelism, and that the activities of Philip there were a natural sequel to Jesus' own preaching.[11]

Who were these Samaritans to whom Philip now turned? One might immediately think of the ethnic Samaritans, who were so closely related to the Jews, whatever the hostilities between them, the descendants of the old Northern Kingdom of Israel, who had their own sanctuary and cult on Mount Gerizim. That might well be what the writer of Acts thought of, too, as he depicted the progressive spread of the gospel from the Jews to those nearest to them, before it finally reached those who were further removed from the Jews. It is the people of the Samaritans who, according to him, heard both Philip's message and, before him, that of Simon Magus (Acts 8.9, 12).

Yet Philip belonged to the group around Stephen and was therefore in all probability Greek-speaking; at any rate, we find him later in the Graeco-Roman city of Caesarea Maritima (Acts 8.40; 21.8). Furthermore the text of Acts 8.5 is uncertain: it is unclear whether Philip travelled to a city of Samaria or to the city of Samaria, which would presumably mean the main city of that region, the former Samaria, now called Sebaste. If the latter is meant, then one must recall that the city had been sacked by the Macedonians in 331 BCE and had then been settled with Macedonian veterans; it was sacked again by John Hyrcanus in 108–7 BCE, but then refounded by Herod the Great with the name of Sebaste, in honour of Augustus (Greek *sebastos*), with six thousand colonists and a temple of Augustus and a shrine of the Greek goddess Persephone. In the first century CE Sebaste was therefore in many ways a thoroughly pagan city, loyal to Rome and the source of many of Rome's auxiliary troops.[12] If this city was meant, then it is questionable how far Philip would have been in contact with the native Samaritans; it would be more likely that he was preaching to gentiles,[13] but that would not fit the pattern of missionary outreach envisaged by the author of Acts.

Many feel, however, that the textual reading 'a city' is better suited to the context,[14] and that could mean one with a less dominantly Graeco-Roman culture. Yet, if it was to offer a congenial refuge for the Greek-speaking Philip and scope for missionary work, it is likely that it possessed a certain measure of Greek culture, as indeed the word 'city' itself might suggest.[15] According to Justin Martyr (*Apol.* 26.2), writing over a century later, but himself from Samaria, Simon Magus came from the Samaritan village of Gitta, but that does not necessarily mean that he heard Philip there – Irenaeus (*Haer.* 1.23.2 [ed. Harvey 1.16.2]) links him with a certain Helena whom he had found living as a prostitute in Tyre; that tradition, too, presupposes a certain mobility. And the magical activities of Simon seem to point to a religiously syncretistic environment rather than to adherents of the Samaritan cult on Gerizim, wherever they were to be found.

It is, at any rate, apparently the ethnic Samaritans (*to ethnos tēs Samareias*) who are led astray by the message of Simon Magus (Acts 8.9), who then, at least according to Luke, comes to faith in Christ along with many other Samaritans,[16] and to this enigmatic figure is attributed not only the origin of the Simonian gnostic group, but the origin of all heresies (Iren. *Haer.* 1.23.2 [ed. Harvey 1.16.2]) – despite the contrition apparently expressed in Acts 8.24. Enigmatic above all is the account of his message given in Acts: he said that he was someone great and the Samaritans described him as the power of God which is called great (Acts 8.9–10). Simon's self-designation is hardly very informative and that of his admirers is little better. Need it mean much more than the presence in him of divine powers, presumably attested by the performing of acts of magic (Acts 8.9, 11)?[17] At any rate, it would be unwise to attach too much weight to the legends which sprang up around him and still less to interpret him in the light of the theology of the group which later bore his name or of the work attributed to him, the *Megalē apophasis*,[18] as if he claimed to be the creator from whom Helena had sprung as his thought (*ennoia*) in the manner of a gnostic emanation from the supreme deity (Iren. *Haer.* 1.23.2 [ed. Harvey 1.16.2]).[19]

Even if the whole welter of *gnostic* teachers and groups attested from the late first century onwards cannot be traced back to the figure of Simon Magus, the hotly disputed question of the origins of this movement is one which cannot be ignored. Is it a purely Christian phenomenon, an 'acute secularization of Christianity',[20] or did it in fact arise independently of Christianity or indeed before it (in which case it is plausible to postulate gnostic influences upon earliest Christianity)? Or must one distinguish between the earlier movement, as 'gnosis' (i.e. 'knowledge' in the sense of esoteric knowledge leading to redemption), and the later 'gnosticism' in the sense of the more clearly defined movements evident from the second century on? If, however, there are gnostic texts which betray no clearly recognizable Christian influence or input or at most a probably secondary Christian veneer,[21] then that suggests that the movement or movements cannot be considered a wholly internal Christian development. On the other hand it would be harder to find gnostic texts which showed no signs of either Christian *or Jewish* features, and indeed many gnostic myths and texts are quite demonstrably a daring retelling and also re-evaluation of Jewish traditions, particularly the story of the creation and fall (cf., for example, The Apocryphon of John, The Hypostasis of the Archons, On the Origin of the World). That might seem to speak for an origin in the context of syncretistic Judaism, but the reversal of the values in the Jewish texts, as, for instance, when eating of the tree of the knowledge of good and evil is positively evaluated (e.g. Hyp. Arch. 90.5–10), is most easily explained as reflecting that hostility between early Judaism and early Christianity which stemmed from the former's rejection of the claims of the latter.[22] That rejection would be felt most deeply and acutely by Jewish Christians, and we will see in Chapter 8 the proximity of a number of forms of 'Jewish Christianity' to gnostic thought.

On the other hand, various features of gnosis or gnosticism are quite clearly earlier than Christianity; in particular, its negative view of matter and of the material body has its antecedents in that Greek dualistic anthropology which is associated with the Orphic and Pythagorean traditions, but then found its way into the Platonic tradition; for these traditions the body is but the prison of the immortal soul. That basically negative view is, however, then undergirded, perhaps also radicalized, by the gnostics with their often highly fanciful and complicated accounts of the origins of the world and of humanity, which trace the human predicament back to some catastrophe, a fall, in the divine world, be it a sin or an error at some level in the many-tiered divine order. That would suggest that any traces of such an anthropological dualism which we can detect in the earliest Christian traditions do not compel us to postulate gnosticism as their source; it is only if we also find the influence of gnostic myths as the bearers of that anthropology that the probability increases that it has been influenced from that quarter. (Correspondingly the mere occurrence of the term *ennoia*, 'thought', in Justin's account of Simon Magus may not be sufficient justification to read into it the whole of the later Simonian myth which speaks of *ennoia* or *epinoia* as a divine emanation, even if it is quite conceivable that by Justin's time the figure of Simon was invested with mythical features. Even more tenuous is the argument that *epinoia* in the sense of the wicked thought of Simon which needs to be forgiven – Acts 8.22 – reflects and presupposes this same mythology.)[23] Even to point to the more radical form of this dualism present in the negative use of 'soul' (*psychē*) and its adjective *psychikos*, in contrast to the Greek view of the soul as the divine and immortal in human nature, is not conclusive. On the one hand there is Philo of Alexandria, who, in common with the mystically inclined Platonic tradition in which he stands, is also conscious of the imperfections of the material world, but nevertheless attributes it ultimately to the one creator God;[24] accordingly he distinguishes between 'soul' in different senses: a higher sense ('the soul of the soul')[25] and a lower sense, that of the natural capacities of a human being. On the other the Christian belief that their salvation came, not from their innate powers, but from an external force, the indwelling Spirit of God, inevitably led to a realignment and re-evaluation of the anthropological terms which they used: if there was something in human nature which answered to the Spirit of God, it was, like the divine Spirit, also 'spirit', and not 'soul' (cf. 1 Cor 2.10–12);[26] that which made redemption possible was, nevertheless, not this human spirit, but the divine Spirit. In other words, it may well be a quite unnecessary hypothesis to read back later gnostic systems of thought into the world of the earliest Christians; more to the point are parallels in dualistic traditions of Greek thought.

Nevertheless other aspects of that phenomenon which we call 'gnosticism' did make their presence felt at a relatively early date. If Irenaeus is correct, already at the end of the first century Cerinthus was active in Asia Minor, with his teaching that the world was not made by the first God, but by a power far removed and separated from the supreme power, a lower power which did not know that God who is over all things.[27] That he taught thus is the more credible because of the points of contact with Philo's earlier teaching attributing the creation to God's powers and also with the later teaching of Marcion. Over against that there is the tendency nowadays to be cautious about reading back into the earliest figures later labelled 'gnostic' by patristic writers the full-blown theological systems which later became associated with their names.[28] That applies, as suggested, to the very early figure of Simon Magus, but the same is also true of Cerinthus, who is named alongside Simon by the Epistula Apostolorum §1 (12),[29] even though he is almost certainly a somewhat later figure. For example Christoph Markschies firmly rejects the proposition that Cerinthus was an early gnostic. Fundamental to gnosticism is, in his view, the notion that the creator God is either ethically indifferent or evil, and there is little to show that Cerinthus' Christology or cosmology were based on that assumption.[30] In other words, although some despair of being able to say anything concrete about Cerinthus,[31] Cerinthus may well have been wrestling with problems, and coming to answers, similar to those of Philo of Alexandria as noted above, and which owe much to the Platonic world view of the day: he sought an answer to the problem of asserting that the perfect God could make an imperfect world or be identified with weak human nature.[32]

That all means, however, that there is increasingly little room left for gnosis as an independent entity existing prior to early Christianity.[33] What is prior manifests itself in certain traditions of Greek thought, even if in a less extreme form than it was later to take in gnostic circles. And the teaching and thought of figures who are counted among the earliest gnostic teachers seem to lack the decisive, constitutive features of the later gnostic systems. The pronounced Jewish element in many gnostic writings is perhaps more easily explained if these documents stem from Christian Jews disillusioned and dismayed by the way in which their fellow-Jews have treated them.[34]

However, apart from the elusive Simon, the figure of Philip and his activity has recently attracted more attention than was previously the case.[35] And rightly so, since many would agree that the group around Stephen was of decisive importance for the development and spread of early Christianity. In the person of Philip we see something of this development and spread taking concrete shape, focused in the work of this one individual. For, whereas Stephen's activity was, as far as we know, confined to Jerusalem, the persecution set in motion after his death took Philip and others further afield, although we must reckon with the possibility that they had already been active elsewhere. And, while Acts mentions the 'wonders and signs' performed by Stephen (6.8), it is the Spirit-filled wisdom and message of this member of the Seven which is the main focus of that work's portrayal of him (6.10–14; 7.2–53). In the case of Philip, on the other hand, we have one story which concentrates as much on his work of healing and exorcism (8.6–7; cf. v. 13) and another which also depicts him as an interpreter of the Old Testament scriptures (8.35) and as physically controlled by the Spirit (8.29, 39) as well as directed by an 'angel of the Lord' (8.26). In the differing features of these two stories about Philip (8.5–13, 26–40), along with Acts' characterization of Stephen, we can recognize certain recurring features of an early Christian movement found amongst some Greek-speaking Jewish Christians, a movement for which charismatic elements in word and deed were characteristic. The profile of this group differed from that of the leadership of the Jerusalem church as represented by figures like Peter and James, although this was perhaps as much as anything the effect of different circumstances: for it was, as we have seen, Greek-speaking Jewish Christians who would naturally be approached first by Greek-speaking non-Jews and, having been forced to flee by persecution, it was inevitable that they should carry their message to new areas.

4.2. Antioch

Exactly when a Christian community came into being in this major city and centre of Diaspora Jews is uncertain,[36] and Acts' schematization does not help us here. It is a striking feature of the puzzling list of areas represented among the audience at Pentecost in Acts 2.9–11 that Syria is not mentioned there, even though it is hardly credible that pilgrims from that area would not be present on such an occasion. Instead it is to be presumed that, if Christianity spread anywhere outside of Palestine, that province would be among the first to be affected. Acts acknowledges that in its account of the dispersal of Christians from Jerusalem following the death of Stephen (11.19), but also mentions the activity of Christians in that city who came from the neighbouring Cyprus as well as the more distant Cyrene (11.20); in view of Antioch's importance as a trading centre that information should occasion no surprise.

It was these visitors, Acts tells us, who first preached to non-Jews in that city. The author of Acts has carefully prepared the way for that step with the account of Peter's conversion of the gentile Cornelius, but as soon as we question the correctness of Acts' chronology at this point, the action of these visitors to Antioch takes on a yet greater significance. Once removed from the straitjacket of Lucan chronology this piece of tradition raises the question whether this action may not even antedate the outbreak of persecution against Stephen and his group in Jerusalem; it raises the possibility that the openness to gentiles shown in Antioch may be the indirect cause of the persecution of Stephen and the others in Jerusalem, rather than its effect. And yet that would imply a very early dating indeed for this step, since we will see that the constraints of Pauline chronology very likely demand that Paul's conversion, after the outbreak of persecution in Jerusalem, took place not very long after the death of Jesus. It is, of course, very natural that this question of relations with gentiles should present itself in such a cosmopolitan city, and it would seem intrinsically plausible that it presented itself there earlier than in Jerusalem. In the presence in Jerusalem of a figure like Nicolaus, the proselyte from Antioch and one of the Seven (Acts 6.5),[37] one can easily see how the issues discussed in the Antioch church could have been made known in Jerusalem. Yet, if the question had been raised in Antioch, and then found its echo in Greek-speaking Jewish-Christian circles in Jerusalem, it is to be expected that any relaxation of the rules applying to Jews' contact with gentiles would meet with far sharper resistance in Jerusalem. The Jews of Antioch were, in so strongly pagan an environment, compelled to seek some sort of *modus vivendi* with their gentile neighbours, far more so than in Jerusalem where Jews were very much in the majority and the life of the city was dominated by Jewish piety.

For the author of Acts the establishment of a church in this great city had to be endorsed by the Jerusalem church, and so we find Barnabas being sent from that church to supervise developments in the Syrian capital (11.22).[38] That may be too schematic, but there is no reason to deny Barnabas' contacts with that church: apart from Acts' account Paul, too, names Barnabas as a delegate of that church, along with himself, to the Jerusalem conference (Gal 2.1, 9), and also mentions his presence in Antioch when Paul quarrelled with Peter and the emissaries of James (2.13). And, according to Acts, it was Barnabas who was responsible for fetching Paul from his native Tarsus to help him in his work of establishing the church in Antioch (Acts 11.25–6).[39] How far he already knew Paul is harder to determine: for Acts he had already introduced the newly converted Paul to 'the apostles' in Jerusalem (9.27), but if Paul considered him to be an apostle too, as 1 Cor 9.6 may imply, then Gal 1.18–19 would mean that he was one of the apostles whom Paul did not meet during that visit to Jerusalem.[40]

It was first at Antioch, Acts also mentions (11.26), that the new movement received the name of 'Christians' or, Helge Botermann suggests, took this name upon themselves.[41] That is in itself a highly significant step, for it implies that outsiders, above all non-Jews, could recognize the distinct identity of this group in that city, although there is nothing in the mere fact of the bestowal of the name to suggest that they saw it as un-Jewish in any way. Yet, for that distinct identity to become apparent, must the Antioch church have abandoned Jewish ways to such an extent that they could no longer be confused with the other Jews in that city? Does that suggest that features like the table-fellowship between Jewish and gentile Christians which occasioned the intervention of emissaries from the Jerusalem church in Gal 2.11–14 were no new innovation, but had characterized the life of that Christian congregation for quite some time before that incident? But that novelty and distinctiveness was more likely to be apparent to devout Jews, not to their gentile neighbours. The form of the name, with its *-ianos*/ *-ianus* suffix, points, at any rate, to its non-Jewish origins,[42] and that makes it more probable that it was these gentile neighbours who recognized this group as one distinctive part of the Jewish community. For, apart from the somewhat mysterious Herodians whom we encounter in Mark's Gospel (Mark 3.6; 12.13 par.),[43] the form is attested in the Graeco-Roman world, and in the Greek-speaking part of it is to be treated as a Latinism.[44] And yet this distinct identity probably only gradually became clear to more and more of the Christians' neighbours, and only as they had opportunity to observe their behaviour and way of life over a period of time. It is, therefore, intrinsically plausible that it is simply as 'Jews' that the newly arrived Paul and Silas are accused in Philippi in Acts 16.20–1.

The bond between the Jewish community in Antioch and Jerusalem is further illustrated by the account in Acts 11.27–30 (12.25) of the prophecy of Agabus, which led to the sending of aid to Jerusalem to help the church there at a time of food shortage. (However, many question the reliability of this account, particularly in the light of the problems which it presents for reconciling Acts' account of Paul's visits to Jerusalem with that of Gal 1–2; so it is argued, for instance, that 'Luke' has mistakenly included here a doublet of Paul's later visit to Jerusalem with the collection raised among his churches or inserted Paul's name in error;[45] nevertheless there are perhaps more satisfactory ways of dealing with this problem.)[46]

In the account of the choice and commissioning of Paul and Barnabas as missionaries of the Antioch church in Acts 13.1–3 we read of the presence in that church of 'prophets and teachers', who are led by the Spirit to their choice of this pair and commission them for this work by the laying on of their hands. The list of the names of this group of 'prophets and teachers' includes persons who play no further part in Acts' story and are otherwise probably unknown, like Simeon Niger, Lucius of Cyrene and Manaen the companion of the tetrarch Herod (Antipas), and this makes it likely that the writer of Acts has taken them over from tradition. And, while Barnabas is named first, Paul is placed last, for Bernd Kollmann a reflection of the leadership structure in the church there, with Barnabas at its head and Paul, though one of the leaders (as prophet or teacher or both), nevertheless subordinate.[47] If this group forms the leadership of the Antioch church, then it is significant that no other office-bearers such as elders are mentioned. Apart from the absence of 'apostles' this corresponds to the offices mentioned by Paul in 1 Cor 12.28. But whereas Paul speaks as if 'prophets' and 'teachers' were separate offices held by different people, Acts 13.1 could be interpreted as meaning that the five named persons were all both prophets and teachers.[48] The group of five named here then decide to send out two of their number, Barnabas and Saul, as their missionaries (perhaps, as already suggested, as their 'apostles', *apostoloi*, Acts 14.4, 14) to carry the gospel beyond the borders of of Syria and Cilicia.

We will encounter this vitally important centre of earliest Christianity more than once in the further course of the history of earliest Christianity, but one point is to be noted here: Gal 2.11 tells how Peter visited Antioch and initially concurred with the existing practice according to which Jewish and gentile Christians ate together (and presumably celebrated the Eucharist together). That in itself, when known, might be enough to distinguish them from the rest of the Jewish community in Antioch in the eyes of outsiders, for it implies a waiving of those food-regulations which would have prevented any comparable integration into the Jewish community of non-Jews who had not become proselytes.

4.3. Peter and Cornelius

Acts 10.1–11.16 describes an event which is obviously of central importance for the author of Acts, perhaps second in importance only to the conversion of Paul. For not only is this event itself described very fully in chapter 10, but Peter tells of it again in a speech in Jerusalem in 11.1–16 and then alludes to it once more, far more briefly, in 15.7–11.

Although it is clear from the Acts account that this event marks for the author the beginning of the gentile mission, it is not clear that this event has in fact been rightly located in the history of the early church. For if one observes carefully the arrangement of material in Acts, it is clear that 11.19 seems to follow on directly from 8.1, as the following diagram shows:

Acts 8.1: But there began on that day a great persecution of the church in Jerusalem, and all were scattered in the countryside of Judaea and Samaria, apart from the apostles.	
	8.4–25: Mission in Samaria 8.26–40: Conversion of the Ethiopian 9.1–31: Conversion of Saul 9.32–43: Peter in Lydda and Joppa 10.1–11.18: Conversion of Cornelius
11.19–20: Then those who had been scattered as a result of the affliction that came upon Stephen	

went as far as Phoenicia and Cyprus and Antioch and proclaimed the word to none but Jews. But there were some amongst them, men from Cyprus and Cyrene, who came to Antioch and spoke also to the Hellenists/Greeks and preached the gospel of the Lord Jesus.

The material in the right-hand column seems to have been inserted between 8.1 and 11.19 and reasons for this are not hard to find: the mention of a scattering in Samaria leads to the account of Philip's missionary activity there. The author knows of a further episode involving Philip, this time in Judaea, and inserts it after the account of the mission in Samaria.

Also worth mentioning here is Heinrich Kraft's suggestion that Acts 8.26–40 belongs to a period *before* Stephen and his fellows were scattered by the outbreak of persecution. It is likelier that Philip had started from Jerusalem when he met the Ethiopian, rather than from one of the places where he is to be found after he had been driven out of Jerusalem by the persecution, such as Sebaste or Caesarea. That would not only be significant for the question of the origins of the mission to non-Jews but also for that of the causes of the persecution of Stephen's group, for it would indicate that they were prepared, as Kraft recognizes, if not actively to seek non-Jewish converts, at least to respond very positively to any interest shown by non-Jews.[49]

There then follows the account of the conversion of the future gentile missionary, Saul, which is placed here because it too is an immediate sequel to the outbreak of persecution in Jerusalem, as 8.3 shows. But then the focus switches to Peter, who, as one of the apostles, was not affected by the persecution, but nevertheless has left Jerusalem. That is perhaps not to be expected until his later arrest by Herod Agrippa I forced him to leave the city (12.3, 17), although one should not assume that he spent his entire time in that city until then; that may be how 'Luke' sees it, but perhaps we should rather see Peter, like the rest of the Twelve, involved in bringing the gospel to all Israel.[50] And yet Paul did find him in that city on the occasion of his first visit there after his conversion (Gal 1.18). But a theological motive for placing the Peter material here is readily recognizable: the responsibility for initiating the gentile mission lies with this leading apostle. Otherwise it would be left to the anonymous 'men from Cyprus and Cyrene' of Acts 11.20 to take this momentous step (if it had not already been taken by Philip in the conversion of the Ethiopian); for from the context it is clear that non-Jews must be meant by the term 'Hellenists' here, if that is the original reading.[51] But it may well fit Luke's purposes better if this momentous step involves so impeccably respectable a figure as the gentile centurion Cornelius, rather than the, in Graeco-Roman eyes at least, religiously and socially more than a little ambiguous Ethiopian. This purpose may well have led to the story being placed earlier in the historical sequence of events than it should be, if it belongs rather to the period in Peter's life after he had been arrested by Herod Agrippa I and had left Jerusalem, and perhaps even to the period after the conference in Jerusalem in Gal 2.1–10,[52] and also to its being ascribed an importance and significance greater than it in fact merited, assuming, that is, that there is some kernel of historical truth in the story. Detecting this editorial purpose, however, enables us to draw the conclusion that in 'Luke's' original source the preaching to gentiles in Antioch followed far more closely upon the outbreak of persecution than is now the case in Acts' account, if indeed it did not precede that persecution.[53] Nor are we told where the 'men from Cyprus and Cyrene' had come from when they arrived in Antioch, but if they were also victims of the persecution that had broken out in Jerusalem then they too would have come from that city. That, in turn, increases the probability that the outbreak of persecution had something to do with the openness of the group of the persecuted in relation to gentiles.

The story is, at any rate, of the utmost importance in the eyes of the author of Acts, as not only the repeated references to it but also the very length of the account in chapter 10 show. In all likelihood the story is not a complete invention,[54] but rests upon some historical tradition, perhaps from the period of Peter's itinerant ministry after his departure from Jerusalem, which the author of Acts has then relocated and endowed with a programmatic significance.[55] Its importance is enhanced by the double visions, of Cornelius and of Peter, although these are, unlike other examples of this phenomenon in the ancient world, different in content from one another and, in the case of Peter's, by no means self-explanatory: it is the Spirit which must tell him how to react to Cornelius' emissaries (10.19–20), as well as the report of the account of Cornelius' vision given by the men whom he has sent (10.22):

that vision was of an angel who told Cornelius to send men to Peter in Joppa. Indeed, it is by no means clear what Peter's vision concerning clean and unclean animals and foods, with the repeated letting down of a sheet, a tarpaulin or a sail, full of all sorts of living creatures, with the command to kill and eat them, has to do with the story and the issue of the admission of gentiles to the church. At any rate, it leaves Peter puzzled and uncertain as to its meaning. This has given rise to the view that the story was originally concerned, not with the conversion of gentiles, but with the problem of table-fellowship between Jewish and gentile Christians, and that Peter's vision originally had to do with that.[56] Indeed elements of that tradition may have left their mark on chapter 11, or at least on vv. 2 and 3 of that chapter; for although 11.1–18 begins and ends with the admission to the gentiles, the issue of table-fellowship with gentiles surfaces in 11.2–3.[57] The latter question was certainly also a very important issue in the earliest church, as the quarrel at Antioch shows (Gal 2.11–14), but at the same time this story of Peter and Cornelius makes Peter's conduct later in Antioch all the harder to understand – if the story is to be taken at face value. So clear a guidance of God on the matter of eating with gentiles should surely have prevented Peter from ever acceding to the demands of James's emissaries. And Paul at any rate shows no sign of knowing of the story, although it would have provided him with valuable ammunition. In that case one must question whether God's guidance was ever so clear and unmistakable as Acts claims. The experience may have been enough to make Peter initially ready to join in the communal meals of the Antioch church together with gentile Christians, i.e. to follow a practice which was already being followed in that church when he came to it, but it was evidently not enough to counteract the pressure brought to bear on him by these Jerusalem Christians.

The story is, at any rate, also seemingly insufficient to prevent the question of the admission of gentiles to the church and of the terms of their admission being raised once again in Acts 15.1, 5, despite the retelling of the story in 11.1–18 and the seeming agreement of the Jerusalem church that God had indeed acted to convert the gentiles (11.18; cf. also v. 1) – that despite the fact that what first seemed to trouble them was not the admission of the gentiles, but that Peter had accepted the hospitality of a gentile (11.3). In that case we would have here the reverse of the situation which will confront us in chapter 15; that chapter begins with the question whether gentiles may be admitted to the church without circumcision and obedience to the law (15.1, 5) but concludes with an agreement (the 'Apostolic Decree') which says nothing explicitly about either circumcision or obedience to the law, but might make more sense as a regulation to enable Jewish and gentile Christians to live together and also to eat together. Here chapter 11 starts with a question that concerns contact between a Jewish Christian and gentiles, a theme to which Peter's vision in 10.11–16, described at length afresh in 11.5–10, is surely relevant, but ends with a decision on the right of gentiles to be admitted into the church, as Peter emphasizes once more in 15.7–11, and only implicitly an acknowledgement that Peter had been right to act thus. Or are we to understand that only the question of their admission had been settled, but not yet expressly that of the terms on which they could be admitted? Yet there is in fact little to suggest this distinction in the Acts account, and the mission to gentiles immediately gets under way, from 11.20 on. To do that, one needed to have some sort of understanding of what one could offer converts. Indeed it is likely that gentiles had already been admitted to the church, even if not actively evangelized, and that this story of Peter and Cornelius has been chosen by 'Luke' to play this symbolic role because it involves the leading apostle, Peter, and a prestigious and respectable representative of the gentile world, Cornelius.

In short, whether Peter was led by some experience to eat with gentiles, perhaps the original meaning of the story, or to convert and admit gentiles to the church, as Acts understands its significance, in neither case does it seem to have been as decisive as, on the face of it, it should have been. To judge from Gal 2.11–14, Peter was not convinced enough on the matter of eating with gentiles and, to judge from the Acts account itself, the Jerusalem church was not sufficiently convinced on the question of the admission of gentiles to the church. In short, Acts has greatly exaggerated the importance of whatever lay behind this story of Peter and Cornelius.

4.4. Peter

In the earliest days of the church Peter plays a prominent part, both in Paul's account in Galatians and in Acts. He is, above all, the one whom Paul meets in Gal 1.18 and is still among the 'pillars' of the church in 2.9. In Acts he is the spokesman of the Christian community and takes the initiative in filling the gap left by Judas Iscariot (1.15–26). He is prominent in word and deed, as the various speeches and miracles attributed to him attest. Perhaps, too, we are also right to see in his judgement on Ananias and Sapphira (5.3–4, 9) and Simon Magus (8.20–3) the exercise of that power given him in Matt 16.19 to bind and to loose.[58] At any rate, it is clear that he and John, who is also, for Paul, one of the 'pillars', are, in Acts, the two leading figures in the life of the earliest community, and it is always Peter who plays the dominant role in this leading pair, and he is always named first in the various lists of the Twelve.[59] Yet it is hard to be sure what Peter stood for amongst the variety of positions to be found in earliest Christianity, and the situation is complicated by the fact that, in Paul's eyes at least, he at one point shifted his ground dramatically: having initially eaten with gentile Christians he abandoned that practice under pressure from emissaries who came from Jesus' brother James in Jerusalem (Gal 2.11–14). However, lack of evidence unfortunately prevents us from saying definitely whether this shift was a permanent one or a temporary lapse.

For after the Jerusalem conference and the quarrel at Antioch[60] we hear of nothing more for certain of Peter's movements: he fades from the scene in Acts and is, at any rate, not mentioned as present when Paul visits Jerusalem in Acts 21. It is uncertain whether Paul's reference in 1 Cor 1.12 to Peter's supporters in that church means that he had also visited that city. That is possible, particularly if the tradition is correct that he eventually made his way to Rome; as the one responsible for mission to the Jews according to the agreement at the Jerusalem conference (Gal 2.7, 9), he may well have felt compelled to visit that city because of the presence of a large number of Jews there.[61] 1 Clement mentions his death alongside that of Paul (5.4), but does not expressly say that it took place in Rome, and Ign. *Rom.* 4.3 speaks of Peter issuing commands to the church there. Nor do we know how he conducted himself if and when he visited such cities: did he after the quarrel of Gal 2.11–14 take care not to eat with gentile Christians? His travels were presumably in fulfilment of his task of bringing the gospel to Jews and, if the need to avoid undermining that mission had weighed heavily in his decision to act as he did in Antioch,[62] then it is to be assumed that he would have continued to act with a similar care in other cities of the Graeco-Roman world.[63] It is, then, at least possible that he ceased, after the incident at Antioch, to 'live like a gentile' (Gal 2.14), and therein lies the plausibility of attempts to find in a Petrine party in the Corinthian church (1 Cor 1.12) a group which paid far more attention to Jewish scruples than their fellow-Christians in that church.[64] (And yet when Paul mentions those liable to be offended by actions of the Corinthian 'strong' he speaks of them as former pagans and makes no mention of any familiarity with Judaism which made them unprepared for the stance of the 'strong': 1 Cor 8.7.)[65]

Yet by virtue of his personal history Peter was well suited to play a vitally important mediating role in the early church. His authority to speak of the legacy of Jesus was indisputable. He had been recognized by his fellow-Jewish Christians as the one responsible for spearheading the mission among Jews (Gal 2.7–9) and yet he also moved about in areas with a predominantly gentile population and seemingly took part uninhibitedly in the life of mixed congregations of Jewish and gentile Christians. For some scholars his residence at Joppa in the house of a tanner (Acts 9.43; 10.6) suggests one who was not overly concerned with matters of ritual purity – and that would be thoroughly in keeping with the spirit of Jesus' ministry.[66] But if Peter's role had once been a mediating one, bridging the world of Jews and Jewish Christians as well as that of gentiles and gentile Christians, open to the gentile world and not giving a rigorous observance of the Jewish law the highest priority, one has to ask whether all that did not change with the dispute at Antioch in Gal 2.11–14; was Peter's role and work from this point on not anchored far more firmly in the Jewish world and amongst Jews? In other words, when assessing the role and the importance of Peter one has to distinguish quite sharply between the part he played before and after the incident at Antioch. We might expect to learn more from the Book of Acts which had so focused on Peter at many points in the first part of that work, but our ability to reach a judgement on this matter is gravely hindered by the fact that he fades fully from the scene in the latter part of the work, even though it does not mention that quarrel between Peter and Paul; it is therefore uncertain whether Peter is not mentioned any more because he no longer served the author's purpose or whether he in fact was now eclipsed by the figure of Jesus' brother James who was able, from now on, increasingly to dictate the way that Jewish Christians, including Peter, should take. Had he, however, continued to support the gentile mission one would have thought that it would have been worth 'Luke's' while to mention the fact. On the other hand, he is not remembered in early Christian literature as an advocate of a Judaizing form of Christianity; yet the further course of his life after this incident is not remembered much at all, and it is only with the later apocryphal Acts of Peter that we find any attempt to depict that period of his life, but then mainly his last days in Rome, at least in the surviving part of this work.[67]

Despite this eclipse of Peter it is important to note the implications of the existence of 1 Peter even if that letter did not come from Peter's hand.[68] For that letter is addressed to readers spread over an enormous area, a predominantly gentile area in Asia Minor, from the Roman province of Asia in the West to Cappadocia in the East, without the least suggestion that they were Jews or even included any Jews.[69] For the writer of this letter, it seems, Peter's authority was by no means restricted to the Jewish world, but he had a great deal to say to gentile Christians as well, and his message had much in common with that of Paul, even if it was often differently formulated.[70] It is as if we here see a Peter who has been rescued from the clutches of a Judaizing form of Christianity, to which he had seemingly surrendered by his behaviour in Antioch, but which was by this point of time itself eclipsed, thanks largely to the death of Jesus' brother James and even more due to the destruction or dispersal of the authoritative Jerusalem church after the fall of that city; the leading apostle has now been reclaimed and rehabilitated with the help of traditions which bear some resemblance to Paul's theology but are nevertheless distinguishable from it.[71] And the tradition that Peter eventually made his way to Rome points to a wider vision which inspired this apostle, even if his concern was still primarily with the Jews and Jewish Christians in the capital city.

5

Paul – the Hidden Years

We saw at the beginning of this study that it was inevitable that the life and work of Paul would loom large in it, partly because of the decisive role which he played in the history of the earliest church, blazing that path which was to lead to the dominant form of Christianity in the following centuries, but partly also because that life and work serve to anchor so much of the little which we know about the rest of earliest Christianity.

5.1. The Pre-Christian Paul

Paul himself refers relatively seldom to his pre-Christian past, and many of the pieces of information about him which spring to mind come not from him, but from the account in Acts. These are to be treated, as with regard to other matters, with circumspection, so that the amount of certain information which we have is very limited, although that has not prevented scholars writing at great length on the subject. Inevitably, much of what has been written can only be more or less intelligent guesswork.

Starting with the information which Paul himself gives we find a tiny handful of autobiographical passages and references. Perhaps the most extensive is Paul's listing of those thoroughly Jewish 'assets' in his pre-Christian life which he counts as 'losses' for Christ's sake in Phil 3.5–6: his circumcision on the eighth day, his belonging to Israel, to the tribe of Benjamin,[1] a 'Hebrew born of Hebrews', with regard to (observance of) the law a Pharisee, with regard to his zeal a persecutor of the church, with regard to righteousness under the law blameless.[2] Beside that are to be set the brief autobiographical references in Gal 1, especially vv. 13–14, where Paul refers to his former life in Judaism, and his especial efforts to persecute and destroy the church of God, thereby far surpassing many of his Jewish contemporaries in zeal for the traditions of his fathers. His language at this point (Gal 1.14) probably reflects the tradition inaugurated by Phinehas who sought zealously and violently to uproot all evil and uncleanness from Israel (Num 25.6–13).[3]

It is to Acts that we owe many further details: Paul's origins in Tarsus in Cilicia, yet the son of Pharisees, his citizenship of that city as well as being a Roman citizen, his education in Jerusalem under the noted rabbi Gamaliel I, his trade as a 'tentmaker'.[4] Yet how reliable are these details, given the suspicions which surround the credibility of Acts' account in general and particularly in view of the tendency of this work to lionize the apostle, even if it does not often speak of him as an apostle? Yet to some details we may perhaps give credence, particularly when the information seems to serve no particular tendentious purpose of the writer or when it seems to mesh well with other information given in Paul's letters.

So the information which Paul gives, that he belonged to the tribe of Benjamin, is not mentioned in Acts, but fits in with another piece of information in Acts, that Paul had the name Saul (Saoul, Acts 9.4, 17, etc., or Saulos, 7.58 etc.), the name of Israel's first king who also belonged to that tribe.[5] Again, Acts and the letters agree on Paul's Pharisaism, but Acts goes further: he was the son of Pharisees and still is a Pharisee (23.6) and was brought up in Jerusalem and there instructed by Gamaliel I (22.3). In the case of his Pharisee parents it must be asked whether it was likely that one would find Pharisees living in Tarsus, in the case of his training by Gamaliel whether the Paul of the letters shows sufficient signs of Pharisaic learning to make that claim credible.[6] Or is this another part of Acts' attempt to boost the Jewish credentials of Paul?

The mention of his upbringing in Jerusalem raises the question whether Paul's roots in the Judaism of Jerusalem did not run deeper than anything that he owed to the Graeco-Roman world of Tarsus. If one holds that he was taken to Jerusalem even before he was old enough to leave the house,[7] then his debt to the city of his birth might be little indeed, and one could then claim that he only learnt Greek relatively late in life, as he began his Christian missionary work.[8] Convenient as that might be to ward off charges that Paul had been corrupted by paganism, it does not seem to be borne out by the evidence of Paul's letters. His use of the Old Testament draws, in the overwhelming majority of cases, upon a Greek version, and more than once depends upon the Greek version rather than the Hebrew text for its relevance to his argument.[9] It would be possible that Paul, in his writings, was heavily dependent upon his secretaries, but he must also have been able to communicate orally with great effectiveness, even if not with great artistic skill (cf. 2 Cor 10.10; 11.6), to judge from his achievements in winning converts and founding churches. It is, of course, possible that he left Tarsus early, but received an education in Greek in Jerusalem (but hardly from Gamaliel). He shows little sign of that knowledge of classical literature that one would expect from an education in Tarsus, unless, of course, the Jewish community there offered its own schooling to the children of its members.[10] It is, at any rate, in the setting of a Greek-speaking synagogue there that we first encounter him in Acts, in the context of the agitation and action against Stephen in that congregation. It is a setting that is both Jewish and at the same time, by virtue of its language and the cultural content which that language brings with it, very much part of the Graeco-Roman world.

Yet Acts claims more than that: this man was a citizen of the 'not insignificant' city of Tarsus (21.39; 22.3) and a Roman citizen (22.25–8). Many have, however, doubted both claims and put them down to Acts' attempts to exalt Paul's status in the Graeco-Roman world. That Paul stemmed originally from *Tarsus* few have doubted, and it would be hard otherwise to account for the tradition.[11] It would also chime in with Paul's early missionary activity in Cilicia (Gal 1.21) if this were Paul's home province. It is his possession of Tarsan citizenship that is regarded as questionable, for normally this was the preserve of a well-to-do elite and was a privilege which relatively few Jews enjoyed.[12] There are parallels for the use of the term 'citizen' in a looser and broader sense, to mean someone who lived in that city;[13] yet, had Paul moved permanently to Jerusalem, then it is harder to see how he would have qualified as a 'citizen of Tarsus' even in this sense.

A more radical challenge to the whole tradition of Paul's presence in Jerusalem prior to his conversion, let alone having spent a considerable time there, is posed by the puzzling reference in Gal 1.22–4 to the now converted Paul being unknown by sight to Christian communities in Judaea. Does that mean that Paul was never responsible for persecutions in Jerusalem, perhaps had never been there before his conversion (although that was the place to be, if one was a Pharisee)? Some draw that conclusion and argue that Paul persecuted Christians elsewhere, e.g. in Damascus.[14] Or were the Judaean churches here mentioned those in other parts of Judaea and not in Jerusalem.[15] Yet those reputedly scattered through Paul's persecuting activities in Jerusalem fled to places in Judaea (Acts 8.1), so that that distinction between Jerusalem and other parts of Judaea does not really help us here; perhaps one should take the reference to the one 'who persecuted *us*' (Gal 1.23) at face value, although these churches of Judaea could simply be talking of, and identifying themselves with, Christians in general. The same arguments count against the suggestion that the churches in Judaea are the 'Hebrews' alone, whereas Paul only persecuted the 'Hellenists'. Does Paul then just mean that they did not know him as a Christian, although they knew him all too well as a persecutor? That, however, goes beyond what he says in v. 22. Or is he talking only about the period covered by Gal 1.18–24, in other words the period after his conversion, and saying that he was unknown there as a Christian?[16] A yet simpler solution may be to call in question the prominence of the role in the persecution that broke out which Acts ascribes to Paul, at least latterly; for initially his role is not that prominent, but rather that of a sort of cloakroom-attendant for those stoning Stephen (Acts 7.58; cf. 22.20). It is only later that Paul becomes the central figure in the persecution (8.3), so that with his conversion all the churches in Judaea, Galilee and Samaria have a respite from persecution (9.31), as if Paul, and Paul alone, had been responsible for all the persecution.[17] In other words, the question whether Paul had been in Jerusalem prior to his conversion must be kept separate from the question whether he had played an active role in the persecution of Christians there: the answer to the two may be different.

In many ways the claim that he was a *Roman citizen* is easier to accept, though many nevertheless doubt it.[18] There is, at any rate, evidence of Jews with Roman citizenship from the time of the late Republic on, and particularly in Asia Minor.[19] It is true that Paul's letters never mention this status, but when would Paul have had cause to bring it up? He lists his Jewish status symbols in Phil 3.5–6, as we have seen, but over against other Jewish Christians who obviously prided themselves on their Jewishness. We do not know, however, of opponents who boasted of their Roman citizenship. Martin Hengel argues, on the other hand, that much of Paul's thinking and planning is 'Rome-orientated':[20] apart from his time in Arabia (Gal 1.17), it is the Empire and its provinces which are the focus of his attention, including the far west of the Empire, Spain (Rom 15.24, 28), and not non-Roman areas like Parthia in the East, and in all probability his sights were fairly early set on Rome, even if his initial plans were frustrated (Rom 1.13). It is also true that most of the avenues to Roman citizenship, which was not so widely available at this time as it was to be later, are unlikely. The likeliest explanation is that Paul's family had been slaves of a Roman citizen, who were then set free. That is, at any rate, how most of the Jews in Rome who were Roman citizens gained their citizenship.[21]

If one still doubts this information, then it is important to note that the whole rationale of Acts' account of how Paul came to be sent to Rome as a prisoner is thoroughly undermined.[22] As a Roman citizen, according to Acts, Paul has the right to appeal over the head of Porcius Festus, the provincial governor, to Caesar and is, accordingly, sent to Rome to be tried there. If this account is problematic, the difficulty lies in the fact that a right to appeal was usually exercised after sentence had been passed; Paul had apparently not yet been sentenced, and that raises the question whether Festus did not act like Pliny the Younger after him and decide, without an appeal by Paul, to refer the matter to the emperor; that he is most likely to have done if Paul was in fact a Roman citizen. Or, as Peter Garnsey suggests,[23] was this an example of a Roman citizen rejecting trial by one court, in this case to be heard by Festus before his fellow Jews in Jerusalem, and asking to have his case heard in Rome. For, whether they appealed or not, Pliny the Younger later records that accused Christians in Pontus and Bithynia who were Roman citizens were sent to Rome to be dealt with there, whereas those who were not were dealt with there and then.[24] It is hard to see why Festus would put himself to the trouble of sending Paul to Rome or putting Rome to the expense of so long a judicial procedure were he not a Roman citizen.[25] It is true that a half-century later Ignatius of Antioch finds himself on the way to Rome as a prisoner, but that was as fodder for the arena, and there is no tradition that this fate awaited Paul in Rome. If one rejects Paul's Roman citizenship, then one must also say whether one thinks that Paul came to Rome and, if so, under what circumstances.[26]

5.2. The Conversion of Paul

It is perhaps not surprising that Paul mentions his pre-Christian past so seldom, but his reticence about that event in which he was changed from a persecutor of the church to one of its most effective proponents is perhaps more remarkable, particularly if one considers how great a prominence this event has in some scholars' accounts of the origins of his theology. It is to Acts that we owe no less than three accounts of this event, two of them in speeches of Paul (9.1–19; 22.6–16; 26.12–18) and this fact underlines the importance of this event for this work. According to Acts it took place as Paul was on his way to Damascus from Jerusalem, authorized by the high priest to arrest any Christians whom he found in the synagogues there (9.2). Although Paul himself does not say where this event took place, his account in Gal 1 presupposes that he was in the vicinity of Damascus at this time, for, he tells us, after a time in Arabia after his conversion he returned *again* to Damascus (1.17).

What actually happened is less clear. Paul speaks of the revelation of God's Son to him (Gal 1.16) and of seeing Jesus (1 Cor 9.1; cf. 15.8; cf. Acts 9.17; 26.16) and this is compatible with Acts' account of Paul's encounter with a heavenly being who identifies himself as Jesus (Acts 9.5; 22.8; 26.15).[27] The results of the event are more clearly recognizable: Paul ceases to persecute the early Christians and, sooner or later, joins them, becoming eventually one of their most prominent, and at the same time controversial, leaders. How much more Paul himself, or indeed Acts, attributes to this event, or traces back to it, is unclear, and it is therefore important not to read too much into it. Yet the hypothesis advanced earlier still holds good: whereas he had violently repudiated the message and the way of life of those whom he persecuted, he was now forced to acknowledge that they had been right.[28] If there was a theological and Christological content to this experience, we need look no further than the message of the hitherto persecuted Christians; this now became the faith and the life of the converted Paul.[29] Yet not because it was the persecuted Christians who had persuaded him, but rather because, he believed, God had intervened to show him the truth of this. Therefore he can with some justification insist vehemently that this message came to him not from any human source, but from a divine one (Gal 1.11–12).

Human bearers of the message he had violently rejected, so that it was God who had had to convince him.[30]

This way of looking at Paul's experience has important corollaries for the future course of his work. For Paul's statement that the purpose of the revelation of God's Son was 'that I might proclaim him among the gentiles' (Gal 1.16), could be interpreted to mean that this was part of the content of his revelation on the way to Damascus. However, it need not mean that, and we should note the enigmatic account in Acts 22, in which Paul attributes the communication of this purpose to him to a separate, later revelation in Jerusalem (22.17–21).[31] The Galatians passage may simply mean that this was God's ultimate purpose in revealing his Son to Paul, a purpose of which Paul only gradually became aware.[32] At any rate, if that was revealed already at that time to Paul, he showed a relative lack of urgency in going about this task, if he was only in Arabia (Gal 1.17), Jerusalem (briefly: 1.18) and in Syria and Cilicia during the whole period before the conference in Jerusalem (1.21); that is a strikingly small area in comparison with the travels of Paul at a later point in his ministry.

It may be helpful at this stage to bear in mind different possible levels of Paul's awareness: it was argued above that the Christians whom Paul had persecuted were characterized by an openness towards gentiles. If this was the form of Christianity which Paul joined, then it is likely that he was introduced to Christian communities where gentiles were welcome. That does not yet mean gentile 'mission', however, if 'mission' implies going out and deliberately seeking to win people over. It is, nevertheless, likely that Paul after some time took that further step, along with others, and at this point he becomes *a* missionary to the gentiles. It is yet a further step to regard himself as *the* missionary to the gentiles, and this point is perhaps only reached when Paul finds himself in a minority of one among the Jewish Christians in the Antioch church (Gal 2.11–14).

If this divine purpose was not communicated to Paul at this point of time it becomes harder to deny that this experience was a 'conversion' and to insist instead that it was a 'call'. It was a 'call', but a call to what? It was doubtless a 'call' as well, but at this stage a very open-ended and unspecific one, and Paul's language is reminiscent of Isaiah and Jeremiah's calls (Gal 1.15–16 with Isa 49.1, 6; Jer 1.5), but in so far as it involved a drastic switch of course, from persecuting the early Christians to taking their side, it can also legitimately and properly be called a 'conversion'.[33] It was at least a change from one religious grouping within that religion to another.[34] The reversal of values attested in Phil 3.7–9 is further confirmation of the appropriateness of talking here of a 'conversion'. To insist that 'conversion' is a matter of switching from one religion to another narrows the meaning of the term unduly; after all, we talk of conversions from Protestantism to Roman Catholicism and vice versa, without thinking of these as two different religions. And that must be borne in mind, since there is no indication that Paul thought of himself as turning to a new and different religion. He was persuaded that the way of the persecuted was the right way to serve his ancestral God, the truest form of the Judaism, the faith in which he had been brought up. In short, the contribution which this experience made to the development of his thought came more from the convictions of those whom he had previously persecuted and whom he now joined than from the content of his vision itself. Their Lord and their way of serving him became his. In particular, that which he had previously found worthy of persecution in their beliefs and ways had now received a divine seal of approval and endorsement.

5.3. Before the Conference in Jerusalem

In keeping with his stress on his independence from the Jerusalem church Paul tells us that immediately after his conversion he consulted no one and did not go up to Jerusalem, to those who had been apostles before him, but he went away to Arabia and then returned again to Damascus (Gal 1.16–17). The Arabia which he means may not have involved a long journey, but may simply refer to those parts of the Nabataean kingdom which were nearest to Damascus. What is even more uncertain is his purpose in going there.[35] Some have inferred from his reference to the purpose of the revelation of God's Son to him, namely that he might preach him among the gentiles (1.16), that this commission was part of Paul's call experience and that he immediately set about carrying it out in the Nabataean kingdom, perhaps in some of the Hellenized cities of that region like Bostra, Philadelphia, Gerasa and Petra.[36] That implies, however, that Paul immediately knew what he had to proclaim and knew, too, that this message had to be taken more actively to the gentiles than had hitherto been the case, as far as we can tell. Is it not expecting too much of his conversion experience to suppose that it could communicate that much to him so quickly and clearly? It is, however, just as possible, perhaps even more likely, that this purpose of God's was one which was gradually disclosed to Paul over many years. In that case it may not have been the beginnings of his gentile mission which took Paul to Arabia, but rather the need to reflect upon the change in his life and thought necessitated by what he had just experienced.[37] Such a withdrawal to a less populous region has Old Testament and contemporary parallels and is thoroughly plausible in the light of the upheaval that was taking place in Paul's life. And such reflection is surely more plausible than the supposition that, even if his conversion experience had told him to evangelize gentiles, he would have immediately known what to do and say.

After a time Paul returned to Damascus, but then had to flee that city, under circumstances which are somewhat differently portrayed in Acts (9.23–5) and in 2 Corinthians (11.32–3).[38] It is at this point that we should probably place the first of Paul's visits to Jerusalem after his conversion (Gal 1.18; Acts 9.26). According to Galatians this was a brief visit, unless the fifteen days only applies to Paul's stay or contact with Cephas (Peter),[39] and Acts' account may suggest that it was briefer than Paul had intended, for it portrays him as arguing with the 'Hellenists' and consequently running the risk of sharing Stephen's fate (9.29). When they see this, his fellow-Christians bring him to Caesarea and send him back to Tarsus (9.30). All that Paul tells us of this apparently eventful fortnight in Jerusalem is that he visited Cephas, and saw none of the other apostles except James, the brother of Jesus (1.18–19).[40] Whereas in the eyes of some the point of the meeting with Cephas was to enable Paul to gather information from one who had known the earthly Jesus, Acts portrays the information as flowing in the other direction: Paul tells the apostles (plural) of his experiences. It is, in fact, inherently plausible and probable that information would have flowed in both directions; they did, after all, surely have more than enough to say to each other.

Paul tells us that he then departed for the regions of Syria and Cilicia (Gal 1.21). There then follows a long period in Paul's life up to the time of the Jerusalem conference 'after fourteen years' mentioned in Gal 2.1. He mentions activity nowhere else during this whole time. Acts, too, having told of his departure to Tarsus, the chief city of Cilicia, goes on to describe how Barnabas, having been sent by the Jerusalem church to supervise developments in Syrian Antioch, summoned Paul from Tarsus to help him in that work (11.22–6). We would naturally love to know more of the activity of these years, but here self-restraint is called for: neither Paul nor the author of Acts thought it necessary to tell us more (in the case of the latter, if he in fact knew more), and it would be rash to try to fill up this gap in our knowledge. It will be particularly salutary to bear that in mind when we try to reconstruct the chronology of Paul's life and work.

6

Agreement and Strife

In this chapter we are principally concerned with two events which can with some justice be described as of pivotal importance, potentially, at least in the one case, not just for Paul's work, but also for the whole history of the earliest church. The first is that conference in Jerusalem which Paul describes in Gal 2.1–10, the second the quarrel in the Antioch church which he describes in 2.11–14. They can also be regarded as pivotal for our knowledge of the course of Paul's ministry, since he seems to date the conference carefully in relation to his conversion, and the quarrel arguably ushered in a new phase in Paul's work.

6.1. Pauline Chronology

The backbone of any chronological reconstruction of the earliest Christian history is to be found in the information which we have about the course of Paul's life as a Christian, and that in itself is reason enough to devote some time to this question. Unfortunately, however, this information is itself by no means easy to interpret. It is, nevertheless, the best that we have, so that it is worth trying to make some sense of it. It is hard enough at times to be sure of the relative chronology of the events which he mentions, that is, their relation to one another and their sequence, and still harder to be sure of the order in which Paul wrote his various letters and of how they relate to those events. Even harder still is the task of achieving an absolute chronology, that is, relating those events and those letters to other known events in the history of the time and thus coming up with firm dates for the former. Nevertheless, it is part of the information provided by New Testament introductions and other such textbooks that they will confidently assign each of the various Pauline letters to a certain year, sometimes without warning the unwary just how much has to be assumed before making such judgements.

At first sight Paul himself seems to provide us with a good starting-point, the autobiographical information which he gives in Gal 1 and 2. As part of an argument that is most probably intended to show his independence of the Jerusalem church, Paul names the two occasions on which he had visited that church after his conversion, once 'after three years', but then only for a fortnight (1.18), and then again 'after fourteen years' when he went up to Jerusalem for the conference (2.1). If, however, Paul wants to put as much distance between himself and the Jerusalem church, to show his independence of it, then it is probable that he names the longest periods of time that he honestly can – and the accuracy of what he is saying is evidently so important to him that he puts his honesty on oath here (1.20). That means that he may have counted part-years as years, in much the same way as Jesus' resurrection was sometimes spoken of as occurring 'after three days', even when the first of those days was really only the early evening of the Friday and the third just a part of the night between the Saturday and the Sunday.[1] Alfred Suhl goes a step further and argues that the 'three years' are included in the fourteen,[2] but, unless chronology forces us to shorten the time yet further, two successive periods of time do better justice to the repeated 'then' at the start of 1.18 and 2.1. However, we must reckon with the possibility that, if part-years at the beginning and end of each period are counted as if they were whole ones, the total period covered by the three plus fourteen years need not, in theory, be much in excess of thirteen years and, in reality, may not be much longer than fourteen years. Nevertheless, it is important to recognize the constraints which these data impose on any chronology of earliest Christianity: to accommodate them the conversion of Paul must be placed quite early or the Jerusalem conference quite late and it must be asked of any proposed chronology whether it does justice to these chronological data.

Suhl makes the even more important further point that Paul is also trying to put as much geographical distance between himself and the Jerusalem church as possible, and argues, plausibly, that, if Paul says that he was first in Arabia and Damascus before the first Jerusalem visit (1.17), and then in Syria and Cilicia before the second (1.21), then he was no further away from Jerusalem during either of these periods.[3] Now that is a most important point, for there are those who follow Acts 13–14 in placing a missionary journey to Cyprus and to southern Asia Minor before the conference, and others who go even further and say that the journey to Macedonia and Achaea also fell within this period. Suhl rightly asks why, if either of those possibilities were correct, Paul did not strengthen his argument by saying so.

6.1.1. Acts and Galatians

The situation is complicated, however, by the fact that Acts also seems to describe the conference, in chapter 15, but to give a different account of the events preceding it. In particular two differences are to be noted: between Paul's visit to Jerusalem after his conversion and his journey to that city for the conference 'Luke' has inserted another visit, after some prophets come down to Antioch from Jerusalem and one of them, Agabus, prophesies that a great famine will come upon the whole world. The Antioch church then raises a collection and sends Barnabas and Paul to Jerusalem with it (Acts 11.30; cf. 12.25). The second difference is that a first missionary journey of Barnabas and Paul takes place before the conference, in which they travel first to Cyprus and then to southern Asia Minor (chs 13 and 14). It is also to be noted, however, that Acts also records two further visits to Jerusalem. The first is mentioned only very briefly and allusively at the end of Paul's next missionary journey to Macedonia and Achaea in 18.22 – so allusively in fact that Jerusalem is not mentioned: Paul lands at Caesarea, goes up and greets the church, and returns to Antioch. Most are agreed that 'the church' is that of Jerusalem, although others rightly protest.[4] Then there is Paul's final visit to Jerusalem in Acts 21, which leads to his arrest. This last visit takes place after the writing of Galatians, in all probability, for it is the journey for which Paul is preparing when he writes Rom 15, and in which he would bring the money raised in a collection among his churches to the poor in the Jerusalem church.[5] The various visits can be seen from the following diagram, in which their mention in Galatians and Acts are marked as G1, G2, A1, etc., for ease of reference in the following discussion:

Paul's journeys according to Galatians and Acts

Galatians	**Acts**
1.15–16: Paul's conversion	9: Paul's conversion
1.18: Paul's first journey to Jerusalem (after 3 years) = G1	9.26: Paul's first journey to Jerusalem = A1
	10.1–11.18: conversion of Cornelius
1.21: Paul active in Syria and Cilicia	11.30 (12.25): Paul and Barnabas travel to Jerusalem with financial aid = A2 13–14: first missionary journey of Paul and Barnabas to southern Asia Minor
2.1: Paul's second journey to Jerusalem (after 14 years) = G2	15: Paul and Barnabas travel to Jerusalem (conference visit = A3)
2.9: Jerusalem agreement	15.20–1, 28–9: 'Apostolic Decree'
	16–18: Paul's second missionary journey to Macedonia and Greece
2.11–14: Antioch quarrel	18.22: Paul's fourth journey to Jerusalem? (= A4)
	19–20: Paul's third missionary journey (collection journey)
	21: Paul's fifth journey to Jerusalem (with the unmentioned collection?) =A5

The relationship of these accounts to one another is a most complicated issue, which has led to a variety of proposed solutions. One can find proponents for each of three basic solutions, identifying G2 with A2, A3 and A4 respectively, and each of these identifications implies a different pattern and development in the work of Paul and of the mission to the gentiles.

The commonest solution is simply to identify Gal 2.1–10 with the account of a meeting in Acts 15 (i.e. G2=A3). For both meetings seem to have been convened to discuss the matter of the need to circumcise gentile Christians, an issue which has been raised in the Antioch church; in both a delegation including Barnabas and Paul is sent by the Antioch church to represent it in Jerusalem, and the validity of the mission of the Antioch church is recognized. The accounts are in many respects similar, but nevertheless it is disconcerting that Paul would then have omitted to mention the visit with famine relief (A2) in his account in Galatians, despite his oath that he is telling the truth (1.20). Is one then forced to say that either Paul has forgotten this famine-relief visit or that 'Luke' has confused this famine-relief visit with Paul's later final visit to Jerusalem with the collection (although Barnabas was not present on that occasion, having by then parted company with Paul) or has simply assumed that Paul was present when he was not?[6] And even more serious is perhaps Paul's assertion that the leaders of the Jerusalem church imposed nothing further upon him (Gal 2.6); for in the account of Acts the so-called 'Apostolic Decree' is promulgated, which does indeed seem to impose certain, albeit minimal, requirements upon gentile Christians (15.29). And finally there is the supporting argument of Suhl's, that it would have helped Paul's argument in Gal 1 to have been able to say that he was away in southern Asia Minor as well as in Syria and Cilicia during this time. It is unconvincing to say that Paul does not mention that here because he is writing to the churches founded on that occasion and they knew already that he had been there. It would have had all the more point to remind them of that, to call them to witness, too.

A further suggestion, which has enjoyed a perhaps surprising popularity in some recent chronologies, is the identification of the occasion of the conference with the visit alluded to in Acts 18.22 (i.e. G2 = A4).[7] This solution has certain advantages. For a start it helps to fill yet further the otherwise rather empty fourteen years between G1 and G2: not only the journey of Acts 13 and 14, but also the far longer one of Acts 16–18 take place before the conference, although it should not be simply assumed that these years must have been as action-packed as the later phase of Paul's ministry, nor that we would not – could not – be left largely in ignorance about what happened during those years. There is, however, a further major advantage in this suggestion: if one takes the agreement to 'remember the poor' mentioned at the close of the account of the Jerusalem conference in Gal 2.10 to be the cue for Paul's work in gathering his collection among his churches for the poor of the Jerusalem church, then immediately and without further delay Paul sets this process in motion, during that phase of his life which we call the third missionary journey. Otherwise there would be an awkward gap in time between this agreement and the start of Paul's fund-raising activities. That is to assume, however, that Paul's collection, which seems not to have involved the Antioch church, was in direct response to this agreement made with the Antioch church, and also that one cannot account for the delay in other ways, for example, as a result of the quarrel mentioned in Gal 2.11–14. There are further problems, too, with this proposal: if the omission of any reference to the first missionary journey in the regions mentioned in Gal 1.21 was an opportunity lost, then this is even more the case if Macedonia and Achaea have also been omitted. And if Paul's silence about the famine-relief visit in his supposedly exhaustive listing of contacts with Jerusalem in Gal 1 is embarrassing, then it would be even more problematic if there had been yet another visit which was passed over in silence – unless Acts had got it wrong and if it were, for instance, the meeting which promulgated the Apostolic Decree and at which Paul had not in fact been present. In addition Barnabas was with Paul in Gal 2.1–10, whereas in Acts he and Paul have parted company, somewhat acrimoniously, over the question whether John Mark should accompany them (Acts 15.36–41), that is, before the second missionary journey. And, finally, if no Jerusalem visit is in fact mentioned in the original text at this point, then the textual basis for this chronology is lacking.[8]

And lastly there is the identification of the famine-relief visit with the conference visit (G2=A2).[9] This has a number of points in its favour: both accounts are Paul's second visit to Jerusalem since his conversion and he has therefore omitted none in his listing in Gal 1 and 2. When he mentions going up to Jerusalem 'according to a revelation' (Gal 2.2), this could be seen as a reference to Agabus' prophecy (Acts 11.28). The agreement to 'remember the poor' in Gal 2.10, particularly if the present tense is given the sense of 'continue to remember the poor', would make sense if the discussion had taken place in the context of the bringing of aid to these poor. The absence of a reference to the Apostolic Decree could then be explained by saying that that decision still lay in the future. And, finally, the recognition of the mission of the Antioch church to the gentiles would very appropriately be followed by the commissioning of Barnabas and Paul to extend the scope of that mission to new areas, in the first instance to Cyprus and to southern Asia Minor. Similarly, it may well have been the point at which Peter, too, began his missionary travels and many, if not all, of the traditions reflecting his missionary activity away from Jerusalem may belong to this period rather than to that earlier period which Acts' narrative suggests. Nevertheless, if such potentially momentous discussions took place on this occasion it is surprising that no mention is made of them (an argument which applies just as forcibly to G2 = A4), and the conference which then takes place in Acts 15 seems to raise the same issues yet again which had supposedly been dealt with during the earlier visit (A2).

The upshot of this review of the possibilities is, then, the conclusion that none of these three attempts to identify the Acts equivalent of Gal 2.1–10 can be regarded as wholly satisfactory. In the light of that, three further observations may be helpful:

(i) It is important to distinguish between the conditions for admitting gentiles to the church on the one hand, and the regulation of their life together with Jewish Christians, and that of Jewish Christians with them, once they have been admitted, on the other. It is true that these are matters that cannot be entirely separated from one another. If, for instance, it were decided that gentiles could only be admitted once they had become Jewish proselytes, observing the Jewish law like Jews and, if they were male, being circumcised, then problems of living together with Jewish Christians would not arise. It is only if the decision regarding that first question went the other way and if they were allowed to join the Christian community, alongside Jewish Christians, without fully observing the law as a Jew would, that the relations between them and Jewish Christians becomes problematic: can they mix freely within the same community and are they really equal members of that community? Or do the Jewish Christians endanger their Jewishness by consorting with them and does that matter?

This distinction is important, because both Gal 2.1–10 and, at least initially, Acts 15 (G2 and A3) seem to be dealing with the first question, whether to admit gentiles to the church and on what terms. And the answer seems to be that they may be admitted, without circumcision and observance of the law. That means that the second question concerning relations between Jewish Christians and gentile Christians does then become relevant, and that, we will see, is the essence of the problem which is dealt with in Gal 2.11–14: Jewish Christians come to Antioch from Jerusalem and from James, the brother of Jesus, and challenge the answer to this question which has up to that point been given or assumed in the Antioch church.

(ii) One feature of the Acts' account in chapter 15 is noteworthy and at the same time rather puzzling: the decisions reached in the meeting which is described in that chapter are recorded in a letter which is then to be sent to the Christians in Antioch, Syria and Cilicia (15.23). But why only to them? For Acts has just described the founding of new churches further afield in southern Asia Minor (chs 13 and 14) and Paul and Barnabas have just described their missionary successes there to the Jerusalem church (15.4, 12), but the letter is not addressed to these new brothers and sisters in Christ. It is true that Paul does later tell them too of this decision reached by the apostles and elders (16.4), but this reads like an afterthought.

This is one important clue which seems to indicate (a) that 'Luke' uses traditional material here, and (b) that these traditions came from different sources. Another is the fact that what is said in the letter does not expressly answer the question raised by the Antioch church. Implicitly we may be supposed to understand that the trouble caused to the Antioch church (and also to the churches in the rest of Syria and in Cilicia, although they are not otherwise mentioned), which is rather vaguely referred to in 15.24, was the demand that gentile Christians be circumcised and keep the Jewish law, and that in imposing only the four demands of the Apostolic Decree the Jerusalem church was saying that these would suffice. However, all that must be read between the lines. And it is also to be noted how Paul and Barnabas are at first not mentioned as the discussion begins (15.6), then are introduced in v. 12 after Peter's speech, and finally are named as accompanying two delegates of the Jerusalem church, Judas Barsabbas and Silas, back to Antioch with the letter (15.22; cf. v. 25). When all this is coupled with Paul's total silence about the Apostolic Decree in his letters, even when he is dealing with questions that are directly related to the terms of the Decree, as is the case with meat offered to idols in 1 Cor 8.1–11.1, then one is forced to ask whether one is not dealing here with traditions that relate to two different meetings, one at which Paul was present and one at which he was not. The matters discussed at these meetings may be related, but need not be the same. It then becomes possible to say, for instance, that Paul was present when the issue of the admission of gentiles to the church was discussed, but not at a further meeting, which may have been concerned with something else – perhaps the demands to be made of gentile Christians if Jewish Christians were to be able to mix with them and above all eat with them without becoming ritually unclean and forfeiting their Jewishness. Acts 21.25 may then accurately reflect the true situation: Paul is told of this decision during his last visit to Jerusalem, as if he had never heard of it before. These demands apply, however, to a relatively small area, the same as that in which Paul was active before the conference according to Gal 1.21, but perhaps also an area which after the conference remained more directly the responsibility of the Antioch church.[10] The text of the Decree would then apply to this area, but not to those areas where Paul had founded new churches.

(iii) A further distinction is then relevant: one must distinguish between the question where a particular visit to Jerusalem fits into the chronology of Paul's ministry and the question of the purpose and content of that visit. For it then becomes possible to say that chronologically the famine-relief visit of Acts 11 (A2) is to be identified with the conference of Gal (G2), which would then take place before the journey of Acts 13–14, but that, as far as the purpose and content of the visit are concerned, it makes best sense to identify the conference of Galatians with at least part of the account in Acts 15, that part in which Paul himself was actually involved.[11] That would then mean that 'Luke' has separated two things which originally belonged together, the famine-relief visit and the negotiations which took place on that occasion, and has at the same time joined together two things which were originally separate, a meeting about the admission of gentiles, at which Paul was present, and another, at which the Apostolic Decree was promulgated and at which Paul was not present. Such a confusion is easily intelligible if the collective memory of the Christian community functioned in any way like the individual memory, in the days before it possessed archives or other such aids to control its recollections. For certain scenes or episodes and their content remain in my memory from my childhood, without my being able to say with any certainty how old I was at the time or in which sequence the scenes followed one another. The content of a collective memory, in other words, may be preserved independently of any chronological framework. That 'Luke' has combined elements from two meetings, the Jerusalem conference of Gal 2.1–10 and a later meeting, perhaps a response to the quarrel at Antioch, is widely recognized: that means that two scenes out of the collective memory of the church, so to speak, have merged or have been merged with one another. What I wish to suggest is a further chronological dislocation, in that the conference has been postponed, either through ignorance or because it fitted the author's purpose better here – for a start, there was now a tradition of missionary successes which the Jerusalem church could (implicitly) acknowledge, even if it was only what was going on in the Antioch church which was on the agenda of the meeting – and the regulations which followed the Antioch quarrel have been brought forward, to be merged with the content of the conference. The latter relocation is all the easier because Acts contains no account of an Antioch quarrel such as would be appropriately resolved by the Decree.

For both Gal 2.1–10 and the meeting of Acts 15 are followed by accounts of two incidents in which Paul and Barnabas find themselves taking different sides. In the one case there is a fundamental split in the Antioch church over Jewish Christians' table-fellowship with gentile Christians, in which Barnabas sides with Peter and the other Jewish Christians against Paul (Gal 2.11–14), in the other it seems to be more a clash of personalities, involving no more than the question whether it was appropriate for Paul and Barnabas to take John Mark with them on their further missionary travels (Acts 15.36–41). It is tempting to view these accounts as a doublet, which would mean that Acts had removed the theological sting from an otherwise very serious theological disagreement, but is this necessarily so? The quarrel of Acts 15 very clearly takes place before the second missionary journey, because Barnabas and Paul here go their own ways, Barnabas with John Mark to Cyprus, Barnabas' place of origin, Paul with Silas, at first through Syria and Cilicia (Paul's place of origin), and then on to those churches which Barnabas and he had founded on the first missionary journey. Galatians, however, offers us no clue as to exactly when the scene described in 2.11–14 took place. Many assume that at the time of this quarrel Paul and Barnabas were still working together, either in Antioch or elsewhere at the behest of that church. If that is not the case, then it is possible to see this serious theological quarrel as taking place later, after Paul and Barnabas had already gone their separate ways as a result of the earlier quarrel over John Mark. And if further work with the Antioch church would have been difficult, if not impossible, for Paul after the quarrel of Gal 2.11–14, then it makes sense to place that incident at the time of Paul's last known contact with that church – in Acts' account the visit of 18.22 after the second missionary journey.[12]

6.1.2. An Absolute Chronology?

Can one relate this sequence of events in Paul's life, this relative chronology, to other dates in the history of the first century and thus reconstruct an absolute chronology? Most would regard the best starting-point as the report in Acts 18.12–17 of Paul being accused before Gallio, the proconsular governor of the Roman province of Achaea. For we know of this Gallio not only as the brother of the philosopher Seneca, but also from the fragments of an inscription mentioning him.[13] The details given on this inscription make it most likely that his term of office lasted from summer 51 CE to summer 52, unless it was cut short by ill-health.[14] If it seems likelier that this case came before him at the beginning of his term of office, when Paul's Jewish accusers would be faced with a relatively unknown quantity as regards his attitude to such cases,[15] and if Acts is correct in mentioning a period of eighteen months in which Paul was active in Corinth (18.11), then this can be correlated with another datum of Acts' account: in 18.2 it is mentioned that Paul joined up with the Jewish couple Aquila and Priscilla, who had just left Rome, because the emperor Claudius had ordered all Jews to leave Rome.[16] Many years later, at the beginning of the fifth century, the Christian historian Orosius dated this event to Claudius' ninth year, that is, 25 Jan. 49–25 Jan. 50.[17] However, this dating has been challenged and the expulsion has been set in 41, at the beginning of Claudius' reign.[18] Here the evidence of a considerably earlier Roman historian, Cassius Dio (*c.* 164–229+) is important: it is true that nothing like this is mentioned in his account of 49, but for the period from 46 on we are dependent on excerpts and epitomes. More important is the account of the trouble in 41, which led to disciplinary measures against the Jews of Rome, in which Dio expressly states that on this occasion they were not expelled, but forbidden to assemble (60.6.6); that way of putting it has more point if Dio knew that at another point of time Claudius would expel them or that one of Claudius' predecessors had already expelled them, as indeed Tiberius had.[19] And another Roman historian, Suetonius, who also mentions this expulsion gives as the reason that they had *continually* been making trouble.[20] That is compatible with trouble having been simmering since the beginning of Claudius' reign and the later date fits neatly into the timing suggested by Acts' eighteen months coupled with the reference to Gallio: Paul would have arrived in Corinth perhaps towards the end of 49 and would have been brought before Gallio in the summer of 51.

These data give us a reference point for these events in the midst of Paul's ministry that can be dated with a fair amount of probability. With regard to other events in Paul's life we are reduced to making more or less intelligent guesses. Too late a date for Paul's conversion immediately runs into problems if one has to leave room for the two periods of time which Paul mentions in Gal 1.18 and 2.1, particularly if one also has to allow time for the journey of Acts 13–14 between the Jerusalem conference and the journey which took Paul to Corinth in 49. An early date for the crucifixion of Jesus and then a relatively short space of time between that and the conversion of Paul are therefore to be preferred, even if that means that events moved with a breathtaking speed in the early church in Jerusalem. So Rainer Riesner, who dates the crucifixion in 30,[21] points to a string of references in New Testament apocrypha and other sources which mention a period of a year and a half for the duration of the resurrection appearances (despite Acts' forty days) and argues that these cover the time up to the last of those appearances, that mentioned by Paul in 1 Cor 15.8 when Jesus appeared to him.[22] In that case Paul's conversion would have taken place in 32 or even at the very end of 31, but, if one wishes to say that Paul had been present at the death of Stephen, then by that time the two groups of the Hebrews and the Hellenists would have had to have formed and the group around Stephen would have had to have aroused violent opposition. If that seems too much to presuppose in so short a period of time, it is, however, worth remembering that some would postulate just as short a period of time or even less for the ministry of Jesus. Even so, the greater the continuity between Stephen's views and those of Jesus, and the more the latter is sufficient to explain the former, the easier it is to accept that Stephen's death could have taken place so early and so soon after Jesus'.

Some scholars also try to extract chronological information from the reference in 2 Cor 11.32 to the 'ethnarch' of the Nabataean king

Aretas IV Philopatris who tried to arrest Paul in Damascus. Aretas' long reign probably ended with his death around 40 CE or earlier and it is therefore to be assumed that this event took place before that date.[23] Jewett tries to pin the date of this incident down more precisely by arguing that at this point of time Damascus must have belonged to Aretas' domain, although the way in which Paul speaks of Arabia and Damascus in Gal 1.17 rather suggests the contrary;[24] this, Jewett nevertheless maintains, could have come about through Caligula's policy of re-establishing a system of client kings in the east, and is therefore to be dated after 37 CE.[25] That would be a dramatic change of policy indeed in view of the fact that Tiberius had ordered Vitellius, the governor of Syria, to bring him Aretas dead or alive because of the war which he had waged against Herod Antipas.[26] Yet, rather than regarding the ethnarch as Aretas' governor in the city, it is perhaps just as or even more probable that he was the head of the colony of Nabataeans living in that city.[27] Suhl's conclusion that one can only infer that Paul had fled from Damascus some time before Aretas' death is justified in its caution, and would fit any date in the 30s, since Aretas had ruled since 9–8 BCE.[28]

The reference to Agabus' prophecy of a famine that would come upon the entire world and the resultant contribution of aid which the Antioch church sent to Jerusalem (Acts 11.27–8) has also seemed to some to offer a further chronological 'peg'. Acts' assertion that this prophecy was fulfilled in Claudius' reign may be an exaggeration – evidently Antioch, or at least the Antioch church, was not so hard hit, although Glanville Downey argues that this city too would have been affected by the shortage of grain in Egypt between 44 and 46 or 47 –[29] but it is true that various regions in the Empire experienced food shortages at various points of time during his reign.[30] These led to grain prices rising and that bore, of course, more heavily upon the poor. These shortages were at times long-lasting and that is perhaps particularly true of Judaea, which seems to have experienced difficulties throughout the period from 44 to 49.[31] That does not offer a very precise dating.

Others have tried to fix certain events during later stages of Paul's life with more precision. When Paul was arrested in Jerusalem (Acts 21.33) we hear that the Roman tribune who arrested him did so on the assumption that he was 'the Egyptian' who had recently caused a disturbance and had led four thousand 'assassins' (*sikarioi*) out into the desert (21.38).[32] According to Josephus this disturbance took place sometime after the death of Claudius in 54, that is, during the reign of Nero.[33] Since other events that occurred at the start of Nero's reign are mentioned first, a date further into Nero's reign is probable, perhaps 56 or 57.[34] Now the Roman governor at the time was Felix, the brother of Pallas, one of those freedmen who had become so influential under Claudius. According to the Paul of Acts Felix had been a long time in this office (24.10) and it is mostly assumed that his term of office had begun in 52 (or even 49). Paul then remained in prison in Caesarea Maritima for two years, we are told, and at this point Felix was succeeded by Porcius Festus (24.27), who sent Paul as a prisoner to Rome. This most likely took place in 59 or 60 CE, which would mean that Paul arrived in Rome in 60 or 61.[35] Acts tells us that he remained there under house arrest for a further two years, but then the account finishes. And yet Paul's farewell speech in chapter 20 to the elders of the Ephesian church may well indicate that 'Luke' not only knew of Paul's death (v. 25), but also that there would be no release from the imprisonment which awaited him in Jerusalem (v. 23).[36] The 'open end' of Acts has, however, long puzzled and exasperated scholars. It has led one noted commentator to speculate that there might be good reasons for this author's silence about Paul's fate: perhaps Paul was in fact put in a less open prison and left to die there, perhaps deserted and rejected by his fellow-Christians in Rome – despite his earlier letter to that church.[37] In that case Acts' silence in this instance may point to a similar embarrassment to that which may, as we shall see, have caused this writer's reticence about Paul's collection for the Jerusalem church, if that gift was in fact rejected by the Jerusalem church.

There is a tantalizing reference in 1 Clement, written towards the end of the first century, to the effect that Paul taught righteousness to the whole world and reached the boundary of the West and bore witness before the rulers 'and thus passed from the world and was taken up into the Holy Place, – the greatest example of endurance' (5.7). Some regard the boundary of the West as a reference to Spain which Paul had planned to visit and evangelize when he wrote Rom 15.24.[38] Or does the Greek word *terma* here mean 'goal' rather than 'boundary', a metaphor from athletics (cf. 5.1, *athlētas*, 5.2, *ēthlēsan*; also 5.5, *brabeion*, 'prize')? The latter possibility is made more probable by the following words: 'he gave his testimony before the rulers'. In that case Rome could be meant and that would fit in with the reference to Paul's witnessing before the rulers and to his death.[39]

In the light of these considerations one can tentatively propose a chronology such as the following, although a dating of the crucifixion in 27 would allow greater latitude in assigning the events up to the Jerusalem conference, but the further step of placing the Jerusalem conference before the persecution under Agrippa I, attractive as it may seem, would mean that Paul's conversion must be dated very soon after Jesus' death and that the fourteen years of Gal 2.1 *must* be reckoned from Paul's conversion, that is, include the three years of 1.18, or that Jesus' death *must* be dated well before 30 CE.[40] If one hesitates to take either of these steps a plausible chronology is still possible, although it is admittedly a tight fit:

30	Crucifixion of Jesus	
31/32	Conversion of Paul	
	Paul in Arabia, Damascus	3 years (Gal 1.18)
33/34	First visit to Jerusalem	
	Paul in Syria, Cilicia	14 years (Gal 2.1)
44–49	Famine in Judaea	
45/46	Second visit to Jerusalem (conference/Antioch collection)	
46/47	'First missionary journey' (Acts 13–14)	
48–51	'Second missionary journey'	
49	Claudius' edict	
49/50	Paul's arrival in Corinth	[1 Thess]
51/52	Gallio's term of office in Corinth	
51/52	Quarrel in Antioch (Acts 18.22)	[Gal immediately afterwards?]
52–57	'Third missionary journey'/ gathering of collection	
	Apostolic Decree	[1–2 Cor, Rom, Philemon?]
57	Collection journey, Paul arrested	
57–59	Paul's imprisonment in Caesarea	[Philemon?]
59–60	Festus arrives as *procurator*, sends Paul to Rome	
60–?	Paul's Roman imprisonment	[Philippians?]

6.2. The Jerusalem Conference

Here we must note that the chronology argued for above means that all those missionary journeys of Paul described in Acts from chapter 13 onwards are to be placed after the meeting described in Gal 2.1–10. This conference was concerned above all with the question of the admission of gentiles to the church and the terms under which they could be admitted. Could one belong to this church without first becoming a Jew? That was a question of fundamental importance for the future of the Christian church and the decisions reached at this meeting would have been epoch-making, at least if they had proved workable. Paul gives us a first-hand account of this meeting, but we need to bear in mind that his account describes the events as seen from his perspective and tailored to the needs of his argument in Galatians. Others might well have described the outcome of the meeting differently.

Various points of contact between Gal 2 and Acts 11 and 15 have already been mentioned: the revelation referred to in Gal 2.2 could refer to the prophecy of Agabus which had led to the famine-relief visit. That the chief issue to be dealt with is the question whether gentile converts need to be circumcised fits in with the controversy in Antioch mentioned in Acts 15.1–2. The Jewish Christians from Judaea, indeed from the Jerusalem church according to Acts 15.24, who stirred up that trouble may be the same as the false brothers who according to Gal 2.4 had infiltrated the church to 'spy out our freedom which we have in Christ Jesus, in order to enslave us', although it is likely that Paul writes that with more than half an eye on those who have now infiltrated the Galatian churches too, and are working a comparable mischief there. (If Acts 15.5 is right in describing the troublemakers in Jerusalem as Pharisees who had come to faith in Christ, then that would contrast strikingly with the form of Christian faith adopted by another former Pharisee, Paul.) At any rate, the issue of the admission of gentiles, and on what terms, takes a concrete and tangible form in the person of the gentile Christian Titus in Gal 2.1, 3, 5. He is not mentioned in Acts 15, but may well have been among the 'certain others' of Acts 15.2. He was a test case. If he did not need to be circumcised, then no gentile Christians needed to be. And according to the Greek text followed by almost all, he was not required to be circumcised (2.3).[41] And it is hard to understand why Paul could have dared to mention the case if the outcome had been any different, for anything else would have been disastrous for his argument at this point, and would have been far better left unmentioned.

The meeting in Acts is clearly attended by many, the apostles and elders in 15.6, and the whole church as well in the formulation of the letter in 15.22, but it is less clear from Paul's account who was actually involved in the discussion. He set out his message before 'them' (2.2) and, he then adds, 'but privately to those of repute'; never in the whole account does he mention the presence of more than 'those of repute', and 'but privately to those of repute' may therefore be meant as a clarificatory qualification of the 'them'. It is thus plausible that what we sometimes refer to as 'the (apostolic) council' was in fact a very small-scale affair, and this has led to some preferring some less pretentious term than 'council'; I have thus opted for the more modest 'conference'. It is indeed likely that some of the participants would have wanted to attract as little attention as possible. For, if Paul was still remembered by the Hellenist Jews with whom he had sided in persecuting the group around Stephen, and who according to Acts had forced him to flee from Jerusalem on the occasion of his former visit, then he would have been in no little danger if he was spotted. The same is presumably true also for Peter, if he too had already had to flee Jerusalem after he had become a target for Herod Agrippa I's attempt to root out leaders of the Christian community, even if the immediate danger would have lessened with that king's death in 44 (cf. Acts 12.23).[42]

That Paul more than once refers to this group as 'those of repute' (2.2, *hoi dokountes*) or 'those reputed to be something' (2.6) or 'reputed to be pillars' (2.9; is the church viewed as a house or, more likely, a temple, or this is simply a metaphor for those of great piety?),[43] indicates that he is distancing himself from them.[44] That is all the clearer from his parenthetical remark in 2.6 that it made no difference to him what sort of people they were, for God is no respecter of persons. This way of speaking of them is hardly complimentary, as the usage of similar language by Plato shows: perhaps the best thing in the words of Euthydemus and Dionysodorus is that 'they care nothing for most people or for the weighty ones or those who are reckoned to be important' (*Euthydemus* 303C).[45] Paul's coolness does not amount to open polemic and perhaps such a polemic would have been ill-advised in the light of the standing and prestige that these leaders enjoyed in the church. Such was the influence of these figures that Paul could not afford to ignore them, and their decision would have far-reaching implications for his work. Yet the coolness is unmistakable. It is, however, a coolness which probably did not exist at the time of the conference itself, since the relations depicted in this account seem to reflect a considerable degree of cordiality and mutual respect. The coolness may, then, rather reflect subsequent events and what had happened since that meeting to chill relations between Paul and the Jerusalem church. And certainly the events described in Gal 2.11–14 can have done nothing to improve the relations between Paul and two of the 'pillars' mentioned here, James the brother of Jesus, whose envoys stirred up trouble in the Antioch church, and Peter, who backed down in the face of their demands. Only John out of this trio was not directly involved on that occasion.

The other side in the negotiations is also a group, a delegation from the Antioch church, despite the fact that Paul repeatedly speaks here as if the agreements concerned himself alone.[46] That is intelligible because he could argue that what held good for him as a member of this delegation also applied to him later as an individual, when he was no longer a delegate or emissary of that church. At least at times, however, a first person plural shows that he had not entirely forgotten that he was one of a group (2.4, 5, 10) and in 2.9 he mentions that the agreement also concerned his fellow-worker Barnabas, just as, on the other side, in that verse James and John are also responsible for the Jews, along with Peter or Cephas. This personal endorsement of the work of these two delegates of the Antioch church is, however, not an element which Acts 15 mentions, and for much of that account the presence of Paul and Barnabas and their contribution is ignored.

At first sight 2.2 might give the impression that Paul himself doubted whether his message was the right one: 'I did this privately . . . for fear that I was running or had run my race in vain' (NIV). It is, however, extremely unlikely that the Paul who had in the previous chapter so stressed the divine origin of his message wanted or meant to give that impression.[47] Instead his fear was more likely that the authority of the Jerusalem church and its leaders was such that their 'No' to his work would fatally undermine it, whatever he said and however much he protested that it had been divinely endorsed. Those who had heeded him in the past would be forced to reconsider their position and all future success would be immeasurably harder to achieve, if not downright impossible. He would be running his missionary race, so to speak, with his feet weighed down or even tied down.

In fact his work and his message, or rather, in fact, those of Barnabas as well and of the Antioch church, were endorsed and Paul adds that nothing further was imposed upon him (or them). This has usually been taken to mean that no further requirements or preconditions for membership were necessary for gentile converts; that is one reason which gives cause to doubt whether the promulgation of the Apostolic Decree can have been part of the meeting which Paul here describes. For, although the requirements of the Decree are few in number, and 'Luke' views them as no burden, in contrast to the full weight of observance of the law (cf. Acts 15.10), they are none the less requirements. Some of them, like avoiding sexual impurity, may well have been things which Paul would expect in his gentile converts anyway, but Paul's attitude to eating what has been offered to idols is a more nuanced one, based on the effect that doing so will have on others (1 Cor 10.23–11.1) and not on a categorical rule, and it is hard to see how he could have failed to view the prohibition of eating non-kosher meat (the 'blood' of the Decree) as a further imposition.

In many respects the way in which Paul summarizes the contents of the agreement reached in Jerusalem is puzzling, and the language which he uses has suggested to some that he is quoting the terms of the agreement itself.[48] For at first sight he seems to speak in 2.7 as if there were two gospels, one for the circumcised and one for the uncircumcised, despite his insistence in 1.6–8 that there is no other gospel than his. He also uses in 2.7–8 the name Peter instead of the name Cephas which he always uses elsewhere,[49] and whereas he expressly says that Peter's apostleship was recognized (2.8), there is a striking asymmetry in his formulation of that side of the agreement which affected himself: God had been working through Peter's apostleship to the circumcision and had also been working through Paul with regard to the gentiles. Left to himself, would Paul have formulated it like that? Would he not rather have included an explicit reference to his own apostleship manifested in that work as he does in 1 Cor 9.2? Yet, if these peculiarities go back to the wording of the actual agreement, it is unlikely that he is quoting the agreement verbatim, or, if he is, it is likely that he is doing so at least using a Greek translation, for it is improbable that the Jerusalem apostles would use the form 'Peter' rather than 'Cephas'. The possibility that the terms of the agreement are here reflected in Paul's text enables us, however, to ask whether what was agreed was not somewhat ambiguous. Although Paul may have been convinced, for instance, that there was one gospel for all, Jews and gentiles, and that he had been entrusted with the activity of preaching that gospel to gentiles, and Peter with doing the same to Jews, the same formulation could be taken by others to mean that there was one message to be preached to gentiles, and another to Jews.[50] And the recognition referred to in 2.8 could be interpreted to mean that Peter was recognized to be an apostle and was to be designated as such, whereas Paul's work was recognized, without acknowledging that it conferred on him the right to this title and therefore without acknowledging that he was Peter's equal.[51]

Ambiguities also beset the wording of v. 9, partly due to Paul's syntax in the last clause of the verse, for he omits a verb in that clause and translations and commentators have sought to make good that omission. Often it is the verb 'to go' which is supplied: it was agreed that 'we [i.e. Paul and Barnabas] should go to the Gentiles and they [i.e. the three 'pillars', James, Peter and John] to the circumcised' (NRSV, similarly REB).[52] Yet it is questionable whether it is legitimate to supply that verb, for when a missing verb has to be supplied it is far commoner to supply the verb 'to be', and Dieter Georgi has accordingly suggested that we should do so in this case and understand the 'to the gentiles . . . to the Jews' as giving not so much the respective destinations or targets of the two missions, but as designating those whose interests the two churches should serve.[53] The Jerusalem church should feel itself responsible primarily for the Jews, the Antioch church primarily for the gentiles – primarily, but not necessarily exclusively; it was a matter of the main focus of the task of each, not a delimitation of them.[54] This definition of the areas of responsibility should probably be understood in a comprehensive way, in that the responsibility of the Jerusalem church should not be restricted, for instance, to Palestine, since that would mean giving up responsibility for the great majority of Jews living in the ancient world. Nor could one very easily widen their geographical area of responsibility meaningfully, without saying that they were primarily responsible for Jews everywhere in the Diaspora.[55] Correspondingly we find Peter in Gal

2.11 in Antioch, presumably because he was responsible for the mission to Jews there. Yet it would be rather strange if he felt himself unable to say anything to gentiles there if he had the opportunity to do so; it was perhaps after the agreement that he had acceded to Cornelius' invitation and had been responsible for his conversion and that of other gentiles present.[56] That fact, however, highlights the overlap of the two areas of mission in cities where there were communities of Diaspora Jews as well as non-Jews, and that would be true of the majority of the cities in which early Christian communities were founded.

Yet even more important than supplying the missing verb or even than the question whether the division was to be understood geographically or ethnically is the recognition that it was, at least initially, a matter of a division of a shared responsibility, and not of assigning rights of jurisdiction. The two churches regarded each other as partners in a shared enterprise. Yet it should not be assumed that the agreement would continue to be regarded in this way. If Acts is right in giving the impression that there was a Judaizing faction in the Jerusalem church, which wanted to impose law observance and circumcision on gentile converts, then this group was seemingly either persuaded or overruled by the leaders of the church at the conference. We should not too easily assume that the Jerusalem church was united on this matter, even at this stage. The position could, however, change yet again if the balance of power shifted in the Jerusalem church, and that was liable to happen if the church came under increased pressure from nationalistically inclined fellow-Jews. Moreover, if the Jerusalem church was responsible for the mission to Jews, then it could well feel that it was up to it to tell those Jews whom it won over how they should live within the Christian community. And, as the quarrel at Antioch in Gal 2.11–14 shows, that would involve decisions as to how they should behave in relation to gentile Christians within the same church. In other words, this agreement was a brittle one, which was liable to be undermined by rising Jewish nationalism, and, moreover, one which, though admirable in its spirit, had not, in all probability, fully faced up to the practical situation that would arise in mixed congregations.[57] It would not be the first nor the last agreement where the parties to it found afterwards that there were snags and ambiguities that they had not originally envisaged. And if the agreement had been primarily meant to regulate the question of the admission of gentiles to the church, then they might be forgiven for overlooking the implications of this for life together in mixed communities, and particularly its implications for the other constituency in the mixed communities, the Jewish Christians.

Paul then concludes his account of the meeting with the agreement to remember or, it may be suggested, to go on remembering the poor. Most are agreed that the poor of the Jerusalem church are meant.[58] Surprisingly, however, although he speaks of 'our' remembering in the present, he adds the comment that he was eager to do this in the aorist tense. Both the change of person from plural to singular and the change of tense are surprising and call for some explanation. The changes are perhaps most easily intelligible if the agreement was one between the Jerusalem church and the Antioch church. As long as Paul was working together with the Antioch church, he is saying, he eagerly supported this. But, mindful of what he is about to narrate in 2.11–14, he can no longer say that, for the Antioch church and he have parted company and gone their own ways. In other words, this verse provides no support for the widespread view that the collection raised among the Pauline churches which Paul eventually brought to Jerusalem was a direct outcome of this agreement in Gal 2.10.

And yet, if, as argued above (pp. 94–8), the bringing of the famine relief in response to Agabus' prophecy and the meeting of Gal 2.1–10 happened at the same time, then one may perhaps see in the bringing of the famine relief something that foreshadows the role that the later collection was to have in Paul's calculations. For it may well be that the Antioch church hoped that the famine relief might incline their brothers and sisters to support them in the dispute which had arisen because of those who had come and demanded the circumcision of gentile Christians. In this case this material aid seems to have had the desired effect, perhaps in part because the Jerusalem church so needed the aid: the legitimacy of the Antioch church's mission and their preaching to the gentiles was recognized.[59] Paul may well have hoped at a later point of time that a similar gift from his churches would produce a similar favourable attitude towards gentile Christians, but in that he may well have been disappointed, as we shall see.

We have also seen already that Gal 2.6 is difficult to reconcile with the account in Acts 15 of the promulgation of the *Apostolic*

Decree and that there is much to be said for regarding this as something which was decided upon at another meeting, when Paul was not present. It is, however, unlikely that 'Luke' has simply invented this Decree, for too many features of it are puzzling and difficult to understand.[60] We have already seen that the addressees of the letter, in which the terms of the Decree are communicated to them, do not seem to correspond to what one would expect in the flow of the narrative of Acts: we have not been told expressly of churches in Cilicia, but they are among the addressees; we have been told of those in southern Asia Minor founded during the journey of Acts 13–14, but the letter is not sent to them.

Implicitly, too, but only implicitly, the issue which was at stake at the beginning of the chapter is settled by this letter: no further burden is to be placed upon the gentile Christians in those churches than the following four prohibitions. By implication circumcision and observance of the rest of the Jewish law as demanded by the agitators in Antioch and the Pharisaic Christians in Jerusalem (15.1, 5) are not required. But this is only implicitly stated and that may be considered surprising. Is it correct, however, to talk of 'observance of the rest of the Jewish law' as if those four prohibitions were four requirements of the law? That might apply to three of the four prohibitions – things sacrificed to idols, non-kosher meat which still contains blood; and sexual impurity or fornication – but 'things strangled' is curiously specific and curiously hard to relate to an Old Testament regulation. So, are these four things to avoid mentioned because they are four Old Testament prohibitions that were particularly important, or were they chosen for other reasons?

Mostly it is assumed that these four prohibitions summarize the rules in Lev 17–18 which are binding on strangers dwelling in the midst of Israel (the *gērîm* or resident aliens). The reference to defilements of idols (in James's original proposal in v. 20) or food offered to idols (v. 29) is to be linked to the command not to slaughter animals elsewhere than before the tabernacle or to sacrifice offerings to demons (Lev 17.1–9). The prohibition of sexual impurity sums up the whole catalogue of forbidden sexual relationships listed in 18.6–23: intercourse with one's blood relations or with menstruating women, adultery, homosexuality or bestiality (child sacrifice is also mentioned in the midst of this list in v. 21). And finally the prohibition of things strangled and blood must be regarded as a doublet, referring to 17.10–14, where Israelites and resident aliens are forbidden to consume blood, and perhaps also to vv. 15–16, where anything that has died a natural death or been mauled by wild beasts makes the person that eats it unclean. And by implication the status of the gentiles within the church is thereby put on a par with that of resident aliens within Israel. They are allowed to be there, but they are very far from enjoying the same status as God's true children.

However, this all too common explanation is not wholly satisfactory. For one thing these are not the only rules binding on the resident aliens: they were, for instance, also expected to observe the rules for the sabbath (Exod 20.10; 23.12; Deut 5.14) and for the Day of Atonement (Lev 16.29). That keeping the sabbath is not mentioned here is all the more surprising because the otherwise rather enigmatic last verse of James's speech (15.21) has just mentioned the sabbath and the proclamation of Moses' teaching which takes place on it. The reference to not consuming blood is in fact the only convincing connection with Lev 17–18, for the prohibitions of defilements of idols or food offered to idols and of sexual impurity are for differing reasons less than satisfactory summaries of the relevant sections in those chapters. Lev 17.1–9 is as much concerned with the question of where the offering is sacrificed, and if the formulation of Acts 15.29 refers to the same sort of problem which arose in Corinth, in a predominantly pagan environment – of eating meat which might have originated in pagan rites (1 Cor 8.1–11.1) – then this is a problem for which Leviticus does not legislate. It goes without saying that the resident aliens in the midst of Israel might find it rather hard to find non-kosher flesh being offered for sale. And the Greek translation of Lev 18 nowhere uses the term used here for sexual impurity or fornication (*porneia*), although a sexual relationship with a kinswoman, here a stepmother, is described as *porneia* by Paul in 1 Cor 5.1 (cf. Lev. 18.8). He also uses this term for relations with prostitutes in 1 Cor 6.18 (cf. vv. 16–17), but this is not one of the sins dealt with in Lev 18.[61]

It is, however, the reference to things strangled which is hardest to explain. One has the impression that this is a separate prohibition and not just an adjunct to the prohibition of blood.[62] In 15.21 it is indeed mentioned before the prohibition of blood. Outside biblical Greek the word used (*pnikton*) normally referred, not to a method of slaughtering, but to a method of cooking or steaming. Its application to a method of slaughtering an animal would be a linguistic novelty. So puzzling is its occurrence here that it is not surprising that some manuscripts replace it with a negative version of the golden rule: 'and that one should not do to others what one does not want to have done to oneself'.[63]

The reference to 'things strangled' remains the chief problem in Wehnert's attempt to derive the terms of the Decree from Lev 17–18. The phrase refers, he claims,[64] to the flesh of animals which in principle may be eaten, but have been inadequately slaughtered and have not been sufficiently drained of blood. The phrase does stand, however, for a summary of Lev 17.13–16, since this incorrect slaughter was a far greater problem in an urban context than carrion or flesh of an animal injured by some predator, as envisaged in Leviticus. The use of the phrase for incorrect slaughtering can be illustrated from t.Ḥul. 1.7 (end) and m.Ḥul. 1.2. Yet considerable glossing is necessary there to explain why *ḥnq* (usually 'strangle') means to cause the animal to choke on its own blood; the focus on this cause of death, when the issue is the presence of the blood, not the mode of death, suggests that 'strangling' was significant for other reasons, and that this significance led Jews, as well as early Christians, to attach great importance to the avoidance of this 'strangling', even if, with the passage of time, it was no longer so clearly remembered what was so serious about 'strangling' and what its prohibition chiefly aimed to achieve.[65]

In view of these difficulties it may be suggested that these four rules arose, not as a summary of Old Testament rules, but as a prohibition of specific pagan cultic practices.[66] For in all three listings of the four prohibitions (Acts 15.20, 29; 21.25), whatever their order, a reference to idolatry or the food contaminated by it always stands first.[67] Fornication, too, was regularly connected with pagan worship (e.g. 1 Cor 10.7–8; Rev 2.14, 20). Werner Georg Kümmel makes the interesting suggestion that blood is here forbidden because consuming it brought one into contact with demons.[68] And finally the difficult word *pnikton*, whether it refers to a method of cooking or of slaughtering, could be seen as a reference to a strangling which preserved intact the soul of the beast so cooked or slaughtered, so that it could be offered to demons.[69] In short, a demonological interpretation perhaps makes better sense of these prohibitions. In that case, however, it needs to be asked whether 'Luke' intended them as any sort of required minimum of Old Testament rules. Nowhere does he make that clear.[70] And anyway, is his understanding of the rules the original one? Were they meant to avert the possibility of Jewish Christians being contaminated through contact with gentiles who had in turn been contaminated through their contact with pagan rites and the demons that were associated with these? That would be an especially pressing need when table-fellowship between Jewish and gentile Christians was involved, but could well apply to other contacts between them. In other words, although 'Luke' uses this Decree as an answer to the question whether gentiles could be admitted to the church and on what terms, it is likelier that its terms reflect a decision on what should be required of gentile Christians who had already been admitted, in order that they might avoid polluting Jewish Christians, but quite possibly for their own sakes too.[71] For it is unlikely that Paul was alone in considering fellowship with demons or sexual impurity quite incompatible with fellowship with Christ (1 Cor 6.15; 10.21), and if this is where the main emphasis of these four prohibitions lies, then it is probable that gentile Christians were expected to obey them whether they were in contact with Jewish Christians or not. A similar uncompromising position with regard to the eating of meat offered to idols is found in the letters to the churches in Pergamum and Thyatira in Rev 2.14, 20 and in Did 6.3, and is in keeping with the separation between Christians and the world advocated elsewhere in the Book of Revelation.[72] Christians should live already in that purity which was expected at the end (Rev 21.8; 22.15), preparing themselves for the destiny promised to them then. Paul seems, on the other hand, to have chosen another way of dealing with the problem, by refraining from treating food offered to idols as automatically polluting or bringing one into contact with demons (1 Cor 10.23–11.1). In other words the Decree is more bluntly formulated than Paul would wish and allows for no possible exceptions to the prohibition of eating food offered to idols.[73] At the same time it may well be that a disagreement over fellowship with Jewish Christians necessitated some such formulation of such basic rules,[74] and it is perhaps significant that it is directed to the Antioch church and the churches of Syria and Cilicia; it is then probably to be regarded as a measure adopted and endorsed in that area and in that area alone.[75]

6.3. The Quarrel at Antioch

It has been suggested that the quarrel which Paul mentions in Gal 2.11–14 was provoked by the terms of the Decree and that the troublesome envoys from James whom he mentions were trying to impose its terms on the Antioch church.[76] More often, however, one meets the perhaps more plausible suggestion that it was a result of the quarrel at Antioch, not its cause, an attempt to regulate relations between Jewish Christians and gentile Christians in such a way that the latter would not be forced to submit to circumcision and full observance of the law and the former would nevertheless not be imperilled by contact with their gentile brothers and sisters in Christ.[77]

It is logical that this quarrel should arise at this point, after the decisions reached in 2.1–10, and in that case the two episodes are narrated in the correct chronological order.[78] Only after it has been decided that gentiles can join the church without submitting to the fullness of the Mosaic law, do questions of the implications of this for Jewish Christians really arise. And it seems from Paul's account that this was a question which did not initially occur to all Jewish Christians, for he describes how Peter, when he came to Antioch, ate freely with gentile Christians there, as presumably did all the other Jewish Christians there, including Paul and Barnabas. Mostly it is assumed that this meant that they were prepared to waive all ritual commandments like food and purity laws for the sake of fellowship with the gentile Christians, including meeting together at the Lord's Supper. That is not to say that they regarded themselves as totally free from the law, for there were undoubtedly commandments of the law which it was explicitly or tacitly assumed both Jewish and gentile Christians would observe – for instance, prohibitions of the worship of other gods or of theft or murder. But evidently ritual requirements were treated differently.

That is the opinion of most, but Dunn has argued that the Antioch church already observed the basic Jewish food regulations, already avoiding things like eating pork.[79] What the emissaries of James required was a more stringent observing of tithing and ritual purity. Dunn regards it as unlikely that the Jewish Christians at Antioch had completely abandoned such food regulations and thinks that the gentile Christians would be drawn mostly, if not entirely, from the circle of synagogue adherents who would be used to keeping those regulations anyway. (But were common meals part of their attachment to the synagogue?[80] And did not a considerable part of the attraction of Christianity for such circles lie in the fact that it was able to offer them what Judaism could offer, without many of the drawbacks of Judaism in gentile eyes? Apart from circumcision, the Jewish food regulations would undoubtedly have seemed particularly irksome and unnecessary barriers to full integration in the community.) And Traugott Holtz doubts, rightly, whether

Paul's radical stance would have been necessary if it was such a matter of just a 'more or less'.[81] The same would be true of the intervention of James's emissaries if the Antioch church were already observing rules that usually governed relations between Jews and gentiles. Would those Jewish Christians who were not convinced of the rightness of the Pharisaic rules on this matter be so easily persuaded that this further step was necessary? And is it just a polemical exaggeration when Paul says of Peter that he had lived like a gentile (Gal 2.14)? For he would, in Dunn's view, only have lived like a God-fearing, righteous gentile in his previous relations with the Antioch church.

If the Jewish Christians at Antioch had been prepared to waive all Jewish food regulations in their community meals, that would indeed have been a step that was unusual at least among the more devout Diaspora Jews, even if others were laxer in such matters, for a number of passages indicate that this was not an option for devout Diaspora Jews: already Daniel and his companions avoided the normal fare of the royal court and ate only vegetables and drank only water (Dan 1.8, 12; even celebration of the Lord's Supper would, however, involve drinking wine together and, in Jewish eyes, gentile wine was associated with libations to the gods of the pagans) and a similar separation is characteristic of devout Egyptian Jews in 3 Macc 3.4 (cf. Letter of Aristeas 139; Jos. Asen. 7.1; also Jub. 22.16). This is also the impression which outsiders in the Graeco-Roman world had: Diod. Sic. 34.1–4; 40.3.4; Philostr. *VA* 5.33; Tac. *Hist.* 5.5. This would be a problem in any church where gentile Christians were the hosts. (Accordingly it would presumably not be a problem when gentile Christians like Titus visited Jerusalem as in Gal 2.3, since the hospitality would be provided according to Jewish rules.[82] It could, however, be a problem for Peter if he visited churches like those of Corinth or Rome after the quarrel at Antioch; it is intriguing to ask how far he could have taken part fully in the life of those churches if he had indeed changed his practice in Antioch out of conviction.)[83]

That all changed dramatically, however, with the arrival of an emissary or, in the text usually followed here, emissaries who had either come from or had been expressly sent by James, the brother of Jesus.[84] It is not expressly said that they came and acted as they did on James's orders and some are reluctant to assume that he had deliberately provoked the following scene; others find it understandably difficult to distance James from the actions of these persons. And it is wholly intelligible that reports reaching Jerusalem of the practice of the Jewish Christians in Antioch might well have caused consternation among the Christians in Jerusalem and indignation and feelings of outrage among their Jewish neighbours, compelling James to intervene. If the emissaries acted with the authority of the whole Jerusalem church and its leader behind them, their representations would have had to be treated with the utmost seriousness in the Antioch church.

Yet, whether these emissaries acted on their own or with James's approval, it is nevertheless clear that opinion among Jewish

Christians was at this point of time divided. The ensuing quarrel did not ensure unanimity, but it did apparently mean that Paul was left very much in a minority among Jewish Christians in Antioch, and presumably also in Judaea, and that opinion among them swung very much in favour of the more conservative forces around James in Jerusalem. For the newcomers were seemingly able to persuade all the other Jewish Christians in the Antioch church to cease from their table-fellowship with gentile Christians, leaving Paul alone as the only Jewish-Christian advocate in Antioch who still supported the legitimacy of their previous conduct.

Unfortunately, but understandably, Paul's account of this incident is hardly a neutral one: he accuses Peter of hypocrisy and the others of fear of 'those from the circumcision'. We may surmise, however, that the other side could have defended their behaviour. Peter had, after all, been entrusted with the mission to Jews (2.8–9) and such laxity could not but undermine his effectiveness in this task by making him needlessly suspect in the eyes of his fellow-Jews. (James, on the other hand, seems to have enjoyed the respect of his fellow-Jews for his rigorous observance of the law, as we shall see.) Whatever Paul thought of it, it does not follow that the other Jewish Christians would have accepted that their change of course violated the agreement reached in Jerusalem. They may well have felt that this was necessary if the double mission to gentiles and to Jews agreed upon there was to continue to function on both fronts. The fear of 'those from the circumcision' that is meant here presumably refers to fear of non-Christian Jews, for the most that Peter and the other Jewish Christians would have had to fear from Christian Jews was that they would be disapproved of and reproved.[85] Peter perhaps might lose his position as leader and a 'pillar' of the church, but the other Jewish Christians in Antioch had no such loss to fear. It was non-Christian Jews who were in a position to endanger the lives of Jewish Christians, particularly in Judaea, but perhaps also elsewhere in the Diaspora too, if they felt that these followers of Jesus were betraying their race and their religion. It may well be right, therefore, to see both the trouble in Antioch and that in Galatia (cf. Gal 6.12–13) as a Jewish-Christian response to a rise in nationalist sentiments among Jews in Judaea, which placed them in some danger.[86]

It is important to recognize that another reason why the Jewish Christians would not regard themselves as in violation of the

Jerusalem agreement was that they could argue that they were not imposing anything on gentile Christians. It was the Jewish Christians in Antioch upon whom they wished to impose their will, and Jewish Christians were the responsibility of Peter and of the Jerusalem church. That is correct to a point, but Paul would have realized that they could not act in this way without also affecting the gentile Christians. For what were the gentile Christians to do? Must they henceforth exist as a separate church, not even able to celebrate the Lord's Supper with their Jewish brothers and sisters? Or must they indeed submit to and observe at least enough of the Jewish law to enable the Jewish Christians to resume eating with them?[87]

Paul does not mention that his rebukes or his arguments (which may be reflected in Gal 2.15–21)[88] met with any success. We may assume that they did not, since he would surely have told the Galatians so if he had carried the day, and that must have had far-reaching consequences for Paul, his mission and the entire early Christian church. Hitherto he had been an emissary of the Antioch church, carrying on his work with its authority, an authority bestowed upon it at the meeting in Jerusalem. Now he was on his own, with only his own conviction of a divine authority which, in his eyes but not necessarily in the eyes of others, more than made up for the lack of the backing of the Antioch church and, behind it, the Jerusalem church. Because of what he felt was a betrayal of the mission to the gentiles and the whole basis upon which he and others had conducted it up till now, it is plausible to argue that it was from this point on that he considered himself to be *the* apostle to the gentiles, since the other potential apostles to the gentiles, such as Barnabas, had, in his eyes, hopelessly compromised their message and their work.

This quarrel meant, however, that the church was now split into two camps and that the whole future of Paul's work was threatened. Against him stood the enormous authority of the Jerusalem church and now also that of the leading apostle, Peter, after he had changed sides.[89] It is against this background that we must understand at least part of the practical motivation for the collection project which occupied so much of Paul's time and energy during the last period of his life before his arrest in Jerusalem. For the immediate consequences of this quarrel should not be underestimated. It is true that, as Lothar Wehr notes,[90] the quarrel at Antioch does not muddy the waters of early Christianity as evidenced in later texts (it is only alluded to later in the anti-Pauline Ps.-Clem. *Hom.* 17.19.5–6), yet, had other events like the death of James the brother of Jesus and the fall of Jerusalem not intervened, it is to be presumed that the Christian church might well have taken a very different form as a result of this split. On the other hand, there would be good reasons for later supporters of both Peter and Paul to find this incident thoroughly disquieting in its implications and to wish to play it down or to pass over it in silence.

Nevertheless, it is to be noted that by the time of Ignatius in the early second century the church in Antioch of which he was bishop seems to have belonged to the heirs of Paul.[91] To that extent the results of the quarrel may be regarded as temporary,[92] but there is no hint of a reconciliation during Paul's life. Between the quarrel at Antioch and this time lies the catastrophe of the Jewish revolt of 66–70, with all the consequences which that undoubtedly had for the balance of power in the Christian church. After it, Judaizing Christians could not have exerted the same influence and pressure as before, and gentile Christians would be less willing to be identified as belonging to a Jewish community. For, even if Antioch seems to have been spared the outbreaks of anti-Jewish feeling manifested in other cities at the start of the Jewish revolt in 66, the same cannot be said of the following years. Josephus tells how, shortly after Vespasian had landed in Syria (spring 67), a Jew named Antiochus stirred up the non-Jews of the city with the allegation that the Jews planned to burn the city down (*BJ* 7.47), and the persecution of Jews occasioned by this accusation was further aggravated by the outbreak of a fire. Later, when Titus visited the city after the successful completion of the siege of Jerusalem, the Antiochenes asked him to banish the Jews from their city (§§103, 108). Although he refused their request, it is hard to believe that after that there was much incentive for gentile Christians to align themselves with their Jewish sisters and brothers, but at an earlier period, as Paul was defeated over the matter of table-fellowship, the situation was very different. One must assume that after the quarrel the church was initially divided and could not even eat the Lord's Supper together, and that the only hope of unity lay in the gentile Christians' acquiescence in the demands of the Jewish Christians. If, however, as has been suggested,[93] the Antioch church had remained divided between Judaizing Christians and

Paul's followers, it is surely harder to see why Paul apparently had no further contact with the latter. For that reason it is perhaps easier to conclude that, for a time at least, perhaps until the Jewish revolt, the Judaizers won the day and the gentile Christians had to settle for unity on their terms. For even if, as Christian Grappe notes,[94] a community made up of house churches made it possible for groups of Christians representing different viewpoints to exist alongside one another in one and the same city, it is clear that, until the coming of James's emissaries, the Antioch church had not been divided along ethnic lines and, had a separate gentile Christian house church existed which remained true to Paul, it is harder to explain why he seems to have avoided Antioch thereafter.

7

Paul the Missionary

Even if Paul was, as a Christian missionary, no unique figure, at least in the period of earliest Christianity, but one among a number engaged in missionary activity,[1] the extent and the manner of his missionary work are far better attested than those of all others and at the same time have been more deeply influential and formative, not only for earliest Christianity, but also for succeeding generations. These factors alone are more than sufficient justification for looking at his work in more detail.

7.1. The Course of Paul's Missionary Work

One should probably distinguish three phases in Paul's activity as a Christian missionary, and can probably divide the middle phase into two as well. First of all there was the phase before the Jerusalem conference. It is true that Paul does not speak directly of his missionary activities during this time, but at least he says that the churches in Judaea heard that their former persecutor was now proclaiming the faith (Gal 1.23) and it is implicit in his account of the conference that there was already some evidence of God's working through him to win gentiles, which the meeting recognized (2.7–8). Gal 1.21 suggests that this activity was limited to the area of Syria and Cilicia.

Then, after the conference and its recognition of the Antioch church's responsibility for bringing the gospel to the gentiles, and only then according to my chronological reconstruction, there followed a period of missionary activity further afield, commissioned by the Antioch church. At first Paul was partnered with Barnabas, quite probably as the junior partner, and their travels took them first to Cyprus, Barnabas' homeland, and then to the southern part of the Roman province of Galatia.[2] In the account of Acts, as we have already seen, Paul and Barnabas then quarrelled over the question of whether they should take John Mark with them on their next journey (Acts 15.36–41). They parted company over this, and so the second part of this phase of Paul's missionary work as an emissary of the Antioch church is carried out without Barnabas and accompanied by other helpers.[3] While Barnabas and John Mark returned to Cyprus, Paul took Silas and passed through Syria and Cilicia, strengthening the churches there – that was in order, although this area was the immediate responsibility of the Antioch church, for he was still working on behalf of that church. But then he pressed on further, through the churches of southern Galatia, visiting again the churches founded there on his previous journey. But, Acts tells us, the Spirit would not let him evangelize in Asia or Bithynia, so that he came to Troas and from there passed over into Macedonia and then eventually on to Greece, the Roman province of Achaea. After a relatively long time in Corinth, eighteen months according to Acts 18.11, he returned to Antioch, and that he returned there is fitting if he was still working on behalf and at the behest of that church.

If it is at that point that the quarrel of Gal 2.11–14 took place, that must inevitably have meant a decisively new, third phase in Paul's work, in which he was no longer an emissary of the Antioch church. Working together with that church was no longer possible for him, and in Acts' account we never hear of him visiting it again.[4] Instead a period of really independent missionary work began, in which Paul was perhaps for the first time completely free to conduct his missionary work as he wanted, although it is nevertheless hard to believe that the Antioch church could have exercised much control over what he did during his time in Macedonia and Greece. Yet in theory, at least, they could have called him to account for it on his return. Nevertheless, this new phase which now began was not a period in which he could devote himself wholly to missionary work, for much of his time during it was taken up with two other matters, dealing with problems that had arisen in his churches and gathering a collection among them for the Jerusalem church.

For it is probable that during Paul's long stay in Ephesus (Acts 19.1–20.1) one of these problems did not allow him to stay in that city the whole time, but forced him to visit Corinth, a visit about which Acts is silent, perhaps because it was both painful and unsuccessful. For Paul refers in 2 Cor 2.1 to his resolve not to pay the Corinthians another painful visit and declares in 12.14 and

13.1–2 that he is now ready to come to them a third time. From Acts 18 we know of his first and apparently thoroughly successful long first visit, but we hear of no further visits until he is about to set out on his last journey to Jerusalem (Acts 20.2 – 'Greece' probably includes, first and foremost, the city of Corinth and its church).

Hyldahl, in his *Die paulinische Chronologie*, tries to deny the existence of this interim visit: 2 Cor 12.14 refers to Paul's readiness for the third time to come to the Corinthians, not to his coming the third time, and 13.1–2 he interprets as referring to Paul's letter being like a second visit to them; but Paul does say in 13.1 that he is coming for the third time, not just that he is ready for the third time. Bärbel Bosenius takes a similar line, interpreting the present *erchomai* in 13.1 as a present *de conatu* (BDR §319), 'I am coming' in the sense of 'I am trying to come', but it is very hard then to take the 'third time' as referring to the trying rather than the coming.[5]

The references to a third visit also make it difficult to regard 2 Cor 10–13 as earlier than chapters 1–9, as many suppose; if it is a separate letter then it should be dated later or, particularly if one allows for the possibility that fresh news may have arrived in the course of writing the letter, which could explain the sharper tone of these chapters, it may be regarded as part of the same letter, perhaps composed over a considerable period of time as Paul waited for a suitable bearer.[6]

However, it was evidently not just the Corinthian church that presented Paul with problems during this time. Even life at his base in Ephesus does not seem to have been without its difficulties. Paul refers to his having fought with 'wild beasts' in Ephesus (1 Cor 15.32), and most interpret that figuratively, for, short of the sort of miracles that abound in the apocryphal Acts of the apostles, few survived the literal version of such encounters in the arena.[7] Nor does Paul mention any such affliction among those that he names in 2 Cor 11.23–9. It is possibly the same problem to which he alludes in 2 Cor 1.8–10, a deadly peril from which God had rescued him. Yet, despite that, Paul is reluctant to leave Ephesus because of the possibilities for evangelistic work there, adding 'and there are many adversaries' (1 Cor 16.8). Acts 19.23–40 recounts the tumult in the theatre of Ephesus, stirred up by the silversmiths whose trade in miniature shrines of the goddess Artemis was being endangered by the competition presented by the Christian gospel. It is tempting to see here the perils to which Paul refers, but it is not easy to combine this account with Paul's own references. For, on the one hand, Acts alleges that sympathizers among the high-ranking asiarchs prevented Paul himself from going into the theatre and risking his life there (19.30–1); on the other, Paul, quite sensibly, leaves Ephesus immediately after the uproar in Acts 20.1, and yet it is clear that 1 Corinthians, which presupposes some trouble already in Ephesus, also envisages that Paul will stay some time longer in the city and is in no great hurry to leave the place.

Now many wish to find a place for an Ephesian imprisonment as well, or even imprisonments,[8] and confidently assign to it many or all of those letters which Paul has written from prison, or at least those of them which Paul has written himself.[9] Yet others just as stoutly dispute whether Paul was ever in prison in Ephesus and seek another setting for these captivity epistles.[10] In the texts of the New Testament there is certainly no clear evidence of an imprisonment in that city, although it was clearly a place of considerable danger and difficulty for Paul. It may well be that it was not only for the sake of saving time (if indeed it would have saved time)[11] that Paul met the elders of the Ephesian church in Miletus in Acts 20.16, but also or perhaps even more because that city was still too fraught with danger for him if he set foot in it again, despite its importance as a centre of his work in the province of Asia.[12]

We have already noted that throughout his missionary work Paul confined himself almost exclusively to the area of the Roman Empire and indeed to the cities of that Empire. One possible exception is the period in Arabia just after his conversion (Gal 1.17), but we have seen that that may not have been for the purpose of missionary work and would not then count as an exception. Otherwise it seems that he saw himself called on to work within the Roman Empire, above all in cities, and also, as he puts it (Rom 15.20), in places where Christ's name was as yet unknown.

We saw, in looking at the question of Paul's Roman citizenship, that Hengel stresses how Paul conceived of his missionary strategy in Roman terms, concentrating upon the Roman Empire and its provinces. The areas which Paul mentions in his letters are Roman provinces and he uses the names of Roman provinces – Syria and Cilicia (Gal 1.21), Galatia (1 Cor 16.1; Gal 1.2), Asia (Rom 16.5; 1 Cor 16.19; 2 Cor 1.8), Macedonia (Rom 15.26; 1 Cor 16.5, etc.), Achaea (Rom 15.26; 1 Cor 16.15, etc.), and Illyricum (Rom 15.19).[13] Non-Roman areas like Parthia in the east or tribes beyond the northern or southern frontiers of the Empire seem to play no role in his planning. Paul's missionary strategy is, so to speak, Roman-shaped. More difficult to explain is his silence with regard to Egypt and Cyrene, but the principle of Rom 15.20 may play a role here: Christ's name was already known there. People from Egypt and Cyrene are mentioned amongst the audience at Pentecost in Acts 2.10 and Jewish Christians from Cyrene are mentioned as preaching to Greeks or 'Hellenists' in Antioch in 11.20, so that it is certainly conceivable that the Christian message had already been brought to those provinces.[14] Later, too, we will meet Apollos, an Alexandrian Jew, 'instructed in the way of the Lord' (18.25), and it may well be implied that he had received this instruction in his native Alexandria.[15]

Again, it is particularly to provincial capitals and Roman colonies, cities like Pisidian Antioch, Iconium, Lystra, Ephesus, Troas, Philippi and Corinth, that Paul turns in his travels and where he bases his operations. We can then the more readily believe his claim when writing to the Romans that he repeatedly wanted to visit the capital of the Empire too (1.13). He had, however, he explains, been hindered from doing so, although he never explains what had hindered him; one possibility is the expulsion of Jews by Claudius, for not only was Paul a Jew, but also the sort of Jew who was likely to provoke further trouble among the Roman Jews.[16] For, even if not all Jews were in fact expelled, Jewish Christians like Aquila and Priscilla, whose beliefs and practice were offensive to their fellow Jews, were probably a prime target of these disciplinary measures.

Paul also mentions in Rom 15, not only his plan to visit Spain, but also that he had preached the gospel from Jerusalem to Illyricum (15.19). However, Acts mentions no travels of Paul to this province lying on the east side of the Adriatic and, although various maps of Paul's journeys attempt to rectify this, either during the period of his second or that of his third journey, these reconstructions remain speculative. Had he reached the Adriatic coast, say at the ancient port of Dyrrhachium (the modern Durazzo/Durrës), he would have been poised to cross over to Italy, but do Paul's words actually mean that he got thus far? The other end of the great arc of missionary travels which he mentions is Jerusalem, but his letters do not give the impression that he preached the gospel in that city or even in Judaea, but rather that he met there with other Christians.[17] So, does his reference to preaching as far as Illyricum mean rather that he took the gospel up to the borders of Illyricum, where it bordered on Macedonia?[18]

If Macedonia was evangelized,[19] then it was done by planting churches in a number of cities, for his preaching in that province was, as elsewhere, limited to cities and does not seem to have involved the rural areas around those cities.[20] The centres where he spent longest, according to Acts, Corinth and Ephesus, were, moreover, provincial capitals and that is true also of his earlier activity in Syrian Antioch. Paul seems to have been a man of the cities,[21] and his work was correspondingly focused on the Graeco-Roman cities of the Empire and took the form of an urban movement, seemingly ignoring entirely the rural hinterland of these urban cities; nevertheless, this could apparently count in his eyes as completing the work of preaching the gospel in those provinces (Rom 15.19 again), even if he had achieved nothing more than planting tiny groups of Christians, house churches, in those cities.

More difficult to evaluate is his claim in Rom 15.20 that it was his policy not to preach the gospel where Christ's name was already known and so not to build on another's foundation. This leads to considerable tensions within the Letter to the Romans, for it is clear from the first chapter that there were already Christians in Rome, but that Paul nevertheless planned to visit that city and hoped to have some 'fruit' there as amongst the other gentiles (1.13). That tension has led Walter Schmithals to postulate two separate letters that have been fitted together to form our Romans, basing himself on the argument that Paul might contradict himself or perform a U-turn in two separate letters, but not in one and the same letter.[22] Already within chapter 1, however, there is a certain tension as Paul at first seems to adopt the attitude of one who has something to give to the Roman Christians (1.11), but then modifies this to stress that it is to be a mutual exchange of spiritual gifts (1.12). Yet it is also important to note with regard to chapter 15 that preaching where Christ is already known need not necessarily mean building on another's foundation (even if Paul here seems to imply that it does), if by that is meant a church which another Christian missionary has founded. For churches could spring up without the aid of such visiting missionaries, when Christians who had heard and accepted the Christian message elsewhere moved to a particular city and formed themselves together into a Christian community. That seems to have been the way in which many cults of oriental deities, including the Jewish cult, originally sprang up in cities of the Roman Empire, and it is particularly plausible that this happened in the case of the coming of Christianity to Rome: various Christians who had heard the gospel elsewhere came for reasons of trade or business or for other reasons to the capital city, and met together as, and formed themselves into, a Christian community or communities in that place. Nevertheless, preaching in Rome seems to violate at least the first part of the principle of 15.20 ('not where Christ is named'), if not the second ('not on another's foundation'). But, as Schmithals himself notes, Paul cannot really have meant that he would never preach in places where individual Christians already lived;[23] quite apart from the situation in Rome, that would, at least according to Acts' account, probably have prevented his work in Corinth (Acts 18.1–3) and perhaps also in Ephesus (18.18–21).[24]

Whatever difficulties the principle of Rom 15.20 presents in the context of Romans, it does, as I have already suggested, offer a means of making other features of Paul's missionary work intelligible, not only his neglect of Egypt and Cyrene, but perhaps also the mysterious reference to areas where the Spirit did not allow Paul to go according to Acts 16.6–7. No explanation of the nature or purpose of this prohibition is offered, but one possibility is that a Christian mission was already in progress in the Roman provinces of Asia and Bithynia. It is true that we hear nothing of Christian churches in Bithynia until the somewhat indefinite time of 1 Peter and the more precise time of Pliny's governorship of that province and Pontus at the beginning of the second century.[25] Is 1 Peter evidence that Peter or some of his supporters had carried the Christian message to that part of the Empire? At any rate by Pliny's time the Christians there are numerous, and are to be found not only in the cities, as is the case with the Pauline churches, but also in the villages and countryside (*Ep.* 10.96.9). The numbers are not in themselves proof that the origins of Christianity lie far back in the past; they could be relatively recent but spectacularly successful, but it is on the whole likelier that this success is the fruit of a long-term growth. (That Aquila came originally from the neighbouring Pontus – Acts 18.2 – is no proof that he became a Christian there, although that remains a possibility.)

Again, the addressees of 1 Peter are also to be found in the province of Asia, and one can similarly ask whether that means that Peter or his followers had been active there. According to Acts Paul visited Ephesus, the capital of that province, at the end of his second missionary journey. It was apparently a short visit and Acts makes no mention of the existence of a Christian community there; instead Paul preaches in the synagogue (18.19) and the Jews ask him to stay longer, but he would not (18.20) – why we are not told, but he promises to visit them again. This promise is fulfilled in chapter 19: Paul first meets with certain 'disciples' who, like Apollos in 18.25, had only been baptized with John's baptism. By calling them 'disciples' Acts implies that they were Christians, and if they only knew John's baptism then they were presumably Jewish Christians. They are, however, depicted as inadequately instructed in the Christian faith, which would be more comprehensible if there were no properly grounded Christian church in Ephesus.[26] Nevertheless Paul preaches the gospel in Ephesus, despite Rom 15.20, but perhaps because the really decisive part of the principle which he enunciates there is his resolve not to build on another's foundation, and his not preaching where Christ was already known is to be interpreted in the light of this. It is at least clear from his letters that he felt himself to be in no way precluded from evangelizing in Ephesus (1 Cor 16.8–9).

It was another feature of Paul's ministry, we learn, that he declined financial support from the church in a particular city when he was working there, although he was evidently able to accept donations from churches elsewhere (cf. Phil 4.16). Otherwise he would support himself by plying a trade, earning his keep, while at the same time seeking to win converts (cf. 1 Thess 2.9; also Acts 18.3). That would mean that he would have had to combine active and passive missionary roles, not only actively going out to seek converts, but also waiting for potential hearers to come to him as he worked.[27] That would naturally restrict him more, but he wanted to place no obstacle in the way of the progress of the gospel (cf. 1 Cor 9.12; also vv. 4, 18), in part presumably not wanting to be identified with those wandering preachers and philosophers who demanded a fee for the imparting of their wisdom, but also from necessity: many of those he reached and presumably wished to reach could not easily afford a fee. In all probability other Christian missionaries were not so unassuming, doubtless able to appeal to Jesus' instructions (Luke 10.7 par.; cf. 1 Cor 9.14), and the different strategy adopted by Paul could seemingly be exploited and turned against him by his rivals and critics (2 Cor 11.7–11; 12.14–18).[28]

7.2. The Nature of the Pauline Communities

Again and again Acts portrays Paul as preaching initially in the Jewish synagogue as he visits a new city, and in itself this picture is plausible. It made sense to seek out a first point of contact there, both with Jews and with non-Jews already interested in the Jewish message. It also explains how Paul was five times scourged by Jewish authorities (2 Cor 11.24) – they are unlikely to have intervened if he had only been preaching in the market place or in a private house. Preaching in the synagogue was another matter, particularly if it threatened to filter off into the Christian community gentile attenders and sympathizers, who were probably in many cases also financial benefactors of the synagogues.[29] For there is sufficient evidence that many non-Jews found the message and faith of the synagogue attractive, even if they were not prepared to take the further step of becoming full members or proselytes – for males, at least, the need to be circumcised doubtless acted as a considerable deterrent. The attractions of a message such as Paul's, which offered full membership in a religious community without demanding submission to such a rite, must have been considerable. So if, for instance, Paul's preaching led to the conversion to Christianity of Crispus, a synagogue president (*archisynagōgos*, Acts 18.8), then that might well have been a considerable blow to the synagogue, for the bearers of such a title are usually named in inscriptions as benefactors of the synagogue and that is particularly likely in the case of ones with a non-Jewish name, as here.

The picture which Acts paints is of an initial preaching in the synagogue, usually followed by rising opposition among the Jews, and then by the withdrawal of Paul and those synagogue members and sympathizers whom he had won over, and the establishment of a Christian community. The picture is again a plausible one, and if those who left the synagogue were often relatively well-to-do and benefactors of the synagogue, then the irritation of the remaining Jews is understandable, the more so since it was a Jew who was responsible for the loss of these people. Yet the assumption that there were indeed relatively well-to-do members of the Pauline communities is not an uncontroversial one. For opinions on the social status of the members of these churches have varied widely, some stressing the relatively high status of some of them, others seeing them as drawn from the lowest-placed sectors of society. 1 Cor 1.26–8 plays a central, but not unambiguous, role in the discussion here: is Paul understating the case when he asserts that God had not called many powerful members of the Corinthian church, meaning that none had in fact been called, or is his statement to be taken at face value as meaning that there were indeed some powerful ones or at least relatively powerful ones, but not many? (It is another question, how far one can generalize from the Corinthian congregation. Whether or not it was typical of Pauline churches in its social mix, it is, however, the one about which we are best informed, even if the information leaves many questions open.)

For a start, one can assert with confidence that there is no firm evidence at this date of Christians drawn from the very highest or the very lowest levels of Graeco-Roman society. At this stage we know for certain of no Christians who were Roman senators or knights (the *equites*) and even by the end of the first century the evidence for that is far from unambivalent.

Possible examples are then the consul T. Flavius Clemens, who was executed at the orders of his uncle Domitian, and Flavia Domitilla (his wife or, according to Euseb. *Hist. eccl.* 3.18.4, his niece; she is otherwise regarded as Domitian's niece), who was banished by the same emperor, both on the charge of 'atheism'; according to Eusebius Flavia was so punished 'because of her testimony to Christ'; both Jews and Christians could, however, be labelled 'atheists' and their faith could be construed as treasonable if it meant refusing to participate in the imperial cult; the position of members of the aristocracy was far more exposed here than that of the ordinary populace, and even more so that of relatives of the emperor, as in this case. Whether this couple were Jewish or Christian converts is disputed.[30] The name of the far earlier Pomponia Graecina who was tried by her husband for *superstitio externa* and acquitted (Tac. *Ann.* 13.32 – 57 CE) has also been mentioned, but Lampe rightly describes this as 'a very uncertain possibility':[31] were Christianity the cause of her behaviour (seemingly mourning for Drusus' daughter Julia for forty years) would her husband have acquitted her on this charge?

Here Meggitt's rejection of the 'new consensus' that some Christians belonged to the 'elite' of the Graeco-Roman world is to be noted, with the corollary that all belonged to the urban poor who lived near or below the subsistence level.[32] However, even if he is right to deny the existence of a 'middle class' in Graeco-Roman society, it is also necessary to point out that there were gradations of poverty within the 'non-elite', and that some of these could be regarded by others as relatively well off: to have a house or a room to live in, even if one was not an owner-occupier, was better than sleeping in the street or in a tomb. In other words, one should avoid too undifferentiated a picture of the 'non-elite'.

And if the lowest of the low were the slaves who worked on large agricultural estates (*latifundia*), in mines or in medium- or large-scale manufacturing concerns, then we neither know of Christians from these circles nor is it likely that they would have found it easy to belong to Christian communities, such were the conditions under which they lived.[33] But what of those in between these extremes? Pliny in the early second century is confronted by a large number of Christians 'of every rank' in Pontus and Bithynia (*Ep.* 10.96.9); was that already true of an earlier period too?

Here again our most tangible evidence comes from Corinth. While it may be uncertain whether the Erastus who is mentioned in Rom 16.23 and described as treasurer (*oikonomos*) of the city – probably of Corinth, if Romans was written from that city – was a magistrate or a slave owned by the city, it is at least unusual that Paul mentions his office and that may be an argument for the former alternative.[34] On the other hand, such was the power and influence of some slaves that even a slave occupying such a position might merit a special mention.[35] To hold such a post as a magistracy one had to be a full citizen of the city and, in a Roman colony like Corinth, a Roman citizen and possessed of some wealth, for one was expected to meet certain costs out of one's own pocket. The same verse in Rom 16 mentions, however, a certain Gaius who is host to Paul and the whole church (cf. also 1 Cor 1.14), and that again suggests the possession of certain means and perhaps a house large enough to accommodate meetings of the whole Corinthian church, even though Justin Meggitt rightly warns us against overestimating either the size of the church or of the house which would be needed.[36]

It is to be noted that, whereas Gaius can be host to the whole church, most probably in Corinth (Rom 16.23; cf. also 1 Cor 14.23, the whole church in one place), Romans 16, if indeed addressed to Rome, attests a church in the house of Prisca and Aquila (16.5), but perhaps implies that all those greeted in 16.5b–15 met elsewhere, and the phrasing of vv. 14 and 15 may suggest that separate Christian congregations gathered around Asyncritus and his fellows and also around Philologus and Julia and those named with them. That all points to a considerably greater number of Christians in Rome than in Corinth, but at the same time to an even greater potential for division.

Others too are mentioned as possessing houses: Stephanas (1 Cor 1.16; 16.15, 17), Philemon (Philem 2) or Aquila and Prisca (Rom 16.3). The same may be true of Lydia in Acts 16.5, who also possesses an *oikos*, this time in the sense of a household; but from that one may assume that she had somewhere to accommodate it. Equally the ability to travel probably points to the possession of some means, although Meeks points out that it might not be those who travelled who actually possessed those means,[37] and that is true of many whom Paul greets in his letters or who assisted him in his work. Phoebe, whom he commends to the Roman church in Rom 16.1–2, is probably an outstanding example of this. In all probability she held an office (*diakonos*) in the church of Cenchreae, a port of Corinth, and this office may well have involved her in ministering financially to the needs of the church there. Paul also describes her as the *prostatis* of many and of himself and it seems likeliest that this term means that she was the patron of many and of Paul.[38] If so, that also implies a position of greater wealth and higher status than her clients. It is in keeping with this that she can travel, and will visit Rome, perhaps bearing Paul's letter with her. Such people may not have belonged to the uppermost strata of society, but were by no means amongst the poorest either.

Other features of the Corinthian church point in the same direction. It has, for instance, been pointed out that the reference to litigation between Christians in 1 Cor 6.1–8 implies that at least one of the parties to this dispute must have had the financial means to seek this mode of redress, even if it was not necessary to belong to the wealthiest. Poorer members of society were unlikely to be able to do so, and were, moreover, unlikely to have success if their adversary were of a higher social status. The system was heavily weighted in favour of the more well-to-do, for the judges and the jury came from the higher echelons of society and tended to favour their own kind, and for a member of the Corinthian church to venture on such a course it is, therefore, likelier that he was socially relatively well placed.[39]

The existence of more affluent members of the Corinthian church may also be implied by Paul's account of the problems in their celebrations of the Lord's Supper. He rebukes certain members of the church whose conduct at the meal puts the have-nots to shame, and protests by asking whether they had not their own houses where they could eat and drink (1 Cor 11.22).[40] It is plausible to compare this, as Theißen does,[41] with the social distinctions which were often characteristic of meals offered by the wealthier in Graeco-Roman society. It was not unknown for social differences to lead to different treatment of one's guests and even different menus – for the guests of honour better fare and for the dependants and clients of the host something inferior; in that way one honoured the important guests and correspondingly put the others to shame, demonstrating their inferiority and dependence on their patron. Yet, as Meggitt notes,[42] it is to be expected that those lower down the social scale might well ape the ways of those at the very top.

It is, however, likely that such relatively wealthy members of the church were very much in the minority, even in the Corinthian church, although their influence in that church may have been out of all proportion to their numbers if the church was dependent upon their wealth, however modest that may have been, for a place to meet and for providing hospitality for visiting Christians or for travellers who were the basis of their communications with other churches and with their founder, Paul. The rest were doubtless less well off and were probably either slaves (cf. 1 Cor 7.21–2) or traders or manual workers (cf. Acts 18.3) – although these too could sometimes own slaves or travel, as the example of Aquila and Prisca shows (Acts 18.18; cf. Rom 16.3).[43] The Pauline Christian communities were in this respect probably more diverse than many other comparable associations in the Graeco-Roman world, but G. W. Clarke points to the example of an association of fishtraders in Ephesus whose members ranged from Roman citizens to slaves.[44] Nevertheless, the Christian community may have been open to all to a degree exceptional in religious associations in the Greek East, but John Kloppenborg suggests that *collegia* organized around a particular deity were probably the most inclusive.[45] The presence of some such relatively well-to-do individuals in the Pauline communities is the more important because of its bearing on the organization of these communities. Those who had a large enough house for meetings or could support the church materially or financially in other ways inevitably wielded an authority of an informal sort. The structure of the household in the Graeco-Roman world exercised a considerable influence on the structure of the early Christian churches and, whether they were given an office or a title or not, the role of the house-owners in the functioning of these churches was a vitally important one.[46]

For many of the tasks which had to be done there were no office-bearers as such, just people who performed these tasks, even if leading the community was among the tasks to be performed. In his earliest extant letter Paul urges the Thessalonians to recognize those who took such pains in leading and instructing their community (1 Thess 5.12). They are not identified by any title, just by what they do. In the same way, in Rom 12.8 Paul mentions the activity of leading alongside those of admonition, generous giving and exercising compassion – if the last three correspond to no 'office', then there is no need to see one in the leading of the community. Yet there may be a point in naming those who led and those who gave alongside one another: often in ancient society it was above all those who had something to give who exercised leadership roles, whether that was formally recognized by the bestowal of an office or not.[47]

In the light of this informal structure it comes as a surprise that Paul at the beginning of Philippians greets the 'deacons' (*diakonoi*) and 'overseers' (*episkopoi*) (Phil 1.1), so much so that some treat the reference as a later gloss.[48] These apparent 'offices' may, however, as much designate functions which certain persons could fulfil by virtue of their financial means. Just as Phoebe may have been a 'deacon' of the church in Cenchreae, as well as patroness of Paul and others, because she was relatively wealthy, this may apply to the 'deacons' and 'overseers' in Philippi, too.

The word *episkopos*, as well as being used of temple and synagogue overseers, was used in Greek societies and clubs for one who provided certain services and fulfilled certain administrative duties.[49] Performing such functions, however, may come so near to holding an office that it makes no appreciable difference, whether one describes the functions as 'offices' or not, particularly if one had sufficient means to perform such functions over a period of time, and if the competition from other potential candidates was not great. *Diakonoi* are also found in a non-Christian context, and again also in a cultic context: from the third century BCE on the word is found with the sense of a servant or office-bearer in pagan temples or cultic societies, and also in the sense of one who serves at table.[50]

The greeting of these persons at the start of the letter, highly unusual in Paul's letters, which, except in the case of Philemon, begin by greeting a whole church without separately mentioning any individuals in it, may have something to do with the fact that Paul wants, among other things, to express his thanks for the financial support which he has received from the Philippian church (4.16, 18). If the 'deacons' and 'overseers' were those particularly responsible for sending this aid, then Paul's singling them out in this way is the more easily intelligible.[51]

None of the genuine Pauline letters mention the office of 'elders', despite the fact that Acts describes Barnabas and Paul appointing elders, with the laying on of hands, in each of the newly founded churches at the end of their first missionary journey (14.21–3).

Apart from that we meet elders in the leadership of the Jerusalem church (11.30; 15.2, 4, 6, 22–3; 16.4; 21.18) and in the church of Ephesus (20.17). Where one might above all expect them to be mentioned in the Pauline letters, in the lists of offices and functions in 1 Cor 12.8–10, 28 and Rom 12.6–8, they are lacking. Is the mention of them in churches founded by Paul an anachronism on the part of Acts, reading back the church order of its author's own day into the time of Paul and showing thereby, yet again, his nearness to the world of the Pastoral Epistles, which also mention this office? Or is this just an office which Paul, left to his own devices, did not introduce into his churches, but which was favoured by other churches, like that of Jerusalem? Yet, if the Galatian churches are those founded in Acts 13–14, one might expect some reference to, even appeal to, these office-bearers in Paul's letter to those churches, and we find none.

It is striking that this office is also so seldom attested in Jewish inscriptions of that period or somewhat later (instead we find designations like archons, etc.).[52] That is the more surprising in view of the role of elders in the Old Testament (and also in 1 Maccabees). It may then be the latter which was the inspiration for the Christian adoption of the office, and not its existence in contemporary Jewish communities.[53] (It is also found in the secular sphere, as attested in inscriptions and papyri from Egypt, as well as in the sacral sphere in Asia Minor and the Aegean.)[54]

'Elders' are attested elsewhere in the New Testament, apart from the references in Acts and the Pastoral Epistles. Less certain, however, is whether the references are to the office-bearers of a particular church. Jas 5.14 seems to refer to 'elders' of a church, whose role is here to pray for the sick and anoint them with oil, and in Wiard Popkes' opinion it is uncertain whether they are office-bearers or just experienced older members of the congregation.[55] If there is an 'office' in this letter it is perhaps above all that of 'teacher' (3.1). When the pseudonymous writer of 1 Peter exhorts the 'elders' as a 'fellow-elder', but also urges obedience on the younger men, it may be just the two age-groups who are meant (5.1–5). 2 and 3 John are also written by one who introduces himself simply as 'the elder', although it seems likely that this is not meant in the sense of the office-bearer of a particular congregation: this figure has a wider authority. Finally, the Book of Revelation bears witness repeatedly to a heavenly body of elders (4.4, 10, etc.).

Alongside the influence of those who had the financial means to support the church, whether or not they occupied a specific office or not, there was another factor which was of enormous significance in shaping the earliest communities, namely the many and varied manifestations of the Spirit. The Spirit activated and enabled Christians to perform various functions that benefited the church and furthered its growth. The 'charismatic' ordering of the church which stemmed from this pneumatocratic principle has sometimes been contrasted with the rise of 'offices', but any absolute contrast is out of place. Already in Paul's writings the at first sight so dominant charismatic order is tempered by signs that this order was quite compatible with the existence of 'offices'. For the two lists of spiritual gifts which Paul gives in 1 Cor 12 differ markedly in this respect: whereas vv. 8–10 list the various activities that the Spirit empowers, v. 28 starts by naming three groups of persons, apostles, prophets and teachers, before reverting to a listing of gifts; implicit here is that people have these gifts, but there is no one who is designated with the title of a miracle-worker or a healer or a tongues-speaker. It is clear that there are particular people, Paul himself included, who are known as apostles, prophets and teachers, and it is difficult to avoid the conclusion from the 'in the first place . . ., in the second place . . ., thirdly . . .' that these are in an order of precedence, however much that may seem to conflict with the lessons to be drawn from the imagery of the church as a body with many limbs, each complementing the other and mutually dependent upon each other, in vv. 12–27. For, despite his stress on the value of all gifts, when it comes to evaluating the controversial gift of speaking in tongues, Paul seems to place it consistently at the end of the lists (vv. 10, 28, 30). And in chapter 14 it becomes yet clearer that, for Paul, speaking in tongues is much less desirable than prophecy and other forms of intelligible speech (vv. 1–19), at least when not practised in conjunction with an intelligible interpretation.

Equally, however, it is clear that apostles, prophets and teachers, even if they are office-bearers, are charismatically endowed – there is, for a start, no question of Paul wanting to deny that his apostleship is a *charisma*, a gift of God's grace! If there is a distinction to be drawn, it is that between, on the one hand, recognizing the *charisma* already in evidence in a person and therefore bestowing upon her or him a particular office, assured that she or he are equipped by God to exercise it, and, on the other, electing a person to an office, in the expectation that the one so chosen will then be given the spiritual equipment to fulfil the task assigned. It is then a further question whether the latter understanding finds any place in the New Testament,[56] but it is certainly not to be found in the acknowledged letters of Paul. Nevertheless, much remains unclear here. In the case of the apostles we have the criteria which Paul assumes in 1 Cor 9.1, that one has seen the risen Lord and that one has manifested the works of an apostle, here above all in the founding of a church like that in Corinth; it is probably implicit that the vision of the Lord entails a commission to carry out such a missionary work. In the other two cases, the prophets and the teachers (the same two groups as are mentioned in Acts 13.1), the criteria are not mentioned. It is to be presumed that a prophet or prophetess was first recognized as such after he or she had actually prophesied, but there is no indication how much or how often one must prophesy before one was so recognized. Perhaps once was enough. If, however, the gift had first to be there and to be visible, that implies that potentially any member of the community could prophesy who had not hitherto done so, and that this activity was not limited to those recognized as prophets and prophetesses; there had to be a first time and potentially anyone might be able to share a revelation with the assembled church (14.26; cf. v. 31, 'all'). With teachers, however, one would assume some less spectacular, but in Paul's eyes none the less charismatic, manifestation of a God-given ability. Again, however, in 1 Cor 14.26 he seems to assume that potentially anyone might come forward with a piece of teaching, and the analogy with the prophets would suggest that this need not be someone hitherto recognized as a teacher. With both prophets and teachers the bestowal of these titles presumably carried with it the expectation that the ones so designated would continue to prophesy and to teach.

Also uncertain is the relationship between these gifts and designations and ones like the office of deacon (or overseer). If it is correct that such persons were concerned with financial matters and with the material needs of the church, whether the means for doing that came out of their own pockets or whether they were merely administering what had been provided by other members of the church, then it is nevertheless clear that Paul wished to regard their activity as Spirit-led – or at least it should be Spirit-led. For the 'helpful deeds' (*antilēmpseis*) mentioned in the list of gifts of grace in 1 Cor 12.28 seem similar to the role of the deacons, and indeed *diakonia* is mentioned expressly amongst those gifts listed in Rom 12.7, parallel to teaching.

In the Pauline churches one finds, then, a form of church order which was by no means tightly defined in its structure, with relatively few specific offices or titles for their holders, an order which arose out of a number of different factors – social as well as charismatic. And yet it was an order, for, however much his churches may have been led and empowered by the Spirit, Paul insisted that their life should not be unstructured or uncontrolled. For God is not, he insisted, a God of disorder, but one of peace (1 Cor 14.33); everything should be done in a seemly and orderly manner (14.40). That the leading of the Spirit is no excuse for behaving otherwise, is clear from his instructions to prophets in this chapter: only one should speak at a time and 'the spirits of the prophets' should be subject to the prophets (14.30, 32). It is in fact clear that it would be a mistake to think that a charismatic order, even if it could ever exist in a pure form, would have no structure and no hierarchy and no office-bearers or their equivalents, and this is hinted at by the problems in the Corinthian church which probably led Paul to deal with the question of spiritual gifts and the spiritually gifted in the first place. In all probability those possessing the most spectacular gifts, in particular the ability to speak in tongues, which was perhaps seen as the ability to speak in the tongues of angels, i.e. heavenly languages (13.1), had claimed that this was the highest and truest form of spiritual gift, thus devaluing the others and making their fellow-Christians feel second-rate. It was a form of authority which was just as open to abuse as that which stemmed from a higher position in society, and just as damaging to the unity of the church. Paul relegated it to a more lowly position in order to thrust into greater prominence other gifts which he regarded as more beneficial to the growth and edification of the church.

7.3. Problems of the Pauline Communities

This was, however, but one of the many and varied problems which confronted Paul in his various churches, some relatively minor, some extremely serious. We have already seen how Paul was forced to end his connection with the Antioch church and how his relations with the Jerusalem church had been seriously damaged. This disagreement spilled over into his relations with other churches that he had founded or had helped to found, most notably those in *Galatia*. That they were most seriously affected is easier to understand if they were located in that region of southern Asia Minor which Barnabas and Paul had visited in the journey described in Acts 13–14. For that region was the nearest to Syria and Cilicia and the Antioch church, and these churches were, moreover, ones that had originally been founded as part of the first missionary outreach of the Antioch church beyond the borders of Syria and Cilicia and would naturally be regarded as belonging to the sphere of influence and jurisdiction of that church.

Whereas it has been widely held in English-speaking scholarship that Galatians was indeed directed to these churches, German scholarship long thought, and to a large extent still does think, that the churches addressed in this letter were located in central Anatolia, in the region around the ancient Ancyra (modern Ankara), a region settled by the ethnic Galatians, a Celtic people, in the third century BCE. Yet even here there are several voices that have been raised in favour of the other alternative, the churches situated in the southern part of the far larger Roman province of Galatia.[57] There are arguments for the so-called North Galatian theory, like the presumed impropriety of calling the Pisidians and Lycaonians in the southern part of the province 'Galatians', but they are outweighed by other considerations.[58]

The trouble in Galatia is, then, to be seen as intimately bound up with the issues raised by James's emissaries in Antioch, and the arrival of emissaries in Galatia should perhaps be regarded as part of the same movement which had had such devastating consequences in Antioch.

At any rate, the issue is ostensibly the same, both in Antioch and in Galatia: gentile Christians must be circumcised. On that the majority of exegetes are agreed.[59] The Galatian Christians are troubled by some who are in all probability not members of those churches (Gal 1.7–8: 'certain people' over against 'you'; cf. 5.10) and who proclaim 'another gospel'. At the close of the letter Paul writes, perhaps laboriously, with his own hand, that, in compelling the Galatians to be circumcised, the motive of these intruders is really to avoid being persecuted because of the cross of Christ and to be able to 'boast' of the 'flesh', i.e. the mark of circumcision in the flesh, of the Galatians (6.12–13).[60] The similarity to the situation described in Antioch in Acts 15.1 and presupposed by the question of Titus' circumcision in Gal 2.3 is clear enough. Yet two factors have caused scholars to hesitate: one is the shift in Paul's argument in Gal 5.13, where he seems to combat a misuse of Christian freedom in order to give free rein to the 'flesh'; the other is his accusation in 6.13 that his opponents do not themselves keep the law. And yet the troublemakers do not seem to be demanding circumcision alone, for in 4.21 Paul speaks of the Galatians wanting to subject themselves to the law, submitting anew to a yoke of slavery, and he refers to their observing 'days, months, particular seasons and years' (4.10). Indeed, if they let themselves be circumcised, Paul argues, they are obliged to keep the whole law (5.1–3). That may, however, be Paul's interpretation of what law-observance entailed, written from the perspective of a former Pharisee. From that perspective, too, the way in which his opponents themselves kept the law may have seemed deficient and inadequate. That he needs to warn against misuse of Christian freedom need not imply that the Galatians actually were misusing it; this may rather be a reason which his opponents gave for rejecting Paul's version of the gospel, a criticism similar to that which surfaces in Rom 3.8 and 6.1, 15 – Paul's gospel invites immorality and unrighteousness;[61] it may be a theoretical reason in Galatia, although we shall see that in Corinth it could well have become a reality in practice. At the same time, however, his exhortations give the impression of strife amidst members of the Galatian churches (5.15; various expressions for strife and discord are also prominent among the 'works of the flesh' in 5.20), and the message of those who were responsible for this 'other gospel' may well have set the Galatian Christians against one another.

Their proximity to Syria and Cilicia and, therefore, to the influence of the Jerusalem church may have meant that the Galatians were particularly exposed to this form of counter-mission, but there are signs that Paul at least feared that this Judaizing threat might also materialize in other churches. In Rom 16.17–18 and in Phil 3.2, 18–19 he warns his readers against troublemakers who serve not Christ, but their own belly (a reference to the observance of dietary regulations?); these he scornfully names the 'mutilation' as over against the true circumcision and he accuses them of glorying in their shame, which may again be a scornful reference to physical circumcision. The Romans and the Philippians are to look out for these (*skopein*, *blepein*) and this may imply that they are not yet present in those churches.[62]

In the case of *2 Corinthians*, however, it seems that Paul must deal with newcomers who have already arrived, perhaps bearing letters of recommendation (3.1). They are evidently Jewish Christians, 'Hebrews' like Paul himself and descendants of Abraham (11.22), and call themselves apostles and servants (*diakonoi*) of Christ (11.13,

23). They may have appealed to the authority of others whom Paul scornfully calls the 'super-apostles' (11.5; 12.11), for the intruders he labels with the more directly hostile 'false apostles' (11.13),[63] although for many these are the same as the 'super-apostles', and the arguments for their identity seem stronger than those in favour of a distinction.[64] Yet, whoever these troublemakers were, their message and their strategy do not seem to have been the same as those of the Judaizing emissaries known to us from Galatians. There is no mention of demands for circumcision and observance of the law, although the old covenant of the letter is compared unfavourably with the new one of the Spirit in 3.4–18. Moreover, if Paul's skills as a speaker were now decried (10.10), it is to be presumed that the intruders' skills were somewhat greater, and it seems that they set great store on appearances and revelations of the Lord, so that Paul feels himself compelled, under protest, to answer them in kind. For signs and wonders were to be expected of an apostle (12.12).[65] From all this we can deduce something of their style, but singularly little of the content of their message. That is all the more frustrating when Paul implies that they preach another Jesus (11.4). It has been suggested that their message corresponds to that of Q, that hypothetical source – if it ever existed as a self-sufficient statement of the message of Jesus: they revered Jesus as a victorious pneumatic and advertised themselves by claims to revelations and by their miracles. Otherwise the proffered identifications range from libertine pneumatics and gnostics (although evidence for their libertinism, as opposed to that of some of the Corinthians, is harder to find), missionaries whose stance resembled that of the Jerusalem church (but evidently not pressing for circumcision and observance of the law this time) or who belonged to the type of Hellenistic itinerant prophets, magicians and bringers of salvation, or Jewish Christians from Jerusalem who were not prepared to follow the agreement reached at the Jerusalem conference – and yet one must be more precise and say what they disagreed with, if they did not call for circumcision and observance of the law. One is left wondering, then, whether these opponents intervened merely out of a personal rivalry or animosity directed against Paul and his work or whether their message in fact differed from his. Or were they but opportunists who sensed what would appeal to and please those members of the Corinthian church who were dissatisfied with Paul's message and way of ordering the church? If one compares Acts' brief portrayal of Apollos in 18.24–8, then there is something to be said for Berger's suggestion that the opponents were connected with Apollos or at least resembled him in their style of missionary work – even to the extent of bringing with them letters of recommendation (Acts 18.27; 2 Cor 3.1).[66]

For it is clear that the Corinthian church was not united in standing behind Paul, even if none of the members of that congregation had yet gone so far as to repudiate him or deny his right to be an apostle. That some of them preferred others is at least to be seen in the slogans which Paul quotes in 1 Cor 1.12: 'I am Paul's', 'I belong to Apollos', 'I to Cephas'.[67] He does not tell us why some chose the one, others another, and this has led to all manner of attempts to reconstruct the beliefs of the various parties, but the basis for these reconstructions is more than a little speculative. It may indeed be suggested that Paul deliberately makes no attempt to criticize the specific beliefs of the various groups and thereby become involved in the points at dispute between them, concentrating his criticism instead on the building of groups as such.[68] In so doing he reinforces his claim to be 'father' of the entire church and not just leader of one faction within it, as well as avoiding anything that might harden the fronts between the groups. It is sometimes also suggested that Paul is defending his apostleship against attack in chapter 9, but if that is the point then it is hardly in keeping with the main thrust of his argument at this point, which is to use the fact that he has apostolic rights but waives them in order to encourage those who have 'knowledge' not to injure their weaker sisters and brothers by taking their insights to their logical conclusion. It is true that some in Corinth may need to be reminded that Paul is, after all, their apostle, but at the stage of the writing of 1 Corinthians there should be no question of a direct frontal attack upon his right to be an apostle, even if some preferred the leadership of others.

Nor should one really speak of opponents of Paul in *1 Corinthians*. He can still address the whole community and there is no contrast between 'you', the community, and certain others such as we find in 2 Corinthians and Galatians.[69] And if it is true that Paul uses an altogether sharper tone when dealing with intruders who do not belong to his churches, then the tone of 1 Corinthians lacks the bitter edge of parts of Galatians or 2 Corinthians. It is the Corinthian church that is responsible for the problems in it dealt with in 1 Corinthians and it is Paul's church. Indeed, some of those problems may have arisen from an over-zealous following of Paul's teaching or Paul's example on the part of some of his most enthusiastic followers.

For we find Paul quoting certain sayings that sound like slogans and that seem to underlie some of the problems in the church: 'Everything is permitted me' (6.12; 10.23, 'everything is permitted') or 'We all have knowledge' (8.1). One could ask whether the use of the first person is purely a stylistic device, or whether it does not indicate that Paul to some extent identifies himself and sympathizes with the content of these words. That all was ever permitted in an absolute sense is, of course, unlikely – tacitly it must be assumed that things like murder are, nonetheless, not permitted – but such a phrase could have its place in a debate about Christian freedom and in particular freedom from the demands of the Jewish law; 'freedom' is, at any rate, a key concept in chapter 9 as Paul shows himself to be the free apostle who has yet made himself everyone's slave in order to win them for the gospel. It is to be noted that this slogan appears in the context of two sins that were, in Jewish eyes, the chief sins of the gentiles – idolatry and sexual impurity. Did freedom from the Jewish law then mean, it might be asked, that these Jewish prohibitions had lost their force? Even the idea that Christians were, according to Paul, created anew (Gal 6.15; 2 Cor 5.17) could perhaps have encouraged the sexual sin of incest which is condemned in 5.1–5, for were not the relationships that made this sexual liaison sinful and forbidden by the law of Moses (Lev 18.8) part of the old creation?

If this slogan about all being permitted has its origin in Paul's message there is, however, a certain attraction in laying the slogan 'We all have knowledge' at the door of Paul's colleague Apollos, who had apparently consolidated Paul's work in founding the Corinthian church (3.6). It is true that we have no right to expect that every Alexandrian Jew, as Apollos originally was (Acts 18.24), should share the interests, let alone the erudition, of Philo, his Alexandrian Jewish contemporary, but it is unlikely that Paul awakened the Corinthians' fascination with 'knowledge' and the closely related 'wisdom'. At any rate, Paul goes to some lengths to distance himself from what is usually judged to be wisdom and to set in its place the wise foolishness of God (1 Cor 1.17–2.16).[70] If Apollos did introduce these terms, then it is unlikely that the use of them which Paul criticizes also goes back to him, for Paul speaks warmly of him and insists that he has encouraged him to return to visit the Corinthian church (16.12).[71] It is unlikely that he would do that if he had regarded him as likely to lead the church astray or to feed them with unhelpful ideas. Such ideas may not, therefore, stem from some teacher who has visited the church, but may rather be the product of the intellectual climate to be found at least in certain circles of society in that Graeco-Roman city. For Paul it was characteristic of the Greeks that they sought wisdom while the Jews sought signs (1.22). Corollaries of the Christian message which might have seemed unthinkable in its Palestinian homeland now sprang readily to mind and were eagerly adopted.

Both Paul and Apollos had probably encouraged the Corinthians to think of themselves as endowed with the Spirit, perhaps particularly associating the gift of the Spirit with the rite of baptism (cf. 12.13; also 6.11).[72] In all probability Apollos had baptized more than Paul, for Paul stresses how few he had baptized (1.14, 16) and in the context of a horticultural image speaks of Apollos' contribution to the rise of the community as a watering (3.6). But Paul himself spoke in tongues (14.18) and Apollos was according to Acts 'afire with the Spirit' (18.25), although he at that stage apparently knew only the baptism of John. Yet it would be rash to jump to the conclusion that Paul or Apollos were to blame for the over-valuation of the gift of speaking in tongues which probably lies behind the question of the Corinthians about 'spiritual gifts' (or possibly 'spiritual people', 12.1) which Paul deals with in chapters 12–14: the history of charismatic Christianity, from Paul's day to ours, has time and again shown how easy it is for those possessing more spectacular and unusual gifts like speaking in tongues to imagine that only they *really* possess the Spirit and that all those without such gifts are spiritually defective.

Nor can everything else that went wrong in the Corinthian church be laid at the door of Paul or Apollos. The problem of litigation (6.1–8) mentioned above may have stemmed from a culture at certain (higher) levels of Corinthian society that considered this the usual way to settle disputes and could afford to do so. The problems at the Lord's Supper may reflect the importation into the Christian meals of the ways of holding meals current in Graeco-Roman society, in that they were made to mirror the social inequalities between the various participants. Or at least the fact that one was accustomed so to behave at social gatherings and meals may have blinded the Corinthians to the incongruity of what they were doing in Christ's name. It is again the more well-to-do members of the church who had most to gain from a pragmatic solution of the problem of food offered to idols. The higher one rose in Graeco-Roman society, the greater the pressure to achieve some compromise on this matter, and failure to achieve it could lead to social ostracism. For anyone holding a municipal office (Erastus?) or an office in any of those societies or clubs that were so integral to the Graeco-Roman city would be expected to participate in the religious rites that were part and parcel of the life of the city and its institutions. (And declining an office when one could afford to hold it could be regarded as highly antisocial.) This was, however, a problem for many far humbler members of society, for there were various trade associations and clubs of other sorts whose gatherings would at least formally acknowledge and pay their respects to some patron deity or other. It is likely that Christians would therefore find themselves debarred from participation in such clubs. Even at the private level there was the difficulty that one might, even unwittingly, come into contact with idolatry through meat that had been ritually slaughtered, although it is to be noted that consuming meat in a private context was more the prerogative of the better-off. Poorer members of society would be more likely to eat meat at public feasts where the place of pagan ritual was perfectly obvious or else, as Meggitt adds, at one of the far from sacral eating-houses.[73] Wealthier Christians had, therefore, much to gain if they could find a way round the blanket ban on contact with idolatry that seemed to be built into the Judaeo-Christian ethos, and much to lose if they did not. One way was to argue that if idols were nonentities then they could not harm one (cf. 8.4) – yet they could if behind them lurked demons (10.20–1, alluding to Deut 32.17). And anyway, Paul retorts, not all Christians shared this conviction that there was nothing to idols, and might therefore be troubled or harmed by the example of the so-called 'strong' if they followed through the logic of this insight (8.7–13). Paul's one concession to them is that at a private gathering they should not fear the whiff of idolatry in every dish, but should only take evasive action if someone makes an issue of the fact that what is served has been offered to an idol (10.25–30).[74]

It should not, however, be thought that these problems were the only ones confronted then by Christian congregations. They were problems peculiar to Christians seeking to live out Paul's version of the Christian gospel in a predominantly non-Jewish setting. Quite obviously, then, different problems arose for Christians who followed a different version of the gospel or lived in a context where Judaism played a more dominant role, as we shall see. Again, however, it is Paul's churches about which we are better informed and can form a clearer picture. And, just as it was important to pay special attention to Paul's work as a missionary because of the influence which he has had on the course of later history, so, too, it should be recognized that the problems which he confronted, above all in a predominantly non-Jewish environment, were problems which would continue to confront Christians in such an environment, at least until, with the conversion of Constantine two and a half centuries later, that environment and Christianity's relationship to it changed significantly. Not that the problems then disappeared overnight or vanished for good. On the contrary; in the course of the succeeding centuries they have often reappeared, in one form or another.

Other problems stemmed from a more general cultural inheritance that was not limited to the well-to-do. In particular the view of the physical body as at best something temporary that would be snuffed out at death or at worst as an unhealthy impediment to one's moral life was widespread, and probably influenced the Corinthians' sexual ethics and the views of some of them with regard to the resurrection. Paul's remark in 1 Cor 6.13b, 'God will destroy [the stomach] and [foodstuffs]', may well echo the arguments of the Corinthians, but it is quoted in the context of a discussion of whether union with a prostitute is permitted for a Christian. Perhaps an argument that had originally been used in discussing the validity of Jewish food laws had been extended to apply to the realm of sexual intercourse. In that case the fact that the body and parts of it like the stomach were only temporary seems to have been taken to mean that it did not matter what one did with it or them. Intercourse with a prostitute only impinged on something that was ephemeral and had no part in the coming world. The contempt for, and aversion to, the body prevalent among many Greeks, particularly in the Orphic and Pythagorean traditions inherited by Platonism, could equally encourage the asceticism with which Paul must deal in chapter 7, although it is likely that Paul's own example (cf. 7.7) had also played a part in causing some to assert that 'it is good for a man not to have contact with a woman' (7.1). And that same contempt for the body probably led some Christians in Corinth to question whether it was desirable that this despised thing should be raised up in the world to come, despite the fact that 'resurrection', at least that of Jesus, played such a central role in the Christian message.[75]

7.4. The Collection

When so many other problems confronted Paul during this period of his work, it is striking that the apostle was nevertheless prepared to devote so much time and energy in it, the last phase of his ministry before his arrest, to another project, the gathering of a collection for the Jerusalem church. Not only did it take him away from missionary work and founding fresh churches, but it was a project fraught with considerable risks, as the eventual outcome of this journey according to Acts shows. The transport of a large sum of money was in itself perilous enough in those days, with storms and robbers to contend with. If it is correct that the unusually large group of travelling companions named in Acts 20.4 in fact accompanied Paul on this journey, then it is plausible to see in their numbers not only a symbolic function, representing the various Pauline churches, but also a security function, guarding the money which they had gathered. Nevertheless, Paul was prepared to run these risks, and that is in itself an eloquent testimony to the importance which he attached to this enterprise.

Such an enterprise is easier to understand if we bear in mind the situation in which Paul found himself and his churches after the quarrel at Antioch. It seemed as if they were out on a limb, cut off from, and not recognized by, the main body of the church, unless they capitulated and kept at least enough of the Jewish law to enable them to mix with, and above all eat with, Jewish Christians without endangering the latter or undermining their Jewishness. Without that capitulation and abandonment of Paul's gospel the Pauline churches could not hope to be treated by their Jewish sisters and brothers as if they, too, belonged to that renewed people of God which had been called into being by God's action in Jesus. In effect, what Paul sought to do with the collection was to persuade the Jerusalem church to recognize, in accepting the gift of the gentile

Christians, that the latter were their brothers and sisters, part of one and the same people of God.

Paul asks the Roman church to pray, not only for his own safety, but also for the success of the collection project and that the Jerusalem church might accept it (Rom 15.31). There is nothing feigned about this request. According to Acts (21.31), Paul's visit to Jerusalem did indeed nearly cost him his life, and there was equal reason to fear that there might be difficulties in persuading the Jerusalem church to accept the gift. Ten years later zealous Jews would dispute whether it was ever right to accept gifts from impure gentiles.[76] Many scholars therefore wonder whether the gift from Paul's churches was in fact rejected.[77] That would at least explain why Acts never mentions the collection project nor the representative nature of the gift which Paul brought to Jerusalem, although 'Luke' does make Paul refer to the (otherwise unmentioned) gift as if it were an act of purely personal piety (24.17); without Paul's letters we would know nothing of the profound significance which it had for him nor of the role which it was supposed to play in relations between gentile and Jewish Christians. If the Jerusalem church rejected the gift, then that is the more significant because it is unlikely that they had no need of it.

That is disturbing enough, but there may be other disturbing implications in Paul's reports on the churches which contributed to this project.[78] For, although Paul mentions in 1 Cor 16.1 that he has instructed the Galatians about the collection, 2 Cor 8 and 9 mention only the raising of the collection in Macedonia, and Rom 15.26 names only Macedonia and Achaea. Had Paul learnt after writing 1 Corinthians that the Galatians had now finally turned against him and would not be participating in this project?

To that may be added further puzzles presented by the list of names in Acts 20.4, which may well represent a list of the delegates of the Pauline churches who accompanied the apostle on this occasion, on his last journey to Jerusalem with his collection raised for the church there; it is, at any rate, an unusually long list of those accompanying him, even though Acts never says that their purpose was to escort the collection and represent the donor churches (as Paul envisaged in 1 Cor 16.3–4). The Macedonians are well represented with Sopater from Beroea and the two Thessalonians, Aristarchus and Secundus. More surprisingly, no Philippian is mentioned, unless that role is assumed by the mysterious figure who lurks behind the 'we' of vv. 5 and 6. Unexpected, too, are the two representatives from Asia, Tychicus and Trophimus, suggesting that above all the Ephesian church may have contributed, although Paul nowhere mentions their participation. Less certain is the role of Timothy or Gaius from Derbe (or from the Macedonian Doberus according to a number of textual witnesses). It is, however, unlikely that they can make good another conspicuous gap in the participants, the province of Achaea and in particular the Corinthian church. Had it, too, finally turned its back on Paul? Certainly Acts mentions trouble there as Paul was due to set out on this journey to Jerusalem, trouble which this work attributes yet again to 'the Jews' (20.3).

If Paul regarded the collection as so important for the future of his work and for the status of his churches, then the consequences of its failure, if that is what Acts indicates by its reticence concerning the collection and by its report of Paul's near-death and arrest, are all the more serious. They bear both upon Paul's relations with some of his churches and also, still more seriously, upon the relations of all the gentile churches to the church of Jerusalem. Some of Paul's churches may have deserted and repudiated him,[79] and the Jerusalem church would have refused to acknowledge that it and the gentile churches were sisters and brothers in Christ. Had Paul been free to continue his missionary work, he would have found himself faced with an uphill task, for the authoritative church of Jerusalem would have conspicuously rejected any fellowship and partnership with the churches he had founded, and by implication would have cast doubt on the message which he had preached in them. That would in turn raise the question whether the only valid form of Christianity was one which involved the keeping of the Jewish law, in short a Judaizing form of Christianity.

In addition to all that, there is the fact that Acts mentions no attempt of the Jerusalem church as such to help Paul after his arrest in Jerusalem (assuming that Paul's nephew mentioned in 23.16–22 was not acting on its behalf), nor indeed is there any mention of further contact with the church in Caesarea during his imprisonment there, despite the contact with Philip on his way up to Jerusalem (21.8–16). This is in stark contrast to the welcome he gets later from Christians in Puteoli and Rome (28.14–15) and may point to a breakdown in relationships between the Judaean churches and Paul. That seems to leave the Jerusalem church as undisputed leader of the church, at least in this eastern corner of the Mediterranean, but quite possibly further afield as well, and it is accordingly to this threat to Paul's work that we must now turn.

8

Judaizing Christianity

The title of this chapter has been chosen deliberately, in preference to some such phrase as 'Jewish Christianity', above all because of the ambiguity of the latter phrase. For 'Jewish Christianity' could mean the faith of all Jewish Christians, including such radical figures as Paul, who was not only detested by his fellow Jews, but also regarded with considerable suspicion and misgivings by many of his fellow-Jewish Christians, particularly those who are described in Acts 21.20 as zealous for the law. In other words, 'Jewish Christianity' is no homogeneous phenomenon.[1]

The breadth of this possible definition of 'Jewish Christianity' should make us wary of its presumed antithesis, 'gentile Christianity', as well. For this, too, is in some need of definition. If 'Jewish Christianity' could encompass all Jews who have faith in Christ, then 'gentile Christianity' should stand for the gentile community of faith. We have, however, seen (ch. 4) that at this period in the history of the church this concept is an abstraction, an entity which did not yet exist in a pure form. Only when one finds a thoroughgoing gnostic repudiation of Christianity's Jewish heritage and roots can one legitimately or plausibly speak of a Christianity that is not Jewish – that is, if one still wants to call it Christianity at all.

Often, however, when one speaks today of 'Jewish Christianity' one is thinking of those tiny groups of Christians who lived on in the East for some centuries practising a form of Christianity true to the Jewish law, in contrast to the Pauline form of Christianity which had become the majority form in the West. Yet they are relevant for a study of the earliest Christians, in that these groups could and often did claim, with some justification, to be the rightful heirs of the Jerusalem church headed by James, the brother of Jesus, whom they held in a special veneration, and of those like him who upheld a form of Christianity true to the Jewish law. And, like those

Jerusalem Christians, they frequently mistrusted Paul thoroughly, and their polemic against him is reflected above all in the Pseudo-Clementine literature.[2]

That opposition to Paul on the part of these later groups points back, then, to another, earlier form of 'Jewish Christianity', one which is more aptly described as a 'Judaizing Christianity', a term which is meant to place the emphasis on belief and practice rather than ethnic descent, a form which is represented not only by a Jerusalem church that was wary of Paul, but also by those opponents of his who sought to undo, or, as they saw it, redo his work by persuading his churches to observe the Jewish law more or less strictly.[3] It is appropriate to speak of them as Judaizers, as those seeking to compel or at least persuade Paul's gentile converts to Judaize, that is to live more or less like Jews. Nor is it necessary to assume that only ethnic Jews would belong to such a group; conceivably some gentiles may have been persuaded that it was necessary for Christians to live as Jews and they may well have been intolerant of other gentile Christians who denied this. Justin, at any rate, mentions the bitter opposition to Christianity of Jewish proselytes (*Dial.* 122.2) and this may have been equally true at an earlier date. Paul feared that that might become true for the Galatian churches, and perhaps it did – and not only there. In Galatia the Judaizing message of the intruders was a form of Christianity that was a reaction to Paul's mission and as such it differs from the unquestioningly Jewish community of believers which existed initially in Jerusalem. For it was only when a form of Christianity arose which had in their eyes (and, perhaps more important still, in the eyes of non-Christian Jews) departed too far from its Jewish roots that such a reaction became possible, and, if the indignation of non-Christian Jews grew too heated, became necessary for their own survival and well-being. Together with the groups representing such a reaction, however, one can equally describe as 'Judaizing' all those Christians and Christian movements which deliberately sought to maintain a certain level of Jewish practice and ritual, regarding it as necessary for being a Christian and more or less explicitly criticizing other forms of Christianity which no longer held such practices to be necessary. Yet they need not have subscribed to that 'aggressive' form of 'Judaizing' which sought to impose its version of Christianity on others. In short, 'Judaizing' Christians still lived like Jews, more or less, but at any rate more than Paul and his followers, whose views later gained the ascendancy, considered necessary (even if there is room for argument as to what degree of observance of the law was required); there was a considerable difference in the degree to which such Christians sought to impose their interpretation of the gospel on other Christians, and those actively promoting it declined in numbers and influence with the passage of time, but they themselves remained 'Judaizing' in the more passive, non-aggressive sense outlined above.

8.1. James

It is widely held that Jesus' brother had not joined in Jesus' movement before his death and probably distanced himself from it along with other members of Jesus' family, to judge from the usual interpretation of Mark 3.21 and John 7.5. This, however, has been called in question by John Painter, who argues that these passages will not bear the weight of that interpretation. Yet there is at least no hint in the Gospels that James belonged to the inner, and numerically symbolic, circle of Jesus' disciples, the Twelve, in contrast to the prominent role which he was to play later in the history of the early church. Paul, however, lists separately an appearance of the risen Jesus to James (1 Cor 15.7), yet that appearance is not described in any canonical writings, but is described briefly in a fragment of the apocryphal Gospel according to the Hebrews,[4] and some explanation is needed for his decision to join the movement after Jesus' death or, if not, at least for his subsequent prominence in it. This was no particularly comfortable bandwagon to climb onto.

For it is clear that James quite rapidly assumed a position of considerable importance in the early Christian community, an importance which has been obscured and eclipsed by the way in which the early church later developed. Paul mentions that he saw him in Jerusalem during his first visit there after his conversion and in all probability regards him as also, like Peter, an 'apostle' (Gal 1.19); it may be that he thinks this important to mention in view of James's later prominence, but the fact that he met him may also indicate that he was already a key figure in the earliest church, perhaps even already recognized as leader or a leader of the Jerusalem church.[5] By the time of the meeting in Jerusalem fourteen years later not only is he one of the three 'pillars' of the church there, but he is also named first (2.9). That is the more striking in the case of one who was not a member of the Twelve and, as far as we can tell, played no active part in Jesus' ministry even if he had not opposed it.[6] And the way in which his emissaries are able to persuade the Jewish Christians in Antioch, including such weighty figures as Peter and Barnabas, to change their ways (Gal 2.11–14) is further evidence of James's influence. Acts seems to presuppose a similar rise to prominence: Peter, after his arrest and miraculous rescue, especially gives instructions that James should be informed before he goes to 'another place' (12.17).[7] And at the meeting described in chapter 15 it is James who has the last and decisive word after Peter has had his say (15.13–21). If 12.17 refers to Peter's leaving Jerusalem for his own safety, perhaps together with any other members of the Twelve who were still there,[8] then we may see here one reason for James's importance: he could remain at the centre of things in Jerusalem, while Peter had to forsake the city. James's Jewish piety, his Judaizing version of Christianity, kept him safe, and even generally respected, at least for the moment. Even if Peter was able on occasions to visit Jerusalem again – for the conference of Gal 2.1–10, for instance – he seems rather to have travelled around more widely, for we hear of him in Lydda and Joppa (Acts 9.32–43; 10.5–8) and then in Caesarea (10.24–48) as well as in Antioch in Gal 2.11. If one's Jewish piety was suspect in the eyes of one's fellow-Jews, then Jerusalem, that focus of Jewish piety and nationalist aspirations, could be an uncomfortable place to be. And so, when Paul comes to Jerusalem for the last time, in Acts 21, James is in sole command of the church, along with the elders, and it is with him that Paul has to deal (21.18).

Quite possibly a sort of dynastic principle was also at work here and after James's death as well; at any rate there is the tradition that the leadership of the Jerusalem church was subsequently, after the fall and sack of Jerusalem, taken over by Symeon, son of Clopas, who also came from Jesus' family (Euseb. *Hist. eccl.* 3.11.1; 3.32.1; 4.22.4).[9] Nevertheless, it is clear that none of James's successors was as dominant a figure as this brother of Jesus. As we shall see, his significance did not end with his death, for, in some circles, perhaps some quite surprising ones in view of the form of Christian piety for which James stood during his lifetime, he eclipsed all other early Christian leaders in importance. That is clearly expressed in the role accorded him in the Gospel of Thomas §12:

> The disciples said to Jesus, 'We know that you will go away from us; who will be our leader?' Jesus said, 'Wherever you are, go to James the Just; heaven and earth came into being for him.'[10]

And yet it is remarkable that this Christian leader should be given such a role in this work, which elsewhere disparages circumcision (§53) and speaks dismissively of 'the Jews' (§43). If his nickname, 'the Just' or 'the Righteous', was one used not just by Christians, but also by non-Christian Jews, as the account of his death may indicate, then it would point, not just to his standing in Christian circles, but to the respect with which he was regarded by non-Christians too.[11]

James, however, met a violent end at the hands of his fellow Jews, but the details of Josephus' account (*AJ* 20.200–3) are significant: in 62 CE there was an interregnum following the death in office of one Roman governor (Festus) and the arrival of his successor, Albinus, and the high priest Ananus seized the opportunity to convene the Sanhedrin and to place before it charges against James and certain others;[12] he accused them of transgressing the law and had them stoned to death.[13] As a result of this act many, whom Josephus describes as rigorous in their observance of the law, perhaps meaning that they were Pharisees,[14] took offence at his behaviour. They complained to Herod Agrippa II and some of them brought the matter before Albinus, on the grounds that the high priest had no authority to convene the Sanhedrin on his own authority, and Agrippa subsequently deposed him.[15] There is nothing to suggest that those who complained were Christians and that in itself points to the esteem in which James was held by strict Jews. This also raises the perhaps unanswerable question of the nature of the charges brought against James and the 'certain others' (that they were also Christians or had anything to do with the Christian movement is not expressly stated): did the charge of transgressing against the law stem from their belief in Christ? And had they really transgressed or were the charges trumped up ones? That the high priest's conduct caused offence to many law-observant Jews at least indicates that the transgression can only have been perceived as such by the high priest and those who thought like him or, as Richard Bauckham suggests,[16] that this severe penalty was only appropriate in the eyes of a Sadducean judge.

Can one then find another reason for the high priest's wish to get rid of James, a reason for which the charge of transgressing against the law is only a cover? Another possibility is that James was on the side of a popular piety opposed to the actions and the exploitation of that piety by the Jewish aristocracy. Or, more concretely, was James on the side of the priests who were violently deprived by Ananus' servants of the tithes due to them?[17] Were that the case then his stance may well have been similar to that of his brother, if those explanations of Jesus' action in the Temple which see in it a protest against that exploitation and misuse of power are correct.[18] It may, then, be no accident that the letter which is attributed to James shows a great concern for the poor (2.1–12).

8.2. Writings of a Judaizing Christianity

For this *Letter of James* is evidence for the enduring legacy of James, even if it does not come from his hand, or even if the use of his name reflects merely a claim to represent that Palestinian early Christianity associated with him.[19] Against its stemming from James himself is not only the literary niveau of the work, but also the fact that it seems to reflect a more moderate form of Jewish Christianity than the James whose emissaries caused such an upheaval in the Antioch church. On the other hand this 'James' is more easily reconcilable with the James portrayed in Acts who plays a conciliatory role in Acts 15. One may ask, however, whether this portrayal of James, in Acts or in the letter, is any more historically reliable than that of Paul in Acts in comparison with the Pauline letters. Themes which one might expect, particularly in a letter directed to Jewish Christians, as suggested by the fact that it is addressed to the twelve tribes in the Diaspora (1.1), are lacking: circumcision, sabbath, Israel, purity regulations and the Temple.[20] A law, whose giver is God (4.12), seems nevertheless to play an important role in this document, referred to as a 'perfect law' (1.25), a 'royal law' (2.8) and a 'law of freedom' (2.12), and it may well be that this law is ultimately the Jewish law; in that case, however, it is to be noted what is and is not important, as it seems, for the form of Christianity espoused by this document. Prominent is the theme of poverty and riches, also within the Christian community (2.2–4), with a sharp critique of the wealthy (1.10–11; 5.1–6). Wiard Popkes is probably correct in his assessment that the community itself is not, at least for the most part, made up either from the rich or from the very poor who might come into their gathering in filthy clothes (2.2),[21] but, bearing in mind the discussion above of the status of members of Paul's churches, we should avoid assigning them to a 'middle class'.[22] Rather they are probably not that well off, but nevertheless do not belong to the poorest – Popkes describes them as 'upwardly mobile' (90). The interests of traders reflected in 4.13–17 do not necessarily imply great affluence, but, nevertheless, certain means. For Popkes observes, correctly, that the great merchants did not themselves have to travel about as these traders evidently do (cf. 4.13) and the really wealthy invested in land (cf. 5.4–5), and that 4.1–3 probably reflects 'a daily struggle to exist' (56–7). The letter is also noted for its seeming critique of the Pauline doctrine of justification by faith (2.14–26); whether or not that critique is directed against Paul himself or against followers of his – and even if the latter are meant, one can nevertheless ask whether reading some utterances of Paul himself, e.g. Rom 2.28; Gal 2.16, could not lead to the same critique – it again continues the tradition of a form of Christianity markedly different in its emphases from that which that apostle propagated.

In many respects similar to James in the form of Christianity which it presents is the *Gospel of Matthew*. Again many elements of the extremest forms of Judaizing Christianity are lacking, and the ending of the Gospel reflects a Christianity now committed to a gentile mission and preaching a message based on the commandments of Jesus rather than on those of the Jewish law (28.19–20).[23] Nevertheless, for all its openness to the gentile world, this work also reflects an attitude that is strongly critical of that world: a sinning church member who will not listen to the church's admonition is to be to it 'as a gentile and a tax-collector' (18.17; cf. 5.46–7) – seemingly a very different attitude towards the latter compared with that of Jesus, even the Matthean Jesus. At the same time this form of Christianity seems to claim to be one that is in continuity with the teaching of the Pharisees and indeed to surpass them; Jesus' disciples should do what the lawyers and Pharisees teach, but not what they do (23.3; i.e. it is implicit that they do not practise what they preach); instead, Jesus' disciples are to outdo them in righteousness (5.20). And yet, despite this nearness to Pharisaic Judaism, Matthew is sharply hostile towards the lawyers and Pharisees, condemning them as hypocrites (23.13–15). Often groups, particularly religious ones, that are seemingly very similar to one another may be most sharply antagonistic towards one another; the relationship here may aptly be described as a 'family dispute'.[24] That is all the more readily intelligible if this community had recently separated from Judaism or an influential form of it,[25] or had perhaps been forced out in a similar manner to the Johannine community, as we shall see. At the same time, since the hostility of this Gospel is especially directed towards a particular Jewish group, the 'scribes and Pharisees', and is not a blanket condemnation of 'the Jews' as so often in the Fourth Gospel, we can see here a Christian group which views itself as the true heir of Judaism's traditions and feels itself to be still 'Jewish'.[26] (One can compare the vociferous claims of the Qumran community to be God's true people even though seemingly either forced out by the Jerusalem authorities at some point in its history or having decided to sever itself from the holy city.) Matthew's Gospel is also very difficult to reconcile with Paul's message. For it portrays a Jesus who 'fulfils' the law and warns that anyone who discards one of the least of these commandments will be called least in the kingdom of heaven (5.17, 19), and it would be hard to deny that that was precisely what Paul was doing. As Martin Hengel puts it, if Matthew had the first (or the last) word in Christian theology, then Paul would be a heretic.[27]

This Gospel originated, according to the majority of scholars, in Syria, although some favour Galilee; there is less agreement, however, whether it stems from a rural area of that province or from some city, above all Antioch. The references to 'market-places', *agorai* (11.16; 20.3; 23.7), may suggest an urban setting or at least a rural centre of population. Yet the traditions which it reflects seem markedly different from those with which Paul was presumably familiar when he worked in and for the Antioch church, but we have seen that it is likely that the character of that church changed considerably after Paul had been driven out as a result of his quarrel with Peter and the other Jewish Christians there (Gal 2.11–14). Yet Paul is, as we shall see (ch. 9), revered by Ignatius, Bishop of Antioch, early in the second century. Would that mean that the pendulum has swung the other way again in that city, or that Matthew reflects a form of Christianity to be found in rural Syria, or that, as we shall see in the case of Ephesus (ch. 10), various forms and traditions of early Christianity may have existed alongside each other in one and the same urban centre?

The position of *Peter* (not James, however) in this work is also striking (16.18–19) – does that reflect that apostle's work in Syria, and again above all in Antioch, over against the more remote influence of James? Had Peter even stayed on for some time in the Antioch church after Paul's departure, in order to bring order into that divided and wounded Christian community? Yet the same power of binding and loosing is two chapters later granted to the whole community of Jesus' disciples (18.18), and it is the community that must settle disputes between Christians, and no office-bearer (18.15–17).[28] (And it must often have been the case later that Peter was not at hand to settle disputes, particularly if he moved on to Rome and to his eventual death.)[29]

The prominence of Peter in Matthew's Gospel invites the question whether he, too, is then to be seen as a representative of a Judaizing Christianity. Again, however, one must differentiate: there is on the one hand the Peter who not only agreed on the shared work of evangelism at the Jerusalem conference, but also ate together with gentile Christians in Antioch (Gal 2.12). That was not the conduct of a Judaizing Christian. But there was, on the other hand, the Peter who yielded to the pressure of James's emissaries and who thereby, however indirectly, 'compelled the gentiles to Judaize' (2.14). Yet it is nevertheless not Peter who is portrayed as a focus and representative of Judaizing Christianity, but James, and the sort of Christianity which is attributed to Peter in the two letters ascribed to him is, at least in the case of 1 Peter, far nearer to the tenor of Pauline Christianity than to that of a zeal for the Jewish law.

If it is correct to see Matthean Christianity as engaged in a polemic against Pharisaic Judaism on the one side and a form of Christianity which sat loose to the commands of the Jewish law on the other, then something similar may plausibly be suggested as the context of the *Book of Revelation*. For in the letters contained in chapters 2 and 3 we find a sharp polemic against the works of the 'Nicolaitans' and their teaching, which is in turn compared with the teaching of Balaam which had encouraged the Israelites to eat meat offered to idols and to commit fornication (2.6, 14–15). The prophetess Jezebel teaches that, too, in Thyatira (2.20). Is this to be interpreted as polemic against a more accommodating version of the Christian gospel such as Paul advocates in 1 Corinthians?[30] That is at least a possibility, particularly if 'fornication' is used here in a figurative sense of any illegitimate (in the eyes of the author) compromise with pagan religiosity. On the other hand, this author is equally scathing about those who say they are Jews, but in his view are rather a 'synagogue of Satan' (2.9; 3.9). In other words, one could see here too a form of Christianity which distances itself sharply both from Christian groups that seek a compromise with the pagan world and from non-Christian Judaism.

Another writing with a pronounced Jewish-Christian character is the *Didache*, even if it may be addressed to gentiles or at least to those living within a dominantly gentile culture.[31] Its nearness to Jewish traditions is particularly clear in the teaching on the two ways (chs 1–6; cf. 1QS 3.20–1) and in the instructions about fasting, even if the fasts are to take place on different days, so as not to be confused with those of the 'hypocrites' (8.1).[32] Like Matthew, therefore, the Didache combines, at first sight, closeness to Judaism with a strong antagonism to it, but also an openness to the gentiles, for the whole document is now entitled, at least in one version of the text, 'The Lord's teaching to the gentiles by the twelve apostles' – the phrase 'to the gentiles' at the same time shows its Jewish perspective;[33] as we have seen, the circle of the Twelve was important and of symbolic significance at an early stage in the history of the Christian community and emphasized its ties with Israel. If, however, this introduction is a later addition, as is more probable, it may give no clue to the nature of the original document or of the traditions contained in it. Its contents would, nevertheless, confirm its similarity to Matthew at least with regard to its nearness to, and yet separation from, Judaism. At the same time the document shows a remarkable independence of other Christian traditions as well as a markedly primitive character, as can be seen, for instance, in its version of the eucharistic tradition. For, if the solemn meal described in chapters 8 and 9, whose strongly Jewish character has often been noted, is the Didache's equivalent of the Lord's Supper, then it shows no knowledge of the words of institution found in the New Testament, except in that the cup and the bread are mentioned. Such features make it hard to date or place this document within early Christian traditions, apart from observing its closeness in some respects to Matthew's Gospel, even if it is not dependent on that canonical text.

Significant, too, is the church order presupposed by this work (chs 11–13): itinerant apostles and prophets are to be received, but under stringent conditions.[34] An apostle who stays longer than one or two days and demands money is a false prophet (11.5–6) – that seemingly unwelcoming ruling is more intelligible if, as an 'apostle', such a person has been 'sent' to proclaim the gospel in an area where there is as yet no church established (a principle which invites comparison with that of Paul in Rom 15.20).[35] Whether that means that they remain perpetually on the move, as Kurt Niederwimmer supposes,[36] is more doubtful, for in order to fulfil their task in a not yet evangelized area they would surely need to remain longer in order to consolidate their initial preaching. It is a different matter with prophets and teachers who take up residence with them: they deserve their keep and the prophets should receive the first-fruits as if they were high priests (13.1–3). At the same time the readers are apparently instructed to appoint *episkopoi* and *diakonoi* who can fulfil the role of prophets and teachers for them (15.1–2), although this passage is sometimes regarded as a later insertion.[37] If this passage is original, we would have here a combination of itinerant charismatics and local office-bearers, but neither a monarchical episcopate or 'monepiscopate' nor church authorities responsible for the churches of a whole area, nor do office-bearers replace the responsibility of the whole community for its life.[38] If this document stems from Syria, as many suppose, then it reflects a very different structure of church life to that presupposed by the letters of Ignatius of Antioch. Is that because it reflects a very much earlier situation or the circumstances which were to be found in remoter parts of this province, well away from an urban centre like Antioch?

The naming of these various documents as evidence of a 'Judaizing Christianity' should not, however, blind us to the difficulty of definition which still remains: although these works take over many aspects of contemporary Judaism, they are nevertheless determined to distinguish themselves from it, at least from the dominant form or forms of it. Matthew's Jesus roundly condemns the practices of the scribes and Pharisees, while endorsing their teaching (23.3) and urging his followers to exceed the scribes and Pharisees in righteousness (5.20). The Didache urges a fasting practice different to that of Judaism, not by doing away with fasting, but by choosing different days for it (8.1). The term 'Judaizing' here combines a basic similarity to, and adoption of, Jewish beliefs and practices, which justify the label 'Judaizing', with a rejection and critique of the practices of non-Christian Jews and a deliberate choice of a form of life which is nevertheless distinguishable from that of non-Christian Jews.

8.3. The Jerusalem Church

Even if the Jerusalem church was linguistically and quite possibly theologically heterogeneous to start with, it is clear that, at least in part under the pressure of various persecutions, which drove out Stephen's group and then Peter, the church took on more and more the character of a strictly law-observant, that is, Judaizing, Jewish-Christian community. In an increasingly tense and inflamed atmosphere, provoked by a series of insensitive Roman governors, the threat of persecution and violent measures against any Jews who seemed to be untrue to their ancestral traditions increased, so that life in Jerusalem must have become ever more uncomfortable for Jewish Christians who were disposed to relax the strict demands of the law in order to enable them to have more contact with gentile Christians. The only form which had much chance of surviving, let alone flourishing, in that environment was one whose faithfulness to the traditions of Judaism could not seriously be faulted.

The Jewish revolt, however, and the subsequent sack of Jerusalem ended the influence of this church, which may already have been seriously diminished by the death of James. There is a tradition that the Jerusalem church moved from Jerusalem to Pella before the siege,[39] but this has been doubted. For, on the one hand, there is the tradition of a line of fifteen bishops of Jerusalem up to the Bar Kokhba revolt in 132–5, after which Jews were banned from Jerusalem.[40] On the other hand Gerd Lüdemann points not only to the difficulties confronting anyone, and particularly a group of any size, wanting to leave Jerusalem after 67, but also to the fact that Pella was a gentile city that had been sacked by Jews in 66 in retaliation for a massacre of Jews in Caesarea (Josephus *BJ* 2.458). That made it an unlikely destination for any sizable group of Jewish-Christian refugees, at least at this point of time. That need not, however, exclude the possibility that some Jewish Christians from Jerusalem found their way there before or after the war and that on this the church in Pella based a later claim to be heir to the prestigious tradition of the Jerusalem church.[41] Jürgen Wehnert and Stephen Wilson also make the interesting suggestion that we should not couple the flight too closely with the outbreak of war and should instead bear in mind the alarm doubtless created earlier in the Jerusalem church by the execution of James (and possibly other members of the church).[42] A flight then, three or four years before the outbreak of hostilities, avoids the problems confronted by the later date. And yet, were the claim to be heir to the traditions of the Jerusalem church accepted by other churches, one would then have expected the church in Pella to exercise something of the same influence and authority that the Jerusalem church had once enjoyed, but of that there is no trace.

For the centre of gravity of the early church now moved westwards, to Rome. That meant the development of the church now took a different course to what one would have expected had the Jerusalem church retained its influence and authority. For the disappearance of this counterbalance to the authority and influence of Paul was doubtless of crucial importance in deciding what course the Christian church should henceforth follow and which form of Christianity should prevail. It is a sobering thought that it was the Roman legions that in large measure snuffed out the rival to Pauline Christianity and ensured the triumph of the latter. Yet no early Christian writer went so far as to describe Titus as God's anointed, as Deutero-Isaiah had once described Cyrus (Isa 45.1). That, however, is scarcely surprising. For, in the first place, it was one thing so to describe one whose edict (in 538 BCE) had set in motion the return of the Jews from exile and had enabled the rebuilding of the Jerusalem Temple, quite another to do so with one who had been responsible for the destruction of the Temple. And, secondly, the title of Messiah was by now bespoken. And yet, despite the momentous significance of the fall of Jerusalem for the future course of the Christian church, this event and all that it implied for the Jewish race and faith 'seems to have made a surprisingly small impact on the Christian communities' and on their writings.[43]

Christians still remained in Palestine, however, but the centre of power and influence had moved far away from them and from the traditions of the Jerusalem church and others who may have held to a similar form of the Christian faith. The bearers of these traditions, doubtless influenced now by their experience of rejection and marginalization, and betraying their resentment of, and hostility to, that Pauline Christianity which had come to dominate the church, lived on in a number of Jewish-Christian groups such as the

Ebionites, some of which could be described as 'Judaizing', others not. For even here a wide variety of traditions is apparent: while some Christians were violently hostile to Paul,[44] a deep hostility towards Jerusalem and those who used to hold sway there manifests itself in other traditions, in the tradition that the destruction of Jerusalem was a punishment for James's death,[45] and above all in the claim of the Nag Hammadi First Apocalypse of James that Jerusalem was full of a great number of archons (25.18–19).[46] In addition, traits which are frequently labelled 'gnostic' are combined with a stress on the keeping of the law of Moses. With the name of James are associated both docetic traditions implicitly dispensing with the need for Jesus to have a human mother,[47] and the development of the tradition of Mary's sinless virginity, making her worthy to be the mother of the Lord (the Protevangelium of James). However one defines it, 'Jewish Christianity' and perhaps even 'Judaizing Christianity' are terms which embrace a wide range of possibilities, and in these traditions we find forms of Christianity whose proximity to gnostic ways of thinking is all too evident, a proximity which is clearly signalled by the appeal to James in several Nag Hammadi tractates, even if not all of these tractates should be called 'gnostic'; some bearing James's name are, nevertheless, quite clearly gnostic, as when 2 Apoc Jas. 56.20–57.1 identifies the Old Testament God with the demiurge who made the world in ignorance.[48]

Some of these strands of tradition deserve further comment, since, while some are thoroughly predictable, others are less so. It is, for instance, only to be expected that the hostility between James and Paul, the 'enemy' of Ps.-Clem. *Recg.* 1.70.1, 8; 71.3, now representative of the form of Christianity triumphant in the West, should be perpetuated; more surprising is the merging of Paul with the figure of Simon Magus, who appears in the New Testament in opposition to Peter, not James, as in these traditions; this identification of the arch-enemy with the reputed source of gnostic heresies is the more surprising in view of the gnostic appropriation of James in some of these traditions. Yet it is Simon who is described as the first (and evil) missionary to the gentiles (Ps.-Clem. *Hom.* 2.17.3; cf. 11.35.5), and it is Paul's claim to the authority of his heavenly vision which is presumably attacked in *Hom.* 17.13–16, especially 17.16.6, even though it is an answer to Simon's claims. And, in an allusion to Paul's condemnation of Peter in Gal 2.11,

Simon is accused of slandering and reviling Peter (*Hom.* 17.19.5–6). There are only twelve apostles and therefore Simon or Paul cannot be one (*Recg.* 4.35.3–4).

Yet, although these Jewish-Christian documents reject Paul's critique of the law and circumcision,[49] nevertheless the sacrificial cult is regarded as obsolete, an error based on false passages inserted into the law,[50] and is replaced by baptism (*Recg.* 1.39.1–2; 54.1); over against this, other groups like the 'Nazarenes' or 'Nazoraeans' keep the Jewish law without its being said that they differentiated between valid and invalid elements in it (Epiph. *Adv. haeres.* 29.5.4). Despite their veneration for James, the zeal for the law shown in many of these documents manifests itself in ways which Jesus' brother would hardly have countenanced.

In the absence of anti-Pauline traits in the Nag Hammadi James material, Wilhelm Pratscher finds an argument that 'genuine' Jewish-Christian traditions (by which he means above all those of the Pseudo-Clementines) were not the decisive factor in the formation of the ideology of these gnostic groups.[51] Yet, if the observations in Chapter 4 on the origins of the gnostic groups are correct, then we have to reckon with a twofold rejection experienced by Judaizing Christian groups, their rejection by non-Christian Jews and their rejection by the majority of Christians. If the former was felt more strongly, then one would expect a radical re-evaluation of Jewish traditions such as we find in gnostic sources; if the latter, then a sharp attack on the apostle whose views triumphed in mainline Christianity.

And yet some of these traditions and the groups which preserved them claimed, as we have seen, to be the rightful heirs of James and the Jerusalem church. That claim is easier to dismiss as special pleading when appeal is made, in a manner typical of the gnostics, to esoteric teachings, but is less easily set aside when it is a matter of faithfulness to the Jewish law, particularly when one realizes how large a role extraneous factors like the fall of Jerusalem may have played in determining which theological position won the day.[52] These various Jewish-Christian groups were marginalized in the church that was now taking shape, but the principle that 'might is right' sits uncomfortably in Christian theological discourse and argument. In other words, if these groups were rightly marginalized, why is that so? Was their faithfulness to the law, typified in the life of Jesus' brother James, intrinsically incompatible with the

Christian message? Yet, the more one hesitates to speak of Jesus himself criticizing the law as such, the more difficult that position is to maintain. Or was their faithfulness to the law something religiously inferior? Yet that would be an argument that would offend most Jews today. In other words, our evaluation of these Jewish-Christian movements has a very direct relevance to any contemporary discussions between Jews and Christians.

9

Pauline Christianity after Paul

Both during the period of Paul's missionary activity and during that of his successors and their contemporaries we are confronted with the problem of diversity, both synchronically and diachronically. One can speak of a synchronic diversity when at one and the same time there existed alongside each other in the earliest church divergent interpretations of what it meant to be a Christian; such a diversity is plainly to be seen in the quarrel at Antioch and in Paul's struggles with Judaizers, if not before. One can also speak of a diachronic diversity when various movements within earliest Christianity share a common starting-point, but then develop from that common starting-point in differing directions, interpreting their common legacy in different, perhaps even mutually exclusive ways. That could be said of earliest Christianity as a whole, taking the Jesus-tradition and above all the events of Jesus' passion and resurrection as its common starting-point, but it also applies to the tradition or traditions which in turn took as their more recent starting-point Paul's interpretation of the legacy of Jesus.

There was a time when 'trajectories' was an 'in' word in New Testament scholarship to describe such developments, and one could speak of the multiplicity of forms which early Christianity as a whole took by arranging these various forms along a number of different trajectories. To some the German word used to translate this English word, *Entwicklungslinien*, 'lines of development', was preferable, in that it suggested less that the forms which eventually developed were predictable from the start and offered more scope than the ballistic metaphor for a variety of developments from the one point of origin.[1] Moreover, such trajectories and lines of development need not always diverge from one another, but may actually draw near to one another again. In the Book of Acts we have a veneration of Paul, but also, in the earlier part of the work, of Peter, who is depicted as the pioneer of the gentile mission. The tragic and bitter quarrel of Gal 2.11–14 finds no place in this work. In 1 Peter, too, we have a letter sent to churches in an area which overlaps with that of the Pauline mission (Galatia, Asia, 1.1) as well as references to Silvanus and Mark at the close (5.12–13) and a theology comparable in many respects with that of Paul. In both these works, then, the parting of the ways that appeared to take place at Antioch seems to have been healed or bridged over again. In the last analysis the formation of the canon and the role ascribed to it cement this process of reassimilation by asserting the essential unity of all these varied forms and developments, despite the evidence in these documents of bitter strife and quarrels, even between leading apostles (Gal 2.11–14 once more!). That is a step of considerable hermeneutical importance, for it discourages us from hearing any discord in the various voices of the canonized writings.

At any rate, whichever expression one prefers, it is important to recognize both the dynamism at work in these developments and the variety of forms which eventually developed. The later forms may in turn enable us to detect their beginnings in the earlier life of the church, but at the same time to recognize how the first beginnings differed from the later developments. This is all particularly apposite in the case of Paul, for he seems to have set something in motion which developed in more than one direction. At the same time these varied later forms have in common that they often more or less explicitly appeal to Paul as their authority and legitimation, and thus force upon us the question how these so different forms can all claim to be the legacy of this one apostle. Not only have we the pseudonymous letters claiming to be by Paul, but we have Clement of Rome claiming to have behind him the authority of both Peter and Paul, 'noble examples' and 'the greatest and most righteous pillars of the church' (1 Clem 5.1–2), or, even more clearly, Ignatius of Antioch, who addresses the Ephesians as 'fellow-initiates with Paul, who was sanctified, ... in whose footsteps may I be found when I shall attain to God' (*Eph* 12.2–3; cf. *Rom* 4.3).

It is to be noted, however, that in speaking of a Pauline school or of Paulinism one is speaking of an entity which is (a) identified by its starting-point (Paul) and (b) is one which claims to be identifiable by this starting-point (however much their interpretations of Paul differ or are perhaps even mutually incompatible with one another, representatives of this school claim to be interpreters of Paul). That can be distinguished from a category like 'early catholicism', which may also be applied to some branches of the Pauline school, and which is (a) a category employed by modern scholars, as a heuristic device to analyse and investigate the various forms of earliest Christianity, and (b) a phenomenon which is defined, not by its starting-point, but rather by its destination, so to speak: one detects with this category and its defining features approximations to, or movements towards, a phenomenon which is only clearly identifiable at a later stage. Somewhere between these lies the phenomenon described as 'gnosis' or 'gnosticism', in that the identity of the various manifestations of this movement may have been more apparent, rightly or wrongly, to outsiders, including the church fathers and not just modern scholars, whereas the members of these various groups themselves did not perceive themselves as belonging to a unified movement over against the Christian church; they did not form themselves into a church of the gnostic Christ or the like, and probably could not have done so.

9.1. A Pauline School or Pauline Schools?

In the light of these various claims to be the heirs of Paul one needs to ask whether, instead of speaking of a Pauline 'school', as some do, it would not be more appropriate to speak of several Pauline 'schools'. The singular would only be appropriate if the idea of a 'school' were elastic enough to encompass all these varied interpretations of the legacy of the apostle. This variety also has the consequence that one can no longer convincingly imagine such a 'school' as located in one place, for it is clearly no centralized institution.[2] It is more plausible to treat the 'school' as something less highly organized, a bundle of different versions of the Christian faith held together perhaps by little more than a shared veneration for Paul and their competing claims to be his heirs.[3]

This diversity is apparent even in the pseudonymous writings which bear Paul's name, not to mention those like Acts, the apocryphal Acts of Paul, the letters of Ignatius or the various gnostic interpreters of Paul, which all reflect a comparable veneration for the apostle without claiming to have been written by him,[4] and which can therefore, to varying degrees, be described as a penumbra around the Pauline school. It is, however, in the use of Paul's name that it can most clearly be seen that a particular document belongs to this school: each writer thereby claims to be the legitimate interpreter of Paul for their respective community, as they seek to realize the apostle's legacy in an appropriate manner, as they see it, in their churches, churches doubtless already shaped by that legacy.

The *Letter to the Colossians* is perhaps the earliest of these attempts, particularly if it was written while the apostle was still alive.[5] It shows signs of having developed the thought of the apostle, very likely under the impact of a new situation which had arisen in the church there.[6] For the Christians there seem to have been confronted with a form of piety which contained various Jewish features, like observing the sabbath (2.16) and perhaps circumcision too (2.11). Also involved were certain food regulations (2.16, 21), and angels also seem to have played a role (2.18). This form of piety, whether Jewish or Jewish Christian, was evidently ascetic in nature and in the eyes of the author of this letter it thereby neglected or undermined what Christ had achieved on behalf of the Colossians. As a consequence the salvation already achieved by Christ is stressed, and in doing so this letter goes further than Paul himself was prepared to do: already the Colossians have been raised from the dead with Christ (2.12; 3.1); they are already filled with the whole fullness of God in Christ, who is the head over all powers (2.10). By implication a mass of ascetic rules is quite unnecessary to achieve their salvation, since it has already been achieved for them in Christ. The letter can thus in all probability be treated as a witness to a Pauline tradition in western Asia Minor in the second half of the first century which is under threat from an ascetic and seemingly syncretistic Judaism or Judaizing Christianity. The criticism directed against heavenly powers (esp. 2.15) and the stress on Christ's supremacy over them (1.16; 2.10) point to a mystical form of Judaism or, more likely, Judaizing Christianity.[7] And yet, if this is a form of Judaizing Christianity, it is one that is markedly different from that which confronted Paul in Galatia or in Corinth as reflected in 2 Corinthians. The characteristic marks of this form in Colossae may in turn be due to local factors such as the forms of Jewish piety to be found in that area.

The *Letter to the Ephesians* shows many points of contact with Colossians and is mostly thought to be literarily dependent on it, but lacks any references to a specific threat or to competing religious ideas or practices. For that matter it seems to lack any particular points of contact with those addressed, in itself a decisive argument against treating it as a letter written by Paul to the church in Ephesus (the words 'in Ephesus' are in fact lacking in a number of manuscripts). Its thought, too, differs from that of the apostle: whereas Christ is in 1 Cor 3.11 the sole foundation of the church, it is apostles and prophets, presumably here Christian prophets, who are its foundation in Eph 2.20 and Christ is its cornerstone or capstone. Further office-bearers also seem to be named alongside these in 4.11: first evangelists, then pastors and teachers – the pastors are apparently also the teachers. But what situation has occasioned this letter? Here we are very much left in the dark, and this darkness has made some commentators understandably cautious about naming a specific situation. The unity of the church, the new people of God, formed of both Jews and gentiles, is emphasized, but it is not clear why this is stressed. It is not surprising that the attempts to reconstruct this situation have been many and numerous and at the same time so diverse as to underline the speculative nature of such an enterprise and its precarious basis.[8]

Whereas the two letters to the Colossians and the Ephesians reflect a tendency to develop Paul's thought further in a more speculative, indeed mythological direction, the *Pastoral Epistles* reflect a very different approach to the apostle's legacy. They ostensibly reflect a later stage in the apostle's life than that reflected in the Book of Acts, or at least do not correspond to any of the situations depicted in the travel accounts of that work, despite all the points of contact between these works.[9] The concerns of this writer are different to those of Paul: his great concern is church discipline as a bulwark against the ravages of error and heresy, against those who teach something different and who attend to 'myths and endless genealogies' and have gone astray by turning to empty talk (1 Tim 1.3–4, 6) and Timothy should avoid worthless old wives' tales (4.7). There is the danger of those who will turn to 'deceiving spirits and demonic teachings', led astray by those seared in their own consciences (4.1–2). Evidently Jewish traditions still pose a threat in this author's eyes, for those who turn to empty talk wish to be teachers of the law, although they understand nothing of that which they so confidently assert (1.7). It is particularly those 'from the circumcision' who are guilty of the empty talk and deception (Tit 1.10); accordingly Titus should instruct them not to attend to Jewish myths and human commands (1.14). Ascetic features of the false teaching are clearly recognizable in 1 Tim 4.3: they forbid marriage and the partaking of foods which God created for us to enjoy.

Intriguing is the suggestion that in the condemnation of those forbidding marriage and in the restrictive instructions regarding the role of women the Pastorals are already opposing the sort of traditions which later surface in the apocryphal Acts of Paul and Thecla.[10] It seems, at any rate, doubtful whether the traditions in this work are simply based on the material found in the canonical writings of the New Testament, especially the Pastorals, and 1 Clement.[11] If that were the case, then some most remarkable shifts and transformations would have taken place: Hermogenes (2 Tim 1.15; 4.10) is now a coppersmith (§1), but this is the trade of Alexander in 2 Tim 4.4. Now an Alexander also appears in the Acts (§26), a Syrian and one of the leading Antiochenes, who falls in love with Thecla. A Queen Tryphaena seeks to protect her (§§27–39), but is she in any way related to the Tryphaena of Rom 16.12? Yet Richard Bauckham argues, ingeniously, that the Acts of Paul is written as a sequel to the canonical Acts, taking its cue from the seven imprisonments of Paul mentioned in 1 Clem 5.5.[12] (And yet the Acts of Paul seems to describe one single journey of the apostle to Rome and to his death, without an earlier imprisonment in Rome.) Whether dependent on the Pastorals or not, the strongly ascetic Acts of Paul certainly reflects a very different attitude to sexual relations and to the status of women compared with the Pastorals.

Some, however, are quick to identify these false teachers as gnostics, above all on the basis of 1 Tim 6.20: Timothy is to shun worthless empty words and the contradictions (*antitheseis*) of so-called knowledge (*gnōsis*). It is not only the reference to 'knowledge' which is significant here (for not all 'knowledge' needs to be gnostic knowledge), but also the word '*antitheseis*', for this was the title of the work of the arch-heretic Marcion who lived in the middle of the second century. But Helmut Koester rightly observes that Marcion's harsh criticism of the Old Testament (the 'contradictions' in his work were those between the Old and the New Testaments) accords ill with the claim of the false teachers of the Pastorals to be teachers of the law, quite apart from the fact that this would imply a later date for the Pastorals than most are willing to give them.[13] Nevertheless one could see in this false teaching the influence of a syncretistic Judaism (as in Colossians) which showed certain similarities to the later gnosticism, but lacked the radical anti-Judaism of Marcion or, as far as we can tell, the radical rejection of the material world and its creator found in so many gnostic systems.

Not only these false teachers are condemned in the Pastorals, but also a certain Hymenaeus and Philetus who err in saying that the resurrection has already taken place (2 Tim 2.17–18). Their view shows an uncomfortable similarity to the readiness of the authors of Colossians and Ephesians to speak of Christians as already raised with Christ and, in the case of Ephesians, as already in the heavenly regions, and this has led some to point to a serious divergence of views within the Pauline school.[14] Nothing indicates that Hymenaeus and Philetus belong to the same group whose false views are condemned elsewhere in these letters.

Faced by these challenges these letters emphasize the authority to deal with them of the two leaders to whom they are addressed, Timothy and Titus. They are guardians of true teaching, and Timothy is accordingly to remain true to what he learnt and to that of whose truth he has been convinced, knowing from whom he has received it (2 Tim 3.14), and to guard what has been entrusted to him (1 Tim 6.20). Much of the letters is also concerned with enforcing church order. Whereas Colossians and Ephesians in their domestic codes expect Christian households to reflect a form of the ethos then propagated by that branch of philosophy relating to the management of the household,[15] this essentially patriarchal and hierarchical ethos is now applied to the management of the church, a step which was doubtless all the easier in that the early Christian communities were still based upon, and dependent upon, households which offered them a place to meet. In view of the patriarchalism of the household in the Graeco-Roman world this was a step with serious consequences for the role of women in the early church,[16] even if competence in teaching is held to be a virtue in older women (Tit 2.3); the paradox is that a woman is not allowed to teach (1 Tim 2.12).

The similarity of *Acts* to the Pastorals has already been noted, and Paul's speech to the Ephesian elders in ch. 20 is a testament of Paul comparable to that found in 2 Timothy; there, too, the Lucan Paul anticipates his end (20.25). Like the author of the Pastorals he anticipates dangers for the church, 'ravaging wolves' which will not spare the flock, and church members who will seek to lure others away by their false teaching (20.29–30). The elders are therefore to remain watchful over the flock which the Spirit has appointed them to oversee (20.28, *episkopous*, 31).[17] Even though the dangers threatening the church and the institutional measures to counter them are not spelt out so fully as in the Pastorals, the similarity between the envisaged situations is discernible.

More distant in many ways is the relationship of the two letters of Peter to the Pauline tradition. The author of *2 Peter* is, at any rate, aware of the writings of Paul, 'our beloved brother', which he dignifies with the name of 'scriptures', according them implicitly a similar status to the Old Testament writings, but he warns that there are some things in them which are hard to understand, which the ignorant and unstable distort to their own undoing, as they do with the other Scriptures (3.15–16). *1 Peter* has also been treated as reflecting Pauline influence, and the references to Silvanus (5.12; cf. 2 Cor 1.19; 1 Thess 1.1; 2 Thess 1.1) and Mark (1 Pet 5.13; cf. Col 4.10; 2 Tim 4.11; Philem 24) may point to some contact with Paul's fellow-workers and thus to contact between the Christian traditions stemming from, and associated with, these two apostles, or may at least point to the attempt to speak with the combined authority of both. The area to which the letter is sent also overlaps with that of Paul's activity (Galatia and Asia) and many of the theological ideas in the letter echo those of Paul, but are differently formulated.[18]

Paul's influence, or at least a veneration for Paul, can also be seen in 1 Clement, as we have seen, and also in the letters of *Ignatius*; at any rate Paul is mentioned in the latter, but only twice by name. Like the Pastorals these letters betray a church order that has developed beyond that presupposed by Paul's letters; the development has clearly led to the existence of a single overseer or bishop (*episkopos*). Indeed, the development that is reflected in these letters clearly goes beyond anything to be found in the New Testament. Not only is there a clear hierarchy of a single bishop per church, a body of elders and an order of deacons (e.g. Ign. *Magn.* 2.1; *Phld.* 7.1; *Pol.* 6.1), but this developed church order seems to be assumed in all the churches in Asia Minor and Macedonia to which Ignatius writes (but not in that of Rome, perhaps because there was none yet).[19] Furthermore the bishop is invested with an authority and importance to which the nearest parallel in the New Testament is the apostolic authority which Paul claims for himself (although, for Ignatius, it is the elders who take the place of the apostles: *Trall.* 2.2): the Ephesians are to regard the bishop as the Lord himself (6.2), for, as he elsewhere says (*Magn.* 6.1; *Trall.* 3.1), the bishop presides in the place of God and is a type of the Father. Correspondingly, they are to follow their bishop as Christ follows the Father (*Smyrn.* 8.1) and living according to Christ means living in obedience to the bishop (*Trall.* 2.1); nothing is to be done without the bishop (and sometimes the elders are also mentioned: e.g. *Magn.* 7.1).

Again there is the threat of false teaching which is in part described in terms echoing those of the Pastorals (*Magn.* 8.1). At times, as in the Pastorals, it seems clear that this danger comes from the direction of Judaism, for Ignatius here goes on to speak of those living 'according to Judaism' as not having received grace, and, slightly later (*Magn.* 10.3), condemns the enormity of speaking of Christ and practising Judaism (cf. also *Phld.* 6.1).[20] Elsewhere, however, a christological error in the form of the claim that Jesus only appeared to have suffered (*Smyrn.* 2.1; 5.2; *Trall.* 10.1), that is, a form of docetism, is apparently combated. Unless it is conceivable that those holding a docetic Christology could also continue with Jewish practices like sabbath observance, it would seem safer to conclude that Ignatius feels that true doctrine is threatened on two fronts, and that the hierarchical church order which he so robustly propounds is to be regarded as a defence against these twin threats.[21]

9.2. 'Early Catholicism'?

In looking at the form of church structure and order which sprang up in the Pauline churches we have already seen how that order was only in part charismatically based and that other factors shaped the life of these churches. We also saw that it would be a mistake to set *charisma* over against order and the existence of offices and office-bearers. Order was necessary and Paul brought his authority as apostle, undoubtedly an authority which he regarded as Spirit-given, to bear in order to counteract abuses, including abuses arising from an exaggerated and exclusive claim to possess, and be empowered by, the Spirit. If one recognizes the existence and necessity of this order in Paul's churches,[22] then one will perhaps hesitate to make too much of the much greater stress on order and authority in the Pastoral Epistles.

These letters have, nevertheless, often been regarded as one of the prime examples in the New Testament of that phenomenon which is frequently referred to as 'early catholicism'.[23] The stress on order, authority and tradition, which is characteristic of this phenomenon, may be seen as a reaction to a new situation. For in place of the dangers arising from an undue concentration on more spectacular spiritual gifts and a devaluing of more pedestrian ones and those who exercised them, other dangers arose which were just as threatening to the well-being of the church. Claims to special revelations were not only dangerous because those who did not share them felt disadvantaged, but also because of what could be claimed as the content of such revelations, and claimed with an authority which brooked no questioning or contradiction. In short, there was the danger of false teachers who claimed that the Spirit and special revelations had led them to their false teaching. And as time passed, and the founding figures of the earliest church gradually died, this danger grew, for there would soon be no one with a comparable authority who could refute such false teachers.[24]

We can detect certain trends within the New Testament, and above all in writings like the Pastoral Epistles, which can be seen as a reaction to this danger, and these tendencies have been labelled 'early catholic'.[25] Amongst the tendencies that have been linked to this are the following:

1. The church itself becomes part and parcel of the saving event.[26]
2. The operation of the Spirit is tied to the holding of an office, leading in turn to a separation of clergy and laity.[27]
3. The entrusting of the faith to the church or, above all, to its office-bearers is stressed;[28] the ordination of office-bearers is seen as authorizing them to act as stewards of the faith entrusted to them. This entrusted faith becomes in turn the basis of the rule of faith which enables the church to distinguish between true and false teaching.
4. Closely associated with this role of the office-bearers is the notion of an apostolic succession. In the Pastoral Epistles Timothy and Titus are portrayed as delegates of the apostle Paul, and may be regarded as foreshadowing the monarchical bishop or 'monepiskopos', such as we find in the letters of Ignatius, or, if the latter already existed, serving as a prototype for the latter.[29]

The third and fourth features mentioned above can be illustrated from the Pastoral Epistles and also, perhaps, the second, although this depends on how one interprets 1 Tim 4.14 and 2 Tim 1.6.[30] How far are such tendencies detectable elsewhere in the New Testament? In Acts, which is often regarded as a prominent representative of this tendency, there is certainly a clearly recognizable interest in continuity and legitimacy, as attested in the account of Matthias' election to succeed Judas (Acts 1.15–26), but at issue there is the continuity between the apostles and Jesus, not that between the apostles and their successors. It is true that Paul commits the Ephesian church into the hands of its elders, but there is no single delegate mentioned, and he commends them to God's word (20.32). And in the choice of Barnabas and Paul for their missionary task in 13.1–2 it is the Spirit which chooses them. In the oversight exercised by the Jerusalem church over the spread of the faith, on the other hand, it is legitimate to recognize a certain institutionalizing and channelling of the Spirit: the Samaritans cannot receive the Spirit until the leaders of the Jerusalem church have laid their hands upon them (8.17). When one speaks of the church becoming part of the event of salvation, then it is, in the first instance, Acts which springs to mind as an example of this in the New Testament, but this is more a deduction from the existence and presumed *raison d'être* of Acts as such, rather than something which the text itself attests. Yet it must be asked whether this must be the motive which led 'Luke', and 'Luke' alone, to compose this work. Or were other motives at work, above all apologetic ones, for instance with regard to the church's relation to the Graeco-Roman world and its authorities on the one hand, and Israel and its inheritance on the other? In other words, the Pastoral Epistles may seem to have taken some steps in the direction of what is described as 'early catholicism', but the in many respects rather similar Acts gives far less clear signs of doing so. More important, the steps which they have or may have taken are in each case different ones, and in neither the one nor the other do we find evidence of all the features which go to make up this 'early catholicism'.

10

Johannine Christianity

As predicted, most of this account of the earliest Christians has been connected in some way or other with Paul: either it has focused directly on him or it has discussed other figures who were in some way connected or in contact with him. And, given the nature of our sources, that is inevitable: his letters form a primary source of knowledge of this history and in the other main source, the Book of Acts, he is at the centre of interest as well. There is, however, another corpus of literature in the New Testament which might seem to offer the hope of tracing the history of another tradition within earliest Christianity which is less directly connected with him, namely that associated with the name of John. (It is, indeed, perhaps surprising that it is apparently so little connected with the Pauline movement, since John was traditionally associated with Ephesus, a city in which Paul worked for a longer period of time.) The Fourth Gospel, the three Johannine letters and the Apocalypse of John initially might seem to offer us the possibility of reconstructing something of the history of this line of development within earliest Christianity, if not in such great detail as in the case of the Pauline tradition.

Yet such an undertaking is beset with considerable problems and obstacles, so many that they make the investigation of the Pauline tradition seem straightforward by comparison. Even geographically the Johannine community or communities are far harder to locate. While some argue that they were located in Palestine or Syria,[1] one must still account for the rise of the stubborn tradition associating John and the Johannine school with Asia Minor and in particular with Ephesus, a tradition attested already by Papias of Hierapolis in western Asia Minor (he is thought to have lived *c.* 60–130 CE). According to Irenaeus, writing towards the end of the second century, who himself came from Asia Minor and was a pupil of Polycarp, Bishop of Smyrna and a companion of Papias, Papias had himself heard John.[2] Yet, even if the Johannine school eventually settled in Ephesus and even if the Fourth Gospel and some at least of the Johannine letters were written there, that does not mean that John and his followers had always resided there. The Gospel reflects a situation in which the Johannine community has been driven out of the synagogue (9.22; 12.42; 16.2) and 16.2 speaks of the threat to kill them.[3] Particularly the latter aspect is more readily intelligible in a Palestinian context and in the period before the Jewish revolt. And if the expulsion from the synagogue was not only psychologically traumatic but occasioned material difficulties for the community in the form of social ostracism, as some suppose, then that is also far more readily intelligible in a Palestinian setting.[4]

This expulsion from the synagogue has played a prominent role in the various attempts to trace the history of the Johannine community, as well as to pinpoint more accurately the dating of the Fourth Gospel and the circumstances in which it was written. This is readily intelligible in view of the dearth of other information and the subsequent uncertainty about the dating of the Gospel; proposals have ranged from a setting before the Jewish revolt to a final editing of the work in the third quarter of the second century.There is a considerable measure of agreement that the unusual word *aposynagōgos*, 'expelled from the synagogue', reflects the so-called *birkath ha-mînîm*, literally 'the blessing of the heretics' (in reality it is a curse, not a blessing!) which is found as the twelfth of the Eighteen Benedictions:

> For the renegades let there be no hope, and may the arrogant kingdom soon be rooted out in our days, and the Nazarenes and the *minim* perish as in a moment and be blotted out from the book of life and with the righteous may they not be inscribed. Blessed art thou, O Lord, who humblest the arrogant.[5]

It is also widely supposed that this curse was added to this prayer around 80 or 90 CE as a part of the new order set up in Jamnia after the Jewish revolt, at the instigation of R. Gamaliel II. Some have, however, criticized this consensus, and certainly the apparent reference to Christians as 'Nazarenes' is lacking in older versions of this prayer, although it has been suggested that it may already have been introduced after the Bar Kokhba revolt of 132–5, which greatly inflamed relations between Christians and Jews;[6] without it, it would be far harder to see the prayer as directed specifically against Christians. References to a new order introduced at Jamnia, or even to a synod there, may, however, be misleading.[7] Nor is it clear how the introduction of this prayer could be construed as an expulsion from the synagogue in the terms which the Fourth Gospel envisages. Whereas some suppose that the recitation of this prayer forced the Christians to withdraw from the synagogue, perceiving that it was directed against them, John 9.22 and also 16.2 suggest, not a voluntary withdrawal on the part of the Christians, but disciplinary measures initiated by the Jews.[8]

Nor should it be assumed that the expulsion referred to belonged to the very recent past of the Johannine community. For the Fourth Gospel is characterized by an at times very negative attitude to 'the Jews' and its author writes as if 'the Jews' were a group to which he and his community do not belong.[9] That is more readily intelligible if the expulsion from the synagogue now lay some considerable time in the past, long enough for the Johannine community to feel that 'the Jews' were a group of which they were no longer members, but yet not long enough for them to forget the pain occasioned by their expulsion.[10] That pain had in all probability led some members of the Johannine community to desert it and to seek reintegration in the Jewish community.[11] If that crisis can be detached from a particular post-70 situation, it must be asked whether or not a pre-70 situation is not likelier, at a time of acute nationalist pressure. That would make it all the more probable that the expulsion now lay some considerable time in the past. In all likelihood it had, at any rate, been a time in which the community had suffered a severe crisis of identity and orientation, and the Fourth Gospel reflects the need to address that crisis and above all the Jewish rejection of the Johannine Christians' claims about the identity of Jesus. At that time the community and its leader may well also have migrated to another place, and if they had formerly lived in Palestine then the social ostracism occasioned by their expulsion from the synagogue would have provided a powerful motive to seek somewhere else to live, in which their alienation from the Jewish community would no longer be such a disadvantage and would not be felt so keenly. That the roots of this group lay in Palestine and indeed perhaps in Judaea, rather than Galilee, as some infer from the 'other disciple' in John 18.15 who is 'known to the high priest', is in itself plausible.[12] The tradition of the expulsion from the synagogue points, then, to a traumatic separation which caused the group to seek some safer place away from their Judaean homeland. Many places in the Jewish Diaspora would have served this purpose, but the persistence of the Ephesus tradition suggests that this was where they eventually settled.

In that case, however, it is to be noted how diverse the Christianity at Ephesus must have been.[13] It is to be assumed that the influence of Paul and perhaps also of Apollos (Acts 18.24–8; 1 Cor 16.12) and perhaps even Nicolaus of Antioch (cf. Rev 2.6?) was still to be felt there;[14] the influence of Paul was, at any rate, presumably still strong, indeed perhaps dominant, at the time when Ignatius wrote to the church, particularly if the Onesimus who was then its bishop (Ign. *Eph.* 1.3) is the same person as the slave on whose behalf Paul wrote his letter to Philemon, although this identification has not found much favour. Ignatius also addresses this church as Paul's 'fellow-initiates' (12.2). Yet there was also in that city a group to whom the author of the Book of Revelation could write, overwhelmingly positively (Rev 2.1–7), and we have already seen in ch. 6 that this writer in all probability represents a very different tradition to that of Paul, one far less prepared to espouse a way of life which avoided giving unnecessary offence to one's pagan neighbours (cf. 1 Cor 10.32–3). Must one then add to these already very different strands of Christianity a third one, one thoroughly distinctive and hardly to be confused or merged with the other two?[15]

Or should one take seriously the traditional attribution of the Fourth Gospel and the Johannine letters as well as the Book of Revelation to a 'John' and attempt to link the writer of the last-named to those Christians responsible for the Gospel and the letters? But then what is the apocalyptic writer's relation to those Christians? Does he share their views or is he resolutely setting his face against them, on the grounds that they are compromising themselves with the world?[16] Does the diversity of the Ephesian church then reach right into the heart of the 'Johannine school'?

In addition the Fourth Gospel is widely regarded as reflecting, more than do the Synoptics, competition between the Johannine community and followers of John the Baptist (cf. John 1.6–8, 15, 19–37; 3.22–4.3). Is this competition still a present reality in the history of the Johannine community or does the Gospel in this respect, too, reflect circumstances lying further back in the past of the group? In view of the rather surprising tradition in Acts 19.1–7, where Paul encounters in Ephesus 'disciples' who have only received John's baptism, it should not be regarded as impossible that followers of the Baptist were still contemporary rivals of the Johannine community and that in Ephesus, although, as we have seen, it is more likely that the term 'disciples' means that they were Christians, however incomplete ones in 'Luke's' eyes.

It is plausible, too, that the Johannine writings reflect a sense of self-identity which sets this community apart from other Christians. So Raymond Brown argues that this is how we should understand the contrast in the Gospel between the beloved disciple, who may best be regarded as 'the idealization of a historical person',[17] and who was a dominant and formative person in the Johannine tradition, and Peter (13.23–6; 18.15–16; 20.2–10; 21.7, 20–3).[18] Whereas for Mark the disciples of Jesus are all characterized by a failure to understand, the beloved disciple does not seem to share the lack of comprehension characteristic of the other disciples in the Fourth Gospel. Yet, in that case, ch. 21, which seems to have been added on later to the body of the Gospel and should therefore reflect a later stage in the community's history, both maintains the distinctiveness of the privileges of the beloved disciple and at the same time recognizes the pastoral responsibility of Peter for Jesus' flock, and not just for part of it (21.15–17); Cullmann is therefore right to stress that throughout the Gospel Peter is never attacked, however different the position of this author and of the beloved disciple may be.[19]

It is likely that the various Johannine writings reflect differing situations in the history of the Johannine community at different points of time. Reconstructing that history is, however, hindered by uncertainty as to the order in which those documents were written.[20] For, whereas a majority of scholars date the Fourth Gospel before the Johannine letters, a smaller but seemingly increasingly numerous group of others have opted for the opposite sequence.

There are indeed certain considerations which speak for an earlier dating of the letters: they, for instance, reflect a more traditional futuristic eschatology (1 John 2.28; 3.1–2) over against the more pronounced realized eschatology of the Gospel, and they use the term *paraklētos* of Christ, not the Spirit (1 John 2.1), and in a way that is far more readily intelligible in terms of the usual sense of this word to refer to an advocate in court. On the other hand, the Gospel's Christology shows no awareness of the Christological controversies reflected in the letters which have led to the split in the community (1 John 2.19) and the high Christology which the Gospel expounds over against the Jews can plausibly be construed as in part the cause of the Christological problems of the letters. For so concerned is the Fourth Evangelist to stress the divine authority of Jesus that there is the danger that his humanity is lost from sight.

Puzzling, too, is the way in which the author of 2 and 3 John introduces himself simply as 'the elder' (2 John 1; 3 John 1); some identify him, therefore, as that elder John, the disciple of the Lord, to whom Papias of Hierapolis refers.[21] The only New Testament document which speaks of a John as its author is the Book of Revelation (1.1, 4, 9; 22.8), but who is this John and how does his writing relate to the rest of the Johannine corpus?

Whereas the Fourth Gospel is most easily understood as opposing the Jews' denial of the status which this writer wishes to claim for Christ, the Johannine letters reflect internal problems in the Johannine community. False teachers have gone out into the world who deny that Christ comes in the flesh (2 John 7). Like the Didache this community, too, seems to be troubled by itinerant Christian teachers. Above all in *1 John* it is clear that a false Christological teaching is being opposed: condemned are those denying that Jesus is the Christ and the Son (2.22–3) and the recipients of the letter, confronted by false prophets who have come into the world, are called upon to test the spirits: every spirit which confesses that Jesus Christ has come in the flesh comes from God (4.1–3). The threat comes apparently from former members of the Johannine community, those antichrists who have come out from their midst, yet in reality do not belong to them and so have left the community (2.18–19).[22] The danger may consist in a form of docetism, perhaps similar to that which Ignatius condemns in his letter to the church in Smyrna, the denial that the Lord was a 'flesh-bearer' (*Smyrn* 5.2) or that of which Polycarp, Bishop of Smyrna, writes somewhat later (?around 135) in his letter to the Philippians, in terms strongly reminiscent of 1 John (7.1). These letters are sufficiently near to the probable time and place of the Johannine letters, if the latter are set in the Roman province of Asia, for it to be plausibly suggested that all these various writers are referring to one and the same basic problem. Whether this problem can be linked specifically with the name of the heretical Cerinthus is undecided, but Christoph Markschies comments that it is 'largely undisputed' that 1 John is attacking a Christology which separates the divine Christ from the earthly Jesus as

Cerinthus did.[23] He questions, however, whether this is aptly described as 'docetism', for Cerinthus' Jesus really suffered, even if his Christ did not (72). More recently, however, Wolfram Uebele has argued that the error which is being opposed, both in the Johannine letters and in those of Ignatius, is indeed a docetism of a kind which he describes as 'monophysite' in the sense that Jesus Christ is one person who only seems to have a human nature and is in fact divine.[24] This type of 'docetism' is to be compared, not with the views of Cerinthus, but rather with those of the somewhat later Satornilus of Antioch.[25]

At first sight *3 John* seems to have little, if anything, to do with this problem: the elder complains that a certain Diotrephes, who wants to be first, is unwilling to accept 'us' and brings charges against 'us', does not receive the brothers and hinders all who want to do so and turns them out of the church (vv. 9–10). Again it may well be a matter of itinerant teachers, but this time ones who come from the elder, whom this Diotrephes rejects; Diotrephes, on the other hand, is evidently a prominent member of that church to which they come. Why he has acted thus is not clear; the elder merely mentions his ambition. It may just be a matter of a clash of two ecclesiastical structures, as Schnelle suggests,[26] one based on the individual church, the other universal in scope, or more probably embracing a number of churches in a particular area, and linking them together by a series of travelling emissaries. Diotrephes' reaction would then be an attempt to prevent outside interference in a domain which he regarded as his responsibility, although one should be cautious about labelling him a monarchical bishop.[27] (Dominant laypersons in Christian denominations which would shun the label 'bishop' like the plague can be just as officious in defending their local congregation against alien perils.) That the 'elder' then can write to Gaius (3 John 1), who has apparently earned the 'elder's' approval by the way he has received and supported travelling emissaries of his (vv. 5–8), is most easily intelligible if Gaius is responsible for another Christian gathering than that over which Diotrephes presides; that in turn may suggest separate house churches, divided in their attitude to the 'elder'. Only if Diotrephes' reasons were theological would we have a possible link with the false teaching of the first two letters, but it is not clear whether he rejects the elder's emissaries because his own teaching is false or whether he rejects the teaching of the elder. Both may be true, depending on whose viewpoint one adopts: both rejected the other's teaching.[28]

Much of this reconstruction of the history and situation of the Johannine community is, and must be, conjectural, but it at least suggests that this tradition and its leading figure, one far less clearly identifiable than Paul, were equally capable of provoking division and controversy, at least within the probably more confined area in which they operated. Just as the figure of Paul aroused violent antipathy in many of his contemporaries and was a divisive figure in the earliest church, challenging even the authority of the Jerusalem church, so too, on a more modest scale, 'the elder' seems to have provoked dissent and opposition. Just as Paul's teaching and practice were widely criticized and rejected, so too the teaching of the Johannine writings seems to have spawned rejection and division. Just as the inheritance of Paul took markedly different forms, so too the legacy of the traditions found in the Fourth Gospel may well have led in differing directions, both more radical and more conservative.

11

The Church in the Roman Empire

For a number of years the early Christian community was, in the eyes of outsiders, at least non-Jewish ones, and in particular in the eyes of the Roman authorities, a Jewish group, and that was an important factor in the growth and spread of the church. For the Jews, above all by virtue of the services which some of their leaders had rendered, often with an astute sense of the way the political wind was blowing, enjoyed a privileged position during much of the period of the early principate, and the antiquity of their faith and traditions earned them respect in a world in which a venerable pedigree was a considerable asset. They were, consequently, spared some of the impositions which would have clashed with their religious principles, and were regarded as loyal to the ruling family of the Julio-Claudians, even if one should avoid using the category of a 'permitted religion' (*religio licita*).[1] Relations between the Jews and Roman authorities during the time of the Julio-Claudians were often better than those between Jews and their Greek neighbours in the Hellenistic cities of the East, where friction often arose and the Romans had to pour oil on troubled waters.[2] There were, of course, exceptions: offences by individual Jews could lead to disciplinary measures being taken against a whole Jewish community. Several instances of such measures are recorded: the Jewish community in Rome had already suffered under Tiberius because certain Jews were found guilty of the misappropriation of funds and of fraud.[3] One particularly important incident was the repeated (*assidue*) unruly behaviour 'at the instigation of Chrestus' (*impulsore Chresto*) which led to Claudius' expulsion of Jews from Rome.[4] It is widely assumed that 'Chrestus' should be 'Christus',[5] and that the reference is to disturbances in the Jewish synagogues of Rome caused by Christian preachers. If that is so, then it is more likely that they preached a version of the gospel akin to Paul's, rather than the law-observant version associated with James and the Jerusalem church.

Again, when power was exercised by someone unfavourably disposed towards the Jews, then things could be considerably more difficult for the Jews. Lucius Aelius Seianus exercised extensive powers under Tiberius, and Philo charges him with responsibility for the hostility shown towards the Jews under Tiberius as long as Seianus was alive (*Leg.* 159–60). And finally, when an emperor decided to appropriate to himself powers and rights which conflicted with those of the Jewish God, then confrontation was inevitable: that occurred when Gaius Caligula wished to set up an enormous statue in the Jerusalem temple.[6] That situation was only defused thanks to the delaying tactics of the Roman governor of Syria, Publius Petronius, and the timely assassination of Caligula. Yet such was the reputation which Caligula left behind him that the Jews' resistance to him was not held against them by his successors. Thus Claudius, in writing to the Alexandrians, recognized and upheld the right of the Alexandrian Jews to observe their ancestral customs as Augustus had allowed them to do, while at the same time warning them against seeking further rights or engaging in activities which might be interpreted as seditious.[7] As long as Christians were regarded as part of the Jewish community they could expect to enjoy that protection and tolerance which generally characterized the Roman state's treatment of the Jews. In particular, worship of the emperor would not be expected of them.[8] At the same time they might be lumped together with other Jews as victims of disciplinary measures taken against the Jews. That was seemingly the case when Jews were expelled from Rome by Claudius, for it brought Aquila and Priscilla to Corinth (Acts 18.2), and, if Christians were responsible for the disturbances in the first place, it was not only fair but inevitable that they would be caught up in these measures.

With the first of the great Jewish uprisings in 66 CE, however, the public perception of the Jews inevitably changed, even if nothing had happened to call Judaism's antiquity in question, and this change would be reinforced by the later risings in the time of Trajan and again under Bar Kokhba (132–5). So the slaughter of the Roman garrison in Jerusalem at the outbreak of the revolt in 66 was followed by the massacre and expulsion of Jews in Caesarea Maritima (Josephus *BJ* 2.457).[9] That led to Jewish reprisals against Syrian villages and cities and, when they had the upper hand, the

Syrians slaughtered those Jews whom they could catch (§461): Josephus mentions attacks on Jews in Scythopolis, Ascalon, Ptolemais, Tyre, Hippos and Gadara (§§466–78). These were followed by attacks on Jews in Alexandria (§§487, 494–8) and Damascus (§§559–61). After the defeat of the Jews by Titus groups of revolutionary Jews fled to Alexandria and Cyrenaica, causing further unrest in those places (7407–19, 437–46). Again North Africa was the main setting for a further Jewish rising in 115–117, along with Cyprus and Mesopotamia, in which the Jews in Alexandria were put to death and a revolt in Cyrene was put down, with thousands of Jewish casualties (Euseb. *Hist. eccl.* 4.2.2–4).[10] In all these upheavals it would be unrealistic to expect the non-Jews to distinguish too carefully between Christians, Jewish Christians and non-Christian Jews. Apparently the Jews also attacked their non-Jewish neighbours in Cyprus, and thereafter no Jew was allowed on the island, on pain of death.[11] And in 135 the consequence of the rising was the expulsion of all Jews from Jerusalem itself. After all this one could not realistically expect the relationship of the Jewish people to their Roman rulers to be quite the same as it had been throughout much of the Julio-Claudian period, although an isolated individual like Flavius Josephus or Herod Agrippa II might still enjoy the favour and the patronage of the Flavian house, and the treatment of the Jewish people by their Roman rulers shows a perhaps surprising degree of tolerance and pragmatism. Yet the fact that Josephus was time and again compelled in his writings to defend his people and to try to pin the blame for the events of 66 and the following years on small groups of troublemakers in itself surely indicates how much damage limitation was necessary in the relationships between the Jews and the Graeco-Roman public. The same applies to the Roman authorities: as Rajak observes,[12] the friendship (*amicitia*), which had largely characterized relations between the Jews and the Roman rulers from the time of Caesar on, could not be entirely secure; the relationship of patron and client (*clientela*) to which the standing of the Jews had approximated, could turn sour, and Josephus reflects a situation in which the Jews clung desperately to their rights.

With the bestowal of the name 'Christians' in Antioch (Acts 11.26), whenever that took place, we have, however, seen the first sign that the separate, but not yet non-Jewish, identity of this new movement could be, and was, recognized by outsiders. Therein lay a great danger, in that the Roman authorities tended to view with considerable suspicion voluntary associations of many sorts, which we would consider quite innocuous or even positively beneficial.[13] A far more serious sign of that growing awareness, however, is to be found in Nero's selection of Christians as scapegoats for the fire of Rome in 64 CE or at least in his singling them out for punishment as 'a new and noxious superstition'.[14] There is no hint that non-Christian Jews were also involved,[15] so we must assume that the Christian community, be they Jews or non-Jews, was regarded as deserving victims, while other Jews were not. James Walters makes the plausible suggestion that one result of the disturbances in the synagogue or synagogues which prompted Claudius' measures against the Jewish community would be to make the Roman Jews wary of any further contacts with Christians, Jewish or non-Jewish,[16] and such separation could well have enabled the Christian community to become more clearly distinguishable from the Jewish. But the charge against the Christians was not that they were Christians, but, at least according to Tacitus, that they were allegedly guilty of arson.[17] And Trocmé's conjecture is plausible, that it would have taken some considerable time before the Roman church would recover from this devastation.[18] Now Nero may not have enjoyed a better reputation after his death than Caligula, but nevertheless a precedent had been set, at least in the identification of the Christians as a group distinct from the Jews and therefore not necessarily enjoying the same time-honoured privileges and recognition as they did, quite apart from any suspicion which might still be attached to them despite the fact that it was Nero who had thus singled them out.[19] Yet it is clear from Pliny's letter to Trajan concerning the Christians that he, as governor of Bithynia and Pontus, had not taken the initiative in instigating proceedings against Christians, but that he was responding to accusations brought against them by other citizens. In other words, there can be no question here of a systematic persecution instigated by the Roman authorities, such as seemingly occurred after the fire of Rome and such as would occur later in the history of the early church. Nonetheless, when accusations were levelled against Christians, Pliny had no compunction about putting their loyalty to the emperor to the test and, if they declined to prove their loyalty, punishing them for their stubbornness; that in itself was proof enough that they deserved to be punished. Here we see one manifestation of the difficulty which the imperial cult presented for early Christians. It had been recognized that participation in the cult in its usual form was impossible for Jews, and provision had been made for an acceptable substitute that showed their loyalty to Rome and the emperor without imperilling their relationship with their God; it was enough to sacrifice to God twice daily in the Temple 'for Caesar and the Roman nation'.[20] But if Christians were now recognized as a distinct entity – and increasingly Christian Jews were, after all, in the minority – , then they could no longer shelter behind this special dispensation,[21] and it would be expected of them that they prove their loyalty by offering incense and a libation before images of the gods and of the emperor, as Pliny shows. It was not necessary, as Trajan confirms, that the accused should first be convicted of those crimes of which Christians were supposed to be guilty; the reference may well be to the suspicions aroused in the mind of the populace by reports of meals called 'love-feasts' at which flesh and blood were consumed; it needed little imagination to construct the most horrific of orgies out of such reports. To bear the name 'Christian' is apparently sufficient and this situation also seems to be presupposed in 1 Pet 4.16, either as a present reality or as something which may overtake the communities addressed at any moment. It is also significant that Pliny turns to Trajan for guidance, admitting that he has had no experience of proceedings against Christians. The way in which this is phrased suggests that he knew of such proceedings in the past and could in theory have been present at them. Is that an indication that some such similar persecutions had taken place in the recent past, perhaps under Domitian (81–96 CE)? Yet Reichert rightly questions whether Pliny's remark allows us to infer that there had been any such general persecution, and notes that scholars are now wary of accepting at face value the bad reputation which Domitian had subsequently among Christian and non-Christian writers. Rather, she suggests, there were few precedents for Pliny to follow (and we have seen that Nero would not have been considered a good one); it may well be that Pliny is in fact paving the way by setting the ground rules for proceedings against Christians on a firmer basis.[22]

At any rate it is in the reign of Domitian that the persecution has usually been dated which is depicted by the seer of the Book of Revelation, although a number of voices plead for dating this book after the death of Nerva and into the reign of Trajan.[23] It is to be noted that Revelation only names one victim, a certain Antipas in Pergamum (2.13); nor is it stated how Antipas met his end.[24] A dating in the mid 90s is also widely favoured for 1 Clement, which begins with a reference to 'the sudden and repeated misfortunes and calamities which have befallen us' (1.1). Slightly later, too, there took place that persecution under which Ignatius of Antioch suffered, perhaps also around the time of Pliny's letter; at least Eusebius also assigns Ignatius' journey to martyrdom to the time of Trajan (*Hist. eccl.* 3.36.2).

After the Jewish rising of 66 and even more after the further revolts, there could no longer be the same value for Christians in being identified with the Jews,[25] although there was undoubtedly still something to be gained by showing that the roots of the seemingly new movement in fact lay in the time-honoured traditions of the Jews. An ancient pedigree counted for something still in the consciousness of the Graeco-Roman world.[26] Nevertheless, the growing number of Christians of non-Jewish origin could not but affect the self-perception of this generation of Christians.[27]

With justification some scholars also suggest a financial element that may well have played a part in their self-awareness and self-definition, at least for Christian Jews:[28] the emperor Vespasian imposed on Jews who still practised their ancestral religion the tax of two drachmae payable to the *fiscus Judaicus* for the temple of Jupiter Capitolinus in Rome, in place of the previous tax for the Jerusalem Temple which was now destroyed (Cassius Dio 65.7.2). That tax, so defined, would inevitably be a considerable incentive for Jewish Christians in the least inclined to follow Paul's lead to make a clear break with the observance of Jewish customs and laws, although that incentive was in fact only new if practice was now the criterion, not ethnic descent; previously, Jewish Christians would, at least in theory, have remained liable for the Temple tax (but cf. Matt 17.24–7) – if the Jewish authorities and communities were in a position to extract it from them. If the tax was enforced more vigorously under Domitian it is likely that either practice or ethnic descent may have made one liable for it, and that a climate of denouncing those liable on either count arose.[29] Was this then the abuse whose abolition Nerva triumphantly proclaimed?[30] Indirectly, too, that would contribute to the self-understanding of gentile Christians, confirming them in their distancing themselves from Judaism.

The experience of persecution, whether it stemmed from the ill-will of an emperor or from that of their fellow-citizens, resulted in a considerable ambivalence on the part of the early Christians. On the one hand, interests of self-protection suggested that one should avoid causing offence either to the authorities or to one's neighbours, particularly if the latter might otherwise denounce one to the authorities. Such considerations seem to weigh particularly heavily in the instructions given in *1 Peter*: the author appeals to his addressees, as strangers in this world, to lead a respectable life in order that they may not be accused as evil-doers (2.12). With that appeal a great deal of the potentially revolutionary impetus of the Christian movement is curbed. They are to honour all, love their brothers, fear God and honour the emperor (2.17), although the author of this letter makes no claim that the emperor has been appointed by God. In this respect he was nevertheless following a path which Paul himself had already trodden in Rom 13.1–7, a path in which Paul was in turn following Jewish precedents.[31] If the readers of 1 Peter must suffer, they should suffer for the name 'Christian' alone and not because they have committed crimes like murder or theft (4.15–16). The idea of suffering for the name alone immediately recalls Pliny's deliberations, and the parallel is the more significant because Bithynia and Pontus are among the regions named in 1.1 where the recipients of this letter are to be found. In that case it is legitimate to see the concern for the reputation of Christians amongst their neighbours as stemming, at least in part, from the consideration that they might otherwise denounce them to the authorities, as had happened in Bithynia and Pontus.

For it is in the light of this consideration that we should probably view the particular form of the tradition of the so-called 'domestic code' found in this letter.[32] In its more typical form, found in Col 3.18–4.1 and Eph 5.21–6.9, it is purely 'domestic' in that it deals with three pairs of reciprocal relationships within the household: wives–husbands, children–parents, slaves–slave-owners. Nevertheless, the management of a household was viewed as an aspect of political order, on the grounds that 'every state is made up of households' (Arist. *Pol.* 1.2.1.1253b3). The motivation for the 'domestic codes' as found in Colossians and Ephesians may be disputed, but the alterations in the form found in 1 Peter give a clear hint as to the purpose of this form in this case. For here not only do we find an incomplete version of the threefold reciprocal form, in that the initial admonition of slaves finds no answer in a statement of the owners' duties, and the pair children–parents is lacking, but the whole is prefaced by a more general introduction, far fuller than the single short verse of Eph 5.21, 'Be subject to one another out of reverence for Christ' (NRSV). Now the addressees are urged 'as aliens and exiles' to abstain from fleshly desires and to lead an honourable life among the gentiles, 'so that, though they malign you as evildoers, they may see your honourable deeds and glorify God when he comes to judge' (1 Pet 2.12, NRSV). Then the letter goes on to urge, in a manner reminiscent of Rom 13.1–7, submission to every human institution, be it the emperor (*basileus*) or the governors appointed by him. God wills it that by so doing they should silence the ignorance of the foolish. They are God's slaves; they should make use of their freedom, but not as a cloak for evil. Then this introduction ends with the fourfold appeal: 'Honour everyone, love the fellowship of believers [lit. the brotherhood], fear God, honour the emperor' (2.17). With this exhortation to political correctness and loyalty to the emperor is combined a concern for the impression made by Christians on their neighbours in the light of the latter's tendency to think the worst of the Christians. Here we see a policy of 'damage limitation' (being known as a Christian was potentially damaging enough) through conforming oneself as far as possible to the *mores* and norms of contemporary society.

On the other hand the sufferings that the early Christians had already suffered had so burned themselves into their consciousness that it was inevitable that a very different attitude should sometimes also surface and that Rome should be regarded as wickedness and godlessness incarnate, as in the *Book of Revelation*. For it is clear that much of the coded imagery of this work cloaks a damning indictment of Rome as an oppressive power; as Wengst puts it,[33] 'Rome and its actions are only depicted in the darkest colours.' It is a work permeated from start to finish with the thought of the suffering of God's chosen ones, from the (presumably exiled) seer on the island of Patmos, who shares with his readers the experience of persecution (Rev 1.9), to the triumphant final vision in which in the new heaven and new earth and new Jerusalem it is above all death and mourning, crying and pain which will be taken away, and their absence will characterize the new world (21.4). Rome is not always accused of being the cause of all this suffering; the Roman power is not the only one that may have caused slaughter and martyrdom. But when the slaughtering is by beheading with an axe (20.4, *pelekizō*), then it becomes clearer that Rome's judicial murders of the saints are meant.[34] It is those who have held fast to their testimony who suffer this fate, and it is plausible to think once more of a trial setting such as Pliny describes, in which the accused are pressed to renounce Christ, in order to save themselves from execution.[35]

Many accusations are levelled against Rome: in it, described as Babylon (as probably in 1 Pet 5.13, despite all the desire expressed in that work not to give unnecessary offence to the pagan world), is to be found the blood of prophets and saints and all slaughtered on the earth (18.24). The woman who is the 'great city that rules over the kings of the earth' is 'drunk with the blood of the saints' (17.6, 18, NRSV). But besides its thirst for blood, its thirst for wealth and its exploitation are also strongly condemned, and not only allied kings, but also merchants and sea-farers share in the condemnation heaped upon the imperial city (18.3, 9–19). Reflecting, too, the pretensions of the cult of Roma and the emperor, the work remarks on the blasphemy of the names on the heads of the beast that rises out of the sea in 13.1.[36] Above all, Rome is the minion of Satan, represented as the serpent or dragon (12.9; 20.2).[37] The dragon has given its authority to the beast that is Rome, and as a consequence the whole earth (or so it seems to the seer) worships the beast (13.4).[38] The seer's vision does not end with that indictment, however, for he also sees the victory already won over the dragon (13.9; 20.2) and Rome punished in kind for all its misdeeds and paid back in full (18.6–8). In this fate the seer exults and finds comfort in the midst of his own suffering.

Yet it is also Wengst who points out that a probably roughly contemporary work, 1 Clement, and the double work of Luke reflect a very different perspective.[39] In keeping with the injunctions of 1 Peter the former work prays for 'our rulers and governors upon the earth' and that Christians may be subject to them as God wills (1 Clem 60.4–61.2; cf. 21.6).[40] And yet 1 Clement is also a letter in which the reality of persecution is acknowledged (1.1; 5.1–6.2). Nevertheless, there is no hint of blame attaching to the Roman authorities, but implicitly Christians themselves are to blame for the envy and jealousy that has repeatedly led to these persecutions (5.2–5; 6.1).

Particularly in the *Book of Acts* 'Luke' similarly reflects a far more positive approach to Roman rule or at least to 'good' Roman rulers, who are only too ready to recognize the innocence of Christians accused before them, in contrast to the malicious accusations brought against them, in some cases by 'the Jews'.[41] This stance may well be connected with the dedication of this work and the gospel of Luke to Theophilus (Luke 1.3; Acts 1.1) if the address 'most excellent' (*kratiste*) implies that this person, real or feigned, is of some social standing in the Graeco-Roman world.[42] Again, it is a Roman centurion who is held up as a conspicuous example of a pious gentile, who then in turn becomes a prototypical and exemplary gentile convert to Christianity (Acts 10.1–2). It is plausible to see in this an apologetic intent, even if, as Michael Wolter suggests,[43] the judgements of the Romans and other authorities serve also to underline the contention that the Christian movement remains within the traditions of Israel, despite the repeated rejection of it by the Jews. On the other hand, the stress which 'Luke' lays upon the endorsement of the innocence of accused Christians and the way in which he holds up the example of such a respectable Roman figure becoming a convert may reflect the uncomfortable awareness of this author that others may see things differently, regarding Christians as dishonourable and subversive, precisely that impression which the author of 1 Peter seeks to avoid.

In short, around the year 100 CE various attitudes towards the Roman state and Graeco-Roman society are reflected in early Christian literature and, correspondingly, markedly different strategies to cope with the demands of living in a world dominated by the might of Rome. Of the voices we can still hear, however, that of the apocalyptist seer of Revelation is in a minority. Yet that does not necessarily mean that he was then in a minority among the Christians of that day. More cautious and irenic voices are more strongly represented in the New Testament canon, but does that mean that they were then in fact more frequent, or that works containing such tones were easier to live with as the early church sought to establish itself and consolidate its position in the following centuries?

Postscript

> These things happened to them to serve as an example, and they were written down to instruct us ... (1 Cor 10.11, NRSV)

A critical study of the history of the earliest church serves to banish the ideas of a perfect and ideal primal time of the church and of an original perfect unity in doctrine and practice.[1] We cannot simply read off from this story a blueprint for our doctrine and practice today, for the New Testament documents bear witness to differences in doctrine and practice, and by no means insignificant or minor differences at that. Yet, just as the Old Testament stories to which Paul had just referred in the text from 1 Cor 10 quoted above were anything but examples to imitate, but were rather examples to avoid imitating, so too an all-too-human story of a divided church may come to us, not only as something of a relief, but also as a warning of the dangers and pitfalls that beset any community that seeks to be true disciples of Jesus here on earth. It is not just that the story of the first Christians displays a variety of interpretations of this following and not just that our situation today is different; perfection is not to be expected or found in any of the varied forms of early Christian life and belief.

For, if the story of the earliest church can be described as part and parcel of Christianity's 'foundation myth',[2] then this 'myth' illustrates not only moral patterns to follow, but also ones to avoid. Just as Israel's myth of human beginnings in Genesis included not only a good creation and an initially blissful relationship between humanity, God and the world, but also the dislocation of the fall, so too this Christian 'myth' embraces both the positive and the negatives sides of this new beginning, and embraces them from the start, with no sequence of a paradisal ideal only later ruined by a fall. As Robert Wilken comments,[3] 'Luke' was 'too close to the apostles to be able to overlook the problems and shortcomings of the first churches'. That idealizing was to be the task of later hands, but already we can detect a movement in that direction in 'Luke's' work, as we have seen on a number of occasions.

Similarly the variety of forms of early Christianity may find their echo in some of the even more varied forms of that faith which exist today. Recognition of that should not spawn complacency, however, as if differences were unimportant and all forms of the Christian faith, or at least all those bearing some resemblance to New Testament forms, were equally valuable and valid. Rather, the variety of options should provoke us to ask questions like: Which of these forms was most true to its origins? Why did these manifestations of the Christian faith diverge from one another? Did some factor or another lead this or that line of development astray and cause it to lose sight of its roots and its goal? In other words, the various traditions and options for faith in Jesus, then and now, need to be evaluated critically, and in that the study of the history of earliest Christianity may help us to see more clearly how and why the various paths taken by Christian faith diverged and in some cases came together again. To that extent the subject-matter of this work should not be regarded as of purely antiquarian interest, but both salutary and essential information for all those seeking to respond today to that same call to discipleship which those first Christians answered in their diverse ways.

Notes

Chapter 1

1. The first task being 'to select a noble subject which will please [the] readers', the third the decisions which events to include and which to omit (also an old problem!), followed by the distribution and arrangement of the material.
2. *Urchristentum*, 11.
3. *Geschichte*, 5 *et passim*. He deals with the whole period of the 'apostolic writings', although this designation may be almost as misleading as references to an 'apostolic age' (see below). For Fischer, *Urchristentum*, 38, the period of 'Urchristentum' ends with the appearance of a clearer form of the church, by which he evidently means those phenomena often lumped together as manifestations of 'early catholicism' (see ch. 9, pp. 175–7). Theißen, *Theory*, 251, goes further and regards the period of 'Urchristentum' as ending only with the formation of the canon! Goppelt, too, although he concentrates upon the 'apostolic age', includes in his treatment of the 'close of the apostolic period' the time up to the end of the second Jewish revolt under Bar Kokhba, i.e. 135 (*Times*).
4. *Geschichte*, 7; cf. also Fischer, *Urchristentum*, 45.
5. As with the title of Conzelmann's work.
6. *Geschichte* 13: in his opinion such expressions assume the idea of a pure, uncorrupted beginning in contrast to which later developments appear as degenerate (similarly Conzelmann, *Geschichte*, 7); see also the monograph of S. Alkier, *'Urchristentum'*, who instead suggests 'early Christianity' ('Frühchristentum', 265).
7. Caird, *Age*; Goppelt, *Times*, who refers (p. 1) to Euseb. *Hist. eccl.* 3.31.6. Schneemelcher, *Urchristentum* 7, criticizes talk of an 'apostolic age' as 'too much tied up with a particular concept of the unity of the church in the first century'. Curiously, Vouga seems to envisage an 'apostolic age' stretching into the middle of the second century, in that it is the period in which the New Testament writings, the most of them, but not all, ascribed to apostles, came into being (esp. *Geschichte* 5); he recognizes the problem, however, that in the same period many documents were written which regard themselves as post-apostolic (from 1 Clement and the letters of Ignatius on).
8. Cf., e.g. Stowers, *Rereading*, 24–5.
9. Galilee is omitted from the programmatic Acts 1.8. Is that because, in the author's view, the message has already been made known there during Jesus' ministry there?
10. Schneemelcher's sober assessment is correct (*Urchristentum*, 85): 'The earliest

history of Christianity is inconceivable without Galilee. But in the light of the sources one can say no more than that.' Cf. J. T. Sanders, *Schismatics*, 39, 77 (but n.b. also 81). G. W. Clarke is correct in stating that hard evidence for Christians in Palestine (apart from Jerusalem) is chiefly limited to coastal cities (and villages in Samaria: Acts 8.25): 'Origins', 853. Such restraint is the more noteworthy in the light of the readiness of many to trace a history of a Q-community and to use the *Logienquelle* as a source for the various phases of this Galilean Christianity. That readiness has provoked scepticism, e.g. on the part of Hengel, *Gospels*, 172. If Tuckett is correct to leave the time span of Q as broad as the period *c.* 40–70 and its location merely as 'Galilee/Syria' (*Q*, 102–3), then the degree of historical precision that is possible is very limited; even a modest consensus on the various stages leading to the formation of Q (so Schnelle, *Einleitung*, 202–5) hardly arouses confidence, and Tuckett also adds the methodological consideration that whoever produced Q intended not only to represent the views of his or her community but also to challenge or change them (*Q*, 82, following Malherbe, *Aspects*, 13). In that case the views represented in Q may not be typical of the community or communities lying behind them, and the same applies to some extent to the canonical Gospels too (cf. the caution of R. E. Brown, *Community*, 17–20, here – even if he then goes on to offer a detailed reconstruction of the history of the Johannine community!).

11. On Theißen's use of the principle of a 'Präventivzensur' see the criticism of Schmeller, *Brechungen*, 63–6.
12. Becker's caution is here warranted: he asks, for instance, if one can really assign the sayings in source Q, Matthew, the Didache, James as well as Mark and John and the letters of Ignatius all to Syria (he does not mention here all the apocryphal writings which have also been assigned to this area) and Ephesians, Colossians, 1 Peter and Revelation to Asia Minor; if so, then it is at the price of having to accommodate very different theologies within one and the same area (*Urchristentum*, 17 with n. 17). That in itself would not be an insurmountable problem, as we shall see. More serious is the slender evidence, if any, upon which many of these decisions are made, particularly in the case of the writings assigned to Syria; the case for a connection with Asia Minor is clearer.
13. The Jewish floggings are not mentioned in Acts, perhaps because they would contradict the picture of a very Jewish Paul which that work paints, and only one Roman scourging – in 16.22–3.
14. Col 2.1 and 4.13, 15 also presuppose the existence of a church in Laodicea, but do not tell how it was established; one in Hierapolis is also mentioned in 4.13. Perhaps, like the church in Colossae, they arose as a result of the work of Epaphras (1.7).
15. Markschies, *Zwischen den Welten*, 22.
16. Cf. Wedderburn, *Baptism*, 70–1 and n. 10.
17. Cf. Schnelle, *Einleitung*, 86–8, and the relevant sections on the various letters in Broer, *Einleitung* 2.
18. Cf. Aland, 'Entstehung'.
19. This travelling companion was identified as that Luke who is mentioned in Col

4.14; 2 Tim 4.11 and Philemon 24. The 'we'-passages, apart from a variant reading in Acts 11.28, are 16.10–17; 20.5–15; 21.1–18 and 27.1–28.16. The immediate impression given is, accordingly, that the narrator was present with Paul during certain parts of his travels but not during others. For a discussion of the problems associated with this striking stylistic feature cf. Wedderburn, '"We"-Passages'.

20. The classic statement of the differences between Paul's own theology and that which is attributed to Paul in Acts (rather than the theology of the author himself, which could more easily be accounted for by asserting the theological independence of the author) is to be found in Vielhauer, '"Paulinism"'. Someone associated with Paul might well have his own theology, but he is less likely to have been so unable to perceive the distinctive emphases of Paul's own theology and so able to misrepresent and misunderstand the apostle. Hengel ('Der Jude Paulus', 345) makes light of this problem, but, accepting his analogy of the 'metamorphoses' undergone by some modern theologians, it is one thing to say that former students, for example, of Bultmann have developed their own positions, often critical of their former teacher, another to accuse them of seriously failing to understand their teacher's position.
21. Interestingly, M. Y. MacDonald suggests that the Pastorals too were written by a fellow-worker of a fellow-worker of Paul (*Churches*, 204).
22. Eusebius of Caesarea, in his *Hist. eccl.* 2.22.6, cites 2 Tim 4.11, and asserts that Luke was with Paul at his second defence, but not at his first, for then 'no one stood up for me; all left me in the lurch' (2 Tim 4.16). Eusebius accordingly argues that Luke probably continued his account for as long as he was with Paul, but the cessation of the 'we' might point to his having parted from Paul even before that. Eusebius' account also raises the question why Luke did not then resume his account again to cover Paul's second defence.
23. He is referred to here in the masculine, not out of male prejudice, but in keeping with the gender of the participle in Luke 1.3.
24. Cf. Pervo, *Profit*.
25. Cf. Wedderburn, 'Gattung', 310–12.
26. Thornton, *Zeuge*, esp. 351–6, provides a telling series of references to Cicero and others which show how much artistic licence could be allowed to a historian in those days, without it being felt that in exercising it he had ceased to be a historian. But cf. Witherington, *Acts*, 26: Cicero asked Lucceius to make an exception to the usual rules in writing a life of Cicero. And the strictures of some historians against such licence may just as well mean that others saw their task differently. And Cicero also praises L. Coelius Antipater as not only a *narrator* but also an *exornator rerum* (*De or.* 2.12.54). What such an adornment might involve in a rhetorical context can be seen in Quint. 8.3.70: 'And we shall secure the vividness we seek, if only our descriptions give the impression of truth, nay, we may even add fictitious incidents of the type which commonly occur.' Others, too, even if not expressly condoning inaccuracy, mention the historian's need to provide the reader with pleasure (cf. 2 Macc 15.39; Polyb. 1.4.11; Dion. Hal. *Ant. Rom.* 1.8.3; Herodian 1.1.3).
27. For some the word 'sources' will suggest written documents, often of some length. About their existence one may in this case have considerable doubts,

but on the other hand there is some evidence that the writer of Acts had at his disposal more than just a mass of isolated bits of information: one instance is the way in which the scattering of the Stephen group is interrupted after 8.4, only to resume in 11.19, after Peter has inaugurated the gentile mission. It seems fairly clear that 11.19–20 draws on traditional material: the presence of Cypriots anticipates Barnabas and Paul's mission on that island in chapter 13. See also ch. 4, pp. 71–5 below.

Mostly it has been assumed that Acts' sources did not include any of Paul's letters, but this has been challenged by Leppä, *Use*, who argues that 'Luke' knew Galatians and probably other letters; the corollary of this – and the cumulative weight of the linguistic evidence which Leppä cites is considerable – is that 'Luke's' use of this source is highly tendentious and critical of Paul's self-portrayal because it conflicted with his 'ideal picture of the first generation Christians' (184).

28. Among many examples is the account of the conference in ch. 15, which begins with the question of circumcision and observance of the Jewish law (15.1, 5), yet never seems to answer that question precisely or explicitly.
29. On the sources which may, for example, lie behind Acts' account of Pentecost cf. Wedderburn, 'Traditions'.
30. Josephus *BJ* 2.118, 433; 7.253; *AJ* 18.4–8; 20.97–8.
31. Cf. on the one hand Bruce, *Acts*, 147; Witherington, *Acts*, 239; on the other Haenchen, *Apg*, 251.

Chapter 2

1. For example: more than a third of Kraft's *Entstehung* is taken up with accounts of Jesus and John the Baptist.
2. So Theißen–Merz, *Jesus*, esp. 29; Theißen–Winter, *Kriterienfrage*, *passim*. But it also plays, for instance, an important role in much of the argument of E. P. Sanders' *Jesus and Judaism*: e.g. 18, 174, 246 (cf. also Kümmel, *Theologie*, 24). A concrete example would be Jesus' attitude to the Jewish law: were it fully unambiguous, it would be more difficult to explain how Christians were later so divided over the question whether it was still binding on them or not.
3. The danger of this divorce is clear in Bultmann's oft-quoted dictum that after the resurrection 'the proclaimer [Jesus] became the proclaimed' (*Theology* 1, 33), at least if one were to infer from that that the content of the proclaimer's proclamation was of no particular relevance for the way in which he was subsequently proclaimed; Jesus' message is then a presupposition of New Testament theology, not part of it (3). It is, accordingly, no surprise that Bultmann's pupil, Hans Conzelmann, begins his history of earliest Christianity with the words: 'Jesus' life and teaching are the presupposition of church history. ... The history of the church begins after Jesus' death' (*Geschichte*, 1). And yet are not 'presuppositions' part of the whole picture which the historian seeks to recover? (Cf. also H.-F. Weiß in his 'Nachwort' to Fischer, *Urchristentum*, 186–7.)
4. For the same reason I have refrained from giving an outline of the history of those times, such as the account of early Judaism which forms the first chapter of

Hyldahl's *History*. For information on that history the reader is referred to such standard reference works as *The Oxford Classical Dictionary*, *Der Neue Pauly* and *Der Kleine Pauly*, as well as to briefer accounts of the history of the period like Goodman's *The Roman World*, Walbank's *The Hellenistic World* or C. Wells' *The Roman Empire* and, for the history of the Jews in this period, the revised Schürer, *History*.

5. For a more than somewhat agnostic view of the evidence for the nature of the resurrection and its implications for Christian faith, see Wedderburn, *Beyond Resurrection*.
6. Berger, *Auferstehung*; Pesch, 'Entstehung' (cf. Wedderburn, *Beyond Resurrection*, 39–40). It is perhaps significant that U. B. Müller, *Entstehung*, who presents a revised version of this explanation, dependent less on later texts, feels the need also to invoke visionary experiences, stemming from reflection upon Jesus' death in the light of the Old Testament Scriptures and their promises.
7. Mark 8.31; 9.31; 10.33; Matthew, and sometimes Luke, prefer 'on the third day', presumably to fit better into the chronology of Jesus' passion, despite Matthew's appeal to Jonah's 'three days and three nights' in the sea monster (12.40).
8. Only in the Fourth Gospel does the sight of the empty tomb itself seem to be sufficient to evoke faith, at least in the Beloved Disciple: 20.8.
9. Gal 1.16.
10. Cf. Lüdemann, *Auferstehung*, 106–12, but also Wedderburn, *Beyond Resurrection*, 75–7.
11. Esp. in Luke 24.16. See also the later, secondary ending of Mark (16.12) where an appearance, probably that of Luke 24.13–16, takes place 'in a different form'.
12. Cf. Wedderburn, *Beyond Resurrection*, esp. 129–35.
13. 'Come, let us return to the Lord; for it is he who has torn, and he will heal us; he has struck down, and he will bind us up. After two days he will revive us, on the third day he will raise us up, that we may live before him' (NRSV). Yet this passage is not quoted in the New Testament, and there are at least two obstacles to its being applied to Jesus' resurrection, the first person *plural* and the reference to returning to the Lord.
14. In particular Matt 28.16–20; John 21, and it can be argued that Mark 14.28 and 16.7 presuppose this.
15. Here the question arises whether a proper burial, such as is recorded in the Gospels, is likely to have been granted to a condemned criminal. And yet this proper burial in his own tomb is a necessary presupposition for the tradition of the discovery shortly afterwards that the tomb was empty.
16. Gal 1.17–19. Whether Paul did not meet the other apostles on this occasion because they were away from Jerusalem at the time, perhaps evangelizing in other places, or because he had to remain as inconspicuous as possible because of the danger to him, is uncertain.
17. In fact only two candidates are mentioned who are considered suitable (Acts 1.23); does that mean that they were the only ones who could be found, or are other, unmentioned criteria supposed to have come into play which narrowed down the field of choice?

18. Cf. Schneider, *Apg*, 219, 225. It is perhaps also a criterion which Luke has inserted into an earlier tradition, to judge from the tortured syntax of Acts 1.21–2 (e.g. the use of an aorist of the same verb, *synerchomai*, which was used in v. 6 in the sense of 'gathered', but which now occurs in the sense of a continuous action of 'accompanying').
19. E.g. Conzelmann, *Geschichte*, 27; Fischer, *Urchristentum*, 48; Klein, *Apostel*, 34–8; Schmithals, *Office*, 68–71; Schneemelcher, *Urchristentum*, 61. That 1 Cor 15.5 refers to an appearance to the Twelve is a slender piece of evidence for this view and may simply be a loose formulation, because 'the Twelve' were an established institution (so Kraft, *Entstehung*, 210); Matthias had presumably seen the risen Jesus and had thereby qualified to be one of the reconstituted Twelve. For the tradition it was more important that all had seen the risen Jesus than that they had all seen him together.

    This theory is to be distinguished from the far less contentious suggestion that in the re-formation of the group of Jesus' disciples Peter played a decisive role (cf., e.g. Kraft, *Entstehung*, 209, citing Luke 22.32; John 21.15–17; Matt 16.18 as indirect witnesses to this role).
20. Schmithals, *Office*, 70 n. 58; *Theologiegeschichte*, 26 (cf. Klein, *Apostel*, 36 n. 140). That one of the Twelve had betrayed Jesus was something that caused too many theological problems to be plausibly explained as a later invention: had Jesus chosen him knowing the role which he was to play?
21. S. G. Wilson, *Gentiles*, 109 n. 2, calls it 'fantastic'.
22. Something of that dilemma is reflected in Mark 14.21, at least the tension between the necessity of God's will on the one hand and yet the culpability of the one who played this part in bringing that will to pass on the other.
23. The order and the contents of the lists are as follows:

Mark 3.16–19	**Matt 10.2–4**	**Luke 6.14–16**	**Acts 1.13**
*Simon Peter: 1	1	1	1
*James, son of Zebedee: 2	3	3	3
*John, son of Zebedee: 3	4	4	2
*Andrew: 4	2	2	4
Philip: 5	5	5	5
Bartholomew: 6	6	6	7
*Matthew: 7	8	7	8
Thomas: 8	7	8	6
James, son of Alphaeus: 9	9	9	9
*Thaddaeus: 10	10	–	–
*Simon the Cananaean: 11	11	S. the zealot: 10	S. the zealot: 10
*Judas Iscariot: 12	12	12	[vacancy to be filled]
		Judas, son of James: 11	Judus, son of James: 11

* Also in the Gospel of the Ebionites §4 (Schneemelcher 1, 141)/2 (Elliott, 14).

24. Cf., e.g. Roloff, *Kirche*, 77.
25. The role of the disciples as future judges is one example of what Theißen refers to as a 'Messianic collective' ('Gruppenmessianismus'), i.e. a passage where an

activity normally associated with the Messiah as an individual figure is instead attributed to a group of disciples, in this case the group of the Twelve.

26. Campbell, 'Elders', 317–18, dismisses as 'dogmatic speculation' the view that James needed no replacement, but his contention that 'Luke' would have 'taken it for granted that James was replaced' seems even more speculative. Problematic, too, is Campbell's contention that the Twelve, who continued to be twelve in number, then came to be known as the elders, and then only later, as in Acts, as the apostles; against that is the evidence of Acts, that the apostles and the elders seem to be two separate bodies (15.2, 4, 6, 22–3; 16.4), and a distinction between the twelve phylarchs of Israel and the elders is suggested not only by the group of seventy associated with the latter (e.g. Exod 24.1; Num 11.16), but also by a text like Deut 29.10 which Campbell cites as evidence to the contrary. Nor would it be unparalleled if 'the elders' were a subordinate group, since those in Israel are clearly subordinate to Moses at least.
27. The use of lots was presumably a means of ascertaining God's will in the matter. Such a means was used in 67 CE, instead of the prevailing hereditary principle, to choose a new high priest, as Josephus, coming from a priestly and aristocratic family, indignantly narrates (*BJ* 4.153–5; cf. also 1QS (2.23; 6.16, 22)).
28. There, too, the connection with the twelve tribes is presupposed: cf. 21.12.
29. Cf. Acts 1.8, 22, etc., with 22.15; 26.16.
30. Cf., e.g. Barrett, *Acts* 1, 671–2; Berger, *Theologiegeschichte*, 182; Pesch, *Apg* 2, 52; Witherington, *Acts*, 419–20, 437. Although this is a common solution, Clark, 'Role', has recently attempted to argue that 'Luke' has deliberately applied the term to these two to put them on a comparable footing with the Twelve; it is then strange that he does so only here and then reverts in 15.2, 6 to a usage which distinguishes them from 'the apostles'.

    Such a use of *apostolos* in the sense of the delegate or emissary of a church is also found in Paul's letters where he talks of *apostoloi* of the churches or a church (2 Cor 8.23; Phil 2.25). In this usage, as in the use of the term for an apostle of Christ, it is probably correct to see an adaptation of the Jewish concept of a *shaliach*, the authorized emissary of a person or persons (e.g. Roloff in *TRE* 3, 342); naturally, then, the status of the sender and the purpose and the content of the commission make a considerable difference to the status of the emissary.
31. E.g. Dupont, 'La nouvelle Pentecôte', 195; Lüdemann, *Early Christianity*, 38. Cf. throughout this section Wedderburn, 'Traditions', esp. 29–39.
32. The association of Pentecost with the covenant is to be found in some early Jewish documents (esp. Jubilees) and at Qumran (e.g. in 4Q270 frag. 11 col. 1 ll. 17–18: '[The sons of Levi and the men of the camps will meet in] the third month and will cu[rse whoever tends to the right or the left of the law . . .]' (tr. Martinez). But cf. Klauck, *Magic*, 8.
33. So, along with an earthquake, in 1 Kings 19.11–12.
34. *Decal.* 33, 35, 37, 46–7; n.b. also the universality implicit in *Spec. leg.* 2.189. See Wedderburn, 'Traditions', 36–8.
35. The problem of reconciling this dating of the church's endowment with the Spirit with John 20.22 is obvious.

36. Cf., e.g. Gilmour, 'Christophany'; Jeremias, *Theology*, 308; Kraft, *Entstehung*, 211–12 (tentatively: Lüdemann, *Early Christianity*, 43).
37. Notably Horn, *Angeld*, e.g. 160.
38. Cf. Grappe, *Temple*, 51. (See also Acts 1.6 for this expectation at a slightly earlier point of time.)
39. Weiser, *Apg* 1, 79; Jervell, *Apg*, 138.
40. E.g. REB 'staying' – 'inhabitants' (cf. Fitzmyer, *Acts*, 231: 'sojourning' – 'inhabitants').
41. In addition, the variations in the text in v. 5 may suggest that, very early on, the reference to 'Jews' was added to a tradition which originally had spoken simply of pious visitors to Jerusalem (see further Wedderburn, 'Traditions', 39–44). This change may well go back to 'Luke', since there could be no question, in his scheme of things, of non-Jews being admitted to the church so early; that had to wait until chapter 10.
42. Haenchen, *Acts*, 233, following Dibelius, 'Stilkritisches', 16.
43. So Haenchen, *Acts*, 233. It is only 4.34 which is problematic here, for Mary's keeping her house and putting it at the church's disposal is quite compatible with the rather different principle of having all things in common (2.44).
44. E.g. Plato *Resp.* 4.424A; 5.449C; Arist. *Eth. Nic.* 8.9.1 (1159b31).
45. Above all in 2.42–7: the breaking of bread in vv. 42, 46 and perhaps to some extent the sharing of goods (44–5) if that is at least part of the fellowship (*koinōnia*) referred to in v. 42. Striking, too, is the repetition of the verb *kartereō*, translated 'devoted themselves to' in 42 and 'spending much time' in 46 (NRSV). These different senses of a not particularly common word perhaps speak for the editing of traditional material which suggested the use of this word to 'Luke', who then uses it himself with a somewhat different meaning.
46. Unquestionably the account which Philo offers in his *On the Contemplative Life* of the Jewish group of the Therapeutae by Lake Mareotis in Egypt contains many idealistic features, but few would doubt that such a group existed and that certain features of the account have a kernel of truth in them (cf. C. Burchard in *KlP* 5.737).
47. Cf., e.g. Esler, *Community*, 71–109. Particularly to be noted is their prominence in 10.40–1: Jesus' eating with his disciples after his resurrection receives special mention in this short summary of his life.
48. So, rightly, Schneemelcher, *Urchristentum*, 86, and many others.
49. See n. 41 above.
50. That would be even more the case if the group of the Twelve, with all its symbolism, had in fact only been formed after Easter, but even if it existed before Easter, as seems more likely (see above ch. 2, pp. 22–3), its continuance after Easter, indicated by the filling of the gap left by Judas Iscariot, would suggest that this perspective remained in force.
51. E.g. Sanders, *Jesus*, 61–90.
52. Cf. Bauckham, 'Jesus' Demonstration'; C. A. Evans, 'Jesus' Action'; Gnilka, *Jesus*, 279.
53. *Temple*, esp. 88–115. Bauckham, 'Parting', points out that the early Christians also differed from the Qumran community in that the latter expected a new temple to be built in the end-time; the early Christians may have believed the

present temple to be doomed but continued to worship there. Yet does that not raise the question how soon the idea of the Christian community as the new Temple of God arose and how widespread it was? (Although Bauckham argues that this was the view of the early Jerusalem community (p. 143), the texts he cites do not stem directly from this community and it may be significant that it is first attested in Paul, a Diaspora Jew. After all, the parallel in Qumran arose in a Jewish community which had also distanced itself from Jerusalem and its temple cult.)

54. Yet, as Bauckham rightly notes ('Parting', 150 n. 37), much of the sacrificial cult was not concerned with atonement and would not be affected by the rise of the theologumenon of Jesus' death as atoning.
55. Cf. Walter, 'Nikolaos', 206.
56. Grappe, *Temple*, 58, notes that this offence is prominent among those condemned in 1QS (6.24–5); there the penalty is less drastic: exclusion for a year and the loss of a quarter of one's food rations.
57. *Omn. prob.* 76, 85–6. If Philo is correct in supposing that pay (*misthos*, §86) was involved, then that would suggest that these villages were not purely Essene villages, but ones in which Essenes lived as a community within a non-Essene community.
58. *Hypothetica* 11.1; cf. Josephus *BJ* 2.124–5. Grappe, *Temple*, 52–66, finds an important undergirding of his suggestive thesis of widespread Essene influence on early Christianity in the probable existence of an Essene quarter in Jerusalem, near the gate known as that of the Essenes and near, too, to the probable base of the early Christian community on Mount Zion. Cf. also Capper, 'Context', esp. 341–50; Riesner, 'Essenerviertel'.
59. Hengel, *Property*, 32–4; cf. Kraft, *Entstehung*, 223.
60. Cf. j.Taan. 4.5.X.H (Neusner, 18.275).
61. Cf. e.g. Schnelle, 'Taufe', 666. That Jesus submitted to John's baptism is a fact which can hardly be disputed, for this tradition created too many theological problems to be a later invention: it seemed to imply both Jesus' subordination to John (cf. Matt 3.14) and his need for forgiveness of his sins (cf. EvNaz 2 [Schneemelcher]/11 [Elliott]).
62. This tradition is accepted as reliable by, e.g. Becker, *Jesus*, 62; Nodet–Taylor, *Origins*, 78; Rowland, *Origins*, 153, 238.
63. Cf. Meier, *Jew* 2, 122, who sees in the redactional qualification an example of what he calls 'the criterion of embarrassment': the Synoptic tradition was so embarrassed by the tradition of Jesus' baptizing that it omitted it altogether.
64. 'Eschatological' in the sense that an outpouring of the Spirit was expected as a feature of the end-time (cf. Wedderburn, *Baptism*, 268–74).
65. Behind them may lie a prediction of God's baptism with wind (also *ruach*, *pneuma*) and fire, as a symbol of judgement (cf. also Luke 3.17 par.; for God's judgement compared to threshing cf. Isa 27.12; Jer 13.24; 15.7).
66. Particularly in the reference to 'all flesh' in v. 17.
67. Cf. Trocmé, *Childhood*, viii, who maintains that the separation was always initiated by the Jews; but cf. Chapter 11 below.
68. Wander also, just as appropriately, uses the plural 'Trennungsprozesse'.
69. *Schismatics*, 99–151. The use of the term 'model' has been criticized and

rejected by Horrell, *Ethos*, esp. 11–18, but it can be defended in the sense of an observable pattern of social behaviour whose occurrence in other contexts, even when in other respects very different ones, can serve a useful heuristic purpose in the present instance, particularly when the pattern of reaction has, as in this case, a plausible rationale.

70. Despite that, J. H. Elliott, for example, defends the appropriateness of speaking of a 'sect', at least with reference to a second phase of early Christianity, after a first phase in which 'faction' would be more fitting ('Phases').
71. See ch. 8 below.
72. Josephus *AJ* 19.293–6, 300–1, 331–4; m.Bik. 3.4; m.Sot. 7.8 (if the reference is to Agrippa I).
73. And yet, as Schwartz notes (*Agrippa I*, 122–3), the mode of execution suggests a political offence rather than a religious one, if the two can be separated, and 'Luke' has remained quiet about the cause of James's death; Schwartz suggests that James had been prominent in causing a disturbance. The most likely cause of a disturbance was, however, essentially a religious one, associated with the preaching of Jesus.

    Answers to the question how Peter came to be released must remain thoroughly speculative, but Lüdemann revives the suggestion of F. C. Baur that Agrippa found that his execution of James proved unpopular and had Peter released (*Early Christianity*, 145).
74. Cf. Acts 12.21–3; Josephus *AJ* 19.343–50; and also, earlier in his reign, 19.335–7 – hardly the actions of a pious Jew.
75. See Chapter 11 below.
76. But Sanders, *Schismatics*, 140, argues that after 70 CE the 'gentilizing' of Christianity was no longer the main problem; rather those enforcing the boundaries of Judaism had to have 'criminals' to punish in order to strengthen their boundaries; however, their 'crime' lay above all in their tendency to ignore and to transcend those boundaries.
77. Goodman, *Roman World*, 325, maintains that it was the Christians who were the prime movers in the break, but self-identity ('self-definition' was in his eyes their motive for this) was at this point of time a problem, not only for the Christians, but also for the non-Christian Jewish community.

Chapter 3

1. It does not correspond, at any rate, to the formal requirements for a dignified and orderly execution by stoning laid down in the Mishnah tractate *Sanhedrin* (cf. the excerpt in Barrett, §209); for instance, in the Mishnah the clothes of the one to be executed are removed, whereas here it is the ones doing the stoning who remove their clothes – rather like bowlers in a game of cricket handing their sweaters to one of the umpires. But a formal trial provides the opportunity for a formal speech of the accused in his defence, a lynching does not.
2. Cf. Cadbury, 'Hellenists'. In 11.19–20 we read that some of the Christians scattered after the martyrdom of Stephen came to Phoenicia, Cyprus and

Antioch, where some of them, who came from Cyprus and Cyrene, also preached to the *Hellēnas* or *Hellēnistas*. It is difficult to decide which reading is correct. Since the gospel has already been preached to Greek-speaking Jews, and indeed to proselytes too (Acts 2.11; 6.5; 10.1–11.18), it seems that non-Jews are here meant, whichever reading is correct. But has a copyist changed the unusual *Hellēnistas* into the commoner *Hellēnas* or has he even noted that 'Hellenist', if used here, would have a different sense to that in the two previous passages in Acts? (Would that mean that Acts here follows a source which uses *Hellēnistai* in another sense, i.e. as a synonym to *Hellēnes*, compared with that found in the two earlier passages? Or must one postulate a further refinement in the definition of the former term, as Walter does: in 11.20 it refers to non-Jews of Palestinian–Syrian origin – 'Apostelgeschichte 6,1', 205 – or Greek-speaking Syrians who are not Greeks either – 'Diaspora-Juden', 385–6; but why not to Greeks as well?) Or has a copyist been influenced by the two references to 'Hellenists' in chs 6 and 9 and therefore altered the commoner *Hellēnas*? In that case, this is the only instance of the latter word which has been so altered (it occurs regularly from 14.1 on, first, however, as Wasserberg notes [*Aus Israels Mitte*, 54–7], of non-Jewish sympathizers within the synagogue in contrast to the 'gentiles/nations', and then, from 19.10 on, to designate the non-Jewish nations).

3. So, e.g. Schneider, 'Stephanus', 220: it is probable that Stephen's opponents also came from this group.
4. Hengel, 'Jesus', esp. 6–9; Hengel–Schwemer, *Paul*, 33; Schneider, 'Stephanus', 218.
5. Cf. Hengel, 'Jesus', 8.
6. The repetition of the definite article before the mention of the Jews from Cilicia and Asia may imply that they did not belong to this particular synagogue. Cf., e.g. RSV. Barrett, however, treats the Cyrenians and Alexandrians as in apposition to the freedmen (*Acts* 1, 318). 'Synagogue' is, at any rate, in the singular, which makes it hard to speak of up to five synagogues; but cf. Neudorfer, *Stephanuskreis*, 158–61.
7. The mention of this synagogue invites comparison with the Greek Theodotus inscription from Jerusalem (*CIJ* 1404), which commemorates this priest and leader of the synagogue, who had 'built a synagogue for the reading of the Law and the teaching of the commandments, and the guest-house and the rooms and the water supplies as an inn for those who have need when they come from abroad' (tr. Barrett, §53). The dates suggested for this inscription range widely, but arguments for a date after the fall of Jerusalem in 70 CE are not overwhelming, and the reference to Theodotus as a priest, while not a conclusive argument, would make better sense while the Temple was still functioning.
8. Rightly, C. C. Hill, *Hellenists*, 3, who also considers it possible that there were liberal 'Hebrews'; that is more than a possibility, as not only the example of Paul, but also the conduct of Peter before he was called to order by James's emissaries (Gal 2.12), show.
9. A point made succinctly by Schneemelcher, *Urchristentum*, 104, who warns against treating the 'Hellenists' as a homogeneous group. Cf. also Barrett,

'Acts', 21; C. C. Hill, *Hellenists*, esp. 193. Yet such generalizations are unfortunately to be found, as, for instance, in Schenke's *Urgemeinde*, where one time and again finds references to 'the Hellenists'.

On the other hand, Hill himself strays rather too far in the direction of a thorough scepticism, disputing whether one can find any trace of the distinctive theology of the Jerusalem Hellenists. But if it is the theology of Stephen and his group among the Jerusalem Hellenists which we are seeking, a good place to start answering this question would be the later theology of their former persecutor, Paul.

10. Cf., however, contemporary parallels as in Josephus *BJ* 2.124; the difference in that passage is that the aid is there offered to visiting Essenes, whereas here it seems to be a matter of meeting the needs of resident members of the community; in *BJ* 2.134, on the other hand, it may be a matter of aiding destitute neighbours; cf. also CD 14.12–16.
11. Roloff, *Apg*, 109, assumes that it was the poor-relief system of the *Jewish* community which neglected them. Similarly Walter sees the discrimination as arising within the general Jewish poor-relief because of the suspect theological stance of some Diaspora Jews with regard to the law and the Temple ('Apostelgeschichte 6,1', esp. 195–6, 206) – as if all Hellenist Jews thought alike; this discrimination would presumably also have affected non-Christian Hellenists, but then, as Walter sees (206), it would not have been a problem only for the Christian ones. At any rate, Acts would then be incorrect to represent the discontent as directed against fellow-Christians rather than the leaders of the Jewish community.
12. But cf. Jeremias, *Jerusalem*, 130–2. Capper, however, argues plausibly that Philo's account of Essene practice in *Hypothetica* 11.11, which refers to eating together daily, provides a closer analogy to the Acts account than Jeremias' later rabbinic references ('Context', 352).
13. Haenchen, 'Book', 264 (also *Acts*, 268); also Dunn, *Unity*, 268–75; *Partings*, 60–74; Trocmé, *Childhood*, 21.
14. A possibility suggested by Walter, 'Apostelgeschichte 6,1', 201.
15. Acts, at any rate, regards the actions of Barnabas there as characteristic.
16. It is also then unnecessary to postulate that 'Hellenist' widows were either disproportionately numerous or disadvantaged, in comparison with the 'Hebrew' community.
17. The etymology suggested by Grimm–Thayer s.v.
18. Cf. Pesch, *Apg* 1, 229.
19. Cf., e.g. Klauck, *Magic*, 13.
20. Although Acts does not use the word 'deacon' to describe the Seven, it is possible, indeed probable, that its readers were meant to see in the use of the cognate verb (*diakonein*) a foreshadowing of that office.
21. *Analyse*, 14. For Meeks, 'Breaking Away', 57, the 'Greeks' here are Diaspora Jews, but this finds little support among recent commentators.
22. *Philip*, 17, citing Josephus *BJ* 1.562; 2.421; 3.233 (there is little to suggest that this Philip fits these categories); *AJ* 14.249; 17.21, 30; *Vita* 46–61; 177–80, 407–9.
23. E.g. Euseb. *Hist. eccl.* 3.30.1 (= Clem. Al. *Strom.* 3.6.52.5); 31.3–4 (Polycrates

and Proclus); 39.9 (quoting Papias, who had apparently met Philip's daughters); 5.24.2 (Polycrates).

24. A similar problem presents itself in the accounts of Jesus' trial before the Sanhedrin: Mark 14.56 par.
25. That, at any rate, is the thoroughly plausible argument of Walter, 'Apostelgeschichte 6,1', 188.
26. Josephus *BJ* 6.301–5. Jer 26 (cf., e.g. Haacker, 'Stellung', 1528–9) may also be apt as an example of a comparable human reaction to such a speaking against the Temple, but not as a justification of the legitimacy of such a reaction, for Jeremiah was, after all, subsequently recognized and respected as a prophet.
27. Cf. Matt 26.59–61 and Mark 14.56–8 (but no parallel here in Luke; the same is true for Matt 26.61 and Mark 14.58; contrast Luke 23.34 with Acts 7.60 – Luke does not shun parallels between Jesus' death and Stephen's on principle). Jesus had also, according to the Gospels, acted violently in the Temple, which would have been enough to justify his execution in the eyes of Pilate, even if this action, surprisingly, plays no part in the accounts of Jesus' trial(s); no such accusation is levelled against Stephen.
28. E.g. Klein, 'Gesetz', 60: 'These events are only intelligible if one assumes that the "Hellenists" in essence declared the law to be abolished and thus questioned all the religious privileges of Israel.'
29. Cf., e.g. Becker, *Paul,* 64–5; Räisänen, '"Hellenisten"', 1498–9, 1501. Fredriksen, *From Jesus to Christ*, 166 (cf. 'Judaism', 553–5, 558), speaks of the Christian mission admitting or including gentiles from the beginning without requiring them to convert to Judaism; yet can one speak so sweepingly of 'the Christian mission' without distinguishing differing interpretations of the Christian message and its implications?
30. U. B. Müller distinguishes, rightly, between freedom with regard to the law and criticism of the law ('Rezeption', 158 n. 1a), even if his decisions with regard to what is freedom or criticism differ from those proposed here.

    Over against the position advocated here is Schmithals' contention (*Theologiegeschichte*, 112–13, 117, 124) that Paul was converted to a form of Christianity which had broken fully with the law, and then later, for a time and under the threat of persecution, agreed to a far less extreme form of the gospel which could be contained within the institution of the synagogue.
31. Rightly Räisänen, '"Hellenisten"', 1484, argues that it is unlikely that direct criticism of the law, let alone rejection of it, was the basis of the charges against Stephen, for it would be hard to explain how such a critique had arisen if Jesus' own attitude had not been such a negative one as is sometimes supposed. That argument is all the more compelling if one postulates only a very short time between Jesus' death and Stephen's (see further on Pauline chronology below and also Wedderburn, 'Paul and Jesus' 119–22).
32. Cf. Walter, 'Diaspora-Juden', esp. 399: Diaspora Jews who joined the Jesus-movement found in Jesus' openness towards those who had been religiously excluded something which tied in with their conviction of God's openness towards all nations.
33. A further example is Matt 8.5–13 parr.
34. Hahn, *Mission*, 39, 51: 'As Jesus received Gentiles because the Kingdom of

God had drawn near, so Peter accepted non-Jews on the ground of their faith.' Fischer, *Urchristentum*, is more cautious: a mission to gentiles is implicit in Jesus' message, in that the sole condition of salvation is an awareness of one's guilt and need for forgiveness (52).

35. Cf. Jeremias, *Jerusalem*, 5–6, 303–12.
36. In the healing and exorcistic ministry of Philip (Acts 8.7) we can without difficulty see a continuation of this aspect of Jesus' work (cf. v. Dobbeler, *Philippus*, 69–86).
37. *Paul*, 75; cf. also Fredriksen's distinction between receiving and encouraging converts and actively soliciting them: 'Judaism', 538 – Jews only did the former.
38. With regard to the Twelve and the Seven Reinbold's caution may well be justified (*Propaganda*, esp. 43–79, 242–52): a strategy of active mission may perhaps be first detected in the case of Peter (alone amongst the Twelve?) after the Jerusalem conference (although Reinbold denies that his apostolic task involved active mission) and in the case of Philip (alone amongst the Seven?) after Stephen's death (although, again, it remains possible that Philip's activity in Samaria had already begun before that: see below, ch. 4, pp. 72–3). Far more often it was a matter of Christians giving testimony wherever they happened to be (for other reasons) and to whomsoever wanted to hear it, and of Christian leaders visiting Christian individuals or groups to consolidate what already existed.
39. So Räisänen, '"Hellenisten"', 1485, speaks of the beginnings of a life shared with gentiles; yet on p. 1500 he speaks of a mission. But instead of an active 'mission' one should rather speak of a more passive receptivity, and that would be true of the majority of other religious movements at that time: they may have engaged in propaganda of various sorts, through literature or public festivals or making known by means of inscriptions or the like the blessings which they offered, but it is mostly to philosophical movements that we must turn for the nearest parallels to early Christian public preaching and attempts to win over their fellows. (For it is integral to an adequate description of early Christian mission that the early Christians not only made the content of their faith known, but also sought to persuade their fellows to commit themselves to this faith; it was, in other words, a matter of active proselytizing.) Nock's assessment of the religion of an earlier age still held good – a 'picture of piety without conflict and without missionary zeal' (*Conversion*, 21; on the efforts of certain philosophical movements to win converts see ch. 11). In the case of early Christianity, which did not engage in public processions or the like, we must assume an even lower public profile than in the case of Judaism, whose adherents were at least far more numerous, and which in its homeland had certainly a very public profile, even if, despite the impression given by Matt 23.15, it did not engage in missionary outreach either. (That text, Goodman, *Mission*, 70, argues, following Munck, *Paul*, 267, refers to the winning over of other Jews to Pharisaism; a proselytizing mission such as that practised by the early Christians was in his eyes [105] a novelty in the ancient world. That is to take up an interpretation of the verse already suggested by J. Basnage in 1716: see Riesner, 'Mission', 213, who documents the movement in some more recent

scholarship away from the assumption of active Jewish proselytizing; he, too, is unwilling to speak of an intentional activity on their part to gain proselytes. Cf. also Levinskaya, *Book of Acts*, 36–9.) That, at any rate, means that early Christianity was more than usually dependent on personal contacts and it is likely that these came in large measure through the Jewish synagogues with their non-Jewish sympathizers and adherents.

40. Cf., e.g. Esler, *Community*, esp. 73–86.
41. E.g. Holtz, 'Bedeutung', 135–9.
42. But cf. Kraus, *Jerusalem*, 91.
43. *Schismatics*, 8.
44. *Migr. Abr.* 89 (cf. Barrett, §225).
45. But cf. Schenke, *Urgemeinde*, 60; Räisänen, '"Hellenists"', esp. 300. Here it must be asked whether Diaspora Jews who held such views were so likely to be drawn to leave their homes in the Diaspora and settle in Jerusalem.
46. Räisänen, '"Hellenisten"', 1491, 1506, rightly doubts whether such a theology would have arisen so early, but see Kraus, *Jerusalem*, 53–4. (Cf. also ch. 2, n. 54 above.) Grappe, *Temple*, 68 n. 3, 195, uses 1 Cor 5.7 as evidence for such a theology, but, as he rightly recognizes, Diaspora Jews, of whom Paul was one, were used to doing without any regular participation in the Jerusalem cult, and it is therefore a very different matter to say that the earliest Christian community in Jerusalem itself already felt that they could dispense with it.
47. So Haacker, 'Stellung', 1528, argues for the authenticity of the Johannine version of the saying (John 2.19) without its Johannine interpretation, but what historically conceivable self-awareness is then reflected here if Jesus imagined that he could rebuild the Temple? Trocmé, *Childhood*, 21, proposes that Stephen and his companions regarded the Temple authorities as idolatrous, but how could such an idea arise so soon (by his admission within two years of Jesus' crucifixion)?
48. Nor, as noted above, Jesus' followers if they indeed made it their practice to worship in the Temple.
49. Cf. Epiph. *Adv. haeres.* 30.16.7 – combined with a denigration of Paul ('Ascents of James'); Ps.-Clem. *Hom.* 2.44.2; 3.52.1.
50. For this prohibition cf. *OGIS* 598, as in Barrett, §50. Theißen, 'Hellenisten', 340; *Theory*, 253, suggests that Stephen was stoned for proclaiming that the Temple would soon be opened up to gentiles, but it would be far more offensive to say that they already had a right to be there.
51. W. Stegemann, *Synagoge*, esp. 164, notes the similarity between the charge against Stephen and that brought against Paul.
52. Yet Räisänen, '"Hellenisten"', 1488, finds no trace of such a positive attitude to the Temple in Mark.
53. It was also apparently the case earlier in the disciplinary measures taken against the Christian leaders by the Jewish authorities in Jerusalem: Acts 4.1–3; 5.17–18.
54. But cf. Hyldahl, *History*, 175.
55. And yet Peter was in Jerusalem for the apostolic conference in Gal 2.1–10. Is this a reason for setting the conference *before* Agrippa's action (see Bunine, 'Paul';

Fischer, *Urchristentum*, 41; Hahn, *Mission*, 90–1; Suhl, *Paulus*, 62; 'Chronologie', 982)? Chronologically that is difficult (Bunine's attempt to treat *epeita dia dekatessarōn etōn* in Gal 2.1 as meaning 'then sometime in the course of the next fourteen years' is linguistically problematic, and Hahn's proposal is only theoretically possible by virtue of his dating the crucifixion of Jesus to 27 and Paul's conversion to 29 – Pratscher, *Herrenbruder*, 53, even prefers 28 for this). Further, would it mean that the James mentioned in Gal 2.9, and mentioned first of the three 'pillars', was the son of Zebedee, not the brother of Jesus, as most suppose? But then who is the James of 2.12? Or had Paul forgotten in 2.9 that he must be more specific, for two leading figures with this name could be meant at this point of time? (Pratscher, *Herrenbruder*, 51, lays weight on the supposition, based on Mark 8.38–9, that both sons of Zebedee died at the same time; but what motive would 'Luke' have for mentioning the death of the one but not the other?) It is, on the whole, more likely that the death of Agrippa in 44 CE and the restoration of direct Roman rule meant a certain lessening of the danger for Peter, even if a prolonged presence in Jerusalem would still have been unwise. After all, Paul was at the conference too, even if that city was also a place of danger for him.

56. So from F. C. Baur (*Paulus*, 46–8; *Christentum*, 43) on.
57. Cf. Hare, *Theme*, 3.
58. Cf. Räisänen, '"Hellenisten"', 1476, 1497.
59. It would seem to be more than a coincidence that they should have escaped because they all happened to be out of town at the critical moment, as Theißen suggests: 'Hellenisten', 328.
60. It is not enough to say, as C. C. Hill, *Hellenists*, 28–32, does, that non-Christian 'Hellenists' simply disciplined the Christian members of their community, for one then has to explain why the authorities of the Jewish communities to which the 'Hebrews' and the apostles belonged did not take similar action against them. That is hard to explain unless Stephen (and others) had said something which the apostles and their Christian group had not (yet) said. And if indeed there was an attempt to extend the persecution beyond Jerusalem, e.g. to Damascus, then the disciplinary measures are not just confined to one community in Jerusalem.
61. Rightly emphasized, e.g. by Schenke, *Urgemeinde*, 176, 185.
62. As Schneemelcher rightly observes (*Urchristentum*, 105), 'it is striking that the Jews apparently treated the two groups differently'.
63. But Dietzfelbinger, *Berufung*, e.g. 29–42, finds one reason for the persecution in what he calls 'the word of the cross' (which he sees – surely anachronistically – as already the basis of the freedom of the Hellenist Christians from the Jewish law). Schmithals' suggestion (*Theologiegeschichte*, 111) that this persecution consisted of informing the gentile authorities concerning those who no longer belonged to the synagogue but still did not sacrifice to or for Caesar seems anachronistic, and it is a scenario that may not play as important a role at a later point of time as some suppose.
64. *Jesus*, 154–7; 'Judaism', 532, 549, 555–6.
65. Fredriksen speaks of 'fairly subdued' Jewish anti-Christian activity in Jerusalem ('Judaism', 557)!

Chapter 4

1. It is uncertain what this last phrase means and how it fits into 'Luke's' programme. Is it fulfilled in Paul's arrival in Rome? (Conzelmann, *Acts*, 7, compares PsSol 8.15, where Pompey comes 'from the end of the earth' to Jerusalem, but that work is written from a Palestinian-Jewish perspective. Contrast Acts 1.19 where 'their language' betrays a very different viewpoint.) Or does it hint at Paul's journey to Spain, mentioned in Rom 15.28? Of that there is no other hint in Acts. Or is it simply a reference to world-mission and particularly to the gentiles? That would seem to be borne out by Paul's first speech in the work, where he cites Isa 49.6 in support of his role as missionary to the gentiles (Acts 13.47); there the same phrase is used as in 1.8 (cf. Hahn, *Mission*, 132).
2. See ch. 3, p. 46.
3. The geographical programme seemingly envisaged in Acts 1.8 proves too tidy in other ways as well: 8.4–25 seems to mark the advance of the gospel into Samaria, but after that Philip is found back in an area that seems to belong to Judaea rather than Samaria, on the road from Jerusalem to Gaza (8.26). Similarly, after Paul's conversion on the way to Damascus, Acts describes Peter's healing miracles in Lydda and Joppa, and the apostle then travels to the Roman administrative centre of the province of Judaea, Caesarea Maritima (Acts 9.32–10.24).
4. Cf. also 22.12; nothing suggests that this man has newly arrived in Damascus under suspicion of belonging to a group believed to be law-breakers.
5. The fourth-century source which we know as 'Ambrosiaster' states, plausibly, that the Roman church originally followed Jewish rites and observed the Jewish law (*Ad Romanos* 3 [2]).
6. Wilckens, *Röm* 1, 38.
7. So Haenchen, *Acts*, 314; Hahn, *Mission*, 133; Weiser, *Apg*, 253.
8. 'Do not let the eunuch say, "I am just a dry tree." For thus says the Lord: To the eunuchs who keep my sabbaths, who choose the things that please me, and hold fast my covenant, I will give ... a monument and a name ... an everlasting name that shall not be cut off' (NRSV). V. Dobbeler, *Philippus*, 39 (cf. 306), following O. Bauernfeind and G. Schneider, sees Isa 56 lying behind both episodes in Acts 8 and the 'programme' of this group, i.e. the Samaritans as the 'foreigner' of 56.3a (cf. Luke 17.18) and then the eunuch.
9. Matthews, *Philip*, 87–9, argues that Luke regarded him as a proselyte. But that would be no further advance, for, apart from 2.11, Acts mentions that one of the Seven is himself a proselyte (6.5).
10. Cf., e.g. Conzelmann, *Acts*, 67; v. Dobbeler, *Philippus*, 117–23 (although he confuses the picture by referring to a tradition 'common' to the 'Hellenists' and the Jerusalem church, which is reflected in both accounts: 122; cf. 182); Haenchen, *Acts*, 315; Kollmann, 'Philippus', 557, who treat the story of Philip and the Ethiopian as a parallel, and rival, tradition to that about Peter and Cornelius. And Acts 8.40 means that Philip had also seemingly already arrived in Caesarea Maritima before Peter's arrival there in 10.24; need Cornelius have sent his messengers so far afield?
11. Cullmann, *Circle*, 49, sees in the reference to the labours of 'others' in John 4.38

a testimony to the mission of Philip (and others of his group?) in this area.

12. Cf. Hengel, 'Luke', 124.
13. Cf. Kollmann, 'Philippus', 554, 564.
14. Cf. Metzger, *Commentary*, 355–6.
15. Sebaste was not the only Graeco-Roman foundation in Samaria: amongst the 'Hellenistic cities' listed in the second volume of Schürer, *History*, are also to be found the Samaritan cities of Apollonia, Caesarea Maritima and Joppa. Contrast the 'villages of the Samaritans' mentioned in Acts 8.25.
16. Klauck, *Magic*, 17, 21, points out that none of the other sources mentioning Simon say that he became a Christian. Was that because he was later too much associated with heresy for that to be palatable? On the other hand, Berger, 'Propaganda'; *Theologiegeschichte*, 159–62, followed by v. Dobbeler, *Philippus*, 63–4, argues that he was already a representative of a yet earlier Samaritan Christianity. But is that chronologically plausible and is it apt to pose the alternatives as 'Christian or pagan' in the case of a Samaritan? That the Samaritans could produce their own prophetic figures and at least would-be wonder-workers is shown by the incident mentioned in Josephus *AJ* 18.85–6.
17. So Klauck, *Magic*, 15; cf. Beyschlag, *Simon Magus*, 102–6, 121–3.
18. Tr. Foerster, *Gnosis* 1, 251–60; cf. the discussion in Beyschlag, *Simon Magus*, esp. 37–47.
19. But cf. Lüdemann, *Early Christianity*, 100, and 'Acts'.
20. Harnack, 'Versuche'; as Rudolph explains (*Gnosis*, 31–2), by 'secularization' Harnack means 'Hellenization'.
21. Cf., e.g. the discussion in R. McL. Wilson, 'Nag Hammadi', 291–5.
22. Rather than being a reaction to the fall of Jerusalem as Hengel, 'Ursprünge', 222, suggests.
23. *Pace* Lüdemann, *Early Christianity*, 100; 'Acts', 421; he appeals especially to the fact that Hippolytus uses the term *epinoia*, not *ennoia* (*Ref.* 6.19.1–2). Cf. R. McL. Wilson, 'Simon'; J. Holzhausen in *DNP* 11, 572. It is significant that the later Acts of Peter show no more traces of developed gnostic thought in their portrayal of Simon than Acts does, and like that work depict him as a magician.
24. At most he introduces God's powers as intermediaries in the creation of the material world: e.g. *Op. mund.* 72–5 (yet elsewhere God's powers are also involved in the creation of the incorporeal world: e.g. *Conf. ling.* 172).
25. E.g. *Rer. div. her.* 55.
26. Hence the uncertainty whether the divine or the human spirit is meant in Rom 8.10.
27. *Haer.* 1.26.1 (ed. Harvey 1.21). A tradition in Iren. *Haer.* 3.3.4 (=Euseb. *Hist. eccl.* 4.14.6) attributes to Polycarp a story which links Cerinthus with the time of 'John the disciple of the Lord' in Ephesus.
28. Cf. Löhr, 'Christentum' for a survey of research; also Hengel, 'Ursprünge', 195–8, 212–16.
29. Dated in the mid-second century: Schneemelcher 1, 207.
30. 'Kerinth', esp. 73.
31. Cf. Klijn–Reinink, *Evidence*, 19.
32. Cf. also C. E. Hill, 'Cerinthus', esp. 152–3; comparable, too, is Markschies'

Platonic, rather than gnostic, interpretation of the somewhat later Valentinus (*Valentinus Gnosticus?*) in contrast to the views of later Valentinians.

33. As Beyschlag, *Simon Magus*, 127, had already concluded with regard to Simonian gnosticism.
34. However, S. G. Wilson, *Strangers*, 196–207, remarks that 'the most influential current view is that Gnosticism arose among disaffected Jews' (204). Yet such a disaffection is most readily intelligible among Jewish *Christians* disowned by their compatriots.
35. So, roughly simultaneously, v. Dobbeler, *Philippus*; Kollmann, 'Philippus'; Matthews, *Philip*.
36. Antioch-on-the-Orontes was perhaps then the third largest city of the Roman Empire at that time, with probably at least 100,000 inhabitants, although the estimates vary wildly; it was an important trading centre and the chief city of the Roman province of Syria, which also at this time included the area of Cilicia Pedias (according to Magie, *Rule*, 418 [cf. 509], 1271–2 n. 44, 1419–20 n. 68, probably from 44 BCE to 72 CE); Tracey, 'Syria', 236–9, hesitates to call it the 'capital' of the province (over against Berytus, the 'premier colony'), but the articles on Antioch in *OCD*[3] and *DNP* 1 and 11 ('Syria'), not to mention Downey, *Antioch*, esp. ch. 5, show no such caution. (Tac. *Hist.* 2.78 describes the city as *caput* of Syria, parallel to Caesarea in Judaea). Josephus tells us that its large Jewish population (*BJ* 7.43) had Antiochene citizenship (*AJ* 12.119–21; that was unusual, but was apparently also the case in Ephesus; cf. *Ap.* 2.39).
37. Yet one cannot infer that Nicolaus had been converted in Antioch; he might first have heard of Christ in Jerusalem (so Becker, *Paul*, 85).
38. That he is sent from Jerusalem presumably implies that he is not one of those driven out by the persecution like those mentioned in 11.19–20 (cf. Walter, 'Nikolaos', 206). He could doubtless speak Greek, but perhaps preferred to join in the worship and life of the 'Hebrews'. At any rate, Jews from Cyprus are not mentioned among those with whom Stephen quarrelled in Acts 6.9. That may have spared Barnabas from persecution, but where did his theological sympathies lie? Did they change, or was he from early on sympathetic to the line taken by Stephen and his group and later by Paul, with whom he worked for so many years? On the question whether Barnabas was in fact sent from Jerusalem, rather than being already a member of the church there, cf. Dauer, *Paulus*, 16–20.
39. Yet it has been suggested that in fact Barnabas may have found Paul already active there as one of the leaders of the church (Painter, *James*, 46).
40. Cf. Kollmann, *Joseph Barnabas*, 27.
41. *Judenedikt*, 144–88, following E. Bickerman and others; she, too, holds that they took on the name only after others had used it of them. She also stresses that this reference in Acts need not imply that the name was used this early or that Acts records this information at the chronologically appropriate point, and suggests that it arose in the course of the proceedings against Paul in Caesarea (cf. Acts 26.28!) and was then taken up by Christians to explain why they were not liable to pay tax to the *fiscus Judaicus* (i.e. after 70 CE). But that all seems to presuppose a situation where above all it was the authorities in Rome who

first recognized the distinctiveness of the Christian movement. Why should the local authorities in a centre like Antioch and/or the Christians' pagan neighbours there not have been able to recognize this distinctiveness at an earlier date?

42. Cf. Kraft, *Entstehung*, 267.
43. BDAG s.v. explain this term as referring to 'partisans of Herod the Great and his family', and Josephus refers to such supporters of Herod the Great, but as *Herōdeioi* (*BJ* 1.319) or *hoi ta Herōdou phronountes* (*AJ* 14.450).
44. BDR §5.2 and n. 12. Other examples are *Kaisarianoi* (Epict. 1.19.19, of members of Caesar's household) or in Latin *August(i)ani*. Hengel, 'Christentum', 207, draws attention to the Roman factions of *Caesariani* and *Pisoniani* in Antioch in 19 BCE.
45. Leppä, *Use*, 97, appealing to the use of *symparalambanō* and *ho kai poieō*, suggests that Gal 2.10 led to 'Luke's' creation of this account, together with information about a famine.
46. For a brief survey of suggestions cf. Dauer, *Paulus*, 28–35. (Cf. also ch. 6, p. 94–9 below.)
47. Kollmann, *Joseph Barnabas*, 36.
48. Cf. Roloff, *Kirche*, 141–2; Hengel–Schwemer, *Paul*, 235.
49. *Entstehung*, 260–1.
50. Cf. Heiligenthal, ' "Petrus" ', 37.
51. See ch. 3, n. 2 above.
52. Cf., e.g. Reinbold, *Propaganda*, 58–62, following Wehnert, *Reinheit*, esp. 265–6 – perhaps even *en route* to Antioch for the visit referred to in Gal 2.11; also Pesch, *Simon-Petrus*, 82.
53. At this point, at least, Acts seems to be following some source which is more than just a series of isolated incidents or pieces of information. The existence of further clusters of stories about Philip and about Peter may help to explain why the two Philip episodes are placed together in ch. 8 (although Matthews, *Philip*, 75, argues that they were originally unconnected and were first put together by 'Luke') and, above all, why the activities of Peter in Lydda and Joppa are included as a prelude to the story of Cornelius, which is so much more important for this writer's purposes.
54. The reference to the presence in Caesarea of a centurion of the 'Italian' cohort is, however, historically suspect. If a *cohors Italica civium Romanorum* is meant, i.e. a cohort of Roman auxiliaries consisting chiefly of Roman citizens from Italy, then such a unit may have been in Syria shortly before 69 (cf. Hemer, *Book*, 164), but was one to be found in Caesarea in the time just before Herod Agrippa I's death (cf. Haenchen, *Acts*, 346 n. 2 and 360; Schürer, *History* 1, 365 n. 54)? Speidel regards this as quite possible ('Army'). Others date the incident either before Herod's reign (so Bruce, *History*, 261, following Acts' sequence) or more likely after it, unless one supposes that this officer had been seconded to Caesarea, without the rest of his unit (cf. also Hengel, 'Geography', 203–4 n. 111). A more fundamental note of scepticism is struck by Cotter, 'Cornelius', who doubts whether it is at all likely that a person in Cornelius' position could or would have been sufficiently attracted to Christianity to become a Christian.
55. Farmer, 'James', 144, argues that 'Peter was from a very early date – and this

means before the conversion of Paul – an advocate and defender of an apostolic mission that was open to and in favour of admission of Gentiles into the intimacy of table fellowship with apostles of Jesus Christ'; if Peter had already taken this line earlier in Jerusalem, then it is hard to see the point of the Cornelius story.

56. Cf., e.g. Klauck, *Magic*, 33–4; Lüdemann, *Early Christianity*, 133. Less certain is whether the story originally involved an encounter with a gentile who was not yet a Christian (as in Acts) or with one who was already a Christian.
57. That is the point at issue according to Acts and not the admitting of gentiles into the church; but cf. Ascough, 'Christianity', 155.
58. Cf. Grappe, *Temple*, 142.
59. Cf. ch. 2, n. 23 above.
60. See ch. 6, pp. 104–20 below.
61. Very scanty is the evidence for Botermann's suggestion that he had already arrived in Rome at the beginning of Claudius' reign and was responsible for the troubles in the synagogue(s) there (*Judenedikt*, 137–40) – and would presumably then have been expelled again at the same time as Prisca and Aquila (like them he could subsequently have made his way to Corinth). But all that makes it yet harder to understand Paul's contention that he would on principle not evangelize where another had founded a church (Rom 15.20 – see below, ch. 7, pp. 124–7).
62. See further ch. 6, pp. 114–20 below.
63. Yet Becker, *Paul*, 102, reckons with the possibility that Peter subsequently had second thoughts and adopted a more open position towards gentile Christians.
64. Cf., besides the use of a Petrine group by the Tübingen school, the more recent articles of Manson ('Correspondence') and Barrett ('Cephas') and also Painter, *James*, 83, and Wehr, *Petrus*, 95–9, 101 (behind the 'weak' of 1 Cor 8–10, who demanded avoidance of meat offered to idols), as well as the less obvious delineation of a Petrine position in Goulder, *Tale* (*inter alia* sexual asceticism and a spiritual resurrection – for the former position, not to mention for the prototype of a celibate clergy, Peter seems an ill-chosen patron if he was married: Mark 1.30 parr.; 1 Cor 9.5; for Clem. Al. *Strom.* 3.6.52.5 he had even fathered children).
65. In contrast to Rom 14 where the terminology of 'profane' (*koinos*) and 'pure' (*katharos*) suggests that Jewish scruples may lie behind the divide between 'weak' and 'strong' there, even if the differences between them are formulated in more general terms (cf. Sampley, 'Weak').

    In short it remains possible that Peter had at some point made his way to Corinth and had influenced the congregation there, but it is hard to be certain of that on the basis of the Petrine slogan of 1 Cor 1.12 alone; indubitably the Corinthians had heard of him and some were much impressed, and therefore Paul keeps referring to him in that letter (3.22; 9.5; 15.5 – probably quoting tradition), but that does not require his physical presence in Corinth.
66. Cf. ch. 3, pp. 50–2 above.
67. Schneemelcher 2, 243–89/Elliott, 390–430 – Peter is still in Jerusalem when he sets out for Italy.

68. It probably reflects a situation considerably after Peter's death and invites a comparison with that presupposed by Pliny the Younger's letter to Trajan as he was governor of Bithynia and Pontus (*c.* 110–12 CE), two of the areas mentioned in 1 Pet 1.1.
69. Karrer, 'Petrus', 211, notes that 1 Pet 1.12 implies that others than Peter brought the gospel to this region.
70. Cf. ch. 9, pp. 173–4 below.
71. Cf. Herzer, *Petrus oder Paulus?*

Chapter 5

1. A detail also found in Rom 11.1.
2. But cf. Doughty, 'Citizens', who questions the authenticity of this section of Philippians. Even if his thesis were plausible, a number of the autobiographical details in this passage are explicitly or at least implicitly supported by passages in Paul's letters whose authenticity is not in question.
3. Cf. esp. Haacker, 'Berufung'; *Paulus*, 84–90.
4. Acts 18.3. It is disputed both exactly what this trade was and what status it implied (cf. Hengel, *Paul*, 17; P. Lampe, 'Paulus'). At any rate it is harder to judge the income that it would have brought in once Paul was travelling around, for any estimates of the economic status of 'tentmakers' would normally be based on the assumption that such a worker was working full-time and undistracted by other concerns and in one place with a regular clientele (cf. Meggitt, *Paul*, 76). Hock and Malherbe, however, infer from the tone of 1 Cor 4.12 (cf. 9.19?) and 2 Cor 11.7 that Paul was one for whom manual work would normally be beneath his dignity (Hock, 'Tentmaking'; *Context*, 36; Malherbe, *1–2 Thess*, 161; similarly D. B. Martin, *Slavery*, esp. 123), but Meggitt, *Paul*, 88–9 n. 65, is sharply critical of this reading of these passages and quotes Petron. *Sat.* 117 as an instance of a porter not above standing on his dignity; elsewhere (e.g. p. 55) he quotes tellingly from Lucian to show how a trade such as Paul's could entail a considerable degree of poverty. Hengel, however, wants to trace the rabbinic custom of learning and practising a trade back into the first century (*Paul*, 15–16); if that is the case, then Paul nevertheless adopts a stance more typical of Graeco-Roman values when speaking of his manual work.
5. Whence the name Paul (*Paulos*) came is uncertain: did it come from the name of the patron of Paul's family (e.g. the Sergii Paulli, the family of the governor of Cyprus in Acts 13.7, although their name is usually spelled with a double L and Acts only has a single one)? Or was it, more likely, simply chosen as the nearest Latin equivalent to Paul's semitic name (cf., e.g. Fischer, *Urchristentum*, 88; Klauck, *Magic*, 52)?
6. Cf. Haacker, *Paulus*, 48–59. In the case of the Pharisaism of Paul's parents it is arguable that, if they had come to Cilicia from Palestine, they might formerly have been Pharisees, even if living strictly as a Pharisee would have been very difficult in the Graeco-Roman city of Tarsus (cf. Hengel, *Paul*, esp. 31). The same would be true for Josephus living in Rome as a protégé of the Flavian house, even though his earlier life had been influenced by Pharisaic teaching (*Vita* 12).

That Paul might have heard Gamaliel teaching is one thing, to claim that he was his pupil goes far further. And if Gamaliel's forbearance vis-à-vis the early Christian movement were accurately reflected in Acts 5.38–9, then Paul's persecuting zeal would betray a very different stance.

7. Van Unnik, *Tarsus*.
8. Cf. R. A. Martin, *Studies*. Martin's thesis would mean it would be far more difficult plausibly to connect Paul with the action taken against Stephen in the Greek-speaking synagogue in Jerusalem, and Martin therefore postulates that Paul's persecution affected 'Hebrews' similarly critical of the law and the Temple.
9. Cf. Michel's quotation of the dictum of H. Vollmer: 'The apostle lives entirely in and with the Greek text' (*Paulus*, 55, quoting *Die alttestamentliche Zitate bei Paulus* [1895] 10); cf. Koch, *Schrift*, 48 (basically Paul presupposes the LXX text); Strecker–Nolting, 'Paulus', 735.
10. The claim in Strecker–Nolting, 'Paulus', 734, that Paul had passed through all the levels of the Hellenistic school system needs therefore to be treated with some caution. It may be that Paul's Jewish piety kept him from citing classical Greek literature (so 736), but other Hellenistic Jews did not feel so inhibited.
11. Cf. Strecker–Nolting, 'Paulus' 724: this is probably traditional since the author of Acts was more concerned to connect Paul with Jerusalem. The fourth-century church father Jerome also mentions a tradition, in his commentary on Philem 23 and in his *De viris illustribus* 5, that Paul's parents came from Gischala (in Judaea in his account, although the town is in northern Galilee), as the province was devastated by war (*De viris*: by the Romans). Jerome contradicts Acts 22.3 by asserting that Paul's parents brought him to Tarsus as a youth (that he would then have Roman citizenship from birth – 22.28 – is less likely). Nor is it easy to see when the Romans would have captured Gischala. (Titus did in 67 CE, but that is far too late; could this have happened under Pompey in 63 BCE – his route lay far further to the south: Josephus *BJ* 1.134/*AJ* 14.49 – or under Varus in 4 BCE – must we assume that this city, too, shared the fate of Sepphoris further to the south: Josephus *BJ* 2.68/*AJ* 17.289?) In short, this account must be treated with caution!
12. The *varia lectio* of D in 21.39 (and similarly in w and the Peshitta), 'born in Tarsus in Cilicia', may simply be an assimilation to 22.3. Cf. here Trebilco, *Communities*, 172–3; but also Rapske, *Paul*, 75–83 (it is doubtful, however, whether Philostr. *VA* 6.34 can serve as a counter-example as Rapske wishes (79), for, despite the LCL, the text refers only to 'inhabitants of Tarsus' and the 'city' of Tarsus (*polis*, not *politēs*). And did the office of alabarch in Alexandria necessarily entail Alexandrian citizenship as Nock suggests ('Isopoliteia', 960–1)? Schürer, *History* 3, 128–9 rightly interprets Claudius' letter of 41 CE (P. London 1912 = Barrett, §48) as meaning that the Jews of Alexandria did not enjoy the same rights as full citizens; reference is made to the telling correction in *CPJ* 2, §151. On the other hand, the Jews in Syrian Antioch had citizenship and equal rights with the Macedonians and Greeks there according to Josephus *BJ* 7.44; *AJ* 12.119; *Ap.* 2.39 (he claims this also for Ephesus and Ionia).
13. Cf. Hengel, *Paul*, 6; P. Lampe, 'Paulus', cites Dio Chrysostom 34.21, who

speaks of the linen-workers of Tarsus, who are not citizens in the full sense, but were mostly born and brought up in that city and so were citizens in a broader sense (*tropon tina politai*); Dio recommends that they be enrolled even if they cannot manage to pay the usual 500 drachmae (§23). Also relevant may be the reference to the Jewish 'citizens' of Sardis in Josephus *AJ* 14.259 or Ptolemy Philadelphus' reference in 12.46 to the high priest Eleazar's 'citizens' settled in Egypt.

14. Cf., e.g. Conzelmann, *Geschichte*, 47, 64.
15. Cf., however, Dietzfelbinger, *Berufung*, 16: Judaea always included Jerusalem for Paul.
16. So, e.g. Hultgren, 'Persecutions', 105–7; Kraus, *Jerusalem*, 32.
17. So Haenchen, *Acts*, 298: 'he *is* the persecution *in person*' (italics in original).
18. E.g. Lentz, *Portrait*; esp. 43–51; Roetzel, *Paul*, 2; W. Stegemann, 'War der Apostel Paulus ein römischer Bürger?'; Noethlichs, 'Der Jude Paulus', is more agnostic. Omerzu, *Prozeß*, 17–52, is the latest to offer a defence of Paul's citizenship.

    Oft mentioned is the consideration that Paul, were he a Roman citizen, should not have had to suffer three times a scourging with rods (2 Cor 11.25), but Roman citizens were not always spared such punishments (as Noethlichs grants – p. 74; on occasions they might even suffer crucifixion as Cic. *Verr.* 2.5.162, Suet. *Galba* 9, and Josephus *BJ* 2.308 – even Jews of equestrian rank – show; cf. further Hengel, *Paul*, 7 and *Crucifixion*, 39–45; or they might be beheaded rather than being thrown to the beasts like the rest: Euseb. *Hist. eccl.* 5.1.47!). As Hengel drily remarks (*Paul*, 7), in those days one did not have a handy identity card to carry around in one's pocket (and British citizens still do not!).
19. Schürer, *History* 3, 133, citing Josephus *AJ* 14.228, 232, 234–5, 237, 240.
20. *Paul*, 10–11; cf. Markschies, *Zwischen den Welten*, 16; Trocmé, *Childhood*, 39, 46.
21. Cf. Philo *Leg.* 155, 157.
22. Unless Paul travelled to Rome as a free man and was first arrested there (Schmithals, *Apg*, 112–13, 219, 235; *Theologiegeschichte*, 122; also Alvarez Cineira, *Religionspolitik*, 348–70). But against that line of argument cf. Labahn, 'Paulus', 98–9. It is true that Ign. *Rom.* 4.3 speaks of Peter and Paul having issued commands to the Roman church as free men – but Ignatius may be thinking above all of Paul's letter to the Romans which he wrote before his arrest (unlike Ignatius).
23. '*Lex Iulia*', esp. 182–5.
24. *Ep.* 10.96.4; cf. also Josephus *BJ* 2.243 (*AJ* 20.131) and, for a later period, Euseb. *Hist. eccl.* 5.1.43–4 (but also 47!). But Garnsey argues that being citizens ensured those accused before Pliny a full trial, but not necessarily in Rome; it was because of Pliny's uncertainty that he sent them to Trajan (*Status*, 74–5). In the case of Paul, however, he grants that his status played a part in Festus' decision (76).
25. Cf. Hengel, *Paul*, 7.
26. Noethlichs argues that the difficult political situation made it convenient for the governor to ship Paul off to Rome ('Der Jude Paulus', 79); that does not really explain the long time in prison; was Paul's case otherwise so very

different from that of Jesus whom Pilate condemned and executed, thus doing as the Jewish authorities wished?

27. Burchard's distinction (*Zeuge*, 93) between a seeing and a hearing alone must therefore be modified; there is, however, a distinction to be drawn between seeing an apparently earthly Jesus (in the Gospels) and seeing a manifestly heavenly Jesus (in Acts and Paul's letters).
28. Cf. Kraus, *Jerusalem*, 92.
29. Cf. Becker, *Paul*, 64–5, 76; also Schmithals, *Theologiegeschichte*, 70, 84, 110. (More questionable is the distinction the latter makes between a Damascene theology and an Antiochene, which pervades his work – but cf. esp. 90–107. The latter is an elusive entity, the former even more so. Berger's *Theologiegeschichte* also makes use of a pervasive 'Antiochene theology'.)
30. And yet in the accounts in Acts 9 and 22 (but not in 26) a human intermediary, Ananias, plays a vital role in communicating God's will and the meaning of his experience to Paul.
31. This account in Acts 22 is striking and has not been adequately explained. Haenchen mentions that 'Luke' could not have included the call to gentile mission in the account in ch. 9, for that would upstage Peter's role as pioneer in ch. 10. Nonetheless, the addition of a separate vision in ch. 22 is still puzzling, given that ch. 26 incorporates this call without difficulty into Paul's original vision (vv. 17–18), and there is much to be said for Zmijewski's conclusion that this passage stems mainly from tradition, though less for his conclusion that it is not historical (*Apg*, 780).

    It is the account in Acts 26 that dates the revelation of this divine purpose to Paul's experience on the way to Damascus (26.17–18). In the account in Acts 9 the reference to bearing the Lord's name before gentiles, kings and the sons of Israel (9.15) is probably to be connected with the following verse which refers to the need for Paul to suffer (cf. Burchard, *Zeuge*, 101); if 'mission' is the cause of this suffering, then at least it is also mission to the 'sons of Israel', and not to the gentiles alone, and this is true even in ch. 26 (cf. v. 20). It is, therefore, not without good cause that Wasserberg entitles his chapter on Paul's ministry in Acts 'Paul, the unsuccessful missionary to Jews' (*Aus Israels Mitte*, 306–57).
32. Extreme caution is required in gauging the explicit or implicit content of Paul's experience; frankly we do not know, so that the many attempted reconstructions of it are highly speculative, but we can at least draw inferences from his changed behaviour: he ceased to persecute those whom he had persecuted and now joined them in preaching the gospel (Gal 1.23).
33. *Pace* Stendahl, *Paul*, 7–23.
34. Cf. Segal, *Paul*, esp. ch. 3.
35. Riesner quotes here Harnack, *Mission*, 699 n. 5: 'What took [Paul] to Arabia and what he did we simply cannot know.'
36. Hengel–Schwemer, *Paul*, e.g. 118–19, 127; Kraus, *Jerusalem*, 95; Meeks, *Christians*, 10; but cf. Riesner, *Paul's Early Period*, 258–60. G. W. Clarke, 'Origins', 852 argues that the failure of any churches in the southern cities of the Decapolis to claim a Pauline foundation is an argument against Paul's missionary activity in that area. Against the argument that only thus can the

opposition of Aretas' ethnarch in 2 Cor 11.32–3 be explained is the clear impression given by Gal 1.17 that Paul does not reckon Damascus to be part of Arabia (see ch. 6, pp. 100–1 below). The ethnarch in question would not then represent Aretas as ruler of the city, but would be the head of the Nabataean community in that city. The hostility is then more likely to have started when Paul returned from Arabia to Damascus. For, if Paul had offended the Nabataean king, e.g. by evangelism, already while in his kingdom why did he not take steps against him then?

37. Cf. N. Taylor, *Paul*, who speaks of the necessity for Paul to overcome the cognitive dissonance between his former persuasion and his new faith. Kraft, *Offb*, 41, sees missionary activity as incompatible with that not consulting 'flesh and blood' to which Paul refers here.

38. In particular Acts attributes the threat to Paul to 'the Jews', Paul himself to Aretas' ethnarch (cf. Harding, 'Historicity'). Is this difference simply to be explained by Acts' hostility towards the Jews or did both parties for some reason collaborate against Paul (cf. Riesner, *Paul's Early Period*, 88–9)? That the ethnarch was a head of the Jewish colony appointed by Aretas, as Haacker suggests (*Paulus*, 82) in an attempt to reconcile Acts' version with Paul's, is hardly a natural interpretation of Paul's words.

39. A possibility suggested by Martyn, *Gal*, 174. A continued stay in Jerusalem, even if not in Peter's house (did he have one there or was he dependent on another's hospitality?), would increase the possibility and impression of dependence upon the Jerusalem church and it is therefore likelier that Paul means us to understand that this was the total length of his stay in Jerusalem.

40. These two verses are notorious for two ambiguities: (1) whereas the basic meaning of the verb *historein* is given as 'visit (for the purpose of coming to know someone or someth[ing]' (BDAG), others suggest 'get information from' or even 'question, cross-examine' (Farmer, 'James', 136). (Paul does not, at any rate, use the same verb of his contact with James, as Martyn notes: *Gal*, 174.) Karrer, 'Petrus', 214, compares the similar use of this verb in Plut. *De curiositate* 516C, but is careful not to infer that Paul became Peter's pupil as Aristippus became Socrates' in that passage. (2) It is not clear whether Paul implies that he considers James an apostle or not ('none of the other apostles, except James', REB, or 'none of the other apostles – only James', NIV) – see ch. 8, p. 153 below.

That Paul only saw Peter and Jesus' brother James on this occasion (despite Acts 9.27, 'the apostles') need not mean that none of the other leaders of the early Christian community were in Jerusalem; this detail may point either to the dangers still confronting the Christians in Jerusalem or to a continued mistrust of Paul or both.

Chapter 6

1. So Matt 12.40; 27.63; Mark 8.31; 9.31; 10.34.
2. Suhl, *Paulus*, esp. 47; similarly Fischer, *Urchristentum*, 39; Reicke, *Re-Examining*, 36.
3. Suhl, *Paulus*, esp. 43–5. Suhl also summarizes his own and others' attempts to establish a chronology of Paul's life in 'Chronologie'.

4. The NRSV makes it plain that it is the Jerusalem church and the same is presumably meant by Moffatt's reference to 'the capital' (although Caesarea Maritima was the Roman governor's base). The Einheitsübersetzung inserts a 'to Jerusalem' in brackets. For the CEV, however, the church greeted is that of Caesarea (the 'he went up' is omitted). Walter, 'Nikolaos', 209, rightly points out that, although some (later) MSS add a reference to Jerusalem in v. 21, it is unlikely that the text as it stands in the earlier tradition could be so interpreted.
5. Only if one follows Vouga, ('Galaterbrief', esp. 250; *Gal*, 4–5) in preferring to date Galatians after Romans would a dating after this last visit come in question.
6. Cf. ch. 4, p. 70 above.
7. Knox, *Chapters*, 68; Lüdemann, *Paulus* 1, 165–73, 272–3; Jewett, *Dating*, 78–85.
8. See n. 4 above.
9. Cf., e.g. Bornkamm, *Paulus*, 63–4; Fischer, *Urchristentum*, 40, 90; Hahn, *Mission*, 60; Haenchen, *Acts*, 439; Jeremias, 'Untersuchungen', esp. 254; Pesch, 'Abkommen', 122; Schmithals, 'Probleme', 16; Schwartz, *Agrippa I*, 214; Vielhauer, *Geschichte*, 78–9.
10. It acted, however, with the authority of the Jerusalem church, particularly after it had yielded to the wishes of that church in the matter of relations between Jewish and gentile Christians, as in Gal 2.11–14.
11. Cf. Dinkler, 'Brief', 277–8.
12. Cf. further Wedderburn, 'Paul and Barnabas'; also Hengel–Schwemer, *Paul*, 159; Reicke, *Re-Examining*, 18.
13. SIG^3 801D (cf. Barrett §49). The inscription is most easily understood if Gallio, not his successor, was still in office when it was written; when it was written Claudius had been acclaimed as *imperator* for the 26th time; since he was thus acclaimed for the 22nd, 23rd and 24th time in 51 and for the 27th time in the twelfth year of his *tribunicia potestas*, which began on 25 January 52, and that before 1 August 52, the 25th and 26th acclamations probably took place in the first half of 52.
14. Seneca mentions that Gallio fell ill in Achaea and was taken on board a ship: *Ep. morales* 104.1.
15. That is all the more relevant if he shared the antipathy towards the Jews of his brother, as Riesner suggests: *Paul's Early Period*, 209.
16. Sherwin-White, *Society*, 81 suggests that the edict may also lie behind the charge brought against Paul and Silas shortly before in Acts 16.20, that they, 'being Jews', were causing a disturbance in Philippi.
17. *Historiae adv. paganos* 7.6.
18. So Lüdemann, *Paulus* 1, 183–95 (cf. also Horrell, *Ethos*, 74; Levinskaya, *Book of Acts*, 171–7; Murphy-O'Connor, *Paul*, 9–13; Schwartz, *Agrippa I*, 94). That Acts seems to bundle the events together which occurred in a particular city and, with the exception of Ephesus in Acts 18.19–21 and 19.1–20.1, narrates them in connection with Paul's first visit to a particular city, as Lüdemann claims, may have another explanation than simply 'Luke's' narrative technique: the first visits may have been the more eventful, the later ones more a matter of consolidating what had already been achieved. In fact the

second visit to Ephesus seems to have been much more eventful than the first.

19. Cf. the discussions in Alvarez Cineira, *Religionspolitik*, 194–216; Botermann, *Judenedikt*, 114–23, 134–5; Omerzu, *Prozeß*, 229–38; Slingerland, 'Suetonius'; also Theißen, 'Verfolgung', 275.
20. Suet. *Claud.* 25.4 (*assidue*) (cf. Barrett, §9).
21. *Paul's Early Period*, 35–58. However, Scriba, 'Korinth', 161, regards 28 CE as more plausible. Some are prepared to date the crucifixion of Jesus as early as 27 (Hahn, *Mission*, 89, following Hölscher) and that would obviously give a chronology of Paul's life that much more leeway.
22. So the Ophites in Iren. *Haer.* 1.30.4 (ed. Harvey 1.28.2) and the school of Ptolemaeus in 1.3.2 (18 months), the Asc. Isa. 9.16 (545 days), the Apocryphon of James (NHC I/2 2.19–24: 550 days); cf. Riesner, *Paul's Early Period*, 64–71.
23. So, e.g. Suhl, *Paulus*, 315; Riesner, *Paul's Early Period*, 89, although Hyldahl sets the event in 42 (and Paul's conversion as late as 40) and argues that the ethnarch continued to rule in Damascus after Aretas' death (*Chronologie*, 123).
24. So, rightly, Riesner, *Paul's Early Period*, 87–8.
25. *Dating*, 32.
26. Josephus *AJ* 18.115. In other words he would have been a very different beneficiary of Caligula's policy in comparison with the latter's friend Herod Agrippa I or Antiochus IV of Commagene, like Herod a Roman citizen (cf. Millar, *Roman Near East*, 59). Cf. the scepticism of Hengel–Schwemer, *Paul*, 130.
27. Cf. ch. 5, pp. 85–8 above and Riesner, *Paul's Early Period*, esp. 84–9; Kennedy, 'Syria', 735 n. 149.
28. Suhl, *Paulus*, 315; cf. Riesner, *Paul's Early Period*, 89.
29. *Antioch*, 90. But is this more than an inference from Acts 11 and the general likelihood that Antioch would also be affected? Yet, as Downey notes earlier (17–18), Antioch differed from a city like Jerusalem in that it 'was surrounded by a fertile plain' which would make it relatively less dependent on imported food supplies.
30. There was seemingly a shortage in Egypt between 45 and 47 (cf. Gapp, 'Famine'; Ogg, *Chronology*, 52–3; Riesner, *Paul's Early Period*, 129). Josephus *AJ* 20.51–3 (cf. 101; also 3.320) tells us of Queen Helena of Adiabene's aid to the starving inhabitants of Jerusalem, purchased in Alexandria, also during the reign of Claudius. Unfortunately an uncertainty in the text at this point (*epi toutou* [LCL following the *Epitome*] or *epi toutois* [MSS] – but 'in the time of [a person]' would usually be *epi* + gen.) makes it hard to pinpoint this aid more exactly. Helena's aid would cost more once the Egyptian prices had risen. Orosius dates this famine to Claudius' fourth year (Jan. 44–Jan. 45): *Historiae adv. paganos* 7.6.
31. If a sabbatical year fell in 48–9 (Riesner, *Paul's Early Period*, 134), that would have aggravated the situation. If Jeremias is correct in setting it in 47–8 (*Jerusalem*, 143), then the hardship would have been alleviated a year earlier.
32. The term *sikarios* here refers to that movement amongst the various forms of opposition to Roman rule which appeared under the governor Felix and which derived its name from the practice of assassinating political opponents

with short daggers (*sicae*). Cf., e.g. Josephus *BJ* 2.254–7; Schürer, *History* 1, 463.

33. *BJ* 2.261–3 (with 30,000 followers!)/*AJ* 20.169–72.
34. Cf. Scriba, 'Korinth', 170.
35. Because of the lateness of 10 Tishri (Acts 27.9 – the 'Fast' referring to the Day of Atonement) in 59, Scriba, 'Korinth', 171, regards 60 as likelier.
36. Cf. Pokorný, *Theologie*, 105.
37. So Barrett, 'End', 549, who refers to the 'envy and strife' mentioned in Phil 1.15 and the 'jealousy and envy' of 1 Clem 5.2 and Paul's death due to 'jealousy and strife' in 5.5.
38. Cf. Acts Pet. 1–3 (Elliott, 399–401/Schneemelcher 2, 258–61), where Paul's departure for Spain is portrayed (it is hoped, no more, that his absence will not last more than a year) and in ch. 40 his return is anticipated; cf. also the Muratorian Canon ll. 38–9 (Schneemelcher 1, 28).
39. So, e.g. Lindemann, *Paulus*, 77–9. However, Koester argues that 2 Timothy assumes a final imprisonment of Paul in Greece or Macedonia – despite the reference to Rome in 2 Tim 1.17 ('Paul', 61–2); Callahan, 'Paul' seeks to support a Philippian martyrdom by the evidence of the grave of a '*prōtopresbyteros* Paulos' there (Pilhofer, *Philippi* 2, §103 – dated to 4th/5th cent.).
40. See n. 21 above.
41. So most commentators in their sifting of the various readings (Martyn, *Gal*, 197: 'to whom we did not give in even momentarily', 'we did not give in even momentarily', 'to whom we did give in momentarily', 'we did give in momentarily'); the elimination of 'to whom' is easily explained as removing the syntactical problem by supplying an otherwise missing main clause. The removal of the negative is more difficult; is it just to show Paul to be more amenable (so Martyn)? Or in order to bring Paul's policy into line with that of his treatment of Timothy (Acts 16.3; Timothy could, however, perhaps count as a Jew because of his Jewish mother, but scribes may not have appreciated that distinction)? Or could one equally well argue that the negative was felt necessary because of the 'was not compelled' of v. 3? Only if the 'yielding' (without the negative) in v. 5 was interpreted as voluntary as opposed to something imposed could the two vv. be harmonized. But even a voluntary yielding would be very awkward for Paul's argument.
42. Cf. Schwartz, *Agrippa I*, 216.
43. Cf. Walter, 'Die "als Säulen Geltenden"', 88–9.
44. But cf. Schmithals, 'Probleme', 27.
45. Cf. also *Gorg.* 472A; also Walter, 'Die "als Säule Geltenden"', with his reference to Gal 6.3 and other passages. Klein, 'Gal 2,6–9', emphasizes the problems of v. 6 and is probably right to conclude that Paul writes now from the perspective of the time of the writing of Galatians; one could then infer that Paul is saying that he once deferred to the authority of the Jerusalem leaders, but he is no longer bound by their decisions, particularly if they have, in his eyes, gone back on what was agreed in Jerusalem.
46. But cf. Schmithals, 'Probleme', 14.
47. So, rightly, Suhl, 'Konfliktlösungsmodell', 81 n. 2.

48. So Betz, *Gal*, 97, following Dinkler, 'Brief', 279–82; Klein, 'Gal 2,6–9', 283–4; cf. also Schnelle, 'Heide', 98–9.
49. Betz, *Gal*, 96–7, traces back to Karl Holl the attempt to separate Cephas and Peter, but already in Euseb. *Hist. eccl.* 1.12.2 we find Clement of Alexandria's suggestion that the Cephas of Gal 2.11 was one of the Seventy and had the same name as Peter; Bart Ehrman ('Cephas') revived Holl's attempt, but Dale Allison ('Peter') has tried to show how much the one seems then to be a double of the other. Wehr, *Petrus*, 54–6, attempts to explain the variations in usage by Paul's nearness to Peter and his distancing himself from Cephas.
50. That is, *euangelion* on the one hand as an activity-word, referring to the activity of preaching, on the other referring also to the content of the message preached.
51. So Lüdemann, *Paulus* 2, 62.
52. Other possibilities are to supply 'to preach' (Lutherbibel) or 'to work with' (CEV).
53. *Armen*, 21–2: it was a matter of determining where the main emphasis of the work of each church should lie, not fixing the boundary between them.
54. Georgi, *Armen*, 21–2; cf. Lührmann, *Gal*, 40.
55. Munck, for instance, adds to Palestine Syria and oriental areas within and beyond the Roman Empire (*Paul*, 119); but in adding Syria he adds Antioch, with the implication that the Antioch church was not responsible for its own city!
56. Acts 10.44–8; see above ch. 4, pp. 73–5.
57. Some, however, are not ready to believe that the two churches could be so short-sighted as to fail to realize the problems presented by mixed churches of Jewish and gentile Christians: cf. Stowasser, 'Konflikte', 67; Lüdemann, *Paulus* 1, 98. It is often, however, easier to be wiser with the advantage of hindsight and we today have that hindsight. It may also be doubted whether Paul saw the agreement as establishing separate gentile-Christian and Jewish-Christian communities (but cf. Schmithals, 'Probleme', 18, 20) – nor did it establish them as far as we can judge from Gal 2.11–14.
58. Cf. Rom 15.26. Goodman, 'Judaea', 769, remarks that the poor in Jerusalem 'formed an urban proletariat of a size rarely found in this period outside the city of Rome'.
59. Cf. Reicke, *Re-Examining*, 21.
60. *Pace*, e.g. Painter, *James*, 52.
61. Berger, *Theologiegeschichte*, 514 (cf. 538–9), suggests that *porneia* in the Decree refers to mixed marriages, but this corresponds neither to the sexual sins of Lev 18 nor to the usual meaning of the term.
62. *Pace* Wehnert, *Reinheit*, 244, it is hard to make the *kai* between 'things strangled' and 'blood' epexegetic while the other two uses of the word in this text connect separate items.
63. Others seek here an explanation in terms of the Noachide commandments which were regarded as binding on all nations; however, evidence for this tradition is relatively late (so that Justin Taylor, 'Decrees', 373 and n. 3, proposes the term 'proto-Noachide', meaning regulations which foreshadow the later rabbinic rules) and when it does emerge, then the commandments do

not really match this quartet. The same is even more true of the only known pre-Christian foreshadowing of this tradition, in Jub 7.20. Prohibitions of sexual impurity and idolatry are amongst these commandments (usually 6 or 7 in number), but they also include the prohibition of shedding (not eating) blood (as well as eating flesh from a living creature) and have no equivalent to 'things strangled'. Goodman, *Mission*, 53, states bluntly that these prohibitions do not lead to the qualities necessary for being a righteous gentile such as are listed in the Noachide commandments.

64. *Reinheit*, 231.
65. But, against Wehnert, *Reinheit*, 242, it must be asked whether the original point of the prohibition was lost from sight in gentile Christianity, and whether Jewish traditions did not also forget what is meant and this led to this strange use of, and focus on, the term 'strangle'.
66. On this problem cf. further Wedderburn, '"Decree"'; also Witherington, *Acts*, 434, 462–4.
67. It is therefore correct to see in the Decree a defence against idolatry as Jervell proposes ('Aposteldekret', 229, 236; *Apg*, 396–7), even if 'Luke' does not tie these prohibitions to the law as closely as Jervell supposes.
68. Kümmel, 'Form': he compares especially Ps.-Clem. *Recg*. 4.36.4, Origen *Cels*. 6.30; 8.60 (blood as the food of demons), and Basil *Comm. in Jes* §236 on 10.11 (demons feeding on the vapour arising from pagan sacrifices).
69. For references to such shamanistic practices cf. Wedderburn, '"Decree"', 387 and n. 90; cf. also *Papyri graecae magicae* 3.1–50; 12.30–5, which may reflect similar beliefs.
70. Cf. Merkel, 'Gesetz', 128.
71. Bauckham, 'James', 464, rightly points out that the foods excluded would not cover all which would contravene Jewish food laws (e.g. pork, even without any blood, was forbidden). That is intelligible if the focus was avoidance of idolatry, not compliance with the food laws as such.
72. Rev 18.4; contrast 1 Cor 5.10. Cf. Walter, 'Nikolaos', 214–17, 221–2: Nicolaus of Antioch (Acts 6.5) may have been founder of the Ephesian church and other churches in the area, and the polemic against the 'Nicolaitans' may be directed against a *modus vivendi* with the pagan world similar to that advocated by Paul (on the last point cf. also Giesen, 'Reich', 2528; Räisänen, 'Nicolaitans', 1633); for Klauck, 'Sendschreiben', 169, on the other hand, the Nicolaitans are to be located midway between Paul and second-century gnostics who countenanced eating meat offered to idols.
73. It is remarkable, however, that, despite the attempts in certain parts of the early church to follow the dictates of the Decree or even, in the judgement of some, despite the general acceptance of the Decree in the early church (cf. Bauckham, 'James', 464–7, who also stresses that Lev 17 was certainly used to interpret and expand the Decree at a later stage; Holtz, 'Zwischenfall', 355; Kollmann, *Joseph Barnabas*, 57; Wehnert, *Reinheit*, 145–208; but cf. n. 75 below), in more modern times it has been completely ignored, even by the most conservative Christian circles, despite the fact that it was ostensibly endorsed, not only by Paul, but also by the leading authorities of the church. On the other hand, some have tried to insist on applying commands which

seem to stem from Paul alone, like the command that women should be silent in church meetings (1 Cor 14.34). Can it be that Christians have found it harder to forgo their favourite dishes than the spiritual contributions of women?

74. Pratscher, *Herrenbruder*, 87, suggests that, rather than being imposed by James and the Jerusalem church, the prohibitions may have been a voluntary agreement between Jewish Christians and gentile Christians.
75. Cf. Klauck, *Magic*, 38; Merkel, 'Gesetz', 129. Berger, *Theologiegeschichte*, 262, suggests that it applied only to the area of the Petrine mission – but the area of that mission as it was then conceived or as it eventually developed? (For Karrer, 'Petrus', esp. 221, that area was to be, primarily, Syria, i.e. the area to which the Decree was sent.) Suggestive is the proposal of Bockmuehl, 'Antioch', 169–79, 187, that Syria and Cilicia were seen as part of the land of Israel, even if that ideal did not correspond to the political realities of the time. Leppä, *Use*, 131–2, regards the four provisions as reflecting the practice of Christians in this area, but attributes their incorporation in a decree of James and the Jerusalem church to the theology of 'Luke'.
76. Catchpole, 'Paul'; cf. Berger, *Theologiegeschichte*, 254. More recently J. Taylor, 'Decrees', has advanced a theory which also presupposes that the Decree played an important part in the Antioch quarrel, with James interpreting it on the analogy of the later Noachide commandments as keeping Jews and non-Jews separate, and Peter interpreting it in the light of Lev 17 and 18 as giving gentile Christians a comparable status to that of resident aliens. Quite apart from the difficulties in connecting the Decree with either of these Jewish traditions, does that mean that Paul too shared Peter's interpretation or did he not know of how Peter was justifying his eating together with gentile Christians?
77. Cf., e.g. Fischer, *Urchristentum*, 98; Holtz, 'Bedeutung', 124; Roloff, 'Konflikte', 122; Weiser, *Apg* 2, 371–2.
78. Cf., however, Lüdemann, *Paulus* 1, 101–5. Against that Schmithals, *Theologiegeschichte*, 116, argues that Quint. 4.2.83 only approves departing from the chronological order as an exception. There is no sign, however, that the problem dealt with at the Jerusalem conference took the form of the demand that Jewish Christians should break off contact with gentile Christians, and that a questioning of the table-fellowship between the two groups would be impossible after the conference only holds good if the agreement there included something like the Apostolic Decree. But that is widely doubted.

    Bauckham, 'James', 469–70, also sets Gal 2.11–14, and Galatians itself, too, before the Jerusalem conference, as one way of reconciling Acts and Galatians, but at the cost of demoting Gal 2.1–10 to 'a short-lived arrangement, very soon superseded by a fuller and more authoritative decision'; Paul would hardly have agreed with that assessment!
79. 'Incident', esp. 154–5.
80. Here Holmberg, 'Identity', 402, rightly distinguishes the contact between Jews and gentiles in the 'common or public sphere' and the non-contact in the 'intimate sphere' (food and drink, marriage), yet can one then say that the

gentile Christians had been accustomed as 'God-fearers' to observe 'basic Jewish rules about what is permitted to eat' (*sic*; 405), if shared meals had not been part of their previous contact with Judaism?

81. 'Zwischenfall', 351.
82. Cf. Hengel, 'Jakobus', 94; Holmberg, 'Identity', 402; E. P. Sanders, 'Association', 178.
83. See also ch. 4, pp. 66–7 above. Klauck, *Magic*, 35, argues that, for Jews, eating with gentiles was always difficult, perhaps even impossible, because they must always fear that they were eating unclean foods – at least if gentiles were the hosts.
84. Mostly it is simply assumed that it is a matter of emissaries in the plural, but there is a well-attested reading which has 'a certain person' in the singular and 'when he came' in v. 12. To explain that reading as secondary one would probably have to assume that 'when they came' has been affected by the 'when Cephas came' in v. 11 (*hote de ēlthen*), and that the 'certain persons' was then emended by the deletion of a sigma to fit that; the first alteration, to the verb, is considerably better and more widely attested than that affecting the indefinite pronoun. Yet if it were assumed that 'those from the circumcision' in v. 12 referred to the emissary or emissaries, then that could possibly have led to the introduction of the two plurals.
85. Cf. Schmithals, *Paul and James*, 66–8, but also Wehnert, *Reinheit*, 270.
86. Cf. Jewett, 'Agitators'; Reicke, *Re-Examining*, 12, 14–15, 19, 22. There are those, like Hengel, 'Jakobus', 92, who stress how far James's approach was a conciliatory one – he could have severed the Jewish Christianity which he represented from gentile Christians in order to avoid all suspicions of disloyalty to Judaism, but nonetheless sought the unity of all Christians. Seen from the other side, Paul's action in gathering a collection for the Jerusalem church was similarly conciliatory (see ch. 7, pp. 147–50 below), but some Jews (if not Jewish Christians) evidently found his coming to Jerusalem too provocative, and Paul evidently felt similarly about the action of James's emissaries in Antioch, however well-intentioned it may have been.
87. Which Paul describes as 'compelling them to Judaize' (Gal 2.14).
88. It is not clear where Paul actually switches his attention to the arguments which he must present to the Galatians, but he clearly felt that both the situation in Antioch which had provoked the Jerusalem meeting (Gal 2.4) and the action of the emissaries from James were a sufficiently close parallel to what was happening in Galatia to enable him to argue from the one to the other. Common to all three situations were the arrival of emissaries and their demand that the Jewish law be obeyed.
89. It is one of the weaknesses of the fourfold division of the possible attitudes of Jewish (and Judaizing) Christians to the gentiles which Raymond Brown offers (Brown–Meier, *Antioch and Rome*, 2–8) that, in identifying representatives of the different stances, he does not allow for this change of stance on the part of Peter. And his characterization of Paul seems to owe more to the pious Jewish Paul of Acts than to the Paul who wrote 1 Cor 9.20–1.
90. *Petrus*, 383; cf. Karrer, 'Petrus', esp. 218.
91. It is true that Reinhard M. Hübner has called the authenticity of Ignatius'

letters and indeed the existence of Ignatius himself in question, but cf. the discussion (and literature) in Uebele, '*Verführer*', 20–7.

92. Cf. Hyldahl, *History*, 179.
93. Cf. J. T. Sanders, *Schismatics*, 160.
94. *Temple*, 80–1; this implication of the house churches had already been noted by Filson, 'Significance'.

Chapter 7

1. Others seem to have been given the designation 'evangelist', even if at a somewhat later point of time: Acts 21.8; Eph 4.11. Evangelistic activity at an earlier stage is better attested, e.g. for Peter: Gal 2.8. But Lane Fox, *Pagans*, 282, comments on how few other Christian missionaries are known by name in the whole period up to the time of Constantine; cf. also Euseb. *Hist. eccl.* 5.10.2, and MacMullen, *Christianizing*, 34: 'after St Paul, the church had no mission, it made no organized or official approach to unbelievers; rather it left everything to the individual'. (He does, however, note one or two conspicuous exceptions such as Polycarp and Gregory the Wonderworker, and naturally the situation changed with the conversion of Constantine.) Reinbold, *Propaganda*, goes further: even before and during the period of Paul's activity he was unusual and atypical. It was largely left to individual Christians to spread the word in their daily contacts with non-believers. It may be granted that Paul was exceptional, but the difference was rather one of degree (cf. 1 Cor 15.10: Paul 'worked harder' than the rest, NRSV) and a whole range of other figures may be compared, up to and including the itinerant 'apostles' of the Didache (see ch. 8, pp. 160–1: the instructions here are hard to understand if these 'apostles' are not supposed to be engaged in founding new churches where none had existed before). Paul's sense of his special responsibility for the gentiles was undoubtedly an important extra dimension to his activity, but according to Gal 2.9 Barnabas (who, as Reinbold, 102–6, grants, probably really did share in Paul's missionary activity – or Paul in his), Peter, John and James *should* have felt a similar responsibility.
2. More speculative is the suggestion that the advance from Cyprus into southern Galatia can be explained by connecting it with their alleged success with the governor of Cyprus (Acts 13.12) whose family possessed estates in that region (Breytenbach, *Paulus*, 42; Lane Fox, *Pagans*, 293–4; S. Mitchell, 'Population', 1074 n. 134; Riesner, *Paul's Early Period*, 275 n. 61).
3. *Pace* Koch, 'Barnabas', 100, Acts 15.40 indicates that for this work at least Paul still departs with the blessing of the Antioch church – hardly conceivable after the quarrel of Gal 2.11–14.
4. Cf., e.g. Fredriksen, *From Jesus to Christ*, 170.
5. Bosenius, *Abwesenheit*, 7–13.
6. For those adopting a similar position see the references in Schnelle, *Einleitung*, 98–9, who himself sees the return of Titus with news of a worsened situation as provoking the addition of chs 10–13 to an already composed, but not yet despatched, chs 1–9. Similarly U. B. Müller, *Phil*, esp. 10–11, reckons with Philippians being written over a period of time and possibly with the arrival of

fresh news after 1.1–3.1 had been written, in order to explain the similar unevenness and changes of tone in that letter.

7. So, for instance, Koester prefers to see here a reference to controversies with opponents ('Ephesos', 120).
8. So Koester, 'Ephesos', 122; Trocmé, *Childhood*, 61.
9. The 'captivity epistles' are, of the generally acknowledged Pauline letters, Philippians and Philemon and, from the deutero-Pauline ones, Colossians and Ephesians and presumably 2 Timothy (even if it is often not named amongst 'the captivity epistles') if 2 Tim 1.16; 2.9 imply that Paul is still in chains.
10. E.g. Reicke, *Re-Examining*, 96, 132–3. Schnelle, *Einleitung*, also avoids assigning any of these captivity epistles to an Ephesian imprisonment (e.g. giving Rome as the place of composition of Philemon and Philippians).
11. Conzelmann, *Acts*, 171, notes that it would have taken the Ephesians at least five days to get to Miletus (so also Koester, 'Ephesos', 131).
12. Cf. Fischer, *Urchristentum*, 108; Walter, 'Nikolaos', 211.
13. Spain (Spania; earlier Hispania, but from the first century on the shorter form became more common: *KlP* 2.1185) might seem to be an exception, for this area in fact was made up of three provinces at this stage. 'Spain' could nevertheless serve as a blanket name for the whole Iberian peninsula.
14. Yet Christians from Cyprus are also mentioned in Acts 11.20 (although it is not expressly said that they had already become Christians in Cyprus), even though Barnabas and Paul preach the gospel there in Acts 13.4–12; does that then mean that the principle of Rom 15.20 was one which Paul applied in his own independent missionary work, but which had not been operative earlier when he was Barnabas' partner or an emissary of the Antioch church?
15. Codex Bezae in fact adds the information that he had been instructed in the Lord 'in his homeland'. For an assessment of the sparse information concerning the origins of Alexandrian and Egyptian Christianity cf. Pearson, 'Christianity', and Klijn, 'Christianity'.
16. So, e.g. Trocmé, *Childhood*, 58.
17. Acts gives a somewhat different impression: 9.27–8.
18. Cf. Strecker–Nolting, 'Paulus', 729: the reference here is only to the 'Gesamtrahmen' of Paul's work and does not imply that he had been in Illyricum.
19. Paul even claims that he has brought the preaching of the gospel to completion in that whole area.
20. In the cities at least a Greek speaker could probably expect to be able to communicate freely – yet even in the city of Lystra Paul's audience allegedly broke into Lycaonian (Acts 14.11), although Neumann, 'Kleinasien', 179, suggests that Greek in a Lycaonian dialect is meant. At any rate, Greek was generally known in Asia Minor (172), although some pre-Roman languages (e.g. Phrygian, Galatian: 175, 177) remained in use; however, S. Mitchell, 'Population', 1058, infers from Luc. *Alex.* 51 that not all could speak Greek and, from the rarity of Greek funerary inscriptions in the Galatian heartland, that 'the majority of the rural population did not use Greek' (cf. also *Anatolia* 1, 50). If Syria can be compared, then it is noteworthy that one still had to provide Syriac translations of sermons in Antioch in the fourth century for

countryfolk who had come into the city (Markschies, *Zwischen den Welten*, 35).

21. Meeks, *Christians*, 9: 'Paul was a city person.'
22. *Römerbrief* (1975), esp. 167–71; but cf. Wedderburn, *Reasons*, 25–9.
23. *Römerbrief* (1988), 531.
24. So Schmithals, but see below; the presence of Christians there already is not expressly stated, unless one infers that from the 'disciples' of 19.1.
25. Pliny was appointed *c.* 110 and died *c.* 112. 1 Peter is directed at those who live in the Diaspora in Pontus, Galatia, Cappadocia (the first that we hear of Christian churches in this area too), Asia and Bithynia (1.1).
26. The 'baptism of John' referred to here would then relate to a rite (administered by Apollos? So v. Dobbeler, *Philippus*, 200) whose content lay nearer to that of the Baptist's rite, even if it was now a Christian form of initiation (cf. here the rightly somewhat tentative analysis of v. Dobbeler, 119–215).
27. Cf. Hock, *Context*, 37–42. Paul's work in Corinth was presumably an example of this combination, both working with Aquila and Prisc(ill)a and then devoting himself to preaching when joined by Silas and Timothy (Acts 18.3, 5). Acts does not mention it, but this pair may have made this switch of strategy possible because they brought with them a financial contribution from the Philippian church (cf. Phil 4.16; v. 17 also mentions financial aid when Paul was in Thessalonica).
28. Cf. Theißen, *Setting*, 27–67.
29. The existence of the 'God-fearers', so prominent in Acts, has been doubted by some, but it is hard to deny that there were non-Jewish sympathizers attached to the synagogue without being full members (attested at a later date by a third-century inscription from Aphrodisias in Asia Minor – tr., e.g. in Feldman–Reinhold, *Life*, 142–3 – but also by Josephus *BJ* 7.45, which speaks of a large number of Greeks attracted to the synagogue in Syrian Antioch and 'in some measure' participating in the life of the Jewish community there). Even if Goodman, *Mission*, 47, is correct in arguing that a formal category such as that suggested by the Aphrodisias inscription is a later development, that does not exclude the earlier existence of such supporters of the synagogue. Cf. the studies of Levinskaya, *Book of Acts*, esp. chs 4–7, and Wander, *Gottesfürchtige*.
30. On the unreliability of arguments from the archaeological evidence cf. Frend, *Martyrdom*, 216–17.
31. P. Lampe, *Christen*, 164.
32. Meggitt, *Paul*.
33. It seems, for instance, that such slaves were often kept in chains and treated no better than if they were convicts. Cf., e.g. Apuleius' description of the chained slaves working for a miller (*Met.* 9.12). Meggitt, *Paul*, 44, questions the existence at this time of large-scale manufacturing concerns – at most we have evidence of workshop-based industry, and the miller's establishment is to be understood in those terms. But it is hard to conceive of those treated in the way Apuleius describes being able to participate in the life of a Christian congregation.
34. An Erastus is known to us from a Corinthian inscription, who, having been elected aedile, donated some paving: Kent, *Inscriptions*, No. 232. Theißen,

Setting, 80–3 identifies the two and suggests that *oikonomos* corresponds to the office of quaestor held earlier by Erastus. Meeks, *Christians*, 58–9, is more cautious, but tends to follow Theißen: yet he grants that it may not be the same Erastus and the one mentioned in Rom 16 may have been a slave. Meggitt, *Paul*, 135–41, is thoroughly sceptical of Theißen's whole line of argument.

35. Cf. Martin, *Slavery*, esp. 15–22. The epigraphic evidence gathered by Landvogt, *Untersuchung*, is ambivalent here: he documents the title '*oikonomos* of the city' only in free cities up to the first century BCE and in Asia Minor (16), but at the same time notes that *oikonomoi* in the Roman period were generally slaves of the imperial household or of private households (13). However, cf. the city *oikonomoi* from Macedonia in *SEG* 24 (1969) §496 (2nd–3rd cent. CE: Diadoumenos and his fellow-slaves) and 38 (1988) §710 (Roman period; H. W. Pleket: perhaps a slave).
36. *Paul*, 120–1.
37. *Christians*, 57.
38. For this sense of *prostatis* cf. Lucian *Bis accusatus* 29: Lady Rhetoric as patroness.
39. Cf. here Clarke, *Leadership*, ch. 5; Horrell, *Ethos*, 109–12; A. C. Mitchell, 'Rich'; cf., however, Meggitt, *Paul*, 122–5: members of the 'non-elite' might also engage in litigation. The likely outcome of litigation at this level is, however, unclear: were the scales of justice still weighted in favour of the economically less disadvantaged?
40. Is it just the eucharistic food and drink which the have-nots do not get, as Meggitt suggests (*Paul*, 120; cf. 189–93)? Is the 'after the meal' (not just 'after eating [the bread]') of 1 Cor 11.25 not then harder to understand?
41. Theißen, *Setting*, 153–63.
42. *Paul*, 122.
43. Cf. Theißen, *Setting*, 91–2.
44. 'Origins', 863 n. 48: IEphes. 1a, §20. Kloppenborg, 'Collegia', 23, argues that 'the majority of associations, with the exception of the priestly sodalities, were composed of the urban poor, slaves, and freedmen', yet also notes the role played in these by benefactors of more exalted status.
45. 'Collegia', 23 (the example he quotes is from Philadelphia: *Syll.*[3] §985), but cf. Lane Fox, *Pagans*, 84–9, 325: in the West such associations could be more inclusive.
46. Cf. Fischer, *Urchristentum*, 71, 154–5. It is less clear that the 'elders' would be a natural designation for a group of house-owners in a city gathering together as Campbell suggests (*Elders*); this would be particularly inappropriate if some house-owners were relatively young and others (perhaps of lower social status) were older and possessed an at least comparable spiritual authority, even if it was based on other factors than the possession of a house and financial means. The role of 'elders' within a society such as that of ancient Israel is in many respects inapplicable to the more complex society of a Graeco-Roman city.
47. Those giving should do so *en haplotēti*; the meaning of this phrase is disputed, but if BDAG is correct in interpreting it of 'simple goodness … "without strings attached" ', then one can perhaps see an implicit contrast to the ethos of much of the patronage system of the Graeco-Roman world, where the patron

expected to get something back for his generosity, at least the prestige of having dependent clients, if not more material returns.

48. Cf. Fischer, *Tendenz*, 23–4; Schenk, *Phil*, 78–82. It is true that Polycarp in writing to the Philippians speaks only of the need to be subject to 'elders and deacons' (5.3), but Pilhofer, *Philippi* 1, 140–7, sees in Phil 1.1 a characteristic Philippian love of official titles that manifests itself in the various associations of that city, including religious ones. The title of '*episkopos*' had, however, given way to that of 'elder' by the time Polycarp wrote to them in the following century (227).
49. Cf. Stegemann–Stegemann, *Sozialgeschichte*, 373 n. 118. Such an interpretation of the nature of these designations in *Phil* 1.1 seems to me more plausible than the suggestion that they were particularly responsible for the worship of the Philippian church, for regulating its eucharistic practice in the various house churches (are we sure that there was more than one?), as Roloff suggests, despite his recognizing the secular origin of *episkopos* and the connection of the term there with administration and the rendering of services (*Kirche*, 142). At the most one would perhaps expect the people so designated to play a role there when it came to financing the communal meals of the church, including eucharistic ones.
50. References in H. W. Beyer's article in *TDNT* 2, 91–2.
51. U. B. Müller, *Phil*, 35–6, regards this as a 'possibility worthy of serious consideration'. Wengst, *Didache*, 42, suggests that the *episkopoi* and *diakonoi* of Did 15.1–2 were also particularly concerned with the community's finances (they should not be 'lovers of money').
52. Cf. Claußen, *Versammlung*, 264–73, esp. 271; also Campbell, *Elders*, 52; Karrer, 'Ältestenamt', 156–62. In Karrer's eyes Isa 24.23 may also have played an important part in the development of the Christian institution in Jerusalem: the elders are part of the eschatological vision for that city (167), but the reference back to Moses' time remains.
53. Similarly, the early Christians used the term *ekklēsia* as a self-designation; quite apart from its secular use to denote the civic assemblies of Greek cities (cf. Acts 19.39–40), this was a regular LXX translation for *qāhāl*, the Old Testament assembly of the people of God (69x; of the other four Hebrew words translated by this Greek word Hatch and Redpath note only one occurrence each), although early Jewish apocalyptic may have played an important mediating role (cf. J. Roloff in *EWNT* 1, 1000; also Fischer, *Urchristentum*, 65). It is true that *synagōgē* was also sometimes used to translate this Hebrew word (36x; for *qᵉhillah* 1x), but that translation had been appropriated by the gatherings of the Jews.
54. Cf. G. Bornkamm in *TDNT* 6, 653–4; Karrer, 'Ältestenamt', 183–4.
55. *Adressaten*, 102.
56. Is it to be found, for instance, in 2 Tim 1.6 ('I remind you to kindle the gift of God's grace [*charisma*] which is in you by virtue of the laying on of my hands')? (Is it presupposed that there is only one such gift? Yet that is not expressly stated.) Or perhaps, though not so clearly, in 1 Tim 4.14 ('do not neglect the gift of God's grace which was given to you on the instructions of prophecy with the laying on of the elders' hands') – that seems to correspond very closely to

the scene described in Acts 13.1–3 and there there is no doubt there that all is seen as happening under the sovereign guidance of God's Spirit. There is, however, no explicit appeal to the proof of Barnabas and Paul's previous empowerment by the Spirit as evidenced in missionary work as was the case in Gal 2.7–9, even though such activity has been described in Acts 11.23–6.

57. This is supported by e.g. Breytenbach, *Paulus*; Hengel, *Paul*, 11; Hengel-Schwemer, *Paul*, 261; Riesner, *Paul's Early Period*, 273–91; Trocmé, *Childhood*, 51–2; Witulski, *Adressaten*. As an outspoken representative of the English-speaking world cf. S. Mitchell, *Anatolia* 2, 3–4: 'There is virtually nothing to be said for the north Galatian theory'. As he notes, northern Galatia lies 200 km to the east of any natural route between Lystra and the region of Mysia (cf. Acts 16.6–7). Whereas later inscriptions (e.g. *ILS* 1017) would list all the constituent parts of this extensive province, at this period it was usual simply to refer to the whole as 'Galatia' (cf., e.g. *ILS* 9499; *IGR* 3.263). There is, however, the difficulty that Derbe, visited by Paul and Barnabas in Acts 14.20–1, probably did not belong to the Roman province at this time, but to the kingdom of Antiochus IV of Commagene: J. Taylor, 'St Paul', 1223–4.

58. But cf. the arguments of Koch, 'Barnabas': e.g. it would have been unwise for Paul to mention Barnabas' role in Gal 2.11–14 if he were co-founder of the Galatian churches. Or is it a sign of Paul's boldness that he expressly mentions Barnabas to show that he himself has alone remained true to the interests and rights of the Galatian Christians? And would it not have been probable that the intruders had expressly made an issue of Barnabas' conduct in order to persuade the Galatians?

59. Schmithals, however, treats these opponents in Galatia as gnostics whose reason for demanding circumcision is either tactical – e.g. for the sake of being tolerated by Jews, and is not central to their beliefs nor entails keeping the rest of the law – or it is symbolic of the destruction of the flesh (*Paul and the Gnostics*, 32–43).

60. The avoidance of persecution may well presuppose a rising nationalism in Judaea, which could endanger Jewish Christians there if they were thought to be consorting with gentiles and undermining the integrity of the covenant people; cf. Jewett, 'Agitators'. In the light of the earlier fate of Stephen and of James, the son of Zebedee, the fear of persecution was not unwarranted. 1 Thess 2.14–16 also seems to presuppose further sufferings of the Judaean Christians at the hands of their fellow-Jews. That this hindered the preaching to the gentiles (v. 16) may be due to the fact that the pressure brought to bear upon the Jewish Christians in Judaea induced them in turn to bring pressure on gentile Christians and above all on those Jewish Christians seeking to include gentiles in the church.

61. Cf. Wedderburn, *Reasons*, 108–23.

62. The direct polemic in Rom 16.17–18, which has no parallel in the rest of the letter, which is more apologetic in tone, could be used as an argument for an interpolation, either in vv. 17–20 or in the whole chapter, but, if the threat has not yet become a reality, need not be. Verse 19, at any rate, forms a neat *inclusio* with 1.8.

63. For a similar accusation cf. Rev 2.2.

64. Cf., e.g. the discussions in Furnish, *II Cor*, 502–5; Thrall, *II Cor* (2), 671–6.
65. There are dangers in a 'mirror reading' of Paul's defence in order to reconstruct the position of his opponents, particularly if it can be shown that the apostle is employing certain rhetorical conventions (cf. Sumney, *Identifying*); this is particularly true in the case of those denying the resurrection in 1 Cor 15, where Paul treats them as if they were like the popular conception of the Epicureans (cf. Wedderburn, 'Problem', 40–1). On the other hand it is difficult to see why Paul should write as he did in 2 Corinthians if his opponents were equally weak as orators and had laid no claim to wonders. In order to make such charges against Paul they would surely have had to have a stronger claim to such qualifications themselves.
66. Cf. *Theologiegeschichte*, 463–5.
67. 1.12 adds 'I am Christ's'. Although much has been built on this last slogan, it seems doubtful that it is a slogan of the Corinthians that Paul must repudiate. For one thing his argument in 1.13 implies that Christians should only belong to Christ; it is the other slogans that are inappropriate. For another, he refers back to these slogans later in 3.22–3 and sets belonging to Christ over against the claims of the other three (and 1 Clem 47.3 also refers to the parties of the first three only). That 'I am Christ's' is Paul's addition was suggested already by John Chrysostom (cf., e.g. M. M. Mitchell, *Paul*, 83 n. 101).

    The way in which Paul then introduces the question whom he had baptized (1 Cor 1.13–17) and the emphasis which he places on the theme of baptism suggests that the formation of parties may, at least in part, have had something to do with the administration of this rite – 'at least in part' because, unless Peter had been in Corinth, he could not have baptized there, and the formation of a Christ party on a similar basis is ruled out; Paul implies that *all* are baptized in Christ's name. Above all it is Apollos who may have baptized larger numbers of the community (cf. 3.6 again). For the possibility that sacramental notions current in the Graeco-Roman world may have influenced the way in which the baptized viewed their relationship to the baptizer, see Wedderburn, *Baptism*, 248–9; also Schrage, *1 Kor* (1), 155.
68. So Dahl, 'Paul', 322–3, 326 (also M. M. Mitchell, *Paul*: Paul's critique is of factionalism as such).
69. It is therefore unnecessary to postulate, for example, the arrival of gnostic missionaries (Schmithals, *Gnosis*).
70. The accumulation of 'wisdom' and 'foolishness' in the first chs of 1 Corinthians is quite unparalleled in Paul's letters:

	1 Cor	*1 Cor 1–4*	*Other generally acknowledged Pauline letters*
'wisdom' (*sophia*)	17x	16x	2x
'wise' (*sophos*)	11x	10x	5x
'folly' (*mōria*)	5x	5x	–
'foolish' (*mōros*)	4x	4x	–

71. Others, however, read this verse in a very different way: Pöttner, *Realität*, 37 speaks of a 'concealed invective' against Apollos (cf. also Sellin, '"Geheimnis"', 78–9). But the way Apollos' followers regarded him is not necessarily his

fault – any more than that Paul is necessarily to be blamed for his followers' attitude to him.

72. It is perhaps surprising that v. Dobbeler, *Philippus*, e.g. 197, suggests that the Spirit-filled Apollos preached a form of baptism with which the gift of the Spirit was not associated, but which was a 'baptism of repentance' like John's, binding the baptized to the baptizer. Yet was it not almost inevitable that at least some of those receiving Apollos' baptism would seek to emulate his form of charismatic, prophet-like existence?
73. Theißen, *Setting*, 125–9; Meggitt, *Paul*, 108–12.
74. What is puzzling is that, if such meals brought one into contact with demons, Paul's only criticism in ch. 8 of one who partakes of a meal in an idol's shrine is in terms of the effect that it may have upon his fellow-Christian who is not endowed with such knowledge of the non-existence of idols (v.10). Of the presence of demons there is no word yet. It is true that shrines and temples often had attached dining rooms where gatherings whose function was not primarily cultic could take place, but it is hard to imagine that they took place without at least a libation to the deity in whose buildings they were meeting. It is, then, in the last analysis hard to believe that Paul would not also condemn just as strongly such actions, and not just because of their effect on others, but in his argumentative strategy he seems to hold his fire for the moment.
75. Whether the resurrection of Christians was from the start so central is less certain; at any rate it is hard to see why the Thessalonians would have been so worried about the death of some of their number (1 Thess 4.13–18) if it had been.
76. Josephus *BJ* 2.408–9; cf. Becker, *Paul*, 455; Haacker, *Paulus*, 97; but also the criticism in Horn, 'Jerusalemreise', 31–2.
77. Not, however, Wehnert, *Reinheit*, 271, who suggests that it was perhaps handed over informally without Paul's participation. More plausible, in that it least has some basis in the text of Acts, is Berger's suggestion that it was used to finance the Nazirite vow mentioned in Acts 21.23–6 (*Theologiegeschichte*, 162; cf. Horn, 'Jerusalemreise', 34), but in its entirety or only in part? Alternatively, Trocmé, *Childhood*, 75, speculates that it served to pay the expenses of Paul and his companions over the next two years. For even if it is correct, as Meggitt notes (*Paul*, 93–4), that where an accused person was imprisoned depended on decisions about the seriousness of the charge or the likelihood of guilt, one has to ask how Paul was able to support himself if he was unable to work for his living. In other words, we are at best guessing here.
78. Cf. Wedderburn, 'Collection', 103 and, on Acts 20.4, 105–6.
79. Trocmé, *Childhood*, 91, refers to the demoralization of Paul's churches after the failure of the collection.

Chapter 8

1. There are problems in Dunn's attempt to describe a spectrum of 'Jewish Christianity' which reaches from John at one end to the Ebionite groups at the other (cf. the diagram in *Unity*, 265). Does John, for instance, deserve to be labelled 'Jewish Christian' while Paul does not? And Dunn's attempt to mark

the point where acceptable diversity passes over into the unacceptable runs the risk of ignoring the question 'Acceptable to whom?' – the decision of Peter and the other Jewish Christians at Antioch was unacceptable to Paul, but the terms on which Paul was conducting his mission were unacceptable to James and the Jerusalem church. Nor can the unacceptability of the position of the Ebionites be satisfactorily demonstrated by the fact that they rejected the Pauline faith of the church in the West. It may have been unacceptable to those holding that Pauline faith, and in the end, with the help of Titus' legions, that faith won. But because they were on the losing side does that make the beliefs of the Ebionites any more or less right or wrong than those of the Jerusalem Christians in the days when that church was the centre of the Christian world? In other words, judging where heresy begins and ends is no business for the historian (Dunn's book originated in an investigation of Walter Bauer's *Orthodoxy and Heresy*), and the synchronic model of the spectrum loses sight of the dynamism of the 'trajectory' or 'lines of development' model (see ch. 9 below), which allows more for changes, including in this case changed perceptions and changed sides.

2. Although this literature probably stems from the fourth century, it is likely that it contains earlier traditions.
3. However, S. G. Wilson, *Strangers*, 160–1, following L. Gaston, speaks only of Judaizing gentiles.
4. Frg. 7 (Schneemelcher)/4 (Elliott). Hengel, 'Jakobus', 82, Painter, *James*, 184–5, Pratscher, *Herrenbruder*, 46, and Ward, 'James', 791, point out that the fragment presupposes James's presence at the Last Supper.
5. Hengel and Schwemer suggest that he was already spokesman for the more conservatively inclined wing of Jewish Christianity (*Paul*, 135); see also Bruce, *Gal*, 99 ('perhaps already leader of one group'); Grappe, *Temple*, 82 (in support of this Acts 12.12, 17 may be mentioned: James and the brethren are not present at the meeting in the house of Mary, the mother of John Mark). Painter, *James*, 60, goes further (cf. also Berger, *Theologiegeschichte*, 714): he was already the leader of the church, although in that case it is harder to see why Paul mentions seeing him almost as an afterthought (cf. Klein, 'Gal 2,6–9', 288–90); Painter's answer seems to be that Paul sought contact with Peter first because he thought him 'more sympathetic to Paul's cause'.
6. This is striking even if, as Pratscher, *Herrenbruder*, 69–70, seeks, not altogether convincingly, to argue, James is named first for other reasons than that he now played the leading role in the triumvirate.
7. Roloff, 'Konflikte', 124, sees behind the whole legend of Peter's miraculous rescue James's replacement of Peter as head of the Jerusalem church, because the latter's latitude was viewed with suspicion. Painter, on the other hand, argues that James had to be told what was happening, not because he was to take Peter's place, but because he was already leader of the Jerusalem church (*James*, esp. 44) – but for Pesch, *Simon-Petrus*, 63, only since Peter's arrest.

   Clement of Alexandria records the tradition of the Kerygma Petri (?first half of the second century) that the apostles should, after twelve years, turn from preaching to the Jews to bring the word to the rest of the world (*Strom.* 6.5.43; cf. Schneemelcher 2, 40; also Apollonius in Euseb. *Hist. eccl.* 5.18.14;

Acts of Peter 5 [Schneemelcher 2, 262/Elliott, 401–2]). Is this period of time connected with this persecution? (Cf. Pesch, *Simon-Petrus*, 63.)

8. Cf. Hengel, 'Jakobus', 100.
9. Grappe, *Temple*, 85–6, points to the prevalence of such a principle at that time, above all in the appointment of high priests, but also among those taking the lead in zealous activity on behalf of the law.
10. Tr. Elliott; Hengel, 'Jakobus', 79–80, suggests that the claim made here for James is comparable to that made for the righteous in some rabbinic traditions. For Bauckham, 'James', 451, the saying stems from James's lifetime and implies his authority over the mission of the other apostles, wherever their mission took them.
11. Euseb. *Hist. eccl.* 2.23.4 (named 'righteous' by all).
12. Must the 'others' also be Christians, as some assume?
13. There is little justification in Josephus' account for Frend's claim (*Martyrdom*, 171) that the 'Jerusalem mob' played a part in James's death.
14. Hengel, 'Jakobus', 73; Painter, *James*, 129.
15. In the second century Hegesippus offers us a more legendary account of the martyrdom of this holy man (in Euseb. *Hist. eccl.* 2.23.4–18).
16. 'For What Offence?', 218–32; it is correct that Josephus has just stressed that Ananias belonged to the school of the Sadducees who were harsher in their judicial practice (§199). For Bauckham the likeliest charge is that of leading the people astray.
17. Josephus *AJ* 20.206–7 – the problem was not new: cf. §181. Cf. Painter, *James*, 140–1, 250, but also the criticism of Pratscher, *Herrenbruder*, 257, who sees the cause rather in the early Christian community's threat to political stability. (But why then use the opportunity presented by an interregnum between Roman governors? Could Ananias not reckon then with the governor's support?)
18. Cf. ch. 2, p. 31 and n. 52 above.
19. Hahn–Müller, 'Jakobusbrief', 63.
20. So, e.g. Pratscher, *Herrenbruder*, 211–12; Schnelle, *Einleitung*, 399.
21. *Adressaten*, 54.
22. And Popkes recognizes that there was, strictly speaking, no Roman 'middle class' (*Adressaten*, 86).
23. Scholars are divided as to whether this mission to gentiles replaces any mission to Jews and as to whether this Gospel, for all its Jewishness, regards the Jews as having had their chance and having failed to use it. See, e.g. the differing views of P. Stuhlmacher, H. Kvalbein, U. Luz and O. Skarsaune in Ådna–Kvalbein, *Mission*, 17–83 (although Luz stresses that his views do not differ so much from Kvalbein's as the latter supposes): much hinges on the question whether 'all the nations' in Matt 28.19 includes the Jews or not.
24. Cf. Hengel, 'Christentum', 208–9, appealing to R. L. Rubinstein.
25. Cf. Stanton, *Gospels*, 78. S. G. Wilson, *Strangers*, 47, makes the valuable point that, although the heirs of the Pharisaic traditions may have been on the way to redefining Judaism and consolidating their interpretation of it, we should not overestimate their numbers or influence at this point of time. It is, however, with them above all that Matthew has a bone to pick, despite all the similarities between his version of Jewishness and theirs.

26. Yet Meeks, 'Breaking Away', 112, points to Matt 28.15 as evidence of a similar detachment from 'the Jews', and 'the whole people' accept their responsibility for Jesus' death in 27.5.
27. 'Bergpredigt', 362 (254).
28. Cf. Riches, 'Synoptiker', 176; also Karrer, 'Petrus', 229.
29. In the judgement of Wehr, *Petrus*, 251–90, 378, this work preserves in large measure the theological position of Peter (more than the works which bear his name).
30. See above ch. 6, p. 114.
31. Cf. Milavec, 'Genius', 108–9.
32. Christians fast, not on the second and fifth day of the week (cf. m.Taan. 2.9), but on the fourth and the day of preparation – the same expression as we find in the New Testament and in Josephus for the day before the Jewish sabbath or a festival. See also S. G. Wilson, *Strangers*, 224–7, for further signs of 'dependence [on Judaism] with a distinctive twist' in the Didache.
33. The longest version of the title is found in the MS Hierosolymitanus 54; the Georgian version is similar. It may well be that all versions of the title, long or short ('teaching of the apostles'), are secondary.
34. Niederwimmer, *Didache*, 215, observes that the circle of the 'apostles' is here not yet limited to the Twelve; this group of itinerants is an open one, whose number is not fixed.
35. Cf. Milavec, 'Genius', 114–15.
36. *Didache*, 216.
37. Cf. Milavec, 'Genius', 104, 119–20.
38. Cf. Wengst, *Didache*, esp. 36, 43. 'Monepiscopate' is Markschies' preferred term for this institution (*Zwischen den Welten*, 215): 'monarchical episcopate' implies, anachronistically, features more appropriate to the third and fourth centuries.
39. Euseb. *Hist. eccl.* 3.5.3; cf. also Epiph. *Adv. haeres.* 29.7.7–8; 30.2.7; *De mensuris et ponderibus* 15; Lüdemann, 'Successors', 168; *Paulus* 2, 277, adds Ps.-Clem. *Recg.* 1.37.2; 39.3.
40. Euseb. *Hist. eccl.* 4.5.1–3. Bauckham, *Jude*, 70–9, following R. van den Broek, 'Brief', in utilizing the apocryphal letter of James to Quadratus, argues that Eusebius is wrong in suggesting that all fifteen followed one another; rather we have here three bishops who succeeded one another and a college of twelve elders who governed the church along with James, a college which included some of the 'apostles'. The presence of a Senikus or Seneca(s) among the elders or bishops does not encourage great confidence in the information in either of these lists. Epiphanius also seems to know of a church continuing in Jerusalem after 70 (*De mensuris et ponderibus* 14 – returning from Pella?).
41. Lüdemann, 'Successors', 173, aptly compares the claim of the group of the Ebionites who traced their pedigree back to the 'poor' of Jerusalem: Epiph. *Adv. haeres.* 30.17.2.
42. S. G. Wilson, *Strangers*, 146; Wehnert, 'Auswanderung', 248–52 (with further references to E. Meyer and M. Simon); at about the same time as James's death Jesus b. Ananias must have begun his prophecies foretelling doom for Jerusalem and the Temple (Josephus *BJ* 6.300–9); Wehnert (249) also

compares Ps.-Clem. *Recg.* 1.71.2 with its account of five thousand men leaving Jerusalem in the direction of Jericho after James's death, and also Josephus' account of many Jews leaving Judaea for gentile territories at this time, due either to the misrule of Gessius Florus (*BJ* 2.279; Florus was governor in 64–6) or the destruction wrought by brigands (*AJ* 20.256).

43. G. W. H. Lampe, 'A.D. 70', 153.
44. Cf. the Ebionites according to Iren. *Haer.* 1.26.2 (ed. Harvey 1.22), the Elkesaites in Euseb. *Hist. eccl.* 6.38, the Cerinthians in Epiph. *Adv. haeres.* 28.5.3, or the Encratites in Orig. *Cels.* 5.65.
45. Probably implicit in Hegesippus' account of James's death in Euseb. *Hist. eccl.* 2.23.18.
46. Contrast the Ebionites' adoration of Jerusalem as the house of God in Iren. *Haer.* 1.26.2 (ed. Harvey 1.22); the Ossaeans (Elkesaites?) faced Jerusalem in prayer according to Epiph. *Adv. haeres.* 19.3.5–6.
47. Cf. 1 Apoc. Jas. 24.15; 31.18–23; perhaps reflected too in 2 Apoc. Jas. 50.15–22 (James and Jesus are brothers only because they shared Mary's milk).
48. Apart from Gos. Thom. §12 quoted above cf. the Apocryphon of James (NHC I/2) and the First and Second Apocalypses of James (V/3–4).
49. *Ep. Petri* 2.3–4; *Contestatio* 1.1; also Iren. *Haer.* 1.26.2 (ed. Harvey 1.22); Epiph. *Adv. haeres.* 28.5.3 (followers of Cerinthus).
50. Ps.-Clem. *Hom.* 2.44.2; 3.52.1; cf. Elchasai in Epiph. *Adv. haeres.* 19.3.6 and Gos. Eb. 6 (Schneemelcher)/7 (Elliott) – abolition of sacrifices without the undergirding of a theory about false passages in the Old Testament.
51. *Herrenbruder*, 177.
52. See also the discussion of Dunn's views in n. 1 of this chapter.

Chapter 9

1. Yet Schmithals (*Theologiegeschichte*, 7) points out, with some justification, that these postulated lines of development are often a somewhat daring reconstruction, since the traditions located on them are mostly bereft of any information as to their time and place.
2. *Pace* Conzelmann, 'Paulus', 233, and 'Schule', 88, who located his Pauline school in Ephesus.
3. P. Müller, *Anfänge*, rightly stresses that this phenomenon is a complex one arising from the varied process of handing on and realizing Paul's legacy in different regions and differing situations. Also disputed is whether the term 'school' is appropriately applied to a whole community or rather to those in it 'more active in writing and bearing witness', above all those seeking to pass on the teaching of the school's head by interpretative writings (R. E. Brown, *Community*, 101–2, over against Culpepper, *School*, 274–5).
4. Apart from the apocryphal letter to the Corinthians contained in the Acts of Paul (Schneemelcher 2, 232–4/Elliott, 380–2) or the letters supposedly written by Paul to the philosopher Seneca (Schneemelcher 2, 44–50/Elliott, 547–53).
5. One argument in favour of such an early date is the fact that Colossae was in all probability affected by the earthquake which devastated the neighbouring Laodicea in the early 60s. Even if Colossae itself was not so badly affected

(although some think it ceased to exist – certainly a church there is never mentioned in Revelation or in the letters of Ignatius), the letter mentions the church in Laodicea (2.1; 4.13, 15, 16) and it is hard to imagine that this catastrophe would not be mentioned if it were an event of the recent past. Such a destination for the letter, if it was really sent to that city, only becomes plausible again after a considerable time has elapsed and this disaster has either been forgotten or become a thing of the distant past. (Cf. Reicke, *Re-Examining*, 3–4, 73–5, 81–3.)

6. The clearest sign of development is in the image of the church as Christ's body: whereas in 1 Cor 12.21 the head was just one part of the body among others, here it is set over the whole of the body (1.18; 2.19). Such a development would be particularly hard to explain if Colossians is regarded as written from Ephesus during the period of Paul's third missionary journey, at least if written by Paul himself in any sense, for 1 Corinthians also stems from the same period.
7. Cf. Wedderburn, 'Theology', 4–12.
8. For Fischer, *Tendenz*, Ephesians opposes an episcopal church order (21–33) and a growing anti-Judaism (79–83, 93–4); Mußner emphasizes the need of the various local churches for a sense of belonging together after the deaths of their founders (*Eph*, 34–5); for Pokorný the danger lies in syncretism (*Eph*, 43–6; cf. also Gnilka, *Eph*, 34–5).
9. Euseb. *Hist. eccl.* 2.22.2 mentions the tradition that Paul defended himself, was released, resumed his missionary activity and then returned again to Rome to suffer martyrdom under Nero. This was the setting presupposed by 2 Timothy, which refers back to Paul's 'first defence' (4.16).
10. Cf. D. R. MacDonald, *Legend*, 57–77; Rordorf, 'Verhältnis', 237–8 and 'Nochmals'.
11. But cf. Bauckham, 'Acts'.
12. 'Acts'; but cf. the critique of, e.g. Büllesbach, 'Verhältnis', 232–4; Pervo, 'Act', esp. 17–31 (who, plausibly, sees the Acts of Paul as meant to correct or even supplant both Acts and the Pastorals).
13. Koester, *Introduction* 2, 306; however, he later ('Ephesos', 124) regards a date for these letters in 'the fourth or fifth decade of the second century' as most likely.
14. Above all Conzelmann, 'Schule', 90, who is scathing in his criticism of those whose views of canonicity do not allow them to recognize this clash. It is, however, questionable whether Koester is right to treat the view of Hymenaeus and Philetus as 'typically gnostic' (*Introduction* 2, 306); it was one way among others by which Christian gnostics could come to terms with the for them distinctly unpalatable doctrine of the resurrection (cf. Wedderburn, *Baptism*, 212–18).
15. See also ch. 11 below. For literature see Wedderburn, 'Theology', 20–2, or (more recently) in Woyke, *Haustafeln*, 77–82.
16. Cf. Wagener, *Ordnung*; also M. Y. MacDonald, *Churches*, 208, 210, 228 (particularly incompatible with the ethos of the Pastorals would be female teachers urging abstinence from marriage). Horrell, *Ethos*, 167, insists that it is even less true of Paul himself that his churches mirrored the social hierarchy of the Graeco-Roman household.

17. 'Elders' and 'overseers' seem to be identical; 1 Tim 3.2 speaks, however, of 'the *episkopos*' in contrast to *diakonoi* (3.8) or elders, *presbyteroi* (5.17) in the plural (similarly Tit 1.5, 7).
18. E.g. 2.24 (cf. also 4.1, 13) echoes Paul's language of dying with Christ, dying to sin and living to God, but without the 'with'-compounds and 'to die' with the dative.
19. Cf., e.g. Hengel, 'Jakobus', 103; P. Lampe, *Christen*, 334–45; Markschies, *Zwischen den Welten*, 217.
20. However, Uebele, '*Verführer*', repeatedly interprets the 'Judaizing' in terms of the exegesis of the Old Testament on which the docetists based their Christology; such a sense of *ioudaizein* would be unusual, to say the least.
21. It is an argument against the combination of Jewish practice and docetism that Judaizing is more often found in combination with the opposite of docetism, a stress on Jesus' humanity. On the other hand, we have seen in ch. 4 how the rise of gnosticism can be regarded (a) as propelled by similar concerns to those which exercised Hellenistic Jews of a Platonizing tendency, and (b) as often connected with a violent aversion to Judaism. The first might show itself in a docetic Christology, but the second point is difficult to combine with the observance of Jewish rites.
22. Käsemann, 'Ministry', 88, refers to the disappearance of a church order based on *charisma* from the Pauline churches because it seemed to them 'an ideal incapable of being realized'. Did Paul then think that it was viable or did he share their realism?
23. There is a danger that the use of this label is a theologically loaded one: while Roman Catholic scholars may welcome the discovery of this phenomenon in certain New Testament writings, there is a tendency for Protestant scholars to treat the phenomenon and the writings which manifest it, or traces of it, negatively, viewing them as in some sense degenerate. But it is one thing to question the appropriateness of the label, another to ask whether the tendencies designated by it are detectable in earliest Christianity.
24. It is likelier that we should see in this danger the main impetus to these developments, and not, say, in the delay of the parousia, the return of Christ which had been expected in the immediate future (but cf. Käsemann, 'Paul', 237).
25. Vouga, *Geschichte*, 235, and S. Alkier in *RGG*[4] 3, 402, trace this expression back to Ernst Troeltsch in 1912, but it is above all Ernst Käsemann whose use of the concept led to its popularity and centrality in more recent discussion.
26. Käsemann, 'Paul', 243.
27. Käsemann, 'Paul', 248; cf. 'Ministry', 87–8.
28. Cf. 1 Tim 6.20.
29. The fact that the Pastoral Epistles are usually dated not that much earlier than the letters of Ignatius (e.g. Schnelle, *Einleitung*, 347: around 100 CE) should warn us that this fictional depiction of the role of these two co-workers of Paul's is not necessarily chronologically earlier than the development of a monarchical episcopate or monepiscopate.
30. Cf. ch. 7, n. 56 above.

Chapter 10

1. E.g. Koester, *Introduction* 2, 182–204 (he gives few reasons for this decision).
2. *Haer.* 5.33.4. However, Koester, 'Ephesos', 138–9, treats Irenaeus' account as a fiction, identifying the Fourth Evangelist with the John of Ephesus who wrote Revelation – sources from Asia Minor like the letters of Ignatius or Polycarp show no knowledge of the Fourth Gospel (135). But if this is a fiction then it it is surely disconcerting if, as Koester grants, shortly afterwards Polycrates of Samos (Euseb. *Hist. eccl.* 3.31.3) and the Acts of John assume the death of the author of the Gospel in Ephesus.
3. *Pace* de Boer, *Perspectives*, esp. 58–63, it seems questionable whether the 'death-threat' marks a separate phase in the community's history.
4. Wengst, *Gemeinde*, is, however, far more specific: reflected here is the history of the Johannine community in Gaulanitis and Batanaea under Herod Agrippa II (Schürer, *History* 1, 472, 481: he was given these territories in 53 CE and was to hold them perhaps until 92–3). Most doubt, however, whether the data allow such precision. However, Meeks, 'Breaking Away', 101–3, is more sympathetic to this, adding only that an urban setting is preferable.

   On the form such an ostracism of those regarded as heretics could take in a Jewish context cf. t. Hull. 2.20–1.
5. Barrett, *Documents*, §200. Contrast the version given in Schürer, *History* 2, 457.
6. Cf. S. G. Wilson, *Strangers*, 182–3.
7. Cf. Maier, *Zwischen den Testamenten*, 288: he points out that the reference to the 'Nazarenes' (*notzrim*) is first found in medieval texts; also van der Horst, 'Birkat ha-minim'; S. G. Wilson, *Strangers*, 176–83.
8. J. T. Sanders, *Schismatics*, 58–9, suggests that this addition was meant to prevent heretics from acting as precentors in the synagogue worship, but something more drastic than that seems to be envisaged by the Fourth Gospel (cf. Hare, *Theme*, 54–5).
9. So, rightly, Segal, *Rebecca's Children*, 157: the Fourth Gospel 'was presumably written by a group that may once have felt itself to be Jewish but did so no more'.
10. Hengel, *Question*, 114–17, treats the expulsion from the synagogue as 'a lengthy and painful process' going back to the martyrdom of Stephen and therefore not contemporary with the writing of the Gospel. However, Zumstein, 'Geschichte', 423, tentatively assigns the final redaction of the Fourth Gospel to the point of time when the Johannine group or school left Syria because of synagogal persecution (similarly Uebele, '*Verführer*', 98–100). But the alienation from 'the Jews' rather suggests that the Gospel itself, although not the traditions it contains, is to be dated some time after this break.
11. Reflected in John 6.61, 64, 66? Or, as R. E. Brown, *Community*, 73–80, suggests, did these believers seek refuge in non-Johannine Jewish-Christian or Judaizing communities?
12. Cf. Trocmé, *Childhood*, 22. Cullmann, too, traces the origins of this Christian tradition to the sphere of influence of the 'Jerusalem Hellenists' (*Circle*, 53) and regards the two as analogous, without explicitly identifying the 'Johannine circle' with this group.
13. Cf. Koester, 'Ephesos', 133; Uebele, '*Verführer*', 39–41.

14. Günther, *Frühgeschichte*, 76–123, argues, however, for a break in the tradition in Ephesus: after Paul's departure the tradition for which Apollos stood declined and was replaced by the tradition represented by John the elder.
15. A point of contact, at least with the seer of Revelation, may, however, be its attitude, at least at times, towards 'the Jews' who are accused of being children of the devil (John 8.44); cf. Revelation's references to the 'synagogue of Satan' (2.9; 3.9).
16. Cf. here Frey, 'Verhältnis', esp. 426.
17. Culpepper, *School*, 265.
18. R. E. Brown, *Community*, 81–8.
19. *Circle*, 15.
20. R. E. Brown, *Community*, notes the difficulties in reconstructing this history and in an appendix (171–82) summarizes five attempts that appeared shortly before the writing of his study (between 1975 and 1977), but the increasing reversal of the more usual order of the Gospel and the letters has since complicated the situation yet further.
21. In Euseb. *Hist. eccl.* 3.39.4. In this account the 'elders' all seem to be disciples of Jesus, including a number of the Twelve, amongst them another John (but cf. Körtner, *Papiasfragmente*, 37). Eusebius sees that two Johns are here referred to, and mentions that there were two tombs in Ephesus, where two Johns were allegedly buried (§6). More questionable is Eusebius' claim (§7) that Papias is saying that he heard Aristion and the elder John in person, but only heard the words of others at second hand. The distinction which this quotation from Papias makes is rather one between what Andrew and the others 'said' and what Aristion and the elder John 'are saying', implying that the latter were still alive when Papias wrote this.
22. To that extent Hyldahl's suggestion (*History*, 256) that 'orthodox Jews' are meant is unlikely, and correspondingly it is hard to see Diotrephes as leader of the local synagogue (256, 258).
23. 'Kerinth', 67–8; cf. also Hengel, *Question*, esp. 60. For Cerinthus' Christology cf. Iren. *Haer.* 1.26.1 (ed. Harvey 1.21): Jesus was born of Mary and Joseph, and Christ descended on him after his baptism; at the end Christ separated from Jesus again, and Jesus suffered and was raised from the dead; Christ remained impassible, for he was spiritual. On the definition of 'docetism' cf. Klauck, *Johannesbriefe*, 138–41.
24. '*Verführer*', *passim*.
25. For Satornilus cf. Iren. *Haer.* 1.24.2 (ed. Harvey 1.18): the Saviour was unbegotten and incorporeal and only seemed to be a human being.
26. *Einleitung*, 512–13.
27. Barrett, 'Johanneisches Christentum', 261, describes both structures, the elder's and Diotrephes', as monarchical, the one responsible for a single congregation, the other for a whole area.
28. For Bauer, at any rate, Diotrephes was the heretic over against the orthodox elder (*Orthodoxy*, 93), for Käsemann, however, it was the other way round ('Ketzer', 173–4, 178). Again, however, categories of heresy and orthodoxy are not helpful in a historical study, particularly if both parties regarded themselves as orthodox and their opponents as the heretics (so, rightly,

Schnelle, *Einleitung*, 515). Only if one adopts anachronistically the definition of orthodoxy of a later period of church history and applies it to these two figures can one decide which of them is right. But to do that one would have to have far more information as to the theological issue(s) at the root of this quarrel.

Chapter 11

1. Cf. Rajak, 'Charter', who points out that this term originated a century and a half later with Tertullian. On the other hand, the category of an 'ancient and legal association', applying also to religious associations, existed earlier (Suet. *Aug.* 32.1; cf. Tac. *Ann.* 14.17; Öhler, 'Vereinsrecht', 54–61).
2. Yet Frend, *Martyrdom*, 143, detects a shift in Roman sympathies away from the Jews and towards the Greeks in the 30s and 40s of the first century.
3. Josephus *AJ* 18.81–4.
4. Suet. *Claud.* 25.4 (Barrett, §9); however the translation here, following LCL, could be misleading, in that it refers to 'the Jews' as if all were affected, in other words several thousand of them; if one leaves out the definite article which the translation has supplied here, the reference may only be to Jews who were causing a disturbance. It is Acts which speaks of all Jews being expelled (18.2). Cf. Botermann, *Judenedikt*, 50–4; Smallwood, *Jews*, 216 (summary expulsion of those who were Roman citizens was legally impossible).
5. See the argument of Botermann, *Judenedikt*, 50–102.
6. Cf. Philo *Leg.* 203.
7. P. Lond. 1912, tr. Barrett, §48.
8. Cf. Theißen, *Theory*, 244.
9. Kollmann, 'Philippus', 561–2, suggests that this may have been the occasion of the flight of Philip and his daughters to Hierapolis (Euseb. *Hist. eccl.* 3.31.3–4; 39.9 – but identified with the apostle Philip); similarly v. Dobbeler, *Philippus*, 248.
10. Cf. the texts in Feldman–Reinhold, *Life*, 290–5. G. W. Clarke, 'Origins', 852, suggests that this may have resulted in the virtual annihilation of the Christian communities in Egypt and Cyrene.
11. Cf. Dio C. 68.32.2 – 240,000 non-Jews were allegedly killed.
12. 'Charter', 116, 121–2.
13. E.g. Trajan's suspicion towards the proposal that an association of firemen might be formed in Nicomedia: Plin. *Ep.* 10.33–4.
14. The connection with the fire is mentioned only in Tac. *Ann.* 15.44 – according to Tacitus involving a 'great crowd' of Christians; Suet., *Nero* 16.2 does not connect these measures with the fire; cf. Barrett, §§11–12; Smallwood, *Jews*, 217–18.
15. *Pace* Botermann, *Judenedikt*, 181–2, 187, nothing in Tacitus' or Suetonius' text suggests that non-Christian Jews were involved; that she suggests they were stems from her reluctance to grant that the Roman authorities were by now aware of Christians' distinctiveness.
16. 'Romans', 178–9.
17. So P. Barceló, 'Christenverfolgungen', in *RGG*[4] 2, 247. Botermann, *Judenedikt*, 181, regards the charge against them as being that of causing disturbances.

(The penalties inflicted would then be very extreme compared with Claudius' measures.)

18. Trocmé, *Childhood*, 82. Harnack's bald assertion (*Mission*, 66–7) that Jews had contributed to this persecution and also, more or less, to most later persecutions is surprising, although a number of others have followed him (e.g. Frend, *Martyrdom*, 164–5; more tentatively in *Rise*, 109; Simon, *Israel*, 117, as well as the survey in S. G. Wilson, *Strangers*, 172–6). At most one could say that they must be the envious persons who slandered the Christians before Nero according to Melito in Euseb. *Hist. eccl.* 4.26.9 and that 1 Clement's reference to the jealousy and envy leading to the deaths of Peter and Paul and others refers to them (5.2–6.1; cf. Smallwood, *Jews*, 218–19, but against that Hare, *Theme*, 72–4). But Acts depicts other groups than the Jews who were ready to denounce Christians, above all because their financial interests were affected. At this early stage there is little solid evidence of Jewish denunciations; the tendency of Acts simply to blame 'the Jews', perhaps at least sometimes unjustly, has already been noted, and, from the time of Justin on, Jewish defamation of Christians becomes a regular theme of Christian apologetics (cf. Justin *Dial.* 17.1; 108.2; 117.3; Iren. *Haer.* 4.21.3 [ed. Harvey 4.35.3]). It is true that the Jews are shown as playing a very malignant role in Mart. Pol. (12.2; 13.1; 17.2; 18.1), but this work manifestly seeks to emphasize the parallels between Polycarp's fate and Jesus'. Even if one grants that occasionally Jews had recourse to the Roman or municipal authorities in the hope of ridding themselves of troublesome Christians, as Acts depicts (17.6; 18.12), and even if they might well be justified in doing so if they saw the problems which one or more synagogues in Rome had brought upon themselves by trying to cope unaided with Christians in their midst, that in itself does not justify attributing the Neronian persecution too to their influence.
19. Cf. Lane Fox, *Pagans*, 432, apropos of Paul's death.
20. Josephus *BJ* 2.197; one cause of the war with Rome was, correspondingly, the suspension of these sacrifices: §409.
21. Whether the practice of the twice-daily sacrifice still existed after 70 CE is a moot point; Josephus *Ap.* 2.77 speaks as if the institution were still in force, but cf. Schürer, *History* 1, 521–3.
22. 'Konfusion', esp. 241–6; also P. Barceló, 'Christenverfolgungen', in *RGG*[4] 2, 247.
23. E.g. Frey, 'Verhältnis', esp. 412–14, 427; Günther, *Frühgeschichte*, 133; Kraft, *Offb*, 93–4; Reichert, 'Konfusion', esp. 249–50; Taeger, 'Streitschrift', 296. However Klauck, 'Do They Never Come Back?', esp. 697, argues that Revelation purports to have been written in the time of Vespasian, the sixth king of 17.10, but was actually written in the time of the eighth, Domitian (v. 11). But then there are the ten horns which also stand for kings (vv. 3, 12): should we see here a further updating of the prophecy to the time of Trajan or simply a borrowing from Dan 7.7? One should, however, distinguish the date of receiving the revelation on Patmos from the date of composition, to judge from the past tense used in Rev. 1.9: John has seemingly now left the island (so Charles, *Rev* 1, 21; Müller, *Offb*, 81, but cf. Günther, *Frühgeschichte*, 131).

24. Whether the seer himself is being punished (so, e.g. Müller, *Offb*, 81) is not clear: those of relatively high status (*honestiores*) might be banished (*relegatio*) and Hengel argues that he enjoyed such a status (*Question*, 126). Or was John there simply to receive his revelation (e.g. Kraft, *Offb*, 42)? Yet Garnsey (*Status*, 119; cf. 121) refers to 'the magisterial use of *relegatio* or *leve exilium* as a coercive measure against troublemakers' of lower rank (cf., e.g. Tac. *Ann.* 13.22; 14.62).
25. Cf. Fischer, *Urchristentum*, 130; Lane Fox, *Pagans*, 319; contrast Trocmé, *Childhood*, viii.
26. As Pilhofer, *Presbyteron*, has amply demonstrated: the principle 'what is older is better' had itself a long pedigree and was still very much in force in the Roman world, along with its corollary that 'what is newer is worse'.
27. That perception is surely reflected in the ending of Acts (esp. 28.28): Christianity's future lay with the mission to the gentiles.
28. Cf., e.g. J. E. Taylor, 'Phenomenon', 318.
29. Suet. *Dom.* 12.2: under Domitian those who lived as Jews without acknowledging it and those who concealed their origin were prosecuted for non-payment of the tax – at least allegedly so, as Thompson, 'Domitian', 337, adds – alleged, for example, by informers. Yet, although Thompson correctly argues that, for Dio and other Romans, all those living the 'Jewish life' were regarded as Jews, an element of uncertainty remains, as Suetonius' account betrays: was being circumcised proof that one still lived a 'Jewish life', for this was something which could not so easily be abandoned, whatever else one did or did not do?
30. Cf. Schürer, *History*, 2.272 with n. 59 and 3.123 with n. 67.
31. Josephus *BJ* 2.140, ascribes to the Essenes the conviction that no one holds any office unless God wills it, and to Herod Agrippa II (2.390) the view that Rome would never have acquired so great an empire had God not wanted it. Josephus had, of course, good personal reasons for endorsing the legitimacy of Roman rule.
32. 1 Pet 2.13–3.7. See also ch. 9, p. 173 and n. 15 above.
33. *Pax*, 118.
34. Other less precise references as in 6.9 may then be interpreted in the light of this.
35. Pliny *Ep.* 10.96.3; so Wengst, *Pax*, 120.
36. For a beast arises out of the sea or the abyss (11.7; 17.8) whence the defeated dragon is ultimately consigned (20.2).
37. Cf. Taeger, 'Streitschrift', 310. This identification makes it questionable whether the Jews are responsible for the persecution mentioned in 2.10; the devil may equally control the synagogue (2.9), but the same power lurks behind the Roman rulers (and they, rather than the Jews, would have the power and the means to imprison Christians in the province of Asia); cf. J. T. Sanders, *Schismatics*, 170, 177, 183 (where he rightly suggests, against Stegemann, *Synagoge*, that it is more likely that gentiles were accusing Christians).
38. It is plausible to see in the 'throne of Satan ... where Satan dwells' in Pergamum (2.13) an allusion to the imperial cult, either to the temple of

Augustus and Dea Roma, the first of its kind, erected in 29 BCE or, if Revelation is dated later, to the Trajaneum: cf. Klauck, 'Sendschreiben', 158–61 (cf. also Giesen, 'Reich', 2531–2).

39. *Pax*, 118.
40. The same work also uses the analogy of a military hierarchy in 37.2–3, without the slightest hint that the Roman army was experienced as an instrument of oppression.
41. 'Good' Roman governors are Gallio (18.14–16) and Festus (25.16–21; 26.31); less commendable is the prevaricating and avaricious Felix (24.25–6). Cassidy, *Society*, has criticized the interpretation of Acts as 'political apologetic', which he assesses according to the impression which the book would have made on Roman 'officials'. But 'Theophilus' (1.1) is more likely a Christian or at least a sympathizer who has received instruction in the Christian faith (Luke 1.4), not a Roman official, yet he might still require assurance that this faith is not disreputable. To that extent, Cassidy would probably class this as 'ecclesial apologetic', which he considers equally inappropriate to describe 'Luke's' purpose. To show that 'Luke' does not need to 'whitewash' every aspect of Roman rule does not contradict this interpretation of Acts; it would not be credible to deny that Christians had on occasions been so misunderstood or misinterpreted that their presence and activity had led to disorder. If 'Theophilus' still remained uneasy after reading Acts it could well have been because Christian witness required a firmness of stance which could be so misunderstood or misinterpreted.
42. In Acts 23.26; 24.3 this adjective is used to address the governor Felix and in 26.25 to address Festus.
43. 'Juden': yet these authorities are not just any external observers who confirm the Jewishness of the Christian mission, but observers whose judgement will count for something with a reader like Theophilus. Bormann, 'Verrechtlichung', compares, on the other hand, 'Luke's' procedure with that of Hellenistic Jewish apologetics in a situation where Roman law was gaining ever greater influence, although the legal basis on which 'Luke' had to argue was in many ways very different from that of Jewish apologists.

Postscript

1. Cf. Hegesippus in Euseb. *Eccl. hist.* 3.32.7–8; 4.22.4: only with the death of the apostles did error and heresy begin to flourish.
2. The term used by Norman Perrin, *New Testament*, e.g. 30, but cf. Segal's discussion of Israel's 'myths/root metaphors/conceptual archetypes' in *Rebecca's Children*, esp. 3–4.
3. *Myth*, 35.

Abbreviations

Monographs and articles are identified in the text and its notes with an abbreviated title, commentaries with the usual English or German abbreviation for the biblical text in question; full details will be found below. For the most part abbreviations employed by the *Anchor Bible Dictionary*, the *Theological Dictionary of the New Testament* or the *Oxford Classical Dictionary* (3rd edn) have been used. The following have also been used in addition to those mentioned in §2 'Reference works':

Barrett	*The New Testament Background* (ed. C. K. Barrett)
CEV	*Holy Bible: Contemporary English Version* (New York: American Bible Society, 1995)
Elliott	*The Apocryphal New Testament* (ed. J. K. Elliott)
FS	Festschrift
HBS	Herders Biblische Studien
HUT	Hermeneutische Untersuchungen zur Theologie
IEphes.	*Die Inschriften von Ephesos* (ed. H. Wankel *et al.*, 1974–84)
Iren. *Haer.*	Irenaeus of Lyon, *Adversus haereses*
JBT	Jahrbuch für Biblische Theologie
REB	*The Revised English Bible* (Oxford University Press/Cambridge University Press, 1989)
SCBO	Scriptorum Classicorum Bibliotheca Oxoniensis
Schneemelcher	*Neutestamentliche Apokryphen in deutscher Übersetzung* (ed. W. Schneemelcher)
TANZ	Texte und Arbeiten zum neutestamentlichen Zeitalter
TSAJ	Texte und Studien zum Antiken Judentum
UTB	Uni-Taschenbücher
ZNT	*Zeitschrift für Neues Testament*

Select Bibliography

For the most part only works actually referred to in the text and notes of this study are cited, with the exception of a small number of basic studies (particularly in §3 below). Not included separately are a number of dictionary articles to which reference is also made.

1. Primary Sources

Die ältesten Apologeten, ed. E. J. Goodspeed (Göttingen: Vandenhoeck & Ruprecht, 1914, repr. 1984).

'Ambrosiaster' *Commentaria in epistolam ad Romanos*, ed. H. J. Vogels (CSEL 81.1; Wien: Hoelder–Pichler–Tempsky, 1966).

The Apostolic Fathers:

— *The Apostolic Fathers*, tr. K. Lake (LCL; London: Heinemann/New York: Macmillan, 1912–13).

— *Didache (Apostellehre), Barnabasbrief, Zweiter Klemensbrief, Schrift an Diognetus*, ed. K. Wengst (Schriften des Urchristentums 2; Darmstadt: Wissenschaftliche Buchgesellschaft, 1984).

— *Papiasfragmente; Hirt des Hermas*, ed. U. H. J. Körtner and M. Leutzsch (Schriften des Urchristentums 3; Darmstadt: Wissenschaftliche Buchgesellschaft, 1998).

Apuleius, *Metamorphoses*, tr. J. A. Hanson (LCL; Cambridge MA/London: Harvard University Press, 1989).

Aristotle *Ethica Nicomachea*, ed. I. Bywater (Oxford: Clarendon Press, 1894).

— *Politics*, ed. H. Rackham (LCL; Cambridge MA: Harvard University Press/London: Heinemann, 1932).

Barrett, C. K., *The New Testament Background: Selected Documents* (London: SPCK, rev. edn 1987).

Basil *Commentary on Isaiah* (Migne PG 30; Paris, 1857; repr. Turnholt: Brepols, 1977).

Cassius Dio *Roman History*, tr. E. Cary (LCL; Cambridge MA: Harvard University Press/London: Heinemann, 1914–27).

Cicero *De oratore*, tr. E. W. Sutton and H. Rackham (LCL; Cambridge MA: Harvard University Press/London: Heinemann, 1942).

— *The Verrine Orations*, tr. L. H. G. Greenwood (LCL; Cambridge MA: Harvard University Press/London: Heinemann, 1928, 1935).

Clement of Alexandria *Stromata*, ed. O. Stählin (GCS 15, 17; Leipzig: Hinrichs, 1906–9).

Corpus inscriptionum iudaicarum, ed. J.-B. Frey (Sussidi allo studio delle antichità Cristiane 1, 3; Rome: Inst. of Christian Archaeology, 1936, 1952).

Corpus papyrorum judaicorum, ed. V. Tcherikover (Cambridge MA: Harvard University Press, 1957–64).

Dead Sea Scrolls:

— *The Dead Sea Scrolls Translated: The Qumran Texts in English*, ed. F. G. Martinez (Leiden: Brill, 1994; ET of Madrid: Trotta, 1992).

— *Die Texte aus Qumran*, vol. 1 ed. E. Lohse (München: Kösel, 1964); vol. 2 ed. A. Steudel (Darmstadt: Wissenschaftliche Buchgesellschaft, 2001).

— *Die Qumran-Essener: Die Texte vom Toten Meer*, ed. J. Maier (UTB 1862, 1863, 1916; München/Basel: Reinhardt, 1995–6).

Dio Chrysostom *Discourses*, tr. J. W. Cohoon (LCL; London: Heinemann/New York/Cambridge MA: Harvard University, 1932–51).

Diodorus Siculus *Bibliotheca*, tr. C. H. Oldfather *et al.* (LCL; London: Heinemann/Cambridge MA: Harvard University, 1933–67).

Dionysius of Halicarnassus *Antiquitates Romanae*, tr. E. Cary (LCL; London: Heinemann/Cambridge MA: Harvard University Press, 1937–50).

Epictetus, *The Discourses as Reported by Arrian, the Manual, and Fragments*, ed. W. A. Oldfather (LCL; Cambridge MA: Harvard University/London: Heinemann, 1925, 1928).

Epiphanius *Haereses*, ed. K. Holl (GCS 25, 31, 37; Leipzig: Hinrichs, 1915, 1922, 1933).

— *De mensuris et ponderibus* (Migne PG 43; Turnholt: Brepols, n.d.).

Eusebius of Caesarea *Historia ecclesiastica*, tr. K. Lake, J. E. L. Oulton and H. J. Lawlor (LCL; London: Heinemann/Cambridge MA: Harvard University Press, 1926, 1932).

Feldman, L. H. and M. Reinhold, *Jewish Life and Thought among Greeks and Romans: Primary Readings* (Minneapolis: Augsburg Fortress/Edinburgh: T&T Clark, 1996).

Gnosis: A Selection of Gnostic Texts 1: Patristic Evidence, ed./tr. W. Foerster and R. McL. Wilson (Oxford: Clarendon Press, 1972).

Herodian *History of the Empire after Marcus*, tr. C. R. Whittaker (LCL; Cambridge MA: Harvard University Press/London: Heinemann, 1969–70).

Hippolytus of Rome *Refutatio omnium haeresium*, ed. M. Marcovich (PTS 25; Berlin/New York: de Gruyter, 1986).

Die Inschriften von Ephesos, ed. H. Wankel *et al.* (Inschriften griechischer Städte aus Kleinasien 11.1–17.2; Bonn: Habelt, 1974–84).

Inscriptiones Graecae ad res Romanas pertinentes, ed. R. Cagnat *et al.* (Paris: Académie des Inscriptions et Belles Lettres, 1911–27).

Inscriptiones Latinae selectae, ed. H. Dessau (1892–1916, repr. Chicago: Ares 1979).

Irenaeus *Adversus Haereses*, ed. W. W. Harvey (Cambridge: Cambridge University Press, 1857).

Jerome *Opera* (Migne PL 22–30; Paris, 1845).

Josephus *Opera*, tr. H. St. J. Thackeray, R. Marcus *et al.* (LCL; London: Heinemann/Cambridge MA: Harvard University Press, 1926–65).

Kent, J. H., *The Inscriptions 1926–1950* (Corinth, Results of Excavations 8/3; Princeton, 1966).

Klijn, A. F. J. and G. J. Reinink, *Patristic Evidence for Jewish-Christian Sects* (NovTSup 36; Leiden: Brill, 1973).

Lucian of Samosata, tr. A. M. Harmon, K. Kilburn and M. D. MacLeod (LCL; London: Heinemann/Cambridge MA: Harvard University Press, 1913–67).

The Mishnah, tr. H. Danby (London: Oxford University Press, 1933).

The Mishnah: A New Translation, tr. J. Neusner (New Haven/London: Yale University Press, 1988).

New Testament Apocrypha:

— *The Apocryphal New Testament*, tr. J. K. Elliott (Oxford: Clarendon Press, 1993).

— *Neutestamentliche Apokryphen in deutscher Übersetzung*, ed. W. Schneemelcher (Tübingen: Mohr–Siebeck, 5th/6th edn 1989–90).

Novum Testamentum Graece, ed. E. and E. Nestle, B. and K. Aland *et al.* (Stuttgart: Deutsche Bibelgesellschaft, 27th edn 1993).

The Old Testament Pseudepigrapha, ed. J. H. Charlesworth (London: Darton, Longman & Todd, 1983, 1985).

Orientis Graeci inscriptiones selectae, ed. W. Dittenberger (Leipzig: Hirzel, 1903–05).

Origen *Contra Celsum*, ed. P. Koetschau (GCS; Leipzig: Hinrichs, 1899).

P. Orosius *Historiarum adversus paganos libri VII*, ed. C. Zangemeister (CSEL 5; Wien, 1882; repr. Hildesheim: Olms, 1967).

Papyri Graecae magicae, ed. K. Preisendanz (Leipzig, 1928–31, 2nd edn Stuttgart: Teubner, 1974).

Petronius *Satyricon*, tr. M. Heseltine and E. H. Warmington (LCL; Cambridge MA: Harvard University Press/London: Heinemann, 1913, rev. edn 1969).

Philo of Alexandria, tr. F. H. Colson, G. H. Whitaker and R. Marcus (LCL; London: Heinemann/Cambridge MA: Harvard University, 1929–62).

Philostratus *Vita Apollonii*, tr. F. C. Conybeare (LCL; Cambridge MA/London: Harvard University Press, 1912, 1989).

Plato *Opera*, ed. J. Burnet (SCBO; Oxford Press: Clarendon, 1900–07).

Pliny *Epistulae*, ed. R. A. B. Mynors (SCBO; Oxford: Clarendon Press, 1963).

Plutarch *Moralia*, tr. F. C. Babbitt *et al.* (LCL; Cambridge MA: Harvard University Press/London: Heinemann, 1927–69).

Polybius *Histories*, tr. W. R. Paton (LCL; Cambridge MA: Harvard University Press/London: Heinemann, 1922–7).

Pseudo-Clementine *Homilies*, ed. B. Rehm, J. Irmscher and F. Paschke (GCS 42; Berlin: Akademie, 2nd edn 1969).

— *Recognitions*, ed. B. Rehm and F. Paschke (GCS 51; Berlin: Akademie, 1965).

Quintilian *Institutio oratoria*, tr. H. E. Butler (LCL; Cambridge MA: Harvard University Press/London: Heinemann, 1920–2).

Seneca *Ad Lucilium epistulae morales*, tr. M. Rosenbach (Darmstadt: Wissenschaftliche Buchgesellschaft, 1995).

Septuaginta, ed. A. Rahlfs (Stuttgart: Württembergische Bibelanstalt, 1935, 7th edn 1962).

Suetonius *De vita Caesarum*, tr. J. C. Rolfe (LCL; London: Heinemann/Cambridge MA: Harvard University Press, 2nd edn 1951).

Sylloge inscriptionum Graecarum, ed. W. Dittenberger (Leipzig, 3rd edn 1915–24; repr. Hildesheim: Olms, 1960).

Tacitus *Annales*, ed. C. D. Fisher (SCBO; Oxford: Clarendon Press, 1906).

— *Historiae*, ed. C. D. Fisher (SCBO; Oxford: Clarendon Press, 1911).
The Talmud of the Land of Israel: A Preliminary Translation and Explanation, tr. J. Neusner (Chicago/London: University of Chicago Press, 1984–93).
The Tosefta, tr. J. Neusner (New York: KTAV, 1977–86).

2. Reference Works

BDAG = *A Greek–English Lexicon of the New Testament and Other Early Christian Literature*, ed. F. W. Danker (Chicago/London: University of Chicago Press, 3rd edn 2000).
BDR = F. Blass, A. Debrunner, F. Rehkopf, *Grammatik des neutestamentlichen Griechisch* (Göttingen: Vandenhoeck & Ruprecht, 15th edn 1979).
DNP = *Der Neue Pauly: Enzyklopädie der Antike* (Stuttgart/Weimar: Metzler, 1996–).
EWNT = *Exegetisches Wörterbuch zum Neuen Testament* (Stuttgart: Kohlhammer, 1978–80, 2nd edn 1992).
Grimm–Thayer = *A Greek–English Lexicon of the New Testament*, ed. J. H. Thayer (Edinburgh: T&T Clark, 4th edn 1901).
Hatch, E. and H. A. Redpath, *A Concordance to the Septuagint and the Other Greek Versions of the Old Testament* (Oxford: Clarendon Press, 1897, repr. Grand Rapids: Baker, 1987).
KlP = *Der Kleine Pauly: Lexikon der Antike* (München: Druckenmüller, 1975/ München: dtv, 1979).
OCD = *The Oxford Classical Dictionary*, ed. S. Hornblower, A. Spawforth (Oxford/ New York: Oxford University Press, 3rd edn 1996).
RGG[4] = *Religion in Geschichte und Gegenwart: Handwörterbuch für Theologie und Religionswissenschaft* (Tübingen: Mohr–Siebeck, 4th edn 1998–).
TDNT = *Theological Dictionary of the New Testament*, ed. G. Kittel and G. Friedrich (Grand Rapids: Eerdmans, 1964–76; ET of Stuttgart: Kohlhammer, 1933–79).

3. General Works on the History of Earliest Christianity

Baur, F. C., *Das Christentum und die christliche Kirche der ersten drei Jahrhunderte* (Tübingen: Fues, 2nd edn 1860).
Becker, J., *Das Urchristentum als gegliederte Epoche* (SBS 155; Stuttgart: Katholisches Bibelwerk, 1993).
Becker, J., *et al.*, *Die Anfänge des Christentums* (Stuttgart: Kohlhammer, 1987).
Berger, K., *Theologiegeschichte des Urchristentums: Theologie des Neuen Testaments* (UTB; Tübingen/Basel: Francke, 1994).
Brown, S., *The Origins of Christianity: A Historical Introduction to the New Testament* (Oxford/New York: Oxford University Press, 1984).
Bruce, F. F., *New Testament History* (1969; Garden City NY: Doubleday, 1971).
Caird, G. B., *The Apostolic Age* (London: Duckworth Press, 1955).
Clarke, G. W., 'The Origins and Spread of Christianity', in *CAH* 10 (1996) 848–72.
Conzelmann, H., *Geschichte des Urchristentums* (GNT 5; Göttingen: Vandenhoeck &

Ruprecht, 1969, 6th edn 1989; ET: *History of Primitive Christianity* [Nashville: Abingdon, 1973]).

Filson, F. V., *A New Testament History* (London: SCM Press, 1965).

Fischer, K. M., *Das Urchristentum* (Kirchengeschichte in Einzeldarstellungen I/1; Leipzig: Evangelische Verlagsanstalt, 1985, 2nd edn 1991).

Frend, W. H. C., *The Rise of Christianity* (Philadelphia: Fortress Press, 1984).

Goppelt, L., *Apostolic and Post-Apostolic Times* (London: Black, 1970) = ET of *Die apostolische und nachapostolische Zeit* (Die Kirche in ihrer Geschichte: Ein Handbuch 1; ed. K. D. Schmidt, E. Wolf and B. Moeller; Göttingen: Vandenhoeck & Ruprecht, 1962, 2nd edn 1966).

Hyldahl, N., *The History of Early Christianity* (Studies in the Religion and History of Early Christianity 3; Frankfurt am Main: Lang, 1997).

Kraft, H., *Die Entstehung des Christentums* (Darmstadt: Wissenschaftliche Buchgesellschaft, 1986).

Lietzmann, H., *A History of the Early Church* (London: Lutterworth Press, 1961; ET of 3rd edn 1953).

Lüdemann, G., *Primitive Christianity: A Survey of Recent Studies and Some New Proposals* (Edinburgh: T&T Clark, 2003; enlarged ET of *Arbeiten zur Religion u. Geschichte des Urchristentums* 12; Frankfurt am Main: Lang, 2002).

Nodet, E. and J. Taylor, *The Origins of Christianity: An Exploration* (Collegeville MN: Liturgical Press, 1998; ET of Paris: Cerf, 1998).

Rowland, C., *Christian Origins: An Account of the Setting and Character of the Most Important Messianic Sect of Judaism* (London: SPCK, 1985).

Schenke, L., *Die Urgemeinde: Geschichtliche und theologische Entwicklung* (Stuttgart: Kohlhammer, 1990).

Schmithals, W., *Theologiegeschichte des Urchristentums: Eine problemgeschichtliche Darstellung* (Stuttgart: Kohlhammer, 1994).

Schneemelcher, W., *Das Urchristentum* (Urban Taschenbücher 336; Stuttgart: Kohlhammer, 1981).

Teeple, H. M., *How Did Christianity Really Begin? A Historical–Archaeological Approach* (Evanston: Religion and Ethics Institute, 1992).

Trocmé, E., *The Childhood of Christianity* (London: SCM Press, 1997; ET of Paris: Noêsis, 1997).

Vouga, F., *Geschichte des frühen Christentums* (UTB 1733; Tübingen/Basel: Francke, 1994).

4. Other Secondary Literature

Ådna, J. and H. Kvalbein (eds), *The Mission of the Early Church to Jews and Gentiles* (WUNT 127; Tübingen: Mohr–Siebeck, 2000).

Aland, K., 'Die Entstehung des Corpus Paulinum', in K. Aland, *Neutestamentliche Entwürfe* (München: Kaiser, 1979) 302–50.

Alkier, S., '*Urchristentum*': *Zur Geschichte und Theologie einer exegetischen Disziplin* (BHT 82; Tübingen: Mohr–Siebeck, 1993).

Allison, D. C., 'Peter and Cephas: One and the Same', *JBL* 111 (1992) 489–95.

Alvarez Cineira, D., *Die Religionspolitik des Kaisers Claudius und die paulinische Mission* (HBS 19; Freiburg: Herder, 1999).

Ascough, R., 'Christianity in Caesarea Maritima', in *Religious Rivalries and the Struggle for Success in Caesarea Maritima*, ed. T. L. Donaldson (Studies in Early Christianity and Judaism 8; Waterloo: Wilfred Laurier University, 2000) 153–79.

Barrett, C. K., 'Cephas and Corinth', in *Abraham unser Vater*, FS O. Michel; ed. O. Betz *et al.* (Leiden: Brill, 1963) 1–12.

— 'Acts and Christian Consensus', in *Context: Essays in Honour of Peder Borgen*, ed. P. W. Bøckman and R. E. Christiansen (Relief 24; Trondheim: Tapir, 1987) 19–33.

— 'Johanneisches Christentum', in J. Becker *et al.*, *Die Anfänge des Christentums: Alte Welt und neue Hoffnung* (Stuttgart: Kohlhammer, 1987) 255–74.

— 'The End of Acts', in *Geschichte – Tradition – Reflexion*, FS M. Hengel; ed. P. Schäfer, H. Cancik and H. Lichtenberger (Tübingen: Mohr–Siebeck, 1996) 3.545–55.

— *A Critical and Exegetical Commentary on the Acts of the Apostles* (ICC; Edinburgh: T&T Clark, 1994, 1998).

Bauckham, R., 'Jesus' Demonstration in the Temple', in *Law and Religion: Essays on the Place of the Law in Israel and Early Christianity by Members of the Ehrhardt Seminar of Manchester University*, ed. B. Lindars (Cambridge: James Clarke, 1988) 72–89.

— *Jude and the Relatives of Jesus in the Early Church* (Edinburgh: T&T Clark, 1990).

— 'The Acts of Paul as a Sequel to Acts', in *The Book of Acts in Its Ancient Literary Setting* (The Book of Acts in Its First-Century Setting 1, ed. B. W. Winter and A. D. Clarke; Grand Rapids: Eerdmans/Carlisle: Paternoster Press, 1993) 105–52.

— 'The Parting of the Ways: What Happened and Why', *StTh* 47 (1993) 135–51.

— 'James and the Jerusalem Church', in *The Book of Acts in Its Palestinian Setting* (The Book of Acts in Its First-Century Setting 4, ed. R. Bauckham; Grand Rapids: Eerdmans/Carlisle: Paternoster Press, 1995) 415–80.

— 'For What Offence Was James Put to Death?', in *James the Just and Christian Origins*, ed. B. Chilton and C. A. Evans (NovTSup 98; Leiden: Brill, 1999) 199–232.

Bauer, W., *Orthodoxy and Heresy in Earliest Christianity* (Philadelphia: Fortress Press, 1971/London: SCM Press, 1972; ET of BHT 10; Tübingen: Mohr–Siebeck, 1934, 2nd edn 1964).

Baur, F. C., *Paulus, der Apostel Jesu Christi: Sein Leben und Wirken, seine Briefe und seine Lehre: Ein Beitrag zu einer kritischen Geschichte des Urchristentums*, ed. E. Zeller (1845, 2nd edn 1866–7; repr. Osnabrück: Zeller, 1968).

Becker, J., *Paul: Apostle to the Gentiles* (Louisville KY: Westminster/John Knox, 1993; ET of Tübingen: Mohr–Siebeck, 1989).

— *Jesus von Nazaret* (Berlin/New York: de Gruyter, 1996).

Berger, K., *Die Auferstehung des Propheten und die Erhöhung des Menschensohnes: Traditionsgeschichtliche Untersuchungen zur Deutung des Geschickes Jesu in frühchristlichen Texten* (SUNT 13; Göttingen: Vandenhoeck & Ruprecht, 1976).

— 'Propaganda und Gegenpropaganda im frühen Christentum: Simon Magus als Gestalt des samaritanischen Christentums', in *Religious Propaganda and Missionary Competition in the New Testament World*, FS D. Georgi; ed. L. Bormann *et al.* (NovTSup 74; Leiden: Brill, 1994) 313–17.

Betz, H. D., *Galatians: A Commentary on Paul's Letter to the Churches in Galatia* (Hermeneia; Philadelphia: Fortress Press, 1979).

Beyschlag, K., *Simon Magus und die christliche Gnosis* (WUNT 16; Tübingen: Mohr–Siebeck, 1974).

Bockmuehl, M., 'Antioch and James the Just', in *James the Just and Christian Origins*, ed. B. Chilton and C. A. Evans (NovTSup 98; Leiden: Brill, 1999) 155–98.

Bormann, L., 'Die Verrechtlichung der frühesten christlichen Überlieferung im lukanischen Schrifttum', in *Religious Propaganda and Religious Competition in the New Testament World*, FS D. Georgi; ed. L. Bormann *et al.* (NTSup 74; Leiden: Brill, 1994) 283–311.

Bornkamm, G., *Paulus* (Urban Bücher 119; Stuttgart: Kohlhammer, 1969).

Bosenius, B., *Die Abwesenheit des Apostels als theologisches Programm: Der zweite Korintherbrief als Beispiel für die Brieflichkeit der paulinischen Theologie* (TANZ 11; Tübingen/Basel: Francke, 1994).

Botermann, H., *Das Judenedikt des Kaisers Claudius: Römische Staat und Christiani im 1. Jahrhundert* (Hermes Einzelschriften 71; Stuttgart: Steiner, 1996).

Breytenbach, C., *Paulus und Barnabas in der Provinz Galatien: Studien zu Apostelgeschichte 13f.; 16,6; 18,23 und den Adressaten des Galaterbriefes* (AGJU 38; Leiden: Brill, 1996).

Broer, I., *Einleitung in das Neue Testament 2: Briefliteratur, die Offenbarung des Johannes und die Bildung des Kanons* (NEB Ergänzungsband 2/II; Würzburg: Echter, 2001).

Brown, R. E., *The Community of the Beloved Disciple* (New York: Paulist Press, 1979).

Brown, R. E. and J. P. Meier, *Antioch and Rome: New Testament Cradles of Catholic Christianity* (London: Chapman, 1983).

Bruce, F. F., *The Acts of the Apostles* (London: Tyndale, 2nd edn 1952).

— *The Epistle to the Galatians* (NIGTC; Exeter: Paternoster, 1982).

Büllesbach, C., 'Das Verhältnis der Acta Pauli zur Apostelgeschichte des Lukas: Darstellung und Kritik der Forschungsgeschichte', in *Das Ende des Paulus: Historische, theologische und literaturgeschichtliche Aspekte*, ed. F. W. Horn (BZNW 106; Berlin/New York: de Gruyter, 2001) 215–37.

Bultmann, R., *Theology of the New Testament* (London: SCM Press, 1952, 1955 = ET of Tübingen: Mohr–Siebeck, 1948–53 [9th edn 1984]).

Bunine, A. V., 'Paul et les Galates: La véritable occasion de la collecte' (not yet published).

Burchard, C., *Der dreizehnte Zeuge: Traditions- und kompositionsgeschichtliche Untersuchungen zu Lukas' Darstellung der Frühzeit des Paulus* (FRLANT 103; Göttingen: Vandenhoeck & Ruprecht, 1970).

Cadbury, H. J., 'The Hellenists', in F. J. F. Jackson and K. Lake, *The Beginnings of Christianity* 1: *The Acts of the Apostles* 5 (London: Macmillan, 1933) 59–74.

Callahan, A. D., 'Dead Paul: The Apostle as Martyr in Philippi', in *Philippi at the Time of Paul and after His Death*, ed. C. Bakirtzis and H. Koester (Harrisburg PA: TPI, 1998) 67–84.

Campbell, R. A., 'The Elders of the Jerusalem Church', *JTS* 44 (1993) 511–28.

— *The Elders: Seniority within Earliest Christianity* (Studies of the New Testament and Its World; Edinburgh: T&T Clark, 1994).

Capper, B., 'The Palestinian Cultural Context of Earliest Christian Community of Goods', in *The Book of Acts in Its Palestinian Setting* (The Book of Acts in Its First-Century Setting 4; ed. R. Bauckham; Grand Rapids: Eerdmans/Carlisle: Paternoster Press, 1995) 323–56.

Cassidy, R. J., *Society and Politics in the Acts of the Apostles* (Maryknoll NY: Orbis, 1987).

Catchpole, D. R., 'Paul, James and the Apostolic Decree', *NTS* 23 (1976/7) 428–44.

Charles, R. H., *A Critical and Exegetical Commentary on the Revelation of St John* (ICC; Edinburgh: T&T Clark, 1920).

Clark, A. C., 'The Role of the Apostles', in *Witness to the Gospel: The Theology of Acts*, ed. I. H. Marshall, D. Peterson (Grand Rapids/Cambridge: Eerdmans, 1998) 169–90.

Clarke, A. D., *Secular and Christian Leadership in Corinth: A Socio-Historical and Exegetical Study of 1 Corinthians 1–6* (AGJU 18; Leiden: Brill, 1993).

Claußen, C., *Versammlung, Gemeinde, Synagoge: Das hellenistisch-jüdische Umfeld der frühchristlichen Gemeinden* (SUNT 27; Göttingen: Vandenhoeck & Ruprecht, 2002).

Conzelmann, H., 'Paulus und die Weisheit', *NTS* 12 (1965/6) 231–44.

— *Acts of the Apostles* (Hermeneia; Philadelphia: Fortress Press, 1987; ET of HNT 7; Tübingen: Mohr, 2nd edn 1972).

— 'Die Schule des Paulus', in *Theologia Crucis – Signum Crucis: Festschrift für Erich Dinkler zum 70. Geburtstag*, ed. C. Andresen and G. Klein (Tübingen: Mohr–Siebeck, 1979) 85–96.

Cotter, W., 'Cornelius, the Roman Army and Religion', in *Religious Rivalries and the Struggle for Success in Caesarea Maritima*, ed. T. L. Donaldson (Studies in Early Christianity and Judaism 8; Waterloo: Wilfred Laurier University, 2000) 279–301.

Cullmann, O., *The Johannine Circle: Its Place in Judaism, among the Disciples of Jesus and in Early Christianity: A Study in the Origin of the Gospel of John* (London: SCM Press, 1976; ET of Tübingen: Mohr–Siebeck, 1975).

Culpepper, R. A., *The Johannine School: An Evaluation of the Johannine-School Hypothesis Based on an Investigation of the Nature of Ancient Schools* (SBLDS 26; Missoula: Scholars Press, 1975).

Dahl, N. A., 'Paul and the Church at Corinth according to 1 Cor. i. 10–iv. 21', in *Christian History and Interpretation*, FS J. Knox; ed. W. R. Farmer *et al.* (Cambridge: Cambridge University Press, 1967) 313–335 (=idem, *Studies in Paul* (Minneapolis: Augsburg, 1977) 40–61).

Dauer, A., *Paulus und die christliche Gemeinde im syrischen Antiochia: Kritische Bestandaufnahme der modernen Forschung mit einigen weiterführenden Überlegungen* (BBB 106; Weinheim: Beltz Athenäum, 1996).

de Boer, M., *Johannine Perspectives on the Death of Jesus* (Contributions to Biblical Exegesis and Theology 17; Kampen: Kok Pharos, 1996).

Dibelius, M., 'Stilkritisches zur Apostelgeschichte', in M. Dibelius, *Aufsätze zur Apostelgeschichte*, ed. H. Greeven (FRLANT 60; Göttingen: Vandenhoeck & Ruprecht, 3rd edn 1957) 9–28.

Dietzfelbinger, C., *Die Berufung des Paulus als Ursprung seiner Theologie* (WMANT 58; Neukirchen-Vluyn: Neukirchener, 1985).

Dinkler, E., 'Der Brief an die Galater: Zum Kommentar von H. Schlier', in E. Dinkler, *Signum crucis: Aufsätze zum Neuen Testament und zur christlichen Archäologie* (Tübingen: Mohr–Siebeck, 1967) 270–82 (repr. of VF [1953–5] 175–83 with additional note).

Dobbeler, A. von, *Der Evangelist Philippus in der Geschichte des Urchristentums: Eine prosopographische Skizze* (TANZ 30; Tübingen/Basel: Francke, 2000).

Doughty, D. J., 'Citizens of Heaven: Philippians 3.2–21', *NTS* 41 (1995) 102–22.

Downey, G., *Ancient Antioch* (Princeton NJ: Princeton University Press, 1963).

Dunn, J. D. G., *Unity and Diversity in the New Testament: An Inquiry into the Character of Earliest Christianity* (London: SCM Press, 1977, 2nd edn 1990).

— 'The Incident at Antioch (Gal 2;11–18)', *JSNT* 18 (1983) 3–57, repr., with Additional Note, in J. D. G. Dunn, *Jesus, Paul and the Law: Studies in Mark and Galatians* (London: SPCK, 1990) 129–82.

— *The Partings of the Ways between Christianity and Judaism and Their Significance for the Character of Christianity* (London: SCM Press/Philadelphia: TPI, 1991).

Dupont, J., 'La nouvelle Pentecôte (Ac 2,1–11)', in J. Dupont, *Nouvelles études sur les Actes des Apôtres* (LD 118; Paris: Cerf) 193–8.

Ehrman, B. D., 'Cephas and Peter', *JBL* 109 (1990) 463–74.

Elliott, J. H., 'Phases in the Social Formation of Early Christianity: From Faction to Sect – A Social Scientific Perspective', in *Recruitment, Conquest, and Conflict: Strategies in Judaism, Early Christianity, and the Greco-Roman World*, ed. P. Borgen *et al.* (Emory Studies in Early Christianity 6; Atlanta: Scholars Press, 1998) 273–313.

Esler, P. F., *Community and Gospel in Luke–Acts: The Social and Political Motivations of Lucan Theology* (SNTSMS 57; Cambridge: Cambridge University Press, 1987).

Evans, C. A., 'Jesus' Action in the Temple and Evidence of Corruption in the First-Century Temple', *SBL 1989 Seminar Papers*, SBLSP 28, ed. D. J. Lull (Atlanta: Scholars Press, 1989) 522–39.

Farmer, W. R., 'James the Lord's Brother, According to Paul', in *James the Just and Christian Origins*, ed. B. Chilton and C. A. Evans (NovTSup 98; Leiden: Brill, 1999) 133–53.

Filson, F. V., 'The Significance of the Early House Churches', *JBL* 58 (1939) 105–12.

Fischer, K. M., *Tendenz und Absicht des Epheserbriefes* (FRLANT 111; Göttingen: Vandenhoeck & Ruprecht/Berlin: Evangelische Verlagsanstalt, 1973).

Fitzmyer, J. A., *The Acts of the Apostles* (AB 31; New York: Doubleday, 1998).

Fredriksen, P., *From Jesus to Christ: The Origins of the New Testament Images of Jesus* (New Haven/London: Yale University Press, 1988).

— 'Judaism, the Circumcision of Gentiles, and Apocalyptic Hope: Another Look at Galatians 1 and 2', JTS 42 (1991) 532–64 (cf. *Recruitment, Conquest, and Conflict: Strategies in Judaism, Early Christianity, and the Greco-Roman World*, ed. P. Borgen *et al.* [Emory Studies in Early Christianity 6; Atlanta: Scholars Press, 1998] 209–44).

Frend, W. H. C., *Martyrdom and Persecution in the Early Church: A Study of a Conflict from the Maccabees to Donatus* (Oxford: Blackwell, 1965).

Frey, J., 'Erwägungen zum Verhältnis der Johannesapokalypse zu den übrigen Schriften des Corpus Johanneum', in M. Hengel, *Die johanneische Frage* (WUNT 67; Tübingen: Mohr–Siebeck, 1993) 326–429.

Furnish, V. P., *II Corinthians* (AB 32A; New York: Doubleday, 1984).

Gapp, K. S., 'The Universal Famine under Claudius', *HTR* 28 (1935) 258–65.

Garnsey, P., 'The *Lex Iulia* and Appeal under the Empire', *JRS* 56 (1966) 167–89.

— *Social Status and Legal Privilege in the Roman Empire* (Oxford: Clarendon Press, 1970).

Georgi, D., *Die Armen zu gedenken: Die Geschichte der Kollekte des Paulus für Jerusalem* (TF 38; Hamburg-Bergstedt: Reich, 1965, 2nd expanded edn, Neukirchen-Vluyn: Neukirchener, 1994).

Giesen, H., 'Das Römische Reich im Spiegel der Johannes-Apokalypse', in *ANRW* II 26.3 (1996) 2501–614.

Gilmour, S. M., 'The Christophany to More than Five Hundred Brethren', *JBL* 80 (1961) 248–52.

Gnilka, J., *Der Epheserbrief* (HTKNT 10/2; Freiburg: Herder, 1971, 4th edn 1990).

— *Jesus von Nazaret: Botschaft und Geschichte* (Freiburg: Herder, 4th edn 1993).

Goodman, M., 'Judaea', in *CAH* 10 (1996) 737–81.

— *Mission and Conversion: Proselytizing in the Religious History of the Roman Empire* (Oxford: Clarendon Press, 1994).

— *The Roman World 44 BC–AD 180* (London/New York: Routledge, 1997).

Goulder, M., *A Tale of Two Missions* (London: SCM Press, 1994).

Grappe, C., *D'un temple à l'autre: Pierre et l'église primitive de Jérusalem* (Études d'histoire et de philosophie religieuses 71; Paris: Presses Universitaires de France, 1992).

Günther, M., *Die Frühgeschichte des Christentums in Ephesus* (Arbeiten zur Religion und Geschichte des Urchristentums 1; Frankfurt am Main: Lang, 1995).

Haacker, K., 'Die Berufung des Verfolgers und die Rechtfertigung des Gottlosen: Erwägungen zum Zusammenhang zwischen Biographie und Theologie des Apostels Paulus', *TBei* 6 (1976) 1–19.

— 'Die Stellung des Stephanus in der Geschichte des Urchristentums', in *ANRW* II 26.2 (Berlin/New York: de Gruyter, 1995) 1515–53.

— *Paulus: Der Werdegang eines Apostels* (SBS 171; Stuttgart: Katholisches Bibelwerk, 1997).

Haenchen, E., *The Acts of the Apostles: A Commentary* (Oxford: Blackwell, 1971; ET of MeyerK 3; Göttingen: Vandenhoeck & Ruprecht, 1956, 14th edn 1965).

— 'The Book of Acts as Source Material for the History of Early Christianity', in *Studies in Luke–Acts*, FS P. Schubert, ed. L. E. Keck and J. L. Martyn (London: SPCK, 1968) 258–78.

Hahn, F., *Mission in the New Testament* (London: SCM Press, 1965).

— and P. Müller, 'Der Jakobusbrief', *TRu* 63 (1998) 1–73.

Harding, M., 'On the Historicity of Acts: Comparing 9.23–5 with 2 Corinthians 11.32–3', *NTS* 39 (1993) 518–38.

Hare, D. R. A., *The Theme of Jewish Persecutions of Christians in the Gospel of Matthew* (SNTSMS 7; Cambridge: Cambridge University Press, 1967).

Harnack, A. von, 'Die Versuche der Gnostiker, eine apostolische Glaubenslehre und eine christliche Theologie zu schaffen, oder: die akute Verweltlichung des Christentums', in *Gnosis und Gnostizismus*, ed. K. Rudolph (WF 262; Darmstadt: Wissenschaftliche Buchgesellschaft, 1975) = idem, *Lehrbuch der Dogmengeschichte* 1 (Freiburg: Mohr–Siebeck, 1886) 158–85.

— *Die Mission und die Ausbreitung des Christentums in den ersten drei Jahrhunderten* (Leipzig: Hinrichs, 1902/Wiesbaden: VMA, 4th edn 1924).

Heiligenthal, R., '"Petrus und Jakobus, der Gerechte": Gedanken zur Rolle der beiden Säulenapostel in der Geschichte des frühen Christentums', *ZNT* 4 (1999) 32–40.

Hemer, C. J., *The Book of Acts in the Setting of Hellenistic History* (WUNT 49; Tübingen: Mohr–Siebeck, 1989).

Hengel, M., *Property and Riches in the Early Church* (London: SCM Press 1974; ET of Stuttgart: Calwer, 1973).

— *Crucifixion in the Ancient World and the Folly of the Message of the Cross* (London: SCM Press, 1977).

— 'Between Jesus and Paul', in M. Hengel, *Between Jesus and Paul: Studies in the Earliest History of Christianity* (London: SCM Press, 1983) 1–29, 133–56 (ET of *ZTK* 72 [1975] 151–206).

— 'Luke the Historian and the Geography of Palestine in the Acts of the Apostles', in M. Hengel, *Between Jesus and Paul*, 97–128, 190–210; repr. as 'The Geography of Palestine in Acts', in *The Book of Acts in Its Palestinian Setting* (The Book of Acts in Its First-Century Setting 4; ed. R. Bauckham; Grand Rapids: Eerdmans/ Carlisle: Paternoster Press, 1995) 27–78 (ET of *ZDPV* 98 [1983] 147–83).

— 'Jakobus der Herrenbruder – der erste "Papst"?', in *Glaube und Eschatologie*, FS W. G. Kümmel; ed. E. Gräßer, O. Merk (Tübingen: Mohr–Siebeck, 1985) 71–104.

— 'Zur matthäischen Bergpredigt und ihrem jüdischen Hintergrund', *TRu* 52 (1987) 327–400 = idem, *Judaica, Hellenistica et Christiana: Kleine Schriften* 2 (WUNT 109; Tübingen: Mohr–Siebeck, 1999) 219–92.

— *The Johannine Question* (London: SCM Press/Philadelphia: TPI, 1989).

— (with R. Deines) *The Pre-Christian Paul* (London: SCM Press, 1991); ET of *Paulus und das antike Judentum* (ed. idem, U. Heckel; WUNT 58; Tübingen: Mohr–Siebeck, 1991) 177–291.

— 'Die Ursprünge der Gnosis und das Urchristentum', in *Evangelium, Schriftauslegung, Kirche*, FS P. Stuhlmacher; ed. J. Ådna *et al.* (Göttingen: Vandenhoeck & Ruprecht, 1997) 190–223.

— 'Das früheste Christentum als eine jüdische messianische und universalistische Bewegung', in M. Hengel, *Judaica, Hellenistica et Christiana: Kleine Schriften* 2 (WUNT 109; Tübingen: Mohr–Siebeck, 1999) 200–18 (rev. and expanded repr. of *TBei* 28 [1997] 197–210).

— *The Four Gospels and the One Gospel of Jesus Christ: An Investigation of the Collection and Origin of the Canonical Gospels* (Harrisburg PA: TPI, 2000).

— 'Der Jude Paulus und sein Volk: Zu einem neuen Acta-Kommentar', *TRu* 66 (2001) 338–68.

— and A. M. Schwemer, *Paul between Damascus and Antioch: The Unknown Years* (Louisville KY: Westminster John Knox, 1997).

Herzer, J., *Petrus oder Paulus? Studien über das Verhältnis des Ersten Petrusbriefes zur paulinischen Tradition* (WUNT 103; Tübingen: Mohr–Siebeck, 1998).

Hill, C. C., *Hellenists and Hebrews: Reappraising Division within the Earliest Church* (Minneapolis: Fortress Press, 1992).

Hill, C. E., 'Cerinthus, Gnostic or Chiliast? A New Solution to an Old Problem', *Journal of Early Christian Studies* 8 (2000) 135–72.

Hock, R. F., 'Paul's Tentmaking and the Problem of His Social Status', *JBL* 97 (1978) 555–64.

— *The Social Context of Paul's Ministry: Tentmaking and Apostleship* (Philadelphia: Fortress Press, 1980).

Holmberg, B., 'Jewish *versus* Christian Identity in the Early Church?', *RB* 105 (1998) 397–425.

Holtz, T., 'Die Bedeutung des Apostelkonzils für Paulus', *NovT* 16 (1974) 110–48.

— 'Der antiochenische Zwischenfall (Gal 2.11–14)', *NTS* 32 (1986) 344–61.

Horn, F. W., *Das Angeld des Geistes: Studien zur paulinischen Pneumatologie* (FRLANT 154; Göttingen: Vandenhoeck & Ruprecht, 1992).

— 'Die letzte Jerusalemreise des Paulus', in *Das Ende des Paulus: Historische, theologische und literaturgeschichtliche Aspekte*, ed. F. W. Horn (BZNW 106; Berlin/New York: de Gruyter, 2001) 15–35.

Horrell, D. G., *The Social Ethos of the Corinthian Correspondence: Interests and Ideology from 1 Corinthians to 1 Clement* (Studies of the New Testament and Its World; Edinburgh: T&T Clark, 1996).

Hultgren, A. J., 'Paul's Pre-Christian Persecutions of the Church: Their Purpose, Locale, and Nature', *JBL* 95 (1976) 97–111.

Hyldahl, N., *Die paulinische Chronologie* (ATDan 19; Leiden: Brill, 1986).

Jeremias, J., 'Untersuchungen zum Quellenproblem der Apostelgeschichte', in J. Jeremias, *Abba: Studien zur neutestamentlichen Theologie und Zeitgeschichte* (Göttingen: Vandenhoeck & Ruprecht, 1966) 238–55 (repr. of ZNW 36 [1937] 205–21).

— *Jerusalem in the Time of Jesus: An Investigation into Economic and Social Conditions during the New Testament Period* (London: SCM Press, 1969; ET of Göttingen: Vandenhoeck & Ruprecht, 3rd edn 1962).

— *New Testament Theology* 1: *The Proclamation of Jesus* (London: SCM, 1971; ET of Gütersloh: Mohn, 1971).

Jervell, J., 'Das Aposteldekret in der lukanischen Theologie', in *Texts and Contexts: Biblical Texts in Their Textual and Situational Contexts*, FS L. Hartman; ed. T. Fornberg and D. Hellholm (Oslo: Scandinavian University Press, 1995) 227–43.

— *Die Apostelgeschichte* (MeyerK 3; Göttingen: Vandenhoeck & Ruprecht, 1998).

Jewett, R., 'The Agitators and the Galatian Congregation', *NTS* 17 (1970/1) 198–212.

— *Dating Paul's Life* (London: SCM Press, 1979) = *A Chronology of Paul's Life* (Fortress Press, 1979).

Karrer, M., 'Petrus im paulinischen Gemeindekreis', *ZNW* 80 (1989) 210–31.

— 'Das urchristliche Ältestenamt', *NovT* 32 (1990) 152–88.

Käsemann, E., 'Ketzer und Zeuge', *ZTK* 48 (1951) 292–311 = E. Käsemann, *Exegetische Versuche und Besinnungen* 1 (Göttingen: Vandenhoeck & Ruprecht, 3rd edn 1964) 168–87.

— 'Ministry and Community in the New Testament', in E. Käsemann, *Essays on New Testament Themes* (SBT 41; London: SCM Press, 1964) 63–94 = ET of *Exegetische Versuche und Besinnungen* 1, 109–34.

— 'Paul and Early Catholicism', in E. Käsemann, *New Testament Questions of Today* (London: SCM Press, 1969) 236–51 = ET of *Exegetische Versuche und Besinnungen* 2 (Göttingen: Vandenhoeck & Ruprecht, 2nd edn 1965) 239–52.

Kennedy, D., 'Syria', in *CAH* 10 (1996) 703–36.

Klauck, H.-J., 'Das Sendschreiben nach Pergamon und der Kaiserkult in der Johannesoffenbarung', *Bib* 73 (1992) 153–82.

— *Die Johannesbriefe* (Erträge der Forschung 276; Darmstadt: Wissenschaftliche Buchgesellschaft, 2nd edn 1995).

— *Magic and Paganism in Early Christianity: The World of the Acts of the Apostles* (Edinburgh: T&T Clark, 2000; ET of SBS 167; Stuttgart: Katholisches Bibelwerk, 1996).

— 'Do They Never Come Back? *Nero Redivivus* and the Apocalypse of John', *CBQ* 63 (2001) 683–98.

Klein, G., 'Galater 2,6–9 und die Geschichte der Jerusalemer Urgemeinde', *ZTK* 57 (1960) 275–95.

— *Die zwölf Apostel: Ursprung und Gehalt einer Idee* (FRLANT 77; Göttingen: Vandenhoeck & Ruprecht, 1961).

— 'Gesetz III: Neues Testament', *TRE* 13 (1984) 58–75.

Klijn, A. F. J., 'Jewish Christianity in Egypt', in *The Roots of Egyptian Christianity*, ed. B. A. Pearson and J. E. Goehring (Studies in Antiquity and Christianity; Philadelphia: Fortress Press, 1986) 161–75.

Kloppenborg, J., 'Collegia and *thiasoi*: Issues in Function, Taxonomy and Membership', in *Voluntary Associations in the Graeco-Roman World*, ed. J. Kloppenborg and S. G. Wilson (London/New York: Routledge, 1996) 16–30.

Knox, J., *Chapters in a Life of Paul* (New York: Abingdon-Cokesbury, 1950/London: Black, 1954).

Koch, D.-A., *Die Schrift als Zeuge des Evangeliums: Untersuchungen zur Verwendung und zum Verständnis der Schrift bei Paulus* (BHT 69; Tübingen: Mohr–Siebeck, 1986).

— 'Barnabas, Paulus und die Adressaten des Galaterbriefes', in *Das Urchristentum in seiner literarischen Geschichte*, FS J. Becker; ed. U. Mell and U. B. Müller (BZNW 100; Berlin/New York: de Gruyter, 1999) 85–106.

Koester, H., *Introduction to the New Testament* 1: *History, Culture, and Religion of the Hellenistic Age*; 2: *History and Literature of Early Christianity* (Berlin/New York: de Gruyter, 2nd edn 1995, 2000; ET rev. of Berlin/New York: de Gruyter, 1980).

— 'Ephesos in Early Christian Literature', in *Ephesos Metropolis of Asia: An Interdisciplinary Approach to Its Archaeology, Religion, and Culture*, ed. H. Koester (HTS 41; Valley Forge PA: TPI, 1995) 119–40.

— 'Paul and Philippi: The Evidence from Early Christian Literature', in *Philippi at the Time of Paul and after His Death*, ed. C. Bakirtzis and H. Koester (Harrisburg PA: TPI, 1998) 49–65.

Kollmann, B., *Joseph Barnabas: Leben und Wirkungsgeschichte* (SBS 175; Stuttgart: Katholisches Bibelwerk, 1998).

— 'Philippus der Evangelist und die Anfänge der Heidenmission', *Bib* 80 (2000) 551–65.

Kraft, H., *Die Offenbarung des Johannes* (HNT 16a; Tübingen: Mohr–Siebeck, 1974).

Kraus, W., *Zwischen Jerusalem und Antiochia: Die 'Hellenisten', Paulus und die Aufnahme der Heiden in das endzeitliche Gottesvolk* (SBS 179; Stuttgart: Katholisches Bibelwerk, 1999).

Kümmel, W. G., 'Die älteste Form des Aposteldekrets', in W. G. Kümmel, *Heilsgeschichte und Geschichte: Ges. Aufs. 1933–64* (MTS 3; Marburg: Elwert, 1965) 278–88.

— *Die Theologie des Neuen Testaments nach seinen Hauptzeugen: Jesus – Paulus – Johannes* (GNT 3; Göttingen: Vandenhoeck & Ruprecht, 1969).

Labahn, M., 'Paulus – ein *homo honestus et iustus*: Das lukanische Paulusporträt von Act 27–28 im Lichte ausgewählter antiker Parallelen', in *Das Ende des Paulus: Historische, theologische und literaturgeschichtliche Aspekte*, ed. F. W. Horn (BZNW 106; Berlin/New York: de Gruyter, 2001) 75–106.

Lampe, G. W. H., 'A.D. 70 in Christian Reflection', in *Jesus and the Politics of His Day*, ed. E. Bammel and C. F. D. Moule (Cambridge: Cambridge University Press, 1984) 153–71.

Lampe, P., 'Paulus – Zeltmacher', *BZ* 31 (1987) 256–61.

— *Die stadtrömischen Christen in den ersten beiden Jahrhunderten: Untersuchungen zur Sozialgeschichte* (WUNT II 18; Tübingen: Mohr–Siebeck, 1989).

Landvogt, P., *Epigraphische Untersuchung über den oikomnomos: Ein Beitrag zum hellenistischen Beamtenwesen* (Strasbourg: Schauberg, 1908).

Lane Fox, R., *Pagans and Christians in the Mediterranean World from the Second Century A.D. to the Conversion of Constantine* (London: Penguin Press, 1986).

Lentz, J. C., Jr., *Luke's Portrait of Paul* (SNTSMS 77; Cambridge: Cambridge University Press, 1993).

Leppä, H., 'Luke's Critical Use of Galatians' (Dissertation, Helsinki, 2002).

Levinskaya, I., *The Book of Acts in Its Diaspora Setting* (The Book of Acts in Its First-Century Setting 5; Grand Rapids: Eerdmans/Carlisle: Paternoster Press, 1996).

Lindemann, A., *Paulus in ältesten Christentum: Das Bild des Apostels und die Rezeption der paulinischen Theologie in der frühchristlichen Literatur bis Marcion* (BHT 58; Tübingen: Mohr–Siebeck, 1979).

Löhr, W. A., 'Das antike Christentum im zweiten Jahrhundert – neue Perspektiven seiner Erforschung', *TLZ* 127 (2002) 247–62.

Löning, K., 'Der Stephanuskreis und seine Mission', in J. Becker *et al.*, *Die Anfänge des Christentums* (Stuttgart: Kohlhammer, 1987) 80–101.

Lüdemann, G., *Paulus der Heidenapostel* 1: *Studien zur Chronologie* (FRLANT 123; Göttingen: Vandenhoeck & Ruprecht, 1980).

— 'The Successors of Pre-70 Jerusalem Christianity: A Critical Evaluation of the Pella-Tradition', in *Jewish and Christian Self-Definition* 1: *The Shaping of Christianity in the Second and Third Centuries*, ed. E. P. Sanders (London: SCM Press, 1980) 161–73, 245–54.

— *Paulus der Heidenapostel* 2: *Antipaulinismus im frühen Christentum* (FRLANT 130; Göttingen: Vandenhoeck & Ruprecht, 1983).

— *Early Christianity According to the Traditions in Acts: A Commentary* (London: SCM Press, 1989; ET of Göttingen: Vandenhoeck & Ruprecht, 1987).

— 'The Acts of the Apostles and the Beginnings of Simonian Gnosis', *NTS* 33 (1987) 420–6.

— *Die Auferstehung Jesu: Historie, Erfahrung, Theologie* (Göttingen: Vandenhoeck & Ruprecht/Stuttgart: Radius, 1994; ET London: SCM Press, 1995).

Lührmann, D., *Galatians: A Continental Commentary* (Minneapolis: Fortress Press, 1992; ET of ZB; Zürich: TVZ, 2nd edn 1988).

MacDonald, D. R., *The Legend and the Apostle: The Battle for Paul in Story and Canon* (Philadelphia: Westminster, 1983).

MacDonald, M. Y., *The Pauline Churches: A Socio-Historical Study of Instituionalization in the Pauline and Deutero-Pauline Writings* (SNTSMS 60; Cambridge: Cambridge University Press, 1988).

MacMullen, R., *Christianizing the Roman Empire (A.D. 100–400)* (New Haven/London: Yale University Press, 1984).
Magie, D., *Roman Rule in Asia Minor to the End of the Third Century after Christ* (Princeton NJ: Princeton University Press, 1950).
Maier, J., *Zwischen den Testamenten: Geschichte und Religion in der Zeit des zweiten Tempels* (Die Neue Echter Bibel Ergänzungsband zum AT 3; Würzburg: Echter, 1990).
Malherbe, A. J., *Social Aspects of Early Christianity* (Baton Rouge/London: Louisiana State University, 1977).
— *The Letters to the Thessalonians* (AB 32B; New York: Doubleday, 2000).
Manson, T. W., 'The Corinthian Correspondence (1)', in T. W. Manson, *Studies in the Gospels and Epistles* (Manchester: Manchester University Press, 1962) 190–209.
Markschies, C., *Valentinus Gnosticus? Untersuchungen zur valentinischen Gnosis mit einem neuen Kommentar zu den Fragmenten Valentins* (WUNT 65; Tübingen: Mohr–Siebeck, 1992).
— *Zwischen den Welten wandern: Strukturen des antiken Christentums* (Europäische Geschichte; Frankfurt am Main: Fischer, 1997).
— 'Kerinth: Wer war er und was lehrte er?', *JAC* 41 (1998) 48–76.
Martin, D. B., *Slavery as Salvation: The Metaphor of Slavery in Pauline Christianity* (New Haven/London: Yale University Press, 1990).
Martin, R. A., *Studies in the Life and Ministry of the Early Paul and Related Issues* (Lewiston: Mellen Press, 1993).
Martyn, J. L., *Galatians* (AB 33A; New York: Doubleday, 1997).
Matthews, C. R., *Philip: Apostle and Evangelist: Configuration of a Tradition* (NovTSup 105; Leiden: Brill, 2002).
Meeks, W. A., *The First Urban Christians: The Social World of the Apostle Paul* (New Haven/London: Yale University Press, 1983).
— 'Breaking Away: Three New Testament Pictures of Christianity's Separation from the Jewish Communities', in *'To See Ourselves as Others See Us': Christians, Jews, 'Others' in Late Antiquity*, ed. J. Neusner and E. S. Frerichs (Scholars Press Studies in the Humanities; Chico: Scholars Press, 1985) 93–115.
Meggitt, J. J., *Paul, Poverty and Survival* (Studies of the New Testament and Its World; Edinburgh: T&T Clark, 1998).
Meier, J. P., *A Marginal Jew: Rethinking the Historical Jesus 2: Mentor, Message, and Miracles* (New York: Doubleday, 1994).
Merkel, H., 'Das Gesetz im lukanischen Doppelwerk', in *Schrift und Tradition*, FS J. Ernst; ed. K. Backhaus and F.G. Untergaßmair (Paderborn: Schöningh, 1996) 119–33.
Metzger, B. M., *A Textual Commentary on the Greek New Testament* (London/New York: United Bible Societies, 1971).
Michel, O., *Paulus und seine Bibel* (Gütersloh: Bertelsmann, 1929/Darmstadt: Wissenschaftliche Buchgesellschaft, 1972).
Milavec, A., 'The Pastoral Genius of the Didache: An Analytical Translation and Commentary', in *Christianity* (Religious Writings and Religious Systems: Systemic Analysis of Holy Books in Christianity, Islam, Buddhism, Greco-Roman Religions, Ancient Israel, and Judaism 2; ed. J. Neusner *et al.*; Brown Studies in Religion 2; Atlanta: Scholars Press, 1989) 89–125.

Millar, F., *The Roman Near East 31 BC–AD 337* (Cambridge MA/London: Harvard University Press, 1993).

Mitchell, A. C., 'Rich and Poor in the Courts of Corinth: Litigiousness and Status in 1 Corinthians 6.1–11', *NTS* 39 (1993) 562–86.

Mitchell, M. M., *Paul and the Rhetoric of Reconciliation: An Exegetical Investigation of the Language and Composition of 1 Corinthians* (HUT 27; Tübingen: Mohr–Siebeck, 1991).

Mitchell, S., 'Population and Land in Roman Galatia', in *ANRW* II 7.2 (1980) 1053–81.

— *Anatolia: Land, Men, and Gods in Asia Minor* 1: *The Celts in Anatolia and the Impact of Roman Rule*; 2: *The Rise of the Church* (Oxford: Clarendon Press, 1993).

Müller, P., *Die Anfänge der Paulusschule, dargestellt am zweiten Thessalonicherbrief und am Kolosserbrief* (ATANT 74; Zürich: TVZ, 1988).

Müller, U. B., 'Zur Rezeption gesetzeskritischer Jesustradition im frühen Christentum', *NTS* 27 (1980–1) 158–85.

— *Die Offenbarung des Johannes* (ÖTK 19; Gütersloher Verlagshaus/Würzburg: Echter, 1984, 2nd edn 1995).

— *Der Brief des Paulus an die Philipper* (THKNT 11/I; Leipzig: Evangelische Verlagsanstalt, 1993).

— *Die Entstehung des Glaubens an die Auferstehung Jesu: Historische Aspekte und Bedingungen* (SBS 172; Stuttgart: Katholisches Bibelwerk, 1998).

Munck, J., *Paul and the Salvation of Mankind* (London: SCM Press, 1959; ET of Acta Jutlandica 26/1; Århus: Universitet/ Kopenhagen: Munksgaard, 1954).

Murphy-O'Connor, J., *Paul: A Critical Life* (Oxford: Clarendon Press, 1996).

Mußner, F., *Der Brief an die Epheser* (ÖTK 10; Gütersloh: Mohn/Würzburg: Echter Verlag, 1982).

Neudorfer, H.-W., *Der Stephanuskreis in der Forschungsgeschichte seit F. C. Baur* (Gießen/ Basel: Brunnen, 1983).

Neumann, G., 'Kleinasien', in *Die Sprachen im römischen Reich der Kaiserzeit: Kolloquium vom 8. bis 10. April 1974* (Beihefte der Bonner Jahrbücher 40; Köln: Rheinland/Bonn: Habelt, 1980) 167–85.

Niederwimmer, K., *Die Didache* (Kommentar zu den Apostolischen Vätern 1; Göttingen: Vandenhoeck & Ruprecht, 1989).

Nock, A. D., *Conversion: The Old and the New in Religion from Alexander the Great to Augustine of Hippo* (London: Oxford University Press, 1933).

— '*Isopoliteia* and the Jews', in A. D. Nock, *Essays on Religion and the Ancient World* 2, ed. Z. Stewart (Oxford: Clarendon Press, 1972) 960–2.

Noethlichs, K. L., 'Der Jude Paulus – ein Tarser und Römer?', in *Rom und das himmlische Jerusalem: Die frühen Christen zwischen Anpassung und Ablehnung*, ed. R. von Haehling (Darmstadt: Wissenschaftliche Buchgesellschaft, 2000) 53–84.

Oberlinner, L., *Die Pastoralbriefe* (HTKNT XI/2; Freiburg: Herder, 1994–6).

Öhler, M., 'Römisches Vereinsrecht und christliche Gemeinden', in *Zwischen den Zeiten: Neues Testament und Römische Herrschaft: Vorträge auf der ersten Konferenz der European Association for Biblical Studies*, ed. M. Labahn and J. Zangenberg (TANZ 36; Tübingen/Basel: Francke 2002) 51–71.

Ogg, G., *The Chronology of the Life of Paul* (London: Epworth Press, 1968).

Omerzu, H., *Der Prozeß des Paulus: Eine exegetische und rechtshistorische Untersuchung der Apostelgeschichte* (BZNW 115; Berlin/New York: de Gruyter, 2002).

Painter, J., *Just James: The Brother of Jesus in History and Tradition* (University of South Carolina Press, 1997/Studies on Personalities of the New Testament; Edinburgh: T&T Clark, 1999).

Pearson, B. A., 'Earliest Christianity in Egypt: Some Observations', in *The Roots of Egyptian Christianity*, ed. B. A. Pearson and J. E. Goehring (Studies in Antiquity and Christianity; Philadelphia: Fortress Press, 1986) 132–59.

Perrin, N., *The New Testament: An Introduction: Proclamation and Parenesis, Myth and History* (New York: Harcourt Brace Jovanovich, 1974).

Pervo, R. I., *Profit with Delight: The Literary Genre of the Acts of the Apostles* (Philadelphia: Fortress Press, 1987).

— 'A Hard Act to Follow: The *Acts of Paul* and the Canonical Acts', *Journal of Higher Criticism* 2 (1995) 3–32.

Pesch, R., 'Zur Entstehung des Glaubens an die Auferstehung Jesu', *TQ* 153 (1973) 201–28.

— *Simon-Petrus: Geschichte und geschichtliche Deutung des ersten Jüngers Jesu Christi* (Päpste und Papsttum 15; Stuttgart: Hiersemann, 1980).

— 'Das Jerusalemer Abkommen und die Lösung des Antiochenischen Konflikts: Ein Versuch über Gal 2, Apg 10,1–11, 18, Apg 11,27–30; 12,25 und Apg 15,1–41', in *Kontinuität und Einheit*, FS F. Mußner; ed. P. G. Müller and W. Stenger (Freiburg: Herder, 1981) 105–22.

— *Die Apostelgeschichte* (EKKNT 5; Zürich, etc.: Benziger/ Neukirchen-Vluyn: Neukirchener, 1986).

Pilhofer, P., *Presbyteron kreitton: Der Altersbeweis der jüdischen und christlichen Apologeten und seine Vorgeschichte* (WUNT 2/39; Tübingen: Mohr–Siebeck, 1990).

— *Philippi* 1: *Die erste christliche Gemeinde Europas*; 2: *Katalog der Inschriften von Philippi* (WUNT 87, 119; Tübingen: Mohr–Siebeck, 1995, 2000).

Pöttner, M., *Realität als Kommunikation: Ansätze zur Beschreibung der Grammatik des paulinischen Sprechens in 1 Kor 1,4–4,21 im Blick auf literarische Problematik und Situationsbezug des 1. Korintherbriefes* (Theologie 2; Münster: Lit, 1995).

Pokorný, P., *Der Brief des Paulus an die Epheser* (THKNT 10/2; Leipzig: Evangelische Verlagsanstalt, 1992).

— *Theologie der lukanischen Schriften* (FRLANT 174; Göttingen: Vandenhoeck & Ruprecht, 1998).

Popkes, W., *Adressaten, Situation und Form des Jakobusbriefes* (SBS 125/126; Stuttgart: Katholisches Bibelwerk, 1986).

Pratscher, W., *Der Herrenbruder Jakobus und die Jakobustraditionen* (FRLANT 139; Göttingen: Vandenhoeck & Ruprecht, 1987).

Räisänen, H., 'The "Hellenists" – a Bridge between Jesus and Paul?', in H. Räisänen, *The Torah and Christ: Deutsche und englische Aufsätze zur Gesetzesproblematik im Urchristentum* (Publications of the Finnish Exegetical Society 45; Helsinki, 1986) 242–306.

— 'Die "Hellenisten" der Urgemeinde', in *ANRW* II 26.2 (Berlin/New York: de Gruyter, 1995) 1468–1514.

— 'The Nicolaitans: Apoc 2; Acta 6', in *ANRW* II 26.2 (Berlin/New York: de Gruyter, 1995) 1602–44.

Rajak, T., 'Was There a Roman Charter for the Jews?', *JRS* 73 (1983) 107–23.

Rapske, B., *Paul in Roman Custody* (The Book of Acts in Its First-Century Setting 3; Grand Rapids: Eerdmans/Carlisle: Paternoster Press, 1994).

Reichert, A., 'Durchdachte Konfusion: Plinius, Trajan und das Christentum', *ZNW* 93 (2002) 227–50.

Reicke, B., *Re-Examining Paul's Letters: The History of the Pauline Correspondence*, ed. D. P. Moessner and I. Reicke (Harrisburg PA: TPI, 2001).

Reinbold, W., *Propaganda und Mission im ältesten Christentum: Eine Untersuchung der Modalitäten der Ausbreitung der frühen Kirche* (FRLANT 188; Göttingen: Vandenhoeck & Ruprecht, 2000).

Riches, J. K., 'Die Synoptiker und ihre Gemeinden', in Becker, *Anfänge*, 160–84.

Riesner, R., *Paul's Early Period: Chronology, Mission Strategy, Theology* (Grand Rapids/ Cambridge: Eerdmans, 1998; ET of WUNT 71; Tübingen: Mohr–Siebeck, 1994).

— 'Das Jerusalemer Essenerviertel und die Urgemeinde: Josephus, Bellum Judaicum V 145; 11QMiqdasch 46,13–16; Apostelgeschichte 1–6 und die Archäologie', in *ANRW* II 26.2 (1995) 1775–1922.

— 'A Pre-Christian Jewish Mission?', in *The Mission of the Early Church to Jews and Gentiles*, ed. J. Ådna and H. Kvalbein (WUNT 127; Tübingen: Mohr–Siebeck, 2000) 211–50.

Roetzel, C., *Paul: The Man and the Myth* (University of South Carolina Press, 1997/ Minneapolis: Fortress Press, 1999).

Roloff, J., *Die Apostelgeschichte* (NTD 5; Göttingen: Vandenhoeck & Ruprecht, 1981).

— 'Apostel/Apostolat/Apostolizität I: Neues Testament', in *TRE* 3 (1978) 430–45.

— 'Konflikte und Konfliktlösungen in der Apostelgeschichte', in *Die Treue Gottes trauen: Beiträge zum Werk des Lukas: Für Gerhard Schneider*, ed. C. Bussmann and W. Radl (Freiburg: Herder, 1991) 111–26.

— *Die Kirche im Neuen Testament* (GNT 10; Göttingen: Vandenhoeck & Ruprecht, 1993).

Rordorf, W., 'In welchem Verhältnis stehen die apokryphen Paulusakten zur kanonischen Apostelgeschichte und zu den Pastoralbriefen?', in *Text and Testimony*, ed. T. Baarda *et al.* (Kampen: Kok, 1988) 225–41.

— 'Nochmals: Paulusakten und Pastoralbriefe', in *Tradition and Interpretation in the New Testament*, FS E. E. Ellis; ed. G. F. Hawthorne and O. Betz (Grand Rapids: Eerdmans/ Tübingen: Mohr–Siebeck, 1987) 319–27.

Rudolph, K., *Gnosis: The Nature and History of an Ancient Religion* (Edinburgh: T&T Clark, 1983; ET of Leipzig: Koehler & Amelang, 1977).

Sampley, J. P., 'The Weak and the Strong: Paul's Careful and Crafty Rhetorical Strategy in Romans 14:1–15:13', in *The Social World of the First Christians: Essays in Honor of Wayne A. Meeks*, ed. L. M. White and O. L. Yarbrough (Minneapolis: AugsburgFortress, 1995) 40–52.

Sanders, E. P., *Jesus and Judaism* (London: SCM Press, 1965, 3rd edn 1991).

— 'Jewish Association with Gentiles and Galatians 2:11–14', in *The Conversation Continues: Studies in Paul and John*, FS J. L. Martyn; ed. R. T. Fortna and B. Gaventa (Nashville: Abingdon Press, 1990) 170–88.

Sanders, J. T., *Schismatics, Sectarians, Dissidents, Deviants: The First One Hundred Years of Jewish–Christian Relations* (London: SCM Press, 1993).

Schenk, W., *Die Philipperbriefe des Paulus: Kommentar* (Stuttgart: Kohlhammer, 1984).

Schmeller, T., *Brechungen: Urchristliche Wandercharismatiker im Prisma soziologisch orientierter Exegese* (SBS 136; Stuttgart: Katholisches Bibelwerk, 1989).

Schmithals, W., *Die Gnosis in Korinth: Eine Untersuchung zu den Korintherbriefen* (FRLANT 66; Göttingen: Vandenhoeck & Ruprecht, 1956, 2nd edn 1965).

— *The Office of Apostle in the Early Church* (London: SPCK, 1971) =ET of *Das kirchliche Apostelamt: Eine historische Untersuchung* (FRLANT NF 61; Göttingen: Vandenhoeck & Ruprecht, 1961).

— *Paul and James* (SBT 46; London: SCM Press, 1965; =ET of FRLANT 85; Göttingen: Vandenhoeck & Ruprecht, 1963).

— *Paul and the Gnostics* (Nashville/New York: Abingdon Press, 1972; ET of Hamburg: Reich, 1965).

— *Die Apostelgeschichte des Lukas* (ZB 3.2; Zürich: TVZ, 1982).

— *Der Römerbrief als historisches Problem* (SNT 9; Gütersloh: Mohn, 1975).

— *Der Römerbrief: Ein Kommentar* (Gütersloh: Mohn, 1988).

— 'Apg 20,17–38 und das Problem einer "Paulusquelle" ', in *Der Treue Gottes trauen: Beiträge zum Werk des Lukas*, FS G. Schneider; ed. C. Bussmann and W. Radl (Freiburg: Herder, 1991) 307–22.

— *Johannesevangelium und Johannesbriefe: Forschungsgeschichte und Analyse* (BZNW 64; Berlin/New York: de Gruyter, 1992).

— 'Probleme des "Apostelkonzils" (Gal 2,1–10)', *Hervormde Teologische Studies* 53 (1997) 6–35.

Schneider, G., 'Stephanus, die Hellenisten und Samaria', in *Les Actes des Apôtres: Traditions, rédaction, théologie*, ed. J. Kremer (BETL 48; Gembloux: Duculot/ Leuven: Leuven University Press, 1979) 215–40.

— *Die Apostelgeschichte* (HTKNT 5; Freiburg u.a: Herder, 1980, 1982).

Schnelle, U., *Einleitung in das Neue Testament* (UTB 1830: Göttingen: Vandenhoeck & Ruprecht, 3rd edn 1999).

— 'Taufe II: Neues Testament', in *TRE* 32 (2001) 663–74.

— 'Muß ein Heide erst Jude werden, um Christ sein zu können?', in *Kirche und Volk Gottes*, FS J. Roloff; ed. M. Karrer *et al.* (Neukirchen-Vluyn: Neukirchener Verlag, 2000) 93–109.

Schrage, W., *Der erste Brief an die Korinther* (EKKNT 7; Zürich, etc.: Benziger/ Neukirchen-Vluyn: Neukirchener Verlag, 1991–2001).

Schürer, E., *The History of the Jewish People in the Age of Jesus Christ (175 B.C.–A.D. 135)*, rev. edn by G. Vermes, F. Millar, P. Vermes and M. Black (Edinburgh: T&T Clark, 1973–87).

Schwartz, D. R., *Agrippa I: The Last King of Judaea* (TSAJ 23; Tübingen: Mohr-Siebeck, 1990).

Schweizer, E., *Der Brief an die Kolosser* (EKKNT; Zürich, etc.: Benziger/Neukirchen-Vluyn: Neukirchener Verlag, 1976).

Scriba, A., 'Von Korinth nach Rom: Die Chronologie der letzten Jahre des Paulus', in *Das Ende des Paulus: Historische, theologische und literaturgeschichtliche Aspekte* ed. F. W. Horn (BZNW 106; Berlin/New York: de Gruyter, 2001) 157–73.

Segal, A. F., *Rebecca's Children: Judaism and Christianity in the Roman World* (Cambridge MA/London: Harvard University Press, 1986).

— *Paul the Convert: The Apostolate and Apostasy of Saul the Pharisee* (New Haven/ London: Yale University Press, 1990).

Sellin, G., 'Das "Geheimnis" der Weisheit und das Rätsel der "Christuspartei" (zu 1 Kor 1–4)', *ZNW* 73 (1982) 69–96.

Sherwin-White, A. N., *Roman Society and Roman Law in the New Testament* (Oxford: Clarendon Press, 1963).

Simon, M., *Verus Israel: A Study of the Relations between Christians and Jews in the Roman Empire* (Lettman Library of Jewish Civilization; Oxford: Oxford University Press, 1986; ET of Paris: de Boccard, 1964).

Slingerland, D., 'Suetonius *Claudius* 25.4 and the Account in Cassius Dio', *JQR* 79 (1989) 305–22.

Smallwood, E. M., *The Jews under Roman Rule from Pompey to Diocletian: A Study in Political Relations* (SJLA 20; Leiden: Brill, 1976, 1981).

Speidel, M. P., 'The Roman Army in Judaea under the Procurators: The Italian and the Augustan Cohort in the Acts of the Apostles', in M. P. Speidel, *Roman Army Studies* 2 (Mavors Roman Army Researches 8; Stuttgart: Steiner, 1992) 224–32.

Stanton, G. N., *The Gospels and Jesus* (Oxford: Oxford University Press, 1989).

Stegemann, E. W. and W. Stegemann, *Urchristliche Sozialgeschichte: Die Anfänge im Judentum und die Christusgemeinden in der mediterranen Welt* (Stuttgart: Kohlhammer, 1995).

Stegemann, W., 'War der Apostel Paulus ein römischer Bürger?', *ZNW* 78 (1987) 200–29.

— *Zwischen Synagoge und Obrigkeit: Zur historischen Situation der lukanischen Christen* (FRLANT 152; Göttingen: Vandenhoeck & Ruprecht, 1991).

Stendahl, K., *Paul among Jews and Gentiles and Other Essays* (Philadelphia: Fortress Press, 1976).

Stowasser, M., 'Konflikte und Konfliktlösungen nach dem Galaterbrief', *TTZ* 103 (1994) 56–79.

Stowers, S. K., *A Rereading of Romans: Justice, Jews, and Gentiles* (New Haven/London: Yale University Press, 1994).

Strecker, G. and T. Nolting, 'Der vorchristliche Paulus: Überlegungen zum biographischen Kontext biblischer Überlieferungen zugleich eine Antwort an Martin Hengel', in *Texts and Contexts: Biblical Texts in Their Textual and Situational Contexts*, FS L. Hartman; ed. T. Fornberg and D. Hellholm (Oslo: Scandinavian University Press, 1995) 713–41.

Suhl, A., *Paulus und seine Briefe: Ein Beitrag zur paulinischen Chronologie* (SNT 11; Gütersloh: Mohn, 1975).

— 'Ein Konfliktlösungsmodell der Urkirche und seine Geschichte', *BK* 45 (1990) 80–6.

— 'Paulinische Chronologie im Streit der Meinungen', in *ANRW* II 26.2 (Berlin/New York: de Gruyter, 1995) 939–1188.

Sumney, J. L., *Identifying Paul's Opponents: The Question of Method in 2 Corinthians* (JSNTSup 40; Sheffield: Sheffield Academic Press, 1990).

Taeger, J.-W., 'Eine fulminante Streitschrift: Bemerkungen zur Apokalypse des Johannes', in *Krisen und Umbrüche in der Geschichte des Christentums*, FS M. Greschat; ed. W. Kurz *et al.* (Gießener Schriften zur Theologie und Religionspädagogik des Fachbereichs Evangelische Theologie und Katholische Theologie und deren Didaktik der Justus-Liebig-Univ. 9; Gießen, 1994) 293–311.

Taylor, J., 'St Paul and the Roman Empire: Acts of the Apostles 13–14', in *ANRW* II 26.2 (1995) 1189–1231.

— 'The Jerusalem Decrees (Acts 15.20, 29 and 21.25) and the Incident at Antioch (Gal 2.11–14)', *NTS* 46 (2001) 372–80.

Taylor, J. E., 'The Phenomenon of Early Jewish-Christianity: Reality or Scholarly Invention?', *VigChrist* 44 (1990) 313–34.

Taylor, N., *Paul, Antioch and Jerusalem: A Study in Relationships and Authority in Earliest Christianity* (JSNTSup 66; Sheffield: JSOT, 1992).

Theißen, G., *The Social Setting of Pauline Christianity* (Studies of the New Testament and Its World; Edinburgh: T&T Clark/Philadelphia: Fortress Press, 1982).

— 'Gruppenmessianismus: Uberlegungen zum Ursprung der Kirche im Jüngerkreis Jesu', in *Volk Gottes, Gemeinde und Gesellschaft* (JBT 7; Neukirchen-Vluyn: Neukirchener Verlag, 1992) 101–23.

— 'Hellenisten und Hebräer (Apg 6,1–6): Gab es eine Spaltung der Urgemeinde?', in *Geschichte – Tradition – Reflexion*, FS M. Hengel; ed. P. Schäfer, H. Cancik and H. Lichtenberger (Tübingen: Mohr–Siebeck, 1996) 3.323–43.

— *A Theory of Primitive Christian Religion* (London: SCM Press, 1999; ET of Gütersloh: Gütersloher Verlagshaus, 1999).

— 'Die Verfolgung unter Agrippa I und die Autoritätsstruktur der Jerusalemer Gemeinde: Eine Untersuchung zu Apg 12,1–4 und Mk 10,35–45', in *Das Urchristentum in seiner literarischen Geschichte*, FS J. Becker; ed. U. Mell and U. B. Müller (BZNW 100; Berlin/New York: de Gruyter, 1999) 263–89.

— and A. Merz, *Der historische Jesus: Ein Lehrbuch* (Göttingen: Vandenhoeck & Ruprecht, 1996).

— and D. Winter, *Die Kriterienfrage in der Jesusforschung: Von Differenzkriterium zum Plausibilitätskriterium* (NTOA 34; Freiburg: Universität/Göttingen: Vandenhoeck & Ruprecht, 1997).

Thompson, L. A., 'Domitian and the Jewish Tax', *Historia* 31 (1982) 329–42.

Thornton, C.-J., *Der Zeuge des Zeugen: Lukas als Historiker der Paulusreisen* (WUNT 56; Tübingen: Mohr–Siebeck, 1991).

Thrall, M. E., *II Corinthians* (ICC; Edinburgh: T&T Clark, 1994, 2000).

Tracey, R., 'Syria', in *The Book of Acts in Its Graeco-Roman Setting* (The Book of Acts in Its First-Century Setting 2; ed. D. W. J. Gill and C. Gempf; Grand Rapids: Eerdmans/Carlisle: Paternoster Press, 1994) 223–78.

Trebilco, P., *Jewish Communities in Asia Minor* (SNTSMS 69; Cambridge: Cambridge University Press, 1991).

Tuckett, C. M., *Q and the History of Early Christianity: Studies on Q* (Edinburgh: T&T Clark, 1996).

Uebele, W., '*Viele Verführer sind in die Welt ausgegangen*'*: Die Gegner in den Briefen des Ignatius von Antiochien und in den Johannesbriefen* (BWANT 151; Stuttgart: Kohlhammer, 2001).

van den Broek, R., 'Der *Brief des Jakobus an Quadratus* und das Problem der judenchristlicher Bischöfe von Jerusalem (Eusebius, *HE* IV,5,1–3)', in *Text and Testimony*, FS A. F. J. Klijn; ed. T. Baarda *et al.* (Kampen: Kok, 1988) 56–65.

van der Horst, P. W., 'The Birkat ha-minim in Recent Research', *ExpTim* 105 (1994/5) 363–8.

van Unnik, W. C., *Tarsus or Jerusalem? The City of Paul's Youth* (London: Epworth

Press, 1962) = idem, *Sparsa Collecta* 1 (NovTSup 29; Leiden: Brill, 1973) 259–320.

Vielhauer, P., 'On the "Paulinism" of Acts', in *Studies in Luke–Acts*, FS P. Schubert; ed. L. E. Keck and J. L. Martyn (London: SPCK, 1968) 35–50 (ET of *EvT* 10 [1950–1] 1–15).

— *Geschichte der urchristlichen Literatur: Einleitung in das Neue Testament, die Apokryphen und die Apostolischen Väter* (Berlin/New York: de Gruyter, 1975).

Vouga, F., 'Der Galaterbrief: Kein Brief an die Galater?', in *Schrift und Tradition*, FS J. Ernst; ed. K. Backhaus and F. G. Untergaßmair (Paderborn: Schöningh, 1996) 243–58.

— *An die Galater* (HNT 10; Tübingen: Mohr–Siebeck, 1998).

Wagener, U., *Die Ordnung des 'Hauses Gottes': Der Ort von Frauen in der Ekklesiologie und Ethik der Pastoralbriefe* (WUNT 2/65; Tübingen: Mohr–Siebeck, 1994).

Walbank, F. W., *The Hellenistic World* (Fontana History of the Ancient World; Glasgow: Collins, 1981).

Walter, N., 'Apostelgeschichte 6,1 und die Anfänge der Urgemeinde in Jerusalem', *NTS* 29 (1983) 370–93 = idem, *Praeparatio evangelica: Studien zur Umwelt, Exegese und Hermeneutik des Neuen Testaments*, ed. W. Kraus and F. Wilk (WUNT 98; Tübingen: Mohr–Siebeck, 1997) 187–211.

— 'Hellenistische Diaspora-Juden an der Wiege des Urchristentums', in *Praeparatio*, 383–404.

— 'Die "als Säulen Geltenden" in Jerusalem – Leiter der Urgemeinde oder exemplarische Fromme?', in *Kirche und Volk Gottes*, FS J. Roloff; ed. M. Karrer *et al.* (Neukirchen-Vluyn: Neukirchener Verlag, 2000) 78–92.

— 'Nikolaos, Proselyt aus Antiochien, und die Nikolaiten in Ephesus und Pergamon: Ein Beitrag auch zum Thema: Paulus und Ephesus', *ZNW* 93 (2002) 200–26.

Walters, J. C., 'Romans, Jews, and Christians: The Impact of the Romans on Jewish/Christian Relations in First-Century Rome', in *Judaism and Christianity in First-Century Rome*, ed. K. P. Donfried and P. Richardson; (Grand Rapids/Cambridge: Eerdmans, 1998) 175–95.

Wander, B., *Trennungsprozesse zwischen Frühem Christentum und Judentum im 1. Jh. n. Chr.: Datierbare Abfolgen zwischen der Hinrichtung Jesu und der Zerstörung des Jerusalemer Tempels* (TANZ 16; Tübingen/Basel: Francke, 1994, 2nd edn 1997).

— *Gottesfürchtige und Sympathisanten: Studien zum heidnischen Umfeld von Diasporasynagogen* (WUNT 104; Tübingen: Mohr–Siebeck, 1998).

Ward, R. B., 'James of Jerusalem in the First Two Centuries', in *ANRW* II 26.1 (1992) 779–812.

Wasserberg, G., *Aus Israels Mitte – Heil für die Welt: Eine narrativ-exegetische Studie zur Theologie des Lukas* (BZNW 92; Berlin/New York: de Gruyter, 1998).

Wedderburn, A. J. M., 'The Problem of the Denial of the Resurrection in I Corinthians XV', *NovT* 23 (1981) 229–41.

— *Baptism and Resurrection: Studies in Pauline Theology against Its Graeco-Roman Background* (WUNT 44; Tübingen: Mohr, 1987).

— *The Reasons for Romans* (Studies of the New Testament and Its World; Edinburgh: T&T Clark, 1988).

— 'Paul and Jesus: Similarity and Continuity', in *Paul and Jesus: Collected Essays*, ed.

A. J. M. Wedderburn (JSNTSup 37; Sheffield: Sheffield Academic Press, 1989) 117–43 (rev. of *NTS* 34 [1988] 161–82).
— 'The Theology of Colossians', in A. T. Lincoln and A. J. M. Wedderburn, *The Theology of the Later Pauline Letters* (New Testament Theology; Cambridge: Cambridge University Press) 3–71, 167–9, 173–8.
— 'The "Apostolic Decree": Tradition and Redaction', *NovT* 35 (1993) 362–89.
— 'Traditions and Redaction in Acts 2.1–13', *JSNT* 55 (1994) 27–54.
— 'Zur Frage der Gattung der Apostelgeschichte', in *Geschichte – Tradition – Reflexion*, FS M. Hengel; ed. P. Schäfer, H. Cancik and H. Lichtenberger (Tübingen: Mohr–Siebeck, 1996) 3.303–322.
— *Beyond Resurrection* (London: SCM Press/Peabody: Hendrickson, 1999).
— 'Paul and Barnabas: The Anatomy and Chronology of a Parting of the Ways', in *Fair Play: Diversity and Conflicts in Early Christianity*, FS H. Räisänen; ed. I. Dunderberg, C. Tuckett and K. Syreeni (NovTSup 103; Leiden: Brill, 2001) 291–310.
— 'The "We"-Passages in Acts: On the Horns of a Dilemma', *ZNW* 93 (2002) 78–98.
— 'Paul's Collection: Chronology and History', *NTS* 48 (2002) 95–110.
Wehnert, J., *Die Wir-Passagen der Apostelgeschichte: Ein lukanisches Stilmittel aus jüdischer Tradition* (GTA 40; Göttingen: Vandenhoeck & Ruprecht, 1989).
— 'Die Auswanderung der Jerusalemer Christen nach Pella – historisches Faktum oder theologische Konstruktion? Kritische Bemerkungen zu einem neuen Buch', *ZKG* 102 (1991/2) 231–55.
— *Die Reinheit des 'christlichen Gottesvolkes' aus Juden und Heiden: Studien zum historischen und theologischen Hintergrund des sogenannten Aposteldekrets* (FRLANT 173; Göttingen: Vandenhoeck & Ruprecht, 1997).
Wehr, L., *Petrus und Paulus – Kontrahenten und Partner: Die beiden Apostel im Spiegel des Neuen Testaments, der Apostolischen Väter und früherer Zeugnisse ihrer Verehrung* (NTA 30; Münster: Aschendorff, 1996).
Weiser, A., *Die Apostelgeschichte* (ÖTK 5; Gütersloh: Mohn/Würzburg: Echter Verlag, 1981, 1985).
Wellhausen, J., *Kritische Analyse der Apostelgeschichte* (Abh. der königl. Gesellschaft der Wissenschaften zu Göttingen, phil.-hist. Klasse NF 15.2; Berlin: Weidmann, 1914).
Wells, C., *The Roman Empire* (Fontana History of the Ancient World; Glasgow: Collins, 1984).
Wengst, K., *Bedrängte Gemeinde und verherrlichter Christus: Der historische Ort des Johannesevangeliums als Schlüssel zu seiner Interpretation* (Biblisch-Theologische Studien 5; Neukirchen-Vluyn: Neukirchener Verlag, 1981, 4th edn: *Bedrängte Gemeinde und verherrlichter Christus: Ein Versuch über das Johannesevangelium* [Kaiser Taschenbücher 114; München: Kaiser, 1992]).
— *Pax Romana and the Peace of Christ* (London: SCM Press, 1987; ET of München: Kaiser, 1986).
Wilckens, U., *Der Brief an die Römer* (EKKNT 6; Zürich, etc.: Benziger/Neukirchen-Vluyn: Neukirchener Verlag, 1978–82).
Wilken, R. L., *The Myth of Christian Beginnings: History's Impact on Belief* (Garden City NY: Doubleday, 1971).

Wilson, R. McL., 'Simon and Gnostic Origins', in *Les Actes des Apôtres: Traditions, rédaction, théologie*, ed. J. Kremer (BETL 48; Gembloux: Duculot/Leuven: Universiteit Leuven, 1979) 485–91.

— 'Nag Hammadi and the New Testament', *NTS* 28 (1982) 289–302.

Wilson, S. G., *The Gentiles and the Gentile-Mission in Luke–Acts* (SNTSMS 23; Cambridge: Cambridge University Press, 1973).

— *Related Strangers: Jews and Christians 70–170 C.E.* (Minneapolis: Fortress Press, 1995).

Witherington, B., *The Acts of the Apostles: A Socio-Rhetorical Commentary* (Grand Rapids/Cambridge: Eerdmans/Carlisle: Paternoster Press, 1998).

Witulski, T., *Die Adressaten des Galaterbriefes: Untersuchungen zur Gemeinde von Antiochia ad Pisidiam* (FRLANT 193; Göttingen: Vandenhoeck & Ruprecht, 2000).

Wolter, M., 'Die Juden und die Obrigkeit bei Lukas', in *Ja und Nein: Christliche Theologie im Angesicht Israels*, FS W. Schrage; ed. K. Wengst and G. Saß (Neukirchen-Vluyn: Neukirchener Verlag, 1998) 277–90.

Woyke, J., *Die neutestamentlichen Haustafeln: Ein kritischer und konstruktiver Forschungsüberblick* (SBS 184; Stuttgart: Katholisches Bibelwerk, 2000).

Zmijewski, J., *Die Apostelgeschichte* (RNT; Regensburg: Pustet, 1994).

Zumstein, J., 'Zur Geschichte des johanneischen Christentums', *TLZ* 122 (1997) 417–28.

Index of Primary Sources

1. Old Testament

2. Other Jewish Sources

3. New Testament

4. Other Early Christian Literature and Gnostic Sources

5. Other Graeco-Roman Literature and Sources

Index of Authors (Secondary Literature)

Index of Subjects